SLOW COOKER RECIPES

by
Jean Paré

companyscoming.com
visit our web-site

Dedication

For busy households everywhere—
ready when you are!

Cover Photo

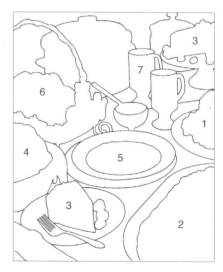

Props Courtesy Of: Creations By Design; Le Gnome;
Scona Clayworks; Stokes; The Basket House

cooking
tonight?

A selection of
feature recipes
are only a
click away—
absolutely **FREE!**

Visit us at **companyscoming.com**

table of Contents

Foreword

Imagine entering your home to the aroma of food cooking away in your slow cooker. It's a wonderful feeling, knowing that while you were elsewhere, dinner was progressing nicely at home.

Some of these recipes can be prepared in the morning and left to cook all day—others won't require cooking for quite that long, but can still offer you freedom of time to garden, shop, or run errands.

Slow cookers offer many benefits that most of us aren't aware of. For instance, a slow cooker can also serve as an extra pot anytime you cook; it won't heat up your kitchen, and, unlike most other conventional cooking methods, it won't dry out food. Meals can be served right from a slow cooker, but for a more impressive presentation, you may want to place food in a serving bowl and add a few garnishes.

For more tips and information on how to make the best use of your slow cooker, check out pages 8 and 9.

Now it's time to plug in your slow cooker and have some fun. For something to simmer all day, you must try Beef Barley Soup. A quicker dish, like Macaroni

And Cheese, will satisfy even the fussiest family member. Amaze everyone that you made Banana Bread in your slow cooker!

Featuring a wide range of recipe ideas to suit practically any occasion, SLOW COOKER RECIPES offers you the chance to take life a little easier.

Jean Paré

Each recipe has been analyzed using the most updated version of the Canadian Nutrient File from Health and Welfare Canada which is based upon the United States Department of Agriculture (USDA) Nutrient Data Base. If more than one ingredient is listed (such as "hard margarine or butter"), then the first ingredient is used in the analysis. Where an ingredient reads "sprinkle" or "optional", it is not included as part of the nutrition information.

Margaret Ng, B.Sc. (Hon), M.A.
Registered Dietitian

TIPS & HINTS

BEVERAGES: Slow cookers make an excellent warmer for any hot drink. As a general rule, always heat beverages on Low. When ready, simply leave your slow cooker on, ready to serve hot drinks to your guests.

BREADS & CAKES: Slow cookers will successfully cook yeast breads and scratch cakes, but you should expect slightly different results in appearance. For instance, they may or may not dome slightly in the center. Also, because moisture is retained in a slow cooker, both breads and cakes will appear more porous with larger air holes and a slightly coarser texture.

If you would like to warm dinner rolls in your slow cooker, wrap them securely first in foil. Cover and heat on Low for 2 to 3 hours, or on High for 1 to 1½ hours.

DAIRY PRODUCTS: Most dairy products don't tolerate long periods of heat. Add during the last hour of cooking whenever possible. Processed cheese and cheese spreads do better than harder cheeses.

DESSERTS: As a general rule of thumb, most desserts (such as puddings and cakes) are cooked on High. Also, because some dessert recipes call for a pan or dish to be set inside the slow cooker, make sure everything fits before you begin.

MEATS: Less tender cuts of meat work well in a slow cooker. Increased moisture and longer cooking times break down tougher cuts, producing a more tender result. There is also less shrinkage of meat because of the low heat and long cooking duration. A meat thermometer, especially an instant one, is a big help in determining the doneness of meat—but avoid checking it too often, and do it as quickly as you can to prevent loss of heat and moisture. For best results using ground beef, scramble-fry or precook before adding to the slow cooker. Meat should be defrosted before cooking, however for safety reasons we do not recommend that you use your slow cooker to defrost.

PASTA: Pasta should not be included in ingredients that you are assembling the night before, because they tend to become mushy.

PREPARATION: As a convenience to avoiding rushed mornings, most ingredients can be prepared, measured and put into a slow cooker the night before. Note that rice and pasta are an exception to this, and should only be added just before cooking begins. If meat, milk or eggs, are included in the recipe, be sure to place your assembled ingredients in the refrigerator overnight.

RICE: The best form of rice to use in a slow cooker is converted rice, because it is less likely to become too sticky or mushy.

SETTINGS: Most slow cookers use only two settings—Low and High. It is virtually impossible to overcook foods on Low, but overcooking may become a problem on High. For best results, you should develop a "feel" for your slow cooker by keeping track of cooking times that produce the results you want. When cooking on Low, try to avoid removing the lid too often since it takes a long time to build up lost heat and moisture.

SIZES: Regular slow cookers range in size from 3½ qts. to 6 qts, and may or may not have a removable liner. In addition, you may find smaller sizes on the market, about .5 qt. (.5 L). These are primarily used for making dips and sauces, and are an ideal size for serving chocolate or cheese fondue. Each recipe identifies what size of slow cooker was used during testing.

TIMING: All of our recipes (with a few exceptions) give an approximate time for both Low and High settings. If you use a different size of slow cooker than what is listed, keep in mind that it should be at least half full for times and results to be reliable. The actual cooking time of a recipe will also depend on the type of food, the starting temperature of the food, and the size, or various sizes, the food is cut into.

VEGETABLES: Because fresh, raw vegetables take longer to cook than meats, they should be thinly sliced or cut into small pieces and then placed on the bottom of the slow cooker. Frozen or canned vegetables may be added to the top if desired.

SNACK MIX

An easy way to whip up a bowl of munchies. Very addictive!

Hard margarine (or butter)	¼ cup	60 mL
Seasoning salt	1½ tsp.	7 mL
Garlic powder	¼ tsp.	1 mL
Onion powder	¾ tsp.	4 mL
Celery salt	¼ tsp.	1 mL
Grated Parmesan cheese	1 tbsp.	15 mL
Pretzel sticks	1½ cups	375 mL
Salted peanuts	1½ cups	375 mL
O-shaped toasted oat cereal	2 cups	500 mL
Whole wheat cereal squares	2 cups	500 mL

Combine first 6 ingredients in 5 quart (5 L) slow cooker. Cook on High to melt margarine. Turn heat to Low.

Add remaining 4 ingredients. Stir well. Cover. Cook for 3½ hours. Remove cover. Stir. Cook for about 30 minutes, stirring once or twice. Makes 7 cups (1.75 L).

½ cup (125 mL): 194 Calories; 12.5 g Total Fat; 537 mg Sodium; 6 g Protein; 17 g Carbohydrate

Pictured on page 17.

PACIFIC PECANS

Dark colored with good spicy flavor.

Hard margarine (or butter)	2 tbsp.	30 mL
Soy sauce	1 tbsp.	15 mL
Salt	½ tsp.	2 mL
Garlic powder	¼ tsp.	1 mL
Onion powder	¼ tsp.	1 mL
Cayenne pepper	⅛ tsp.	0.5 mL
Pecan halves	2 cups	500 mL

Stir first 6 ingredients in 3½ quart (3.5 L) slow cooker. Cook on High to melt margarine.

Add pecans. Stir well. Reduce heat to Low. Cover. Cook for 1½ hours, stirring at half-time. Turn heat to High. Remove cover. Cook for 20 minutes, stirring twice. Spread on tray to cool. Makes 2 cups (500 mL).

2 tbsp. (30 mL): 106 Calories; 10.8 g Total Fat; 161 mg Sodium; 1 g Protein; 3 g Carbohydrate

Ribs in golden juice. Deliciously sweet and tangy.

White vinegar	½ cup	125 mL
Granulated sugar	1 cup	250 mL
Ketchup	⅔ cup	150 mL
Onion flakes	1 tbsp.	15 mL
Worcestershire sauce	1 tbsp.	15 mL
Water	1 cup	250 mL
Pork spareribs, cut into short lengths and into single rib pieces	3 lbs.	1.4 kg

Place first 6 ingredients in 5 quart (5 L) slow cooker. Stir well.

Add ribs. Stir. Cover. Cook on Low for 10 to 12 hours or on High for 5 to 6 hours. Makes about 37 ribs.

1 rib: 73 Calories; 3.4 g Total Fat; 79 mg Sodium; 4 g Protein; 7 g Carbohydrate

Nice curry flavor. Very good.

Natural almonds with brown skin (1⅓ cups, 325 mL)	½ lb.	225 g
Hard margarine (or butter)	1 tbsp.	15 mL
Salt	¼ tsp.	1 mL
Curry powder	1½ tsp.	7 mL

Place all 4 ingredients in 3½ quart (3.5 L) slow cooker. Cook on High to melt margarine. Stir well. Cover. Cook on Low for about 2 hours. Stir. Turn heat to High. Cook, uncovered, for about 1 hour, stirring at half-time. Spread on tray to cool. Makes 1⅓ cups (325 mL).

2 tbsp. (30 mL): 130 Calories; 11.7 g Total Fat; 76 mg Sodium; 4 g Protein; 4 g Carbohydrate

Pictured on page 17.

SALTED ALMONDS: Simply omit curry powder.

SWEET AND SOUR WINGS

In dark flavorful sauce. These are among the first appetizers to disappear.

Whole chicken wings (or drumettes)	**3 lbs.**	**1.4 kg**
Brown sugar, packed	**1 cup**	**250 mL**
All-purpose flour	**¼ cup**	**60 mL**
Water	**½ cup**	**125 mL**
White vinegar	**¼ cup**	**60 mL**
Ketchup	**1½ tbsp.**	**25 mL**
Soy sauce	**¼ cup**	**60 mL**
Garlic powder	**¼ tsp.**	**1 mL**
Onion flakes	**1 tbsp.**	**15 mL**
Salt	**½ tsp.**	**2 mL**
Prepared mustard	**½ tsp.**	**2 mL**

Discard tip and cut wings apart at joint. Place chicken pieces in 5 quart (5 L) slow cooker.

Mix brown sugar and flour well in saucepan. Add water, vinegar and ketchup. Stir. Add remaining 5 ingredients. Heat and stir until boiling and thickened. Pour over wings. Cover. Cook on Low for 8 to 9 hours or on High for 4 to 4½ hours until tender. Serve from slow cooker or remove to platter. Makes about 28 wing pieces or about 18 drumettes.

1 wing piece: 99 Calories; 5 g Total Fat; 4.3 mg Sodium; 241 g Protein; 10 g Carbohydrate

Pictured on page 17.

If only you could cross an octopus with a hen, you would get chicken with drumsticks for everyone.

When you dip down with a sturdy chip or spoon, you get different layers. Wrecks many a diet. Serve with chips.

Light cream cheese, softened	**2 x 8 oz.**	**2 x 250 g**
Canned flakes of ham, with liquid, mashed together	**6.5 oz.**	**184 g**
Grated medium Cheddar cheese	**3 cups**	**750 mL**
Medium or hot salsa	**1/2 cup**	**125 mL**
Canned chopped green chilies, drained	**4 oz.**	**114 mL**
Chili powder	**1/2-1 tsp.**	**2-5 mL**

Mash cream cheese with fork in bowl. Spread in bottom of 3½ quart (3.5 L) slow cooker.

Sprinkle ham evenly over top. Sprinkle with Cheddar cheese.

Stir salsa and green chilies together. Spoon over top.

Sprinkle with chili powder. Cover. Cook on Low for 2 to 2½ hours until quite warm. Do not stir. Makes 4¼ cups (1 L).

1 tbsp. (15 mL): 42 Calories; 3.4 g Total Fat; 173 mg Sodium; 2 g Protein; 1 g Carbohydrate

Fairly mild dip, but good. Serve with crackers, chips or chunks of bread.

Light cream cheese, softened	**8 oz.**	**250 g**
Light sour cream	**1/4 cup**	**60 mL**
Worcestershire sauce	**1 tbsp.**	**15 mL**
Grated onion	**1 tbsp.**	**15 mL**
Lemon juice	**1 tbsp.**	**15 mL**
Salt	**1/2 tsp.**	**2 mL**
Garlic powder	**1/8 tsp.**	**0.5 mL**
Canned minced clams, drained	**5 oz.**	**142 g**

Combine first 7 ingredients in bowl. Mix until well blended.

Add clams. Mix. Turn into 3½ quart (3.5 L) slow cooker. Cover. Cook on Low for 1¾ hours, stirring occasionally, until quite warm. Makes 2 cups (500 mL).

1 tbsp. (15 mL): 21 Calories; 1.4 g Total Fat; 121 mg Sodium; 2 g Protein; 1 g Carbohydrate

BEEFY CHIP DIP

Thick, meaty and cheesy. Add more chili powder to suit your taste. Serve with chips.

Lean ground beef	1 lb.	454 g
Grated Monterey Jack cheese (¾ lb., 340 g)	3 cups	750 mL
Worcestershire sauce	2 tsp.	10 mL
Canned chopped green chilies	4 oz.	114 mL
Medium or hot salsa	1 cup	250 mL
Chili powder	½ tsp.	2 mL
Onion powder	½ tsp.	2 mL

Scramble-fry ground beef in non-stick frying pan until no longer pink. Drain. Use fork to mash and break up beef. Turn into 3½ quart (3.5 L) slow cooker.

Add next 6 ingredients. Stir. Cover. Cook on Low for 1¾ to 2 hours, stirring occasionally, until quite warm. Makes 4 cups (1 L).

1 tbsp. (15 mL): 33 Calories; 2.2 g Total Fat; 103 mg Sodium; 3 g Protein; 1 g Carbohydrate

SPINACH DIP

Mild and tasty. Popeye's favorite. Serve with chunks of bread or chips.

Light cream cheese, softened	8 oz.	250 g
Light salad dressing (or mayonnaise)	½ cup	125 mL
Lemon juice	2 tsp.	10 mL
Salt	½ tsp.	2 mL
Garlic powder	⅛ tsp.	0.5 mL
Worcestershire sauce	½ tsp.	2 mL
Chopped green onion	½ cup	125 mL
Frozen chopped spinach, thawed and squeezed dry	10 oz.	300 g

Mash first 7 ingredients together with fork in bowl.

Add spinach. Stir. Turn into 3½ quart (3.5 L) slow cooker. Cover. Cook on Low for 1½ hours, stirring every 30 minutes, until quite warm. Makes generous 2 cups (500 mL).

1 tbsp. (15 mL): 29 Calories; 2.2 g Total Fat; 149 mg Sodium; 1 g Protein; 1 g Carbohydrate

Pictured on page 35.

ARTICHOKE DIP

Cream colored. Delicious flavors of Parmesan cheese and artichokes. Serve with chunks of bread.

Light cream cheese, softened	4 oz.	125 g
Salad dressing (or mayonnaise)	1/2 cup	125 mL
Light sour cream	1/4 cup	60 mL
Grated Parmesan cheese	1/2 cup	125 mL
Garlic powder	1/4 tsp.	1 mL
Onion powder	1/4 tsp.	1 mL
Chopped green onion	1 tbsp.	15 mL
Jars marinated artichoke hearts, drained and chopped	2 × 6 oz.	2 × 170 mL

Beat cream cheese, salad dressing and sour cream together in bowl until smooth. Stir in Parmesan cheese, garlic powder, onion powder and green onion.

Add artichokes. Turn into 3½ quart (3.5 L) slow cooker. Cook on Low for about 2 hours, stirring occasionally, until quite warm. Makes 2 cups (500 mL).

1 tbsp. (15 mL): 31 Calories; 2.2 g Total Fat; 119 mg Sodium; 1 g Protein; 2 g Carbohydrate

REFRIED BEAN DIP

A smooth bean mixture with cheese and green onion. Serve with chips and vegetables.

Refried beans (less than 1% fat)	14 oz.	398 mL
Grated medium or sharp Cheddar cheese	1 cup	250 mL
Chopped green onion	1/4 cup	60 mL
Chili powder	1 tsp.	5 mL

Put beans, cheese, green onion and chili powder into 3½ quart (3.5 L) slow cooker. Stir. Cover. Cook on Low for 1½ hours, stirring every 20 minutes, until melted and quite warm. Makes 2 cups (500 mL).

1 tbsp. (15 mL): 29 Calories; 1.3 g Total Fat; 77 mg Sodium; 2 g Protein; 3 g Carbohydrate

HOT WINGS

Dip these nippy little fellows into Blue Cheese Dip for a special treat.

White vinegar	4 tsp.	20 mL
Granulated sugar	2 tsp.	10 mL
Hot pepper sauce	1/4 cup	60 mL
Paprika	1 tsp.	5 mL
Whole chicken wings (or drumettes)	3 lbs.	1.4 kg
BLUE CHEESE DIP		
Light salad dressing (or mayonnaise)	1/2 cup	125 mL
Blue cheese, crumbled	1/4 cup	60 mL
Lemon juice	1 tbsp.	15 mL
Onion powder	1/4 tsp.	1 mL
Garlic powder	1/4 tsp.	1 mL
Worcestershire sauce	1/2 tsp.	2 mL
Non-fat (or regular) sour cream	1/2 cup	125 mL

Combine first 4 ingredients in small cup. Stir. Discard tip and cut wings apart at joint. Brush sauce over both sides of chicken pieces. Place pieces in 3 1/2 quart (3.5 L) slow cooker. Cover. Cook on Low for 7 to 8 hours or on High for 3 1/2 to 4 hours until tender. Serve from slow cooker. Makes about 28 pieces of wing or 18 drumettes.

Blue Cheese Dip: Combine all 7 ingredients in bowl. Beat until smooth. Makes 1 1/8 cups (280 mL). Serve with wings.

1 wing piece (with dip): 81 Calories; 5.8 g Total Fat; 76 mg Sodium; 5 g Protein; 1 g Carbohydrate

1. Cranberry Warmer, page 57
2. Sweet And Sour Wings, page 12
3. Curried Almonds, page 11
4. Carrot Onion Casserole, page 150
5. Stuffed Pork Roast, page 93
6. Applesauce, page 79
7. Snack Mix, page 10

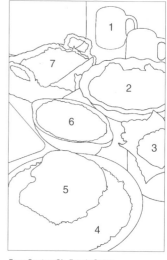

Props Courtesy Of: Eaton's; Stokes;
The Basket House;
The Bay

South of the border. Great served with chips.

Velveeta cheese, cubed	1 lb.	454 g
Canned chopped green chilies	4 oz.	114 mL
Medium or hot salsa	1¼ cups	300 mL

Combine cheese, green chilies and salsa in 3½ quart (3.5 L) slow cooker. Stir. Cover. Cook on Low for 1½ hours, stirring occasionally, until quite warm. Makes a generous 3 cups (750 mL).

1 tbsp. (15 mL): 34 Calories; 2.2 g Total Fat; 258 mg Sodium; 2 g Protein; 2 g Carbohydrate

ORIENTAL CHICKEN WINGS

Soy sauce flavor is always a favorite. These marinate as they cook.

Whole chicken wings (or drumettes)	3 lbs.	1.4 kg
Soy sauce	1 cup	250 mL
Brown sugar, packed	¾ cup	175 mL
Water	½ cup	125 mL
Lemon juice	1 tsp.	5 mL
Dry mustard	¼ tsp.	1 mL
Garlic powder	¼ tsp.	1 mL
Salt	½ tsp.	2 mL
Ground ginger	¼ tsp.	1 mL

Discard tip and cut wings apart at joint. Place pieces in 3½ quart (3.5 L) slow cooker.

Measure remaining 8 ingredients into bowl. Mix well. Pour over chicken pieces. Cover. Cook on Low for 8 to 9 hours or on High for 4 to 4½ hours until tender. Serve from slow cooker or remove to platter. Makes about 28 pieces of wing or about 18 drumettes.

1 wing piece (with sauce): 91 Calories; 4.3 g Total Fat; 692 mg Sodium; 6 g Protein; 7 g Carbohydrate

If you have a rabbit and a lawn sprinkler, you have hare spray.

BEEF 'N' BEANS

Lots of beef, beans and rice. A meal in one.

Lean ground beef	1 lb.	454 g
Canned mixed beans, with liquid	19 oz.	540 mL
Canned black-eyed peas, with liquid	14 oz.	398 mL
Canned tomatoes, with juice, broken up	14 oz.	398 mL
Finely chopped onion	1/2 cup	125 mL
Mild or medium salsa	1 cup	250 mL
Uncooked long grain converted rice	2/3 cup	150 mL
Salt	1 tsp.	5 mL
Pepper	1/4 tsp.	1 mL
Garlic powder	1/4 tsp.	1 mL
Water	1 cup	250 mL

Scramble-fry ground beef in non-stick frying pan. Drain well. Turn into 3 1/2 quart (3.5 L) slow cooker.

Add remaining 10 ingredients. Stir. Cover. Cook on Low for 8 to 9 hours or on High for 4 to 4 1/2 hours. Makes a generous 8 cups (2 L).

1 cup (250 mL): 281 Calories; 5.7 g Total Fat; 1303 mg Sodium; 19 g Protein; 39 g Carbohydrate; excellent source of Dietary Fiber

OVERNIGHT BAKED BEANS

When you start the beans cooking, have the rest of the ingredients measured and ready to add when needed.

Dried navy beans	2 cups	500 mL
Water	4 cups	1 L
Diced bacon, cooked crisp (about 5 slices)	3/4 cup	175 mL
Ketchup	1/4 cup	60 mL
Brown sugar, packed	1/3 cup	75 mL
Molasses (not blackstrap)	2 tbsp.	30 mL

Combine beans and water in 3 1/2 quart (3.5 L) slow cooker. Stir well. Cover. Cook on Low for 8 to 10 hours or overnight until beans are soft.

Add remaining 4 ingredients. Stir well. Cover. Cook on High for about 30 minutes to blend flavors. Makes 4 cups (1 L).

1/2 cup (125 mL): 256 Calories; 2.7 g Total Fat; 183 mg Sodium; 13 g Protein; 47 g Carbohydrate; good source of Dietary Fiber

Saucy, beany and meaty. Serve with crusty rolls.

Dried chick peas (garbanzo beans), 2½ cups (625 mL)	1 lb.	454 g
Chopped onion	1½ cups	375 mL
Medium carrots, cut julienne	2	2
Dried sweet basil	½ tsp.	2 mL
Pepper	¼ tsp.	1 mL
Water	5½ cups	1.4 L
Beef (or pork) stew meat, cut into ½ inch (12 mm) cubes	1 lb.	454 g
Cooking oil	1½ tsp.	7 mL
Canned tomatoes, drained, juice reserved	14 oz.	398 mL
Beef bouillon powder	1 tbsp.	15 mL
Salt	1 tsp.	5 mL
Reserved tomato juice		
All-purpose flour	3 tbsp.	50 mL

Combine first 6 ingredients in 3½ quart (3.5 L) slow cooker.

Brown beef quickly in hot cooking oil in frying pan. Add to slow cooker. Cover. Cook on Low for 8 to 10 hours or on High for 4 to 5 hours.

Add tomato, bouillon powder and salt.

Slowly whisk tomato juice into flour in small bowl. Stir into slow cooker. Cover. Cook on Low for 2 hours or on High for 1 hour. Stir before serving. Makes 9½ cups (2.3 L).

1 cup (250 mL): 300 Calories; 8.1 g Total Fat; 589 mg Sodium; 21 g Protein; 37 g Carbohydrate

Pictured on page 125.

If you hear a loud knock, it isn't opportunity. It's a relative.

BOSTON BAKED BEANS

When served as a breakfast dish in Boston in years past, it contained diced salt pork.

Dried navy beans (or peas), 1 lb. (454 g)	2¼ cups	560 mL
Chopped onion	1½ cups	375 mL
Water	5 cups	1.25 L
Ketchup	½ cup	125 mL
Molasses (not blackstrap)	⅓ cup	75 mL
Brown sugar, packed	⅓ cup	75 mL
Dry mustard	1 tsp.	5 mL
Salt	1 tsp.	5 mL
Pepper	¼ tsp.	1 mL

Combine beans, onion and water in 3½ quart (3.5 L) slow cooker. Stir. Cover. Cook on Low for 8 to 10 hours or on High for 4 to 5 hours.

Add remaining 6 ingredients. Stir well. Cover. Cook on High for about 30 minutes to blend flavors. Makes 6 cups (1.5 L).

½ cup (125 mL): 195 Calories; 0.6 g Total Fat; 380 mg Sodium; 9 g Protein; 40 g Carbohydrate; good source of Dietary Fiber

RANCH-STYLE BEANS

Thick and meaty. A touch on the sweet side. Contains both beef and ham.

Extra lean ground beef	1 lb.	454 g
Diced smoked ham (or 1 can, 6.5 oz., 184 g, with liquid)	1 cup	250 mL
Chopped onion	1 cup	250 mL
Canned beans in tomato sauce	2 x 14 oz.	2 x 398 mL
Canned kidney beans, drained	19 oz.	540 mL
Ketchup	½ cup	125 mL
Molasses (not blackstrap)	¼ cup	60 mL
Brown sugar, packed	¼ cup	60 mL
Salt	¾ tsp.	4 mL
Pepper	⅛ tsp.	0.5 mL
Liquid gravy browner	¼ tsp.	1 mL

Measure all 11 ingredients into 3½ quart (3.5 L) slow cooker. Mix well to break up and distribute beef and ham. Cover. Cook on Low for 8 to 9 hours or on High for 4 to 4½ hours. Stir before serving. Makes 8 cups (2 L).

1 cup (250 mL): 385 Calories; 9.7 g Total Fat; 1273 mg Sodium; 27 g Protein; 51 g Carbohydrate; excellent source of Dietary Fiber

A variety of pastel colors—green, yellow and cream—with little bits of red showing. A hearty vegetable.

Frozen lima beans	2 cups	500 mL
Chopped onion	1½ cups	375 mL
Sliced celery	½ cup	125 mL
Frozen corn	2 cups	500 mL
Chopped pimiento	2 tbsp.	30 mL
Garlic powder	¼ tsp.	1 mL
Dried sweet basil	¼ tsp.	1 mL
Salt	½ tsp.	2 mL
Pepper	⅛ tsp.	0.5 mL
Condensed cream of mushroom soup	10 oz.	284 mL

Grated medium Cheddar cheese, sprinkle

Measure first 10 ingredients into large bowl. Stir together well. Put into 3½ quart (3.5 L) slow cooker. Cover. Cook on Low for 8 to 10 hours or on High for 4 to 5 hours.

Stir. Sprinkle with cheese before serving. Makes 4 cups (1 L).

½ cup (125 mL): 136 Calories; 3.4 g Total Fat; 509 mg Sodium; 5 g Protein; 24 g Carbohydrate; good source of Dietary Fiber

Pictured on page 107.

If you meet a fire-breathing dragon, douse him with water so he'll let off steam.

BEANS AND BACON

To have more of a nip, use medium salsa. A touch on the sweet side. Good mixture.

Bacon slices, diced	8	8
Canned beans in tomato sauce, drained	2 x 14 oz.	2 x 398 mL
Chopped onion	1 cup	250 mL
Medium green pepper, chopped	1	1
Brown sugar, packed	1/2 cup	125 mL
Ketchup	1/2 cup	125 mL
Worcestershire sauce	1 tsp.	5 mL
Liquid smoke	1/4-1/2 tsp.	1-2 mL
Mild or medium salsa	1/2 cup	125 mL
Prepared mustard	1 tsp.	5 mL

Cook bacon in frying pan until crispy. Drain well. Turn into 3 1/2 quart (3.5 L) slow cooker.

Add remaining 9 ingredients. Stir. Cover. Cook on Low for 6 to 7 hours or on High for 3 to 3 1/2 hours. Makes 6 cups (1.5 L).

1/2 cup (125 mL): 153 Calories; 2.5 g Total Fat; 670 mg Sodium; 5 g Protein; 30 g Carbohydrate; excellent source of Dietary Fiber

PINEAPPLE BAKED BEANS

The pineapple flavor really complements this dish.

Canned beans in tomato sauce, with liquid	2 x 14 oz.	2 x 398 mL
Canned kidney beans, drained	14 oz.	398 mL
Minced onion flakes	3 tbsp.	50 mL
Hickory smoked barbecue sauce	1/2 cup	125 mL
Canned crushed pineapple, drained	14 oz.	398 mL
Brown sugar, packed	1/2 cup	125 mL
Prepared mustard	1 1/2 tsp.	7 mL

Place all 7 ingredients in 3 1/2 quart (3.5 L) slow cooker. Stir well. Cover. Cook on Low for 6 to 8 hours or on High for 3 to 4 hours. Makes 6 1/2 cups (1.6 L).

1/2 cup (125 mL): 140 Calories; 0.6 g Total Fat; 397 mg Sodium; 5 g Protein; 31 g Carbohydrate; excellent source of Dietary Fiber

Tastes just like lasagne but doesn't have layers.

Lasagne noodles, broken into bite-size pieces	8	8
Boiling water	3 qts.	3 L
Cooking oil (optional)	2 tsp.	10 mL
Salt	2 tsp.	10 mL
Lean ground beef	1½ lbs.	680 g
Finely chopped onion	¾ cup	175 mL
Canned tomatoes, with juice, broken up	2 x 14 oz.	2 x 398 mL
Tomato paste	5½ oz.	156 mL
Creamed cottage cheese	1 cup	250 mL
Grated mozzarella cheese	2 cups	500 mL
Granulated sugar	2 tsp.	10 mL
Parsley flakes	1 tsp.	5 mL
Dried whole oregano	½ tsp.	2 mL
Garlic powder	¼ tsp.	1 mL
Dried sweet basil	¼ tsp.	1 mL
Salt	1¼ tsp.	6 mL
Pepper	½ tsp.	2 mL

Cook lasagne noodle pieces in boiling water, cooking oil and salt in large uncovered Dutch oven for 14 to 16 minutes until tender but firm. Drain.

Scramble-fry ground beef in non-stick frying pan until browned. Drain well. Turn into 3½ quart (3.5 L) slow cooker.

Add remaining 12 ingredients. Stir well. Add lasagne noodle pieces. Stir. Cover. Cook on Low for 7 to 9 hours or on High for 3½ to 4½ hours. Makes 10 cups (2.5 L).

1 cup (250 mL): 295 Calories; 12.4 g Total Fat; 708 mg Sodium; 24 g Protein; 22 g Carbohydrate

Paré Pointer

If you smashed a clock, would you be convicted of killing time?

HAMBURGER CASSEROLE

Slight tomato flavor with carrot and peas adding color.

Lean ground beef	1½ lbs.	680 g
Medium potatoes, thinly sliced	3	3
Medium onion, thinly sliced	1	1
Medium carrots, thinly sliced	3	3
Celery rib, thinly sliced	1	1
Frozen peas	10 oz.	300 g
Salt	1 tsp.	5 mL
Pepper	¼ tsp.	1 mL
Condensed tomato soup	10 oz.	284 mL
Beef bouillon powder	2 tsp.	10 mL
Water	½ cup	125 mL

Scramble-fry ground beef in frying pan until browned. Drain well. Turn into 3½ quart (3.5 L) slow cooker.

Add next 7 ingredients. Stir.

Mix soup, bouillon powder and water in bowl. Add to slow cooker. Stir. Cover. Cook on Low for 8 to 10 hours or on High for 4 to 5 hours. Makes 8 cups (2 L).

1 cup (250 mL): 238 Calories; 8 g Total Fat; 842 mg Sodium; 19 g Protein; 22 g Carbohydrate; good source of Dietary Fiber

HAMBURGER STROGANOFF

Stroganoff over noodles makes a favorite dish.

Lean ground beef	1½ lbs.	680 g
All-purpose flour	2 tbsp.	30 mL
Salt	1 tsp.	5 mL
Pepper	¼ tsp.	1 mL
Chopped onion	1 cup	250 mL
Condensed cream of chicken soup	10 oz.	284 mL
Red wine vinegar	1 tsp.	5 mL
Prepared orange juice	2 tbsp.	30 mL
Light sour cream	1 cup	250 mL
Fettuccine noodles	1 lb.	454 g
Boiling water	4 qts.	4 L
Cooking oil (optional)	1 tbsp.	15 mL
Salt	1 tbsp.	15 mL

(continued on next page)

Scramble-fry ground beef in non-stick frying pan until browned. Do not drain.

Mix in flour, first amount of salt, pepper and onion. Stir in soup, vinegar and orange juice. Turn into 3½ quart (3.5 L) slow cooker. Cover. Cook on Low for 5 to 6 hours or on High for 2½ to 3 hours.

Stir in sour cream. Heat through. Makes 5 cups (1.25 L).

Cook noodles in boiling water, cooking oil and second amount of salt in large uncovered Dutch oven for 5 to 7 minutes until tender. Drain. Serve stroganoff over noodles. Serves 6.

1 serving: 631 Calories; 24.1 g Total Fat; 946 mg Sodium; 34 g Protein; 67 g Carbohydrate

BEEF STROGANOFF

Rich tasting and colorful. Does double duty. Serve as-is or as a topping for noodles or rice.

All-purpose flour	⅓ cup	75 mL
Salt	1 tsp.	5 mL
Pepper	¼ tsp.	1 mL
Paprika	½ tsp.	2 mL
Beef round steak, cut into ½ inch (12 mm) thick strips	2 lbs.	900 g
Chopped onion	1½ cups	375 mL
Garlic powder	¼ tsp.	1 mL
Canned tomatoes, with juice, broken up	14 oz.	398 mL
Ketchup	¼ cup	60 mL
Beef bouillon powder	2 tsp.	10 mL
Sherry (or alcohol-free sherry)	2 tbsp.	30 mL
Sliced fresh mushrooms	2 cups	500 mL
Light sour cream	1 cup	250 mL

Combine flour, salt, pepper and paprika in plastic bag. Place a few strips of steak in at a time. Shake to coat. Place in 3½ quart (3.5 L) slow cooker.

Mix next 7 ingredients in bowl. Pour over steak. Cover. Cook on Low for 7 to 9 hours or on High for 3½ to 4½ hours.

Stir in sour cream last 30 minutes of cooking time. Serves 6.

1 serving: 365 Calories; 13.6 g Total Fat; 1008 mg Sodium; 40 g Protein; 19 g Carbohydrate

SPICY SPAGHETTI SAUCE

Serve this over spaghetti, noodles or other pasta. A chunky sauce.

Canned diced tomatoes	19 oz.	540 mL
Ketchup	1/4 cup	60 mL
Canned sliced mushrooms, drained	10 oz.	284 mL
Chopped green pepper	1/3 cup	75 mL
Lemon juice	1 1/2 tbsp.	25 mL
Dried whole oregano	3/4 tsp.	4 mL
Dried sweet basil	1/2 tsp.	2 mL
Bay leaf	1	1
Chili powder	2 tsp.	10 mL
Garlic powder	1/4 tsp.	1 mL
Granulated sugar (optional)	1 tsp.	5 mL
Salt	1 1/2 tsp.	7 mL
Pepper	1/4 tsp.	1 mL
Lean ground beef	1 lb.	454 g
Chopped onion	1 cup	250 mL

Combine first 13 ingredients in 3 1/2 quart (3.5 L) slow cooker.

Scramble-fry ground beef and onion in non-stick frying pan until beef is no longer pink. Drain well. Add to slow cooker. Stir. Cover. Cook on Low for 6 to 7 hours or on High for 3 to 3 1/2 hours. Discard bay leaf. Makes 5 1/4 cups (1.3 L).

1 cup (250 mL): 193 Calories; 7.8 g Total Fat; 1267 mg Sodium; 18 g Protein; 14 g Carbohydrate; good source of Dietary Fiber

Pictured on page 107.

BEEFY RICE CASSEROLE

A mild chili flavor addition. Good mixture.

Cooking oil	1 tbsp.	15 mL
Lean ground beef	1 1/2 lbs.	680 g
Canned tomatoes, with juice	28 oz.	796 mL
Chopped onion	1 1/2 cups	375 mL
Chopped green pepper	1/4 cup	60 mL
Uncooked long grain converted rice	1 cup	250 mL
Salt	1 1/2 tsp.	7 mL
Chili powder	1 tsp.	5 mL
Water	1 cup	250 mL

(continued on next page)

Heat cooking oil in frying pan. Add ground beef. Scramble-fry until browned. Drain well. Turn into 3½ quart (3.5 L) slow cooker.

Add remaining 7 ingredients. Stir. Cover. Cook on Low for 6 to 8 hours or on High for 3 to 4 hours. Makes 7½ cups (1.8 L).

1 cup (250 mL): 285 Calories; 7.4 g Total Fat; 766 mg Sodium; 14 g Protein; 29 g Carbohydrate

MEATY SPAGHETTI SAUCE

Thick dark reddish sauce with just the right spice mixture. Leftover sauce may be frozen.

Canned tomatoes, with juice, mashed	28 oz.	796 mL
Tomato paste	5½ oz.	156 mL
Finely chopped onion	1 cup	250 mL
Garlic powder	½ tsp.	2 mL
Prepared mustard	2 tsp.	10 mL
Dried whole oregano	½ tsp.	2 mL
Parsley flakes	1 tsp.	5 mL
Granulated sugar	2 tsp.	10 mL
Bay leaf	1	1
Liquid gravy browner	½ tsp.	2 mL
Beef bouillon powder	1 tsp.	5 mL
Salt	1¼ tsp.	6 mL
Pepper	¼ tsp.	1 mL
Lean ground beef	1 lb.	454 g
Canned sliced mushrooms, drained	10 oz.	284 mL

Combine first 13 ingredients in large bowl. Stir well.

Add ground beef and mushrooms. Mix. Turn into 3½ quart (3.5 L) slow cooker. Cover. Cook on Low for 7 to 9 hours or on High for 3½ to 4½ hours. Discard bay leaf. Makes 6 cups (1.5 L).

½ cup (125 mL): 121 Calories; 6.1 g Total Fat; 546 mg Sodium; 9 g Protein; 8 g Carbohydrate

CHILI

Nice mild and dark chili. To make more fiery, simply add more chili powder.

Lean ground beef	1 lb.	454 g
Chopped onion	1 cup	250 mL
Green pepper, chopped	1	1
Canned kidney beans, with liquid	14 oz.	398 mL
Canned sliced mushrooms, drained	10 oz.	284 mL
Condensed tomato soup	10 oz.	284 mL
Chili powder	1 tsp.	5 mL
Seasoning salt	1/4 tsp.	1 mL
Granulated sugar	1 tsp.	5 mL
Salt	1/2 tsp.	2 mL
Pepper	1/8 tsp.	0.5 mL

Scramble-fry ground beef in non-stick frying pan until browned. Drain well.

Place onion and green pepper in bottom of 3½ quart (3.5 L) slow cooker.

Combine remaining 8 ingredients in bowl. Stir well. Add ground beef. Stir. Add to slow cooker. Cover. Cook on Low for 6 to 7 hours or on High for 3 to 3½ hours. Stir before serving. Makes 5½ cups (1.3 L).

1 cup (250 mL): 252 Calories; 8.2 g Total Fat; 1109 mg Sodium; 21 g Protein; 25 g Carbohydrate; excellent source of Dietary Fiber

PANIC ROAST!

Take roast out of freezer and place in slow cooker without defrosting. Make this easy one-step roast when time is of the essence.

Frozen boneless beef roast	3 lbs.	1.4 kg
Boiling water, to completely cover		

Place roast in 3½ quart (3.5 L) slow cooker. Pour boiling water over top. Cover. Cook on Low for 7 to 8 hours. Serves 10.

1 serving: 230 Calories; 9.5 g Total Fat; 78 mg Sodium; 34 g Protein; 0 g Carbohydrate

SWISS STEAK MEDITERRANEAN

Lots of deep rusty red gravy with steak, onion and mushrooms.

Spaghetti sauce	2 cups	500 mL
Dried whole oregano	1/2 tsp.	2 mL
Salt	1 tsp.	5 mL
Pepper	1/4 tsp.	1 mL
Beef round steak, trimmed of fat, cut into 6 pieces	1³/₄ lbs.	790 g
Medium onions, cut into chunks	2	2
Small whole fresh mushrooms (about 2 cups, 500 mL)	1/2 lb.	225 g

Stir first 4 ingredients together in bowl.

Place steak pieces in 3¹/₂ quart (3.5 L) slow cooker. Pour ¹/₃ of sauce over and between pieces.

Sprinkle onion and mushrooms over top. Pour remaining ²/₃ of sauce over all. Cover. Cook on Low for 7 to 9 hours or on High for 3¹/₂ to 4¹/₂ hours. Serves 6.

1 serving: 253 Calories; 7.4 g Total Fat; 943 mg Sodium; 28 g Protein; 19 g Carbohydrate

Pictured on page 35.

AEGEAN BEEF

Spiced with oregano and thyme.

Boneless beef chuck steak, cut into 1¹/₂ inch (3.8 cm) cubes	2.2 lbs.	1 kg
Chopped or sliced onion	2 cups	500 mL
Condensed cream of chicken soup	10 oz.	284 mL
Dried whole oregano	1/2 tsp.	2 mL
Ground thyme	1/4 tsp.	1 mL
Salt	3/4 tsp.	4 mL
Pepper	1/4 tsp.	1 mL
Liquid gravy browner	1/2 tsp.	2 mL

Place beef cubes in 3¹/₂ quart (3.5 L) slow cooker. Add onion over top.

Mix remaining 6 ingredients in bowl. Pour over top. Cover. Cook on Low for 7 to 9 hours or on High for 3¹/₂ to 4¹/₂ hours. Serves 8.

1 serving: 337 Calories; 23.7 g Total Fat; 645 mg Sodium; 23 g Protein; 7 g Carbohydrate

BEEF BRISKET

Brown and tender with chunks of carrot as well. Use leftover meat for sandwiches.

Medium carrots, cut diagonally into thin slices	6	6
Boneless beef brisket, trimmed of fat	4½ lbs.	2 kg
Red (or alcohol-free) wine	½ cup	125 mL
Water	½ cup	125 mL
Beef bouillon powder	2 tsp.	10 mL
Onion powder	½ tsp.	2 mL
Liquid gravy browner	½ tsp.	2 mL
Ground rosemary	¼ tsp.	1 mL
Pepper	¼ tsp.	1 mL

Place carrot in 6 quart (6 L) slow cooker. Lay brisket over top. If cooker is smaller, cut brisket in half.

Combine 7 remaining ingredients in small bowl. Pour over top. Cover. Cook on Low for 10 to 12 hours or on High for 5 to 6 hours until very tender. Serves 12.

1 serving: 243 Calories; 10.1 g Total Fat; 190 mg Sodium; 30 g Protein; 5 g Carbohydrate

POT ROAST

An old-fashioned meal in a pot.

Medium potatoes, cut into chunks	4	4
Medium carrots, cut into chunks (or use peeled baby carrots)	4	4
Medium onions, cut into chunks	2	2
Boneless beef chuck roast (or other)	3 lbs.	1.4 kg
Boiling water	½ cup	125 mL
Beef bouillon powder	1 tsp.	5 mL
Liquid gravy browner	½ tsp.	2 mL

Lay potato, carrot and onion in bottom of 5 quart (5 L) slow cooker.

Place roast on top.

Combine remaining 3 ingredients in small bowl. Stir. Pour over top. Cover. Cook on Low for 10 to 12 hours or on High for 5 to 6 hours. Serves 8 to 10.

⅛ recipe: 302 Calories; 9.9 g Total Fat; 182 mg Sodium; 35 g Protein; 17 g Carbohydrate

Pictured on front cover.

CHILI CON CARNE

A great chili with lots of beans and beef.

Canned tomatoes, with juice, broken up	14 oz.	398 mL
Envelope dry onion soup mix	1 x 1¹/₂ oz.	1 x 42 g
Pepper	¹/₄ tsp.	1 mL
Chili powder	2 tsp.	10 mL
Ketchup	¹/₄ cup	60 mL
Liquid gravy browner	¹/₂ tsp.	2 mL
Garlic powder (optional)	¹/₄ tsp.	1 mL
Dried sweet basil	¹/₄ tsp.	1 mL
Chopped onion	2 cups	500 mL
Canned kidney beans, with liquid	2 x 14 oz.	2 x 398 mL
Lean ground beef	1¹/₂ lbs.	680 g

Combine first 10 ingredients in 3¹/₂ quart (3.5 L) or 5 quart (5 L) slow cooker. Stir well.

Scramble-fry ground beef in non-stick frying pan until browned. Drain. Add to slow cooker. Stir. Cover. Cook on Low for 8 to 9 hours or on High for 4 to 4¹/₂ hours. Makes 8 cups (2 L).

1 cup (250 mL): 270 Calories; 8 g Total Fat; 1085 mg Sodium; 23 g Protein; 28 g Carbohydrate; excellent source of Dietary Fiber

STUFFED STEAK

Stuffing changes this steak into a scrumptious completely different dish. Also called Mock Duck.

Beef round steak, trimmed of fat, pounded ¹/₄ inch (6 mm) thick	1³/₄ lbs.	790 g
Box of stuffing mix, prepared as per package directions	4¹/₄ oz.	120 g
Beef bouillon powder	2 tsp.	10 mL
Hot water	1¹/₂ cups	375 mL

Lay steak out on flat surface. Spread stuffing over top. Roll up. Tie with string. Depending on size of your slow cooker, you may need to cut beef roll into 2 pieces, such as for the 3¹/₂ quart (3.5 L) slow cooker.

Stir bouillon powder into hot water. Pour over all. Cover. Cook on Low for 8 to 10 hours or on High for 4 to 5 hours. Cuts into 10 slices.

1 slice: 146 Calories; 4.6 g Total Fat; 337 mg Sodium; 17 g Protein; 9 g Carbohydrate

HUNGARIAN GOULASH

Super good dish. Beef cubes cook in a medium-thick gravy.

Beef stew meat (or round steak), cut into ¾ inch (2 cm) cubes	1½ lbs.	680 g
Chopped onion	1½ cups	375 mL
Garlic clove, minced (or ¼ tsp., 1 mL, garlic powder)	1	1
All-purpose flour	2 tbsp.	30 mL
Paprika	2 tsp.	10 mL
Salt	1 tsp.	5 mL
Pepper	¼ tsp.	1 mL
Canned tomatoes, with liquid	14 oz.	398 mL
Liquid gravy browner	½ tsp.	2 mL
Beef bouillon powder	2 tsp.	10 mL
Granulated sugar	1 tsp.	5 mL
Sour cream	½-1 cup	125-250 mL

Combine first 7 ingredients in 3½ quart (3.5 L) slow cooker. Stir well to coat beef and onion with flour.

Stir tomato, gravy browner, bouillon powder and sugar together in bowl. Pour over beef mixture. Stir. Cover. Cook on Low for 8 to 10 hours or on High for 4 to 5 hours.

Spoon off a few spoonfuls of juice into bowl. Add sour cream. Stir. Pour back into slow cooker. Stir before serving. Serves 6.

1 serving: 272 Calories; 13.1 g Total Fat; 851 mg Sodium; 27 g Protein; 11 g Carbohydrate

1. Swiss Steak Mediterranean, page 31
2. Scalloped Potatoes, page 110
3. Salmon Loaf, page 86
4. Tasty Mex Casserole, page 49
5. Spinach Dip, page 14

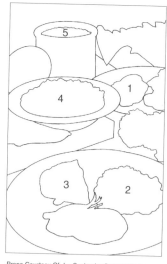

Props Courtesy Of: La Cache; Le Gnome; Stokes; The Bay; Tile Town Ltd.

Dark meatloaf with kidney beans peeping through. Enchilad. adds the final touch.

ENCHILADA SAUCE

Condensed cream of mushroom soup	10 oz.	284 mL
Canned tomatoes, with juice, broken up	14 oz.	398 mL
Canned chopped green chilies	4 oz.	114 mL
Sour cream	1/4 cup	60 mL
Granulated sugar	1 tsp.	5 mL
Garlic powder	1/8 tsp.	0.5 mL
Onion powder	1/8 tsp.	0.5 mL

MEATLOAF

Large eggs, fork-beaten	2	2
Canned tomatoes, with juice, broken up	14 oz.	398 mL
Canned kidney beans, drained	14 oz.	398 mL
Minced onion	1/2 cup	125 mL
Chili powder	1 tbsp.	15 mL
Salt	2 tsp.	10 mL
Pepper	1/4 tsp.	1 mL
Dried whole oregano, generous measure	1/2 tsp.	2 mL
Garlic powder	1/4 tsp.	1 mL
White vinegar	1 1/2 tbsp.	25 mL
Lean ground beef	2 lbs.	900 g
Coarsely crushed corn chips	3/4 cup	175 mL
Grated medium or sharp Cheddar cheese	3/4 cup	175 mL

Enchilada Sauce: Combine all 7 ingredients in bowl. Stir well. Set aside.

Meatloaf: Combine first 10 ingredients in large bowl. Measure 1/4 cup (60 mL) enchilada sauce and add to tomato mixture. Mix well. Cover remaining sauce and refrigerate until meatloaf is done.

Add ground beef and corn chips. Mix very well. Shape into round loaf. Pack in 5 quart (5 L) slow cooker. Cover. Cook on Low for 8 to 10 hours or on High for 4 to 5 hours.

Transfer remaining enchilada sauce to saucepan. Heat, stirring often, until hot. Pour over meatloaf. Sprinkle with cheese. Cook on High until cheese is just melted. Serves 10.

1 serving: 357 Calories; 22.5 g Total Fat; 1189 mg Sodium; 24 g Protein; 15 g Carbohydrate

MEATLOAF STEW

Quite different to have meatloaf in a stew.

Water	¼ cup	60 mL
Medium potatoes, peeled and cut bite size	5-6	5-6
Medium carrots, peeled and cut bite size	6	6
Salt, sprinkle		
Pepper, sprinkle		
Large egg, fork-beaten	1	1
Ketchup	⅓ cup	75 mL
Beef bouillon powder	2 tsp.	10 mL
Finely chopped onion	⅓ cup	75 mL
Ground thyme	¼ tsp.	1 mL
Water	¼ cup	60 mL
Soda cracker crumbs	⅓ cup	75 mL
Salt	1 tsp.	5 mL
Pepper	¼ tsp.	1 mL
Lean ground beef	1½ lbs.	680 g

Pour first amount of water into 6 quart (6 L) slow cooker. Add potato and carrot. Sprinkle with first amounts of salt and pepper.

Combine next 9 ingredients in bowl. Mix well.

Add ground beef. Mix well. Place over vegetables. Cover. Cook on Low for 8 to 10 hours or on High for 4 to 5 hours. Serves 6.

1 serving: 409 Calories; 18.9 g Total Fat; 1010 mg Sodium; 26 g Protein; 34 g Carbohydrate; good source of Dietary Fiber

EASY MEATLOAF

An extra good meatloaf.

Large eggs, fork-beaten	2	2
Ketchup	6 tbsp.	100 mL
Envelope dry onion soup mix	1 × 1½ oz.	1 × 42 g
Quick-cooking rolled oats (not instant)	½ cup	125 mL
Garlic powder	⅛ tsp.	0.5 mL
Parsley flakes	1 tsp.	5 mL
Salt	½ tsp.	2 mL
Lean ground beef	2 lbs.	900 g
Ketchup	3 tbsp.	50 mL

(continued on next page)

Combine first 7 ingredients in large bowl.

Add ground beef. Mix well. Place in 3½ quart (3.5 L) slow cooker.

Smooth second amount of ketchup over top. Cover. Cook on Low for 6 to 8 hours or on High for 3 to 4 hours. Serves 8.

1 serving: 318 Calories; 18.9 g Total Fat; 961 mg Sodium; 24 g Protein; 12 g Carbohydrate

TRADITIONAL MEATLOAF

Cheese adds extra protein and more flavor. Good spices added.

Large eggs, fork-beaten	2	2
Milk	¼ cup	60 mL
Dry bread crumbs	1 cup	250 mL
Worcestershire sauce	1 tsp.	5 mL
Salt	1 tsp.	5 mL
Pepper	¼ tsp.	1 mL
Dried sweet basil	¼ tsp.	1 mL
Ground thyme	¼ tsp.	1 mL
Finely chopped onion	2 cups	500 mL
Lean ground beef	1 lb.	454 g
Lean ground pork	1 lb.	454 g
Grated sharp Cheddar cheese (optional)	1 cup	250 mL
Ketchup	¼ cup	60 mL

Mix first 9 ingredients in large bowl.

Add ground beef and ground pork. Mix well. Press ½ of meat mixture into bottom of greased 5 quart (5 L) slow cooker.

Spread with cheese. Press second ½ of meat mixture over top. Cover. Cook on Low for 10 to 11 hours or on High for 5 to 5½ hours. Smooth ketchup over meat mixture during last hour of cooking. Serves 6 to 8.

⅙ recipe: 405 Calories; 18 g Total Fat; 875 mg Sodium; 36 g Protein; 23 g Carbohydrate

Paré Pointer

If you don't get everything you want, think of the things you do get that you don't want.

BEEF DIP

Lean over bowls of dipping sauce, dunk and enjoy.

Boneless beef chuck (or blade) roast	2½ lbs.	1.1 kg
Boiling water		
Beef bouillon powder	4 tsp.	20 mL
Onion powder	½ tsp.	2 mL
Salt	½ tsp.	2 mL
Pepper	⅛ tsp.	0.5 mL
Hamburger buns, split (buttered, optional)	10	10

Place roast in 3½ quart (3.5 L) slow cooker. Add boiling water until halfway up sides of roast. Cover. Cook on Low for 7 to 9 hours or on High for 3½ to 4½ hours. Remove roast. Strain beef juice. Skim off any fat. Add hot water to beef juice, if needed, to make 3 cups (750 mL).

Add bouillon powder, onion powder, salt and pepper. Stir.

Slice beef thinly. Insert slices into each bun. Serve with a small bowl of beef juice for dipping. Makes 10 buns and 3 cups (750 mL) beef juice.

1 bun with ⅓ cup (75 mL) beef juice: 253 Calories; 8.3 g Total Fat; 636 mg Sodium; 19 g Protein; 24 g Carbohydrate

BEEF IN WINE

Just the right amount of wine flavor. Meat is tender with a delicate blend of flavors. Serve over rice or noodles.

Boneless beef blade steak, cut into 2 inch (5 cm) cubes	2⅛ lbs.	1 kg
Hot water	½ cup	125 mL
Beef bouillon powder	2 tsp.	10 mL
Condensed cream of mushroom soup	10 oz.	284 mL
Canned mushroom pieces, drained	10 oz.	284 mL
Envelope onion soup mix	1 × 1½ oz.	1 × 42 g
Red (or alcohol-free) wine	½ cup	125 mL

(continued on next page)

Place beef cubes in 6 quart (6 L) slow cooker.

Stir hot water and bouillon powder together in medium bowl.

Add soup, mushroom pieces, soup mix and wine. Stir. Pour over beef cubes. Cover. Cook on Low for 7 to 9 hours or on High for 3½ to 4½ hours. Makes 6⅔ cups (1.65 L). Serves 6 to 8.

⅙ recipe: 473 Calories; 32.9 g Total Fat; 982 mg Sodium; 31 g Protein; 9 g Carbohydrate

Pictured on page 125.

SWEDISH MEATBALLS

Make a bunch so you can freeze some; cut the recipe in half for a smaller crowd. Gravy adds the extra touch.

Milk	1 cup	250 mL
Fine dry bread crumbs	1¼ cups	300 mL
Large eggs, fork-beaten	2	2
Chopped onion	1¼ cups	300 mL
Salt	1½ tsp.	7 mL
Pepper	¼ tsp.	1 mL
Ground allspice	⅛ tsp.	0.5 mL
Lean ground beef	1½ lbs.	680 g
Lean ground pork	½ lb.	225 g
SAUCE		
All-purpose flour	¼ cup	60 mL
Salt	½ tsp.	2 mL
Condensed beef consommé	10 oz.	284 mL
Water	1 cup	250 mL

Mix first 7 ingredients in bowl. Stir well.

Add ground beef and ground pork. Shape into 1½ inch (3.8 cm) balls. Arrange on broiler tray. Brown quickly under broiler, turning once. Pile balls into 5 quart (5 L) slow cooker.

Sauce: Measure flour and salt in saucepan. Whisk in consommé and water gradually until no lumps remain. Heat until it boils and thickens a bit. Pour over meatballs. Cover. Cook on Low for 8 to 10 hours or on High for 4 to 5 hours. Makes 57 meatballs.

3 meatballs (with sauce): 151 Calories; 7 g Total Fat; 467 mg Sodium; 12 g Protein; 9 g Carbohydrate

PORCUPINE MEATBALLS

Very colorful with rice being the quills.

Lean ground beef	1½ lbs.	680 g
Onion flakes (or ¼ cup, 60 mL, diced onion)	1½ tbsp.	25 mL
Salt	1 tsp.	5 mL
Pepper	¼ tsp.	1 mL
Large egg, fork-beaten	1	1
Uncooked long grain converted rice	⅔ cup	150 mL
Fine dry bread crumbs	½ cup	125 mL
Milk	2 tbsp.	30 mL
Tomato juice	3 cups	750 mL
Water	1 cup	250 mL
Granulated sugar	1 tsp.	5 mL
Salt	½ tsp.	2 mL
Liquid gravy browner	½ tsp.	2 mL

Combine first 8 ingredients in large bowl. Mix well. Shape into 1½ inch (3.8 cm) balls. Place in 3½ quart (3.5 L) slow cooker.

Pour tomato juice and water into bowl. Add sugar, second amount of salt and gravy browner. Stir. Pour over meatballs. Cover. Cook on Low for 8 to 10 hours or on High for 4 to 5 hours. Makes 36 meatballs.

3 meatballs (with sauce): 204 Calories; 9.3 g Total Fat; 652 mg Sodium; 13 g Protein; 16 g Carbohydrate

SMOKY MEATBALLS

A hint of smoked flavor makes these irresistible.

Chili sauce	¾ cup	175 mL
Granulated sugar	⅔ cup	150 mL
Worcestershire sauce	1 tsp.	5 mL
Large egg, fork-beaten	1	1
Water	½ cup	125 mL
Fine dry bread crumbs	⅔ cup	150 mL
Chopped onion	½ cup	125 mL
Liquid smoke	2 tsp.	10 mL
Garlic powder	¼ tsp.	1 mL
Chili powder	1 tsp.	5 mL
Salt	1 tsp.	5 mL
Pepper	¼ tsp.	1 mL
Lean ground beef	1½ lbs.	680 g

(continued on next page)

Measure first 3 ingredients into bowl. Stir well. Set aside.

Combine next 9 ingredients in bowl. Stir well.

Add ground beef. Mix well. Shape into 1½ inch (3.8 cm) balls. Place in 3½ quart (3.5 L) slow cooker. Spoon chili sauce mixture over top, covering all balls that are visible. Cook on Low for 8 to 10 hours or on High for 4 to 5 hours. Makes 36 meatballs.

3 meatballs (with sauce): 221 Calories; 9.4 g Total Fat; 565 mg Sodium; 13 g Protein; 22 g Carbohydrate

PINEAPPLE MEATBALLS

Sure to please with pineapple flavor coming through.

Fine dry bread (or soda cracker) crumbs	¾ cup	175 mL
Milk	2 tbsp.	30 mL
Large eggs, fork-beaten	2	2
Finely chopped onion	¾ cup	175 mL
Garlic powder	¼ tsp.	1 mL
Ground ginger	¼ tsp.	1 mL
Salt	1¼ tsp.	6 mL
Pepper	¼ tsp.	1 mL
Lean ground beef	1½ lbs.	680 g
SAUCE		
Canned crushed pineapple, with juice	14 oz.	398 mL
Brown sugar, packed	1 cup	250 mL
White vinegar	½ cup	125 mL
Soy sauce	3 tbsp.	50 mL
Cornstarch	1 tbsp.	15 mL
Water	1 tbsp.	15 mL

Stir first 8 ingredients together well in bowl.

Add ground beef. Mix well. Shape into 1½ inch (3.8 cm) balls. Place in 3½ quart (3.5 L) or 5 quart (5 L) slow cooker.

Sauce: Put first 4 ingredients into saucepan on medium. Stir. Bring to a boil.

Stir cornstarch and water together in small cup. Stir into boiling mixture until slightly thickened. Pour over meatballs. Cover. Cook on Low for 8 to 10 hours or on High for 4 to 5 hours. Makes about 36 meatballs.

3 meatballs (with sauce): 268 Calories; 9.8 g Total Fat; 653 mg Sodium; 13 g Protein; 32 g Carbohydrate

CURRIED BEEF

Rich dark color with a good tangy taste.

Beef stew meat, cut into 1½ inch (3.8 cm) thick cubes or strips	2 lbs.	900 g
Medium onions, cut into small chunks	2	2
All-purpose flour	3 tbsp.	50 mL
Salt	1½ tsp.	7 mL
Pepper	½ tsp.	2 mL
Garlic powder (or 1 clove, minced)	¼ tsp.	1 mL
Curry powder	1½ tsp.	7 mL
Tomato sauce	2 × 7.5 oz.	2 × 213 mL
Beef bouillon powder	2 tsp.	10 mL
Liquid gravy browner	½ tsp.	2 mL
Granulated sugar	½ tsp.	2 mL

Combine first 7 ingredients in 3½ quart (3.5 L) slow cooker. Stir well to coat with flour.

Stir remaining 4 ingredients in small bowl. Pour over top. Cover. Cook on Low for 8 to 10 hours or on High for 4 to 5 hours. Makes 6 cups (1.5 L).

1 cup (250 mL): 314 Calories; 13.3 g Total Fat; 1425 mg Sodium; 35 g Protein; 13 g Carbohydrate

ORIENTAL BEEF

Pea pods and bean sprouts are added 30 minutes before serving. They add great flavor.

Beef steak, cut across the grain into thin slices	1½ lbs.	680 g
Beef bouillon powder	1 tbsp.	15 mL
Hot water	2 cups	500 mL
Liquid gravy browner	½ tsp.	2 mL
Soy sauce	3 tbsp.	50 mL
Ground ginger	¼ tsp.	1 mL
Garlic powder	¼ tsp.	1 mL
Cornstarch	2 tbsp.	30 mL
Water	2 tbsp.	30 mL
Frozen pea pods, thawed	6 oz.	170 g
Bean sprouts, handful	1	1

(continued on next page)

Place steak strips in 5 quart (5 L) slow cooker.

Stir next 6 ingredients together in bowl. Pour over top. Cover. Cook on Low for 8 to 10 hours or on High for 4 to 5 hours.

Mix cornstarch and second amount of water in small cup. Add to slow cooker. Stir. Stir in pea pods and bean sprouts. Cover. Cook on High for about 20 minutes until thickened and tender. Serves 6 to 8.

1/6 recipe: 221 Calories; 8.7 g Total Fat; 907 mg Sodium; 27 g Protein; 7 g Carbohydrate

CORNED BEEF DINNER

Since corned beef is cooked in liquid, vegetables are placed on top which means it takes longer to cook. So good and so colorful.

Boiling water	2 cups	500 mL
Whole cloves	2	2
Brown sugar, packed	1 tbsp.	15 mL
Bay leaf	1	1
Pepper	1/4 tsp.	1 mL
Corned beef	3 1/3 lbs.	1.5 kg
Small cabbage (about 2 lbs., 900 g), cut into 8 wedges	1	1
Medium carrots, cut up	6	6
Medium onions, cut up	2	2
Medium potatoes, peeled and cut up	4	4

Stir first 5 ingredients together in bowl. Pour liquid mixture into 6 quart (6 L) slow cooker.

Place corned beef in liquid mixture.

Add remaining 4 ingredients. Cover. Cook on Low for 10 to 12 hours or on High for 5 to 6 hours. Discard bay leaf. Serves 12.

1 serving: 298 Calories; 17 g Total Fat; 1028 mg Sodium; 18 g Protein; 18 g Carbohydrate; good source of Dietary Fiber

Paré Pointer

If you have a doorbell and a baseball player, you have a dingbat.

BBQ BEEF RIBS

Awesome flavor and so tender.

Cooking oil	2 tbsp.	30 mL
Beef short ribs, trimmed of fat	3 lbs.	1.4 kg
Barbecue sauce	1 cup	250 mL
Molasses (not blackstrap)	2 tbsp.	30 mL
White vinegar	2 tbsp.	30 mL
Salt	1½ tsp.	7 mL
Pepper	½ tsp.	2 mL
Soy sauce	1 tbsp.	15 mL
Chopped onion	½ cup	125 mL

Heat cooking oil in frying pan. Add ribs. Brown all sides. Drain. Place ribs in 5 quart (5 L) slow cooker.

Mix next 6 ingredients well in bowl.

Stir in onion. Pour over short ribs. Cover. Cook on Low for 8 to 10 hours or on High for 4 to 5 hours. Serves 6.

1 serving: 310 Calories; 15.9 g Total Fat; 1415 mg Sodium; 27 g Protein; 13 g Carbohydrate

BEEF SHORT RIBS

A very tender economical meat dish.

Beef short ribs, trimmed of fat	4 lbs.	1.8 kg
Salt, sprinkle		
Pepper, sprinkle		
Medium onions, sliced or chopped	2	2
Beef bouillon powder	2 tsp.	10 mL
Liquid gravy browner	½ tsp.	2 mL
Warm water	1½ cups	375 mL

Sprinkle short ribs with salt and pepper.

Lay onion in bottom of 5 quart (5 L) slow cooker. Arrange ribs over top.

Stir bouillon powder and gravy browner into warm water. Pour over ribs. Cover. Cook on Low for 7 to 9 hours or on High for 3½ to 4½ hours. Serves 8.

1 serving: 215 Calories; 11.9 g Total Fat; 203 mg Sodium; 23 g Protein; 3 g Carbohydrate

POLYNESIAN STEAK STRIPS

This is easy to cut in half for a family of four. Dark strips of beef have a ginger soy sauce flavor.

Beef steak, cut across the grain into thin slices	2 lbs.	900 g
Water	1/2 cup	125 mL
Ketchup	2 tbsp.	30 mL
Oyster sauce	1 tbsp.	15 mL
Soy sauce	1/4 cup	60 mL
Ground ginger	1/2 tsp.	2 mL
Garlic powder	1/4 tsp.	1 mL
Granulated sugar	1 tsp.	5 mL
Liquid gravy browner	1/4 tsp.	1 mL
Salt	1 tsp.	5 mL
Pepper	1/4 tsp.	1 mL

Place steak strips in 3½ quart (3.5 L) slow cooker.

Mix remaining 10 ingredients in small bowl. Pour over strips. Stir. Cover. Cook on Low for 8 to 10 hours or on High for 4 to 5 hours. Serves 6.

1 serving: 263 Calories; 11.2 g Total Fat; 1480 mg Sodium; 34 g Protein; 5 g Carbohydrate

Pictured on page 143.

ITALIAN-STYLE ROAST

Topped with red sauce, this is very tender.

Beef sirloin tip roast	3 lbs.	1.4 kg
Canned mushroom pieces, drained	10 oz.	284 mL
Chopped onion	1 cup	250 mL
Spaghetti sauce	1 cup	250 mL
Garlic salt	1/2 tsp.	2 mL

Gravy, page 48

Place roast in 3½ quart (3.5 L) slow cooker. Add mushroom pieces and onion.

Stir spaghetti sauce and garlic salt together in bowl. Pour over all. Cover. Cook on Low for 8 to 10 hours or on High for 4 to 5 hours.

Make gravy with remaining liquid. Serves 6 to 8.

1 serving: 407 Calories; 14.4 g Total Fat; 797 mg Sodium; 54 g Protein; 13 g Carbohydrate

ROAST BEEF

Mmm! Roast beef and gravy. Bring on the potatoes and vegetables.

Boneless beef roast (such as eye of round)	3 lbs.	1.4 kg
Beef bouillon powder	1 tsp.	5 mL
Boiling water	½ cup	125 mL
Gravy, below		

Place beef in 3½ quart (3.5 L) slow cooker.

Stir bouillon powder and boiling water together in small cup. Pour over beef. Cover. Cook on Low for 8 to 10 hours or on High for 4 to 5 hours.

Make gravy with remaining juice from beef. Serves 6 to 8.

1 serving: 396 Calories; 16 g Total Fat; 442 mg Sodium; 57 g Protein; 2 g Carbohydrate

GRAVY

Whether you want a little gravy or a lot, simply use this method.

All-purpose flour	2 tbsp.	30 mL
Salt (see Note)	¼ tsp.	1 mL
Pepper	¹⁄₁₆ tsp.	0.5 mL
Meat juice or liquid, strained if needed, fat removed, plus water to make	1 cup	250 mL
Bouillon powder (use beef bouillon for beef, pork or lamb; chicken bouillon for poultry)	1 tsp.	5 mL
Liquid gravy browner, enough to make a pleasing color (optional)		

Combine flour, salt and pepper in saucepan. Stir.

Gradually whisk in meat juice and water until no lumps remain. Heat and stir until boiling and thickened.

Taste, adding bouillon powder for more flavor if needed. Stir in gravy browner to color. Add more salt and pepper if needed. Makes 1 cup (250 mL).

Note: The more bouillon powder used, the less salt required. Salt may be added as the last step.

¼ cup (60 mL): 17 Calories; 0.1 g Total Fat; 318 mg Sodium; 1 g Protein; 3 g Carbohydrate

Lots of color. Green chilies add flavor.

Lean ground beef	1½ lbs.	680 g
White vinegar	3 tbsp.	50 mL
Chili powder	1 tbsp.	15 mL
Dried whole oregano	1 tsp.	5 mL
Garlic powder	¼ tsp.	1 mL
Salt	1½ tsp.	7 mL
Pepper	¼ tsp.	1 mL
Chopped onion	1½ cups	375 mL
Medium green pepper, chopped	1	1
Canned chopped green chilies, drained (optional)	4 oz.	114 mL
Canned kernel corn, drained	12 oz.	341 mL
Elbow macaroni, partially cooked, drained and rinsed	1 cup	250 mL
Canned tomatoes, with juice, broken up	2 x 14 oz.	2 x 398 mL
Chili powder	2 tsp.	10 mL
Parsley flakes	1 tsp.	5 mL
Dried whole oregano	½ tsp.	2 mL
Granulated sugar	2 tsp.	10 mL
Salt	½ tsp.	2 mL
Pepper	¼ tsp.	1 mL

Mix first 7 ingredients in bowl. Scramble-fry in non-stick frying pan until browned. Drain.

Put onion into 3½ quart (3.5 L) or 5 quart (5 L) slow cooker. Add green pepper, green chilies, corn and partially cooked macaroni. Add beef mixture. Stir.

Combine remaining 7 ingredients in bowl. Stir well. Pour over top. Stir. Cover. Cook on Low for 8 hours or on High for 4 hours. Makes 10 cups (2.5 L).

1 cup (250 mL): *206 Calories; 6.5 g Total Fat; 874 mg Sodium; 16 g Protein; 23 g Carbohydrate*

Pictured on page 35.

Paré Pointer

If you've been growling all day, you will be dog tired at night.

BEEF BOURGUIGNONNE

Cubes of beef with onion and mushrooms have that food cooked-in-wine taste.

Boneless beef chuck roast, cut into 1 inch (2.5 cm) cubes	1½ lbs.	680 g
Sliced white onion	1 cup	250 mL
Small whole mushrooms	2 cups	500 mL
Condensed cream of mushroom soup	10 oz.	284 mL
Red (or alcohol-free) wine	¼ cup	60 mL
Beef bouillon powder	1 tsp.	5 mL
Water	½ cup	125 mL
Salt	¾ tsp.	4 mL
Pepper	¼ tsp.	1 mL

Place beef cubes in 3½ quart (3.5 L) slow cooker. Add onion and mushrooms.

Combine 6 remaining ingredients in bowl. Stir vigorously. Pour over top. Cover. Cook on Low for 8 to 10 hours or on High for 4 to 5 hours. Serves 6.

1 serving: 193 Calories; 9.7 g Total Fat; 882 mg Sodium; 17 g Protein; 8 g Carbohydrate

STEAK AND MUSHROOMS

In its own gravy. Ready and waiting.

Beef round steak (about 1 inch, 2.5 cm, thick), cut into cubes	1 lb.	454 g
Salt, sprinkle		
Pepper, sprinkle		
Condensed cream of mushroom soup	10 oz.	284 mL
Canned mushroom pieces, drained (optional)	10 oz.	284 mL
Liquid gravy browner	¼ tsp.	1 mL

Place beef cubes in 3½ quart (3.5 L) slow cooker. Sprinkle with salt and pepper.

Combine soup and mushroom pieces in bowl. Add gravy browner. Stir well. Spoon over steak. Cover. Cook on Low for 7 to 9 hours or on High for 3½ to 4½ hours. Serves 4.

1 serving: 265 Calories; 13.4 g Total Fat; 685 mg Sodium; 29 g Protein: 6 g Carbohydrate

HOT CITRUS PUNCH

A pretty bright yellow. Nice light tang. Good sipping.

Prepared orange juice	4 cups	1 L
Frozen concentrated lemonade, thawed	12½ oz.	355 mL
Lemon-lime soft drink	4 cups	1 L
Ginger ale	4 cups	1 L

Combine all 4 ingredients in 3½ quart (3.5 L) slow cooker. Stir. Cover. Cook on Low for at least 3 hours until quite warm. Makes 12⅔ cups (3.1 L)

1 cup (250 mL): 159 Calories; 0.1 g Total Fat; 17 mg Sodium; 1 g Protein; 41 g Carbohydrate

Pictured on front cover.

APPLE PUNCH

Cinnamon-apple flavor. A great cold day sipper. Doubles or triples easily.

Apple juice	4⅓ cups	1 L
Brown sugar, packed	1 tbsp.	15 mL
Lemon juice	½ tsp.	2 mL
Cinnamon stick (2 inches, 5 cm, in length), broken up and crushed in plastic bag	1	1
Whole cloves	15	15
Orange pekoe tea bag (or 1 tbsp., 15 mL, loose tea)	1	1

Combine apple juice, brown sugar and lemon juice in 3½ quart (3.5 L) slow cooker. Stir.

Tie cinnamon, cloves and tea bag in double layer of cheesecloth. Add to slow cooker. Cover. Heat on Low for at least 3 hours until quite warm. Discard spice bag. Makes 4 cups (1 L).

1 cup (250 mL): 150 Calories; 0.3 g Total Fat; 17 mg Sodium; trace Protein; 38 g Carbohydrate

Pictured on page 125.

MULLED WINE

A very convenient potful, ready for company.

Dry red (or alcohol-free) wine	8 cups	2 L
Corn syrup	⅔ cup	150 mL
Cinnamon sticks, (4 inches, 10 cm, each in length), broken up and crushed in plastic bag	3	3
Whole allspice	1 tsp.	5 mL
Whole cloves	1 tsp.	5 mL
Medium orange, sliced	1	1
Lemon juice	1 tsp.	5 mL
Prepared orange juice (or cranberry cocktail)	2 cups	500 mL

Combine wine and corn syrup in 3½ quart (3.5 L) slow cooker. Stir.

Tie cinnamon, allspice and cloves in double layer of cheesecloth. Add to slow cooker.

Add remaining 3 ingredients. Cover. Cook on Low for at least 3 hours. Discard spice bag. Discard orange slices if desired. Makes 9 cups (2.25 L).

1 cup (250 mL): 267 Calories; 0.1 g Total Fat; 29 mg Sodium; 1 g Protein; 31 g Carbohydrate

1. Dried Fruit Compote, page 78
2. Hot Chocolate, page 55
3. Oatmeal Porridge, page 60
4. Date Loaf, page 63
5. Ham Steaks, page 103
6. Cranberry Loaf, page 64
7. Banana Bread, page 62

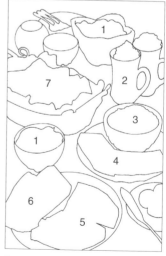

Props Courtesy Of: Creations By Design; Dansk Gifts; Eaton's; La Cache; Stokes

MOCHA HOT SPOT

Triple the flavor with coffee, chocolate and liqueur.

Prepared coffee, warm or cold	8 cups	2 L
Sweetened chocolate drink powder	1/2 cup	125 mL
Powdered coffee whitener	1/4 cup	60 mL
Kahlua (or Tia Maria) liqueur	1/2 cup	125 mL

Frozen whipped topping (in a tub),
    thawed (or whipped cream), optional
Grated chocolate, sprinkle (optional)

Combine first 4 ingredients in 3 1/2 quart (3.5 L) slow cooker. Stir. Cover. Cook on Low for at least 3 hours until hot.

Pour into mugs. Top with a dollop of whipped topping. Sprinkle with chocolate. Makes 8 1/2 cups (2.1 L).

1 cup (250 mL): 110 Calories; 1.4 g Total Fat; 33 mg Sodium; 1 g Protein; 17 g Carbohydrate

HOT CHOCOLATE

Imagine this after a family outing—skating, tobogganing or during a video.

Skim milk powder	4 cups	1 L
Cocoa	3/4 cup	175 mL
Icing (confectioner's) sugar	1 cup	250 mL
Water	10 cups	2.5 L

Frozen whipped topping (in a tub),
    thawed (or marshmallows), optional
Grated chocolate (optional)

Combine first 3 ingredients in 3 1/2 quart (3.5 L) slow cooker. Stir well.

Add water. Stir. Cover. Cook on Low for at least 3 hours until hot. Stir. Ladle into mugs.

Top with whipped topping. Sprinkle with chocolate. Makes 11 1/2 cups (2.85 L).

1 cup (250 mL): 213 Calories; 0.9 g Total Fat; 237 mg Sodium; 17 g Protein; 37 g Carbohydrate

Pictured on page 53.

GLÖGG

This beverage is a good tasty variation of the Swedish drink. To make more authentic, add a few raisins and whole almonds to each mug. Brandy or aquavit (a strong colorless Scandinavian liquor) may also be added.

Cardamom seeds, crushed in plastic bag	20	20
Whole cloves	25	25
Cinnamon sticks (4 inches, 10 cm, each in length), broken up and crushed in plastic bag	4	4
Red wine (or alcohol-free wine)	6 cups	1.5 L
Prepared orange juice	1 cup	250 mL
Lemon juice	¼ cup	60 mL
Granulated sugar	½ cup	125 mL

Tie cardamom, cloves and cinnamon in double layer of cheesecloth. Add to 3½ quart (3.5 L) slow cooker.

Add remaining 4 ingredients. Stir. Cover. Cook on Low for at least 3 hours until quite warm. Discard spice bag. Makes 7⅓ cups (1.8 L).

1 cup (250 mL): 220 Calories; trace Total Fat; 11 mg Sodium; 1 g Protein; 22 g Carbohydrate

RED HOT PUNCH

Clear red color with a subtle strawberry flavor.

Water	6 cups	1.5 L
Tropical punch-flavored crystals with sugar	⅔ cup	150 mL
Lemon-lime soft drink (or ginger ale)	3½ cups	875 mL
Lemon juice	¼ cup	60 mL
Frozen sliced strawberries, in syrup, thawed	15 oz.	425 g

Combine water, flavored crystals, soft drink and lemon juice in 3½ quart (3.5 L) slow cooker.

Add strawberries with syrup. Stir. Cover. Cook on Low for at least 3 hours until quite warm. Remove strawberries with slotted spoon. Discard strawberries. Strain liquid to remove pulp if desired. Makes 10½ cups (2.6 L).

1 cup (250 mL): 126 Calories; 0.1 g Total Fat; 27 mg Sodium; trace Protein; 33 g Carbohydrate

This toddy is easy to take.

Water	12 cups	3 L
Rum	2 cups	500 mL
Brown sugar, packed	1/2 cup	125 mL
Hard margarine (or butter)	1/4 cup	60 mL
Ground cinnamon	1/4 tsp.	1 mL
Ground nutmeg	1/4 tsp.	1 mL
Ground cloves	1/8 tsp.	0.5 mL
Salt	1/16 tsp.	0.5 mL

Combine all 8 ingredients in 5 quart (5 L) slow cooker. Stir well. Cover. Cook on Low for at least 3 hours until quite warm. Makes 13 cups (3.25 L).

1 cup (250 mL): 151 Calories; 3.8 g Total Fat; 60 mg Sodium; trace Protein; 9 g Carbohydrate

Mild with a bit of tang. A pick-me-up rosy drink.

Cranberry cocktail	4 cups	1 L
Pineapple juice	4 cups	1 L
Prepared orange juice	2 cups	500 mL
Brown sugar, packed	1/2 cup	125 mL
Whole cloves	20	20
Cinnamon sticks (4 inch, 10 cm, each in length), broken up and crushed in plastic bag	4	4

Combine first 4 ingredients in 3 1/2 quart (3.5 L) slow cooker. Stir.

Tie cloves and cinnamon in double layer of cheesecloth. Add to slow cooker. Cover. Cook on Low for at least 3 hours until quite warm. Discard spice bag. Makes 10 cups (2.5 L).

Variation: Wine or gin may be added if desired. Use about 2 cups (500 mL) wine or about 1 1/2 cups (375 mL) gin.

1 cup (250 mL): 188 Calories; 0.2 g Total Fat; 9 mg Sodium; 1 g Protein; 47 g Carbohydrate

Pictured on page 17.

IITE BREAD

s bread has a touch more porous texture with the same homemade aroma and flavor as regular bread. No kneading or rising.

Granulated sugar	2 tsp.	10 mL
Warm water	1¼ cups	300 mL
Envelope active dry yeast	1 x ¼ oz.	1 x 8 g
(1 scant tbsp., 15 mL)		
All-purpose flour	2 cups	500 mL
Granulated sugar	2 tbsp.	30 mL
Cooking oil	2 tbsp.	30 mL
Salt	1 tsp.	5 mL
All-purpose flour	1 cup	250 mL

Stir first amount of sugar and warm water together in large bowl. Sprinkle with yeast. Let stand for 10 minutes. Stir to dissolve yeast.

Add first amount of flour, second amount of sugar, cooking oil and salt. Beat on low to moisten. Beat on high for 2 minutes.

Work in second amount of flour. Grease bottom of 3½ quart (3.5 L) slow cooker. Turn batter into slow cooker. Lay 5 paper towels between top of slow cooker and lid. Put wooden match or an object ⅛ inch (3 mm) thick between paper towels and edge of slow cooker to allow a bit of steam to escape. Do not lift lid for the first 1¾ hours cooking time. Cook on High for about 2 hours. Loosen sides with knife. Turn out onto rack to cool. Cuts into 16 slices.

1 slice: 115 Calories; 2 g Total Fat; 170 mg Sodium; 3 g Protein; 21 g Carbohydrate

Pictured on front cover.

BROWN QUICK BREAD

A porous biscuit-like mealtime or coffee break treat.

Whole wheat flour	2 cups	500 mL
All-purpose flour	1 cup	250 mL
Baking powder	1 tbsp.	15 mL
Salt	1 tsp.	5 mL
Molasses (not blackstrap)	2 tbsp.	30 mL
Cooking oil	2 tbsp.	30 mL
Water	1⅓ cups	325 mL

(continued on next page)

Combine first 4 ingredients in bowl. Stir.

Add molasses, cooking oil and water. Mix until moistened. Turn into greased 5 quart (5 L) slow cooker. Place 5 paper towels between top of slow cooker and lid. Put wooden match or an object $\frac{1}{8}$ inch (3 mm) thick between paper towels and edge of slow cooker to allow a bit of steam to escape. Do not lift lid for the first $1\frac{3}{4}$ hours cooking time. Cook on High for about 2 hours. Loosen sides with knife. Turn out onto rack to cool. Cuts into 14 wedges.

1 wedge: 122 Calories; 2.4 g Total Fat; 200 mg Sodium; 3 g Protein; 22 g Carbohydrate

TOMATO HERB BREAD

This gets its color from the tomato sauce.

Granulated sugar	1 tsp.	5 mL
Warm water	$\frac{1}{3}$ cup	75 mL
Envelope active dry yeast (1 scant tbsp., 15 mL)	1 x $\frac{1}{4}$ oz.	1 x 8 g
All-purpose flour	2 cups	500 mL
Granulated sugar	1 tbsp.	15 mL
Finely minced onion	$\frac{1}{4}$ cup	60 mL
Lukewarm tomato sauce, plus water to make 1 cup (250 mL)	7.5 oz.	213 mL
Grated sharp Cheddar cheese	$\frac{1}{4}$ cup	60 mL
Salt	1 tsp.	5 mL
Pepper	$\frac{1}{4}$ tsp.	1 mL
Dried whole oregano	$\frac{1}{2}$ tsp.	2 mL
All-purpose flour	1 cup	250 mL

Stir first amount of sugar into warm water in large warmed bowl. Sprinkle yeast over top. Let stand for 10 minutes. Stir to dissolve yeast.

Add next 8 ingredients. Beat on low to moisten. Beat on high for 2 minutes.

Work in second amount of flour. Turn into greased $3\frac{1}{2}$ quart (3.5 L) slow cooker. Smooth top with wet spoon or hand. Place 5 paper towels between top of slow cooker and lid. Put wooden match or an object $\frac{1}{8}$ inch (3 mm) thick between paper towels and edge of slow cooker to allow a bit of steam to escape. Do not lift lid for the first 2 hours cooking time. Cook on High for about $2\frac{1}{2}$ hours. Loosen sides with knife. Turn out onto rack to cool. Cuts into 14 slices.

1 slice: 124 Calories; 1 g Total Fat; 303 mg Sodium; 4 g Protein; 25 g Carbohydrate

Pictured on page 89.

PUMPERNICKEL BREAD

Dark colored, aromatic and so good. No pre-rising to this.

Granulated sugar	1 tsp.	5 mL
Warm water	1⅓ cups	325 mL
Envelope active dry yeast	1 × ¼ oz.	1 × 8 g
(1 scant tbsp.,15 mL)		
All-purpose flour	1 cup	250 mL
Rye flour	1 cup	250 mL
Molasses (not blackstrap)	2 tbsp.	30 mL
Cooking oil	2 tbsp.	30 mL
Cocoa	2 tbsp.	30 mL
Salt	1 tsp.	5 mL
Caraway seed (optional)	2 tsp.	10 mL
Rye flour	1 cup	250 mL

Stir sugar into warm water in large bowl. Sprinkle yeast over top. Let stand for 10 minutes. Stir to dissolve yeast.

Add next 7 ingredients. Beat on low to moisten. Beat on high for 2 minutes.

Stir in second amount of rye flour. Grease bottom of 3½ quart (3.5 L) slow cooker. Turn dough into cooker. Lay 5 paper towels between top of slow cooker and lid. Put wooden match or an object ⅛ inch (3 mm) thick between paper towels and edge of slow cooker to allow a bit of steam to escape. Do not lift lid for the first 1¾ hours cooking time. Cook on High for about 2 hours. Loosen sides with knife. Turn out onto rack to cool. Cuts into 14 slices.

1 slice: 118 Calories; 2.4 g Total Fat; 196 mg Sodium; 3 g Protein; 22 g Carbohydrate; good source of Dietary Fiber

Pictured on front cover.

OATMEAL PORRIDGE

This will wait for you, even if your overnight is a bit longer. Serve with cream and sugar.

Large flake rolled oats (old-fashioned)	2½ cups	625 mL
Water	5 cups	1.25 L
Salt	½ tsp.	2 mL

Mix all 3 ingredients in 3½ quart (3.5 L) slow cooker. Cover. Cook on Low for 7 to 8 hours overnight. Makes 5½ cups (1.3 L).

¾ cup (175 mL): 105 Calories; 1.7 g Total Fat; 174 mg Sodium; 4 g Protein; 18 g Carbohydrate

Pictured on page 53.

Nicely rounded loaf. Herb colored with good flavor.

Granulated sugar	1 tsp.	5 mL
Warm water	1⅓ cups	325 mL
Envelope active dry yeast	1 x ¼ oz.	1 x 8 g
(1 scant tbsp., 15 mL)		
All-purpose flour	2 cups	500 mL
Granulated sugar	1 tbsp.	15 mL
Cooking oil	2 tbsp.	30 mL
Dried whole oregano	1 tsp.	5 mL
Ground sage	1 tsp.	5 mL
Garlic powder	¼ tsp.	1 mL
Onion powder	¼ tsp.	1 mL
Salt	1 tsp.	5 mL
All-purpose flour	1 cup	250 mL

Stir first amount of sugar in warm water in large warmed bowl. Sprinkle with yeast. Let stand for 10 minutes. Stir to dissolve yeast.

Add next 8 ingredients. Beat on low to moisten. Beat on medium for 2 minutes.

Work in second amount of flour. Turn into greased 3½ quart (3.5 L) slow cooker. Smooth top with wet spoon or hand. Place 5 paper towels between top of slow cooker and lid. Put wooden match or an object ⅛ inch (3 mm) thick between paper towels and edge of slow cooker to allow a bit of steam to escape. Do not lift lid for the first 2 hours cooking time. Cook on High for about 2½ hours. Loosen sides with knife. Turn out onto rack to cool. Cuts into 14 slices.

1 slice: 128 Calories; 2.3 g Total Fat; 195 mg Sodium; 3 g Protein; 23 g Carbohydrate

Pictured on page 71.

Paré Pointer

If your dog's tail gets in the lawn mower, you will have to take him to a retail store.

BANANA BREAD

Makes a large dark loaf. Good flavor. Serve plain or buttered.

Hard margarine (or butter), softened	6 tbsp.	100 mL
Granulated sugar	⅔ cup	150 mL
Large egg	1	1
Mashed banana (about 3 small)	¾ cup	175 mL
All-purpose flour	1½ cups	375 mL
Cocoa	1 tbsp.	15 mL
Baking powder	1½ tsp.	7 mL
Baking soda	¼ tsp.	1 mL
Salt	½ tsp.	2 mL
Chopped walnuts (optional)	½ cup	125 mL

Cream margarine and sugar together in bowl. Beat in eggs. Add banana. Mix.

Add remaining 6 ingredients. Stir to moisten. Turn into greased 9 x 5 x 3 inch (22 x 12 x 7.5 cm) loaf pan. Set pan on wire trivet in 5 quart (5 L) oval slow cooker. Place 5 paper towels between top of slow cooker and lid. Put wooden match or an object ⅛ inch (3 mm) thick between paper towels and edge of slow cooker to allow a bit of steam to escape. Do not lift lid for the first 2 hours cooking time. Cook on High for about 2¼ hours. A wooden pick inserted in center should come out clean. Remove pan to wire rack to cool. Let stand for 20 minutes. Loosen sides with knife. Turn out onto rack to cool. Cuts into 18 slices.

1 slice: 118 Calories; 4.2 g Total Fat; 144 mg Sodium; 2 g Protein; 19 g Carbohydrate

Pictured on page 53.

In reality, a pirate ship is a thug boat.

A large moist loaf. Spread with butter—delicious.

Boiling water	**²/₃ cup**	**150 mL**
Baking soda	**1 tsp.**	**5 mL**
Chopped dates	**1 cup**	**250 mL**
Large egg, fork-beaten	**1**	**1**
Granulated sugar	**²/₃ cup**	**150 mL**
Hard margarine (or butter), melted	**2 tbsp.**	**30 mL**
Vanilla	**¹/₂ tsp.**	**2 mL**
Salt	**¹/₄ tsp.**	**1 mL**
All-purpose flour	**1²/₃ cups**	**400 mL**
Chopped walnuts	**¹/₂ cup**	**125 mL**

Pour boiling water over baking soda in bowl. Stir. Add dates. Stir. Let stand until cool.

Combine egg, sugar, margarine, vanilla and salt in separate bowl. Beat. Add date mixture. Stir.

Add flour and walnuts. Stir. Turn into greased 9 x 5 x 3 inch (22 x 12 x 7.5 cm) loaf pan. Place pan on wire trivet in 5 quart (5 L) oval slow cooker. Place 5 paper towels between top of slow cooker and lid. Put wooden match or an object ¹/₈ inch (3 mm) thick between paper towels and edge of slow cooker to allow a bit of steam to escape. Do not lift lid for the first 2 hours cooking time. Cook on High for about 2³/₄ hours until wooden pick inserted in center comes out clean. Remove pan to rack. Let stand for 20 minutes. Loosen sides with knife. Turn out onto rack to cool. Cuts into 18 slices.

1 slice: 138 Calories; 4 g Total Fat; 134 mg Sodium; 2 g Protein; 24 g Carbohydrate

Pictured on page 53.

Is butter a young goat?

CRANBERRY LOAF

Lots of flavor and most colorful slices.

Large egg	1	1
Prepared orange juice	⅔ cup	150 mL
Hard margarine (or butter), melted	2 tbsp.	30 mL
Granulated sugar	1 cup	250 mL
Salt	1 tsp.	5 mL
Vanilla	½ tsp.	2 mL
All-purpose flour	2 cups	500 mL
Baking powder	1½ tsp.	7 mL
Coarsely chopped fresh (or frozen, thawed) cranberries	1 cup	250 mL

Beat egg in bowl. Add next 5 ingredients. Beat until smooth.

Add flour and baking powder. Stir just to moisten.

Add cranberries. Stir lightly. Turn into greased 9 x 5 x 3 inch (22 x 12 x 7.5 cm) loaf pan. Set pan on wire trivet in 5 quart (5 L) oval slow cooker. Place 5 paper towels between top of slow cooker and lid. Put wooden match between paper towels and edge of slow cooker to allow a bit of steam to escape. Cook on High for about 2½ hours until wooden pick inserted in center comes out clean. Remove pan from slow cooker. Let stand for 20 minutes. Loosen sides with knife. Turn out onto rack to cool. Cuts into 18 slices.

1 slice: 122 Calories; 1.8 g Total Fat; 171 mg Sodium; 2 g Protein; 25 g Carbohydrate

Pictured on page 53.

It is always the last place you look that you find what you're looking for. Naturally. Why else would you keep looking?

A handy cake mix and applesauce combine to make this spicy cake.

Yellow cake mix (2 layer size)	1	1
Instant vanilla pudding (4 serving size)	1	1
Ground cinnamon	½ tsp.	2 mL
Ground nutmeg	¼ tsp.	1 mL
Ground allspice	¼ tsp.	1 mL
Large eggs, fork-beaten	4	4
Canned applesauce	14 oz.	398 mL

Butterscotch Icing, page 68,
   double recipe

Place first 7 ingredients in bowl. Beat on low to moisten. Beat on medium for 2 minutes until smooth. Line greased 5 quart (5 L) round slow cooker with foil. Pour batter over foil. Place 5 paper towels between top of slow cooker and lid. Put wooden match or an object ⅛ inch (3 mm) thick between paper towels and edge of slow cooker to allow a bit of steam to escape. Do not lift lid for at least 2 hours. Cook on High for 2½ hours until wooden pick inserted in center comes out clean. Remove slow cooker liner to rack or turn slow cooker off. Let stand for 20 minutes. Loosen sides of cake with knife. Invert cake onto plate, foil side up, then onto rack, foil side down, to cool. Remove foil before serving.

Cut cake into 2 layers if desired. Ice with Butterscotch Icing. Cuts into 12 wedges.

1 wedge: 464 Calories; 13.1 g Total Fat; 296 mg Sodium; 4 g Protein; 85 g Carbohydrate

Pictured on page 71.

Paré Pointer

It is odd how both a goose and an icicle grow down.

CARROT CAKE

Can be a one or two-layer cake.

Yellow cake mix (2 layer size)	1	1
Ground cinnamon	1½ tsp.	7 mL
Ground nutmeg	½ tsp.	2 mL
Grated carrot	1½ cups	375 mL
Large eggs	3	3
Cooking oil	⅓ cup	75 mL
Water	½ cup	125 mL
CREAM CHEESE ICING		
Cream cheese, softened	4 oz.	125 g
Hard margarine (or butter), softened	2 tbsp.	30 mL
Vanilla	1 tsp.	5 mL
Icing (confectioner's) sugar	2 cups	500 mL

Combine cake mix, cinnamon, nutmeg and carrot in bowl. Mix.

Add eggs, cooking oil and water. Beat on low until moistened. Beat on medium for 2 minutes. Line bottom of 5 quart (5 L) round slow cooker with foil. Pour cake batter over top. Place 5 paper towels between top of slow cooker and lid. Put wooden match or an object ⅛ inch (3 mm) thick between paper towels and edge of slow cooker to allow a bit of steam to escape. Do not lift lid. Cook on High for about 2 hours until wooden pick inserted in center comes out clean. Remove slow cooker liner to rack or turn slow cooker off. Let stand for about 20 minutes. Loosen sides of cake with knife. Invert cake onto plate, foil side up, then onto rack, foil side down, to cool. Remove foil before serving. Slice into 2 layers or leave as is.

Cream Cheese Icing: Beat all 4 ingredients together in bowl until smooth. Makes about 1¾ cups (425 mL). Ice top and sides of cake. Cuts into 12 wedges.

1 wedge: 402 Calories; 18.8 g Total Fat; 248 mg Sodium; 4 g Protein; 56 g Carbohydrate

Pictured on page 89.

Paré Pointer

It is said that the first few missionaries gave the cannibals their first taste of Christianity.

The crowning glory is the pink raspberry icing.

Chocolate cake mix (2 layer size), see Note	1	1
FILLING		
Raspberry (or strawberry) jam	1 cup	250 mL
RASPBERRY ICING		
Hard margarine (or butter), softened	6 tbsp.	100 mL
Raspberry unsweetened drink powder	1 tsp.	5 mL
Icing (confectioner's) sugar	1½ cups	375 mL
Water	¼ cup	60 mL
Icing (confectioner's) sugar	1½ cups	375 mL

Prepare cake mix as directed on package. Line bottom of 5 quart (5 L) round slow cooker with foil. Pour batter over foil. Place 5 paper towels between top of slow cooker and lid. Put wooden match or an object ⅛ inch (3 mm) thick between paper towels and edge of slow cooker to allow a bit of steam to escape. Do not lift lid for at least 2 hours. Cook on High for about 2½ hours until wooden pick inserted in center comes out clean. Remove slow cooker liner to rack or turn slow cooker off. Let stand, uncovered, for 20 minutes. Loosen sides of cake with knife. Invert cake onto plate, foil side up, then onto rack, foil side down, to cool. Remove foil before serving.

Filling: Cut cake into 2 layers. Spread bottom layer with jam. Place second layer on top.

Raspberry Icing: Measure first 4 ingredients into bowl. Beat until creamy.

Add second amount of icing sugar. Beat well. Add more water or icing sugar if needed to make proper spreading consistency. Makes 2 cups (500 mL). Ice top and sides of cake. Cuts into 12 wedges.

Note: Testing showed that white or yellow cake mixes could not be substituted.

1 wedge: 424 Calories; 10.5 g Total Fat; 309 mg Sodium; 2 g Protein; 84 g Carbohydrate

Pictured on front cover.

"SCRATCH" CHOCOLATE CAKE: Combine 1 chocolate cake mix, 1 chocolate or vanilla instant pudding (4 serving size), 4 eggs, ½ cup (125 mL) cooking oil and 1 cup (250 mL) water. Mix and cook as for Chocolate Cake, above.

M CRUMB CAKE ━━━━━━

a neat cake. The graham crumbs take the place of flour.
e.

margarine (or butter), softened	½ cup	125 mL
Granulated sugar	¾ cup	175 mL
Large eggs	2	2
Graham cracker crumbs	2¼ cups	560 mL
Medium coconut	½ cup	125 mL
Baking powder	1½ tsp.	7 mL
Salt	⅛ tsp.	0.5 mL
Milk	½ cup	125 mL
Vanilla	1 tsp.	5 mL
BUTTERSCOTCH ICING		
Brown sugar, packed	6 tbsp.	100 mL
Milk (or cream)	2½ tbsp.	37 mL
Hard margarine (or butter)	3 tbsp.	50 mL
Icing (confectioner's) sugar	1¼ cups	300 mL

Cream margarine and sugar together in bowl. Beat in eggs, 1 at a time. Add graham crumbs, coconut, baking powder and salt. Stir well.

Add milk and vanilla. Stir. Line bottom of greased 5 quart (5 L) round slow cooker with foil. Pour batter over foil. Place 5 paper towels between top of slow cooker and lid. Put wooden match or an object ⅛ inch (3 mm) thick between paper towels and edge of slow cooker to allow a bit of steam to escape. Do not lift lid. Cook on High for 2 hours until wooden pick inserted in center comes out clean. Remove slow cooker liner to rack or turn slow cooker off. Let stand for 20 minutes. Loosen sides of cake with knife. Invert cake onto plate, foil side up, then onto rack, foil side down, to cool. Remove foil before serving.

Butterscotch Icing: Combine brown sugar, milk and margarine in saucepan. Heat and stir until boiling. Boil for 2 minutes. Remove from heat. Cool.

Add icing sugar. Beat until smooth, adding more milk or icing sugar, if needed, to make proper spreading consistency. Makes about 1 cup (250 mL). Ice top and sides of cake. Cuts into 12 wedges.

1 wedge: 354 Calories; 16.7 g Total Fat; 327 mg Sodium; 4 g Protein; 51 g Carbohydrate

Cakes

Maple Whip Icing dresses up any cake.

Yellow cake mix (2 layer size)	1	1
Instant vanilla pudding (4 serving size)	1	1
Water	1 cup	250 mL
Rum flavoring	1 tbsp.	15 mL
Large eggs	4	4
MAPLE WHIP ICING		
Envelope unflavored gelatin	1 x 1/4 oz.	1 x 7 g
Water	1/4 cup	60 mL
Brown sugar, packed	1/4 cup	60 mL
Envelopes dessert topping (not prepared)	2	2
Milk	1 cup	250 mL
Maple flavoring	1 tsp.	5 mL

Combine first 5 ingredients in bowl. Beat on low to moisten. Beat on medium for 2 minutes until smooth. Line greased 5 quart (5 L) round slow cooker with foil. Pour batter over foil. Place 5 paper towels between top of slow cooker and lid. Put wooden match or an object $1/8$ inch (3 mm) thick between paper towels and edge of slow cooker to allow a bit of steam to escape. Cook on High for about $2^1/2$ hours until wooden pick inserted in center comes out clean. Remove slow cooker liner to rack or turn slow cooker off. Let stand for 20 minutes. Loosen sides of cake with knife. Invert cake onto plate, foil side up, then onto rack, foil side down, to cool. Remove foil before serving.

Maple Whip Icing: Sprinkle gelatin over water in small saucepan. Let stand for 1 minute.

Add brown sugar. Heat and stir to dissolve. Cool.

Beat dessert topping, milk and maple flavoring together according to package directions until soft peaks form. Add gelatin mixture. Beat until stiff. Makes $4^2/3$ cups (1.15 L) icing. Cut cake into 2 or 3 layers. Fill and ice top and sides of cake. Cuts into 12 wedges.

1 wedge: 314 Calories; 10.2 g Total Fat; 241 mg Sodium; 5 g Protein; 51 g Carbohydrate

CHERRY WHIP ICING: Omit brown sugar and maple flavoring. Add $1/2$ cup (125 mL) or more chopped maraschino cherries and 1 tsp. (5 mL) each of vanilla and almond flavoring.

STEAMED FRUIT PUDDING

Serve with your favorite pudding sauce. A carefree method for cooking a fruit pudding.

Hard margarine (or butter), softened	³/₄ cup	175 mL
Granulated sugar	³/₄ cup	175 mL
Large eggs	2	2
Prepared orange (or apple) juice	½ cup	125 mL
Raisins	2 cups	500 mL
Cut mixed glazed fruit	1½ cups	375 mL
Fine dry bread crumbs	1 cup	250 mL
Ground cinnamon	1 tsp.	5 mL
Ground allspice	½ tsp.	2 mL
Baking powder	³/₄ tsp.	4 mL
Baking soda	½ tsp.	2 mL
Salt	1 tsp.	5 mL
All-purpose flour	1 cup	250 mL

Cream margarine and sugar together in bowl. Beat in eggs, 1 at a time. Add orange juice. Beat.

Combine remaining 9 ingredients in separate large bowl. Stir together well. Pour orange juice mixture into dry ingredients. Stir until moistened. Turn into greased 8 cup (2 L) pudding pan. Cover with greased foil, tying sides down with string. Place on wire trivet in 5 quart (5 L) slow cooker. Pour boiling water into slow cooker to reach halfway up sides of pudding pan. Cover. Cook on High for 5 hours. Serves 16.

1 serving: 311 Calories; 10.4 g Total Fat; 397 mg Sodium; 3 g Protein; 54 g Carbohydrate

1. Borscht, page 141
2. Herb Bread, page 61
3. Asparagus Bake, page 148
4. Poached Salmon, page 84
5. Glazed Ham, page 102
6. Apple Cake, page 65, with Butterscotch Icing, page 68

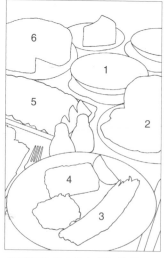

Props Courtesy Of: La Cache; Stokes; The Bay; Tile Town Ltd.

RICE PUDDING

Serve hot or cold. Ice cream or cream finishes this nicely.

Uncooked short grain white rice	¾ cup	175 mL
Skim evaporated milk	13½ oz.	385 mL
Water	2 cups	500 mL
Granulated sugar	⅓ cup	75 mL
Raisins	½ cup	125 mL
Vanilla	1½ tsp.	7 mL
Salt	¾ tsp.	4 mL
Cinnamon stick (3 inches, 7.5 cm, in length)	1	1

Measure all 8 ingredients into 3½ quart (3.5 L) slow cooker. Stir. Cover. Cook on Low for 4 to 5 hours or on High for 2 to 2½ hours, stirring once or twice. Makes 4¾ cups (1.2 L).

1 cup (250 mL): 298 Calories; 0.4 g Total Fat; 532 mg Sodium; 9 g Protein; 64 g Carbohydrate

STEAMED CHOCOLATE PUDDING

No egg in this. Makes a chewy brownie-like dessert. Serve with ice cream and chocolate sauce.

Hard margarine (or butter), softened	1 tbsp.	15 mL
Granulated sugar	½ cup	125 mL
Cocoa	2 tbsp.	30 mL
Milk	½ cup	125 mL
Vanilla	½ tsp.	2 mL
All-purpose flour	1½ cups	375 mL
Baking powder	2 tsp.	10 mL
Salt	½ tsp.	2 mL

Boiling water, to cover

Cream margarine, sugar, and cocoa together in bowl. Add milk and vanilla. Beat well.

Add flour, baking powder and salt. Mix well. Turn into greased 4 cup (1 L) bowl. Cover with greased foil, tying sides down with string. Place wire trivet in 5 quart (5 L) or 6 quart (6 L) slow cooker. Set bowl on top.

Pour boiling water into slow cooker to reach halfway up bowl. Cover. Cook on High for 2½ hours. Serves 6.

1 serving: 221 Calories; 2.7 g Total Fat; 266 mg Sodium; 5 g Protein; 45 g Carbohydrate

PEACH PUDDING

Serve warm with ice cream. A mild spicy flavor.

All-purpose flour	1 cup	250 mL
Granulated sugar	1/2 cup	125 mL
Brown sugar, packed	1/4 cup	60 mL
Baking powder	2 tsp.	10 mL
Salt	1/2 tsp.	2 mL
Ground cinnamon	1/2 tsp.	2 mL
Ground nutmeg	1/4 tsp.	1 mL
Large eggs, fork-beaten	2	2
Cooking oil	2 tbsp.	30 mL
Vanilla	1 tsp.	5 mL
Milk	1 1/8 cups	280 mL
Canned sliced peaches, drained and chopped	14 oz.	398 mL

Measure first 7 ingredients into bowl. Stir.

Add eggs, cooking oil, vanilla and milk. Mix well.

Stir in peaches. Turn into greased 3 1/2 quart (3.5 L) slow cooker. Place 5 paper towels between top of slow cooker and lid. Cook on High for about 2 hours until wooden pick inserted in center comes out clean. Serves 6.

1 serving: 292 Calories; 7.1 g Total Fat; 282 mg Sodium; 6 g Protein; 51 g Carbohydrate

LEMON-SAUCED PUDDING

A yummy lemon flavor. A cake-like top with lemon sauce to spoon over. Serve with ice cream.

All-purpose flour	1 cup	250 mL
Granulated sugar	1/2 cup	125 mL
Baking powder	2 tsp.	10 mL
Grated lemon peel	2 tsp.	10 mL
Salt	1/8 tsp.	0.5 mL
Milk	1/2 cup	125 mL
Cooking oil	2 tbsp.	30 mL
Hot water	1 3/4 cups	425 mL
Lemon juice	1/4 cup	60 mL
Granulated sugar	3/4 cup	175 mL

(continued on next page)

Desserts

Measure first 7 ingredients into bowl. Mix well. Turn into greased 3½ quart (3.5 L) slow cooker.

Stir hot water, lemon juice and second amount of sugar together in separate bowl. Pour carefully over batter. Do not stir. Place 5 paper towels between top of slow cooker and lid. Cook on High for about 2 hours until wooden pick inserted in center comes out clean. Makes 6 small servings.

1 serving: 304 Calories; 5.1 g Total Fat; 76 mg Sodium; 3 g Protein; 63 g Carbohydrate

BUMBLEBERRY COBBLER

Fruity and warm. Serve with ice cream to top it off.

All-purpose flour	1 cup	250 mL
Granulated sugar	½ cup	125 mL
Baking powder	1½ tsp.	7 mL
Ground cinnamon	½ tsp.	2 mL
Salt	½ tsp.	2 mL
Large eggs, fork-beaten	2	2
Cooking oil	2 tbsp.	30 mL
Milk	2 tbsp.	30 mL
Vanilla	1 tsp.	5 mL
Fresh (or frozen) raspberries	1 cup	250 mL
Fresh (or frozen) blueberries	1 cup	250 mL
Sliced fresh (or whole frozen, sliced) strawberries	1 cup	250 mL
Granulated sugar	¾ cup	175 mL
Water	½ cup	125 mL

Stir first 5 ingredients together in bowl.

Add eggs, cooking oil, milk and vanilla. Mix well. Turn into ungreased 3½ quart (3.5 L) slow cooker.

Measure remaining 5 ingredients into saucepan. Heat, stirring occasionally, until boiling. Pour over batter in slow cooker. Place 5 paper towels between top of slow cooker and lid. Cook on High for 1¾ to 2 hours. Serves 6.

1 serving: 353 Calories; 6.9 g Total Fat; 255 mg Sodium; 5 g Protein; 69 g Carbohydrate; good source of Dietary Fiber

...MIX PUDDING

...n-raisin treat with plenty of butterscotch sauce to top it off.

...ose flour	1 cup	250 mL
...ted sugar	2/3 cup	150 mL
Baking powder	2 tsp.	10 mL
Ground cinnamon	1/2 tsp.	2 mL
Salt	1/8 tsp.	0.5 mL
Milk	1/2 cup	125 mL
Cooking oil	2 tbsp.	30 mL
Raisins (or currants)	1/2 cup	125 mL
Vanilla	1/2 tsp.	2 mL
Brown sugar, packed	3/4 cup	175 mL
Vanilla	1/2 tsp.	2 mL
Hot water	1 3/4 cups	425 mL

Stir first 5 ingredients in bowl.

Add milk, cooking oil, raisins and first amount of vanilla. Mix well. Turn into 3 1/2 quart (3.5 L) slow cooker.

Stir brown sugar, second amount of vanilla and hot water together in bowl. Pour carefully over batter in slow cooker. Do not stir. Cover. Cook on High for about 2 hours until wooden pick inserted in center comes out clean. Serves 4 to 6.

1/4 recipe: 559 Calories; 7.7 g Total Fat; 129 mg Sodium; 5 g Protein; 120 g Carbohydrate

BROWN BETTY

Looks and tastes just like Brown Betty.

Medium cooking apples, peeled, cored and sliced (such as McIntosh)	4	4
Brown sugar, packed	3/4 cup	175 mL
Quick-cooking rolled oats (not instant)	1/3 cup	75 mL
All-purpose flour	1/2 cup	125 mL
Salt	1/4 tsp.	1 mL
Hard margarine (or butter), softened	1/3 cup	75 mL

(continued on next page)

Place apple slices in 3½ quart (3.5 L) slow cooker.

Mix remaining 5 ingredients in bowl until crumbly. Sprinkle over apple. Place 5 paper towels between top of slow cooker and lid. Put wooden match between paper towels and edge of slow cooker to allow a bit of steam to escape. Cook on High for 1½ to 2 hours. Serves 4.

1 cup (250 mL): 468 Calories; 17.2 g Total Fat; 374 mg Sodium; 3 g Protein; 79 g Carbohydrate; good source of Dietary Fiber

CHOCOLATE FUDGE PUDDING

No need to heat up the kitchen to enjoy this yummy dessert. Good chocolate flavor with lots of sauce.

All-purpose flour	1 cup	250 mL
Brown sugar, packed	¾ cup	175 mL
Cocoa	2 tbsp.	30 mL
Baking powder	2 tsp.	10 mL
Salt	¼ tsp.	1 mL
Milk	½ cup	125 mL
Cooking oil	2 tbsp.	30 mL
Vanilla	½ tsp.	2 mL
Brown sugar, packed	¾ cup	175 mL
Cocoa	2 tbsp.	30 mL
Hot water	1¾ cups	425 mL

Place first 5 ingredients in bowl. Stir.

Add milk, cooking oil and vanilla. Stir well. Turn into 3½ quart (3.5 L) slow cooker.

Stir second amount of brown sugar and second amount of cocoa together well in bowl. Add hot water. Mix. Pour carefully over batter in slow cooker. Do not stir. Cover. Cook on High for about 2 hours until wooden pick inserted in center comes out clean. Serves 6.

1 serving: 358 Calories; 5.4 g Total Fat; 148 mg Sodium; 4 g Protein; 77 g Carbohydrate

Paré Pointer

Little Susie ate T.N.T. so her hair would grow bangs.

STEWED RHUBARB

This uses frozen rhubarb which takes a long time on Low to start to cook. Just fix it and forget it.

Frozen cut rhubarb	8 cups	2 L
Granulated sugar	1½ cups	375 mL
Water	½ cup	125 mL

Place rhubarb, sugar and water in 3½ quart (3.5 L) slow cooker. Cover. Cook on Low for 6 to 7 hours. Makes 6 cups (1.5 L).

STEWED STRAWBERRY RHUBARB: Substitute 4 cups (1 L) frozen strawberries for 4 cups (1 L) frozen rhubarb.

½ cup (125 mL): 182 Calories; 0.2 g Total Fat; 3 mg Sodium; 1 g Protein; 47 g Carbohydrate

STEWED PRUNES

Worry-free. Juice doesn't have a chance of boiling away as it does on a burner.

Dried pitted prunes	1 lb.	454 g
Water	3 cups	750 mL

Combine prunes and water in 3½ quart (3.5 L) slow cooker. Cover. Cook on Low for 4 to 5 hours or on High for 2 to 2½ hours. Stir. Makes 4¼ cups (1 L).

½ cup (125 mL): 145 Calories; 0.3 g Total Fat; 2 mg Sodium; 2 g Protein; 38 g Carbohydrate; good source of Dietary Fiber

DRIED FRUIT COMPOTE

A good breakfast dish or light dessert.

Dried pitted prunes	8 oz.	225 g
Dried apricots, halved	8 oz.	225 g
Canned sliced peaches, with juice	2 x 14 oz.	2 x 398 mL
Maraschino cherries	12	12
Water	1½ cups	375 mL
Granulated sugar	½ cup	125 mL

Combine all 6 ingredients in 3½ quart (3.5 L) slow cooker. Stir. Cover. Cook on Low for 3½ to 4 hours. Makes 6¾ cups (1.68 L).

½ cup (125 mL): 142 Calories; 0.2 g Total Fat; 5 mg Sodium; 1 g Protein; 37 g Carbohydrate; good source of Dietary Fiber

Pictured on page 53.

STEWED PEARS

Wonderful pear flavor. Cloves add just a bit of zip. Great for brunch or dessert.

Apple juice	1½ cups	375 mL
Granulated sugar	½ cup	125 mL
Lemon juice	1 tbsp.	15 mL
Whole cloves	2	2
Fresh pears (such as Bosc), peeled, cored and thinly sliced (see Note)	4	4

Stir apple juice, sugar, lemon juice and cloves together in 3½ quart (3.5 L) slow cooker.

Add pears. Cover. Cook on Low for 6 to 7 hours or on High for 3 to 3½ hours. Makes 3¾ cups (925 mL).

Note: If using bartlett pears, check for doneness sooner as they soften quickly. The same applies to canned pears. Double cloves for shorter stewing time.

½ cup (125 mL): 104 Calories; 0.1 g Total Fat; 4 mg Sodium; trace Protein; 27 g Carbohydrate

APPLESAUCE

May be served hot or cold.

Medium cooking apples (such as McIntosh), peeled, cored and sliced	8	8
Water	½ cup	125 mL
Granulated sugar (see Note)	½ cup	125 mL

Combine apple and water in 5 quart (5 L) slow cooker. Cover. Cook on Low for 4½ to 5 hours or on High for 2¼ to 2½ hours until apple is soft.

Sprinkle sugar over top. Stir. Makes a generous 4 cups (1 L).

½ cup (125 mL): 124 Calories; 0.4 g Total Fat; trace Sodium; trace Protein; 32 g Carbohydrate

Note: The amount of sugar will vary, depending on sweetness of apple. Add more or less to desired sweetness.

Pictured on page 17.

Variation: No need to peel or core the apples. Just nip out blossom end, and cut up. Press through food mill when cooked. Makes a smooth applesauce.

MARBLED CHEESECAKE

A perfect dessert to make when your oven is already in use.

GRAHAM CRUST

Hard margarine (or butter)	4 tsp.	20 mL
Graham cracker crumbs	1/3 cup	75 mL
Granulated sugar	1 tsp.	5 mL

FILLING

Semisweet chocolate baking squares, cut up	3 x 1 oz.	3 x 28 g
Light cream cheese, softened	12 oz.	375 g
Granulated sugar	3/4 cup	175 mL
Non-fat plain yogurt	1/3 cup	75 mL
Vanilla	1 tsp.	5 mL
Large eggs	4	4
All-purpose flour	1/2 cup	125 mL

Graham Crust: Melt margarine in saucepan. Stir in graham crumbs and sugar. Press in ungreased 8 inch (20 cm) round cake pan.

Filling: Melt chocolate in saucepan over low, stirring often.

Beat cream cheese, sugar, yogurt and vanilla together in large bowl until smooth. Beat in eggs, 1 at a time. Add flour. Mix. Reserve 1¾ cups (425 mL) of cheese mixture. Pour remaining cheese mixture over bottom crust.

Stir melted chocolate into reserved 1¾ cups (425 mL) of cheese mixture. Stir. Drizzle over top of white layer. Cut through in a zig-zag motion to get a marbled look.

Tear off a 16 inch (40 cm) long piece of foil to make a foil strap. Fold lengthwise to make a strip 16 inches (40 cm) long and 4 inches (10 cm) wide. Set cake pan on center of foil strap. Put wire trivet in bottom of 5 quart (5 L) round slow cooker.

Using foil strap, carefully lower pan into slow cooker, leaving foil strap in the slow cooker to use to remove pan when baking is complete. Place 5 paper towels between top of slow cooker and lid. Cook on High for 3 hours. Remove pan. Cool. Refrigerate for several hours or overnight. Cuts into 12 wedges.

1 wedge: 226 Calories; 11 g Total Fat; 362 mg Sodium; 7 g Protein; 26 g Carbohydrate

Pictured on page 107.

Contains ham, chicken and shrimp as well as vegetables. A full mea
dish from the Deep South.

Chopped onion	1½ cups	375 mL
Chopped celery	½ cup	125 mL
Canned tomatoes, with juice, broken up	14 oz.	398 mL
Medium green pepper, chopped	1	1
Cubed smoked ham	1 cup	250 mL
Boneless, skinless chicken breast halves, chopped	2	2
Beef bouillon powder	1½ tsp.	7 mL
Hot water	1 cup	250 mL
Garlic clove (or ¼ tsp., 1 mL, garlic powder)	1	1
Dried whole oregano	½ tsp.	2 mL
Dried sweet basil	½ tsp.	2 mL
Salt	½ tsp.	2 mL
Pepper	¼ tsp.	1 mL
Cayenne pepper	¼ tsp.	1 mL
Parsley flakes	2 tsp.	10 mL
Ground thyme	⅛ tsp.	0.5 mL
Granulated sugar	1 tsp.	5 mL
Cooked fresh (or cooked frozen, thawed) shelled shrimp	½ lb.	225 g
Cooked white (or brown) rice	2 cups	500 mL

Put first 6 ingredients into 3½ quart (3.5 L) slow cooker. Stir.

Stir bouillon powder into hot water in bowl. Add next 9 ingredients. Stir well. Add to slow cooker. Stir. Cover. Cook on Low for 8 to 9 hours or on High for 4 to 4½ hours.

Add shrimp and rice. Stir. Cover. Cook on High for about 30 minutes until shrimp is heated through. Makes 8 cups (2 L).

1 cup (250 mL): 184 Calories; 1.9 g Total Fat; 695 mg Sodium; 19 g Protein; 22 g Carbohydrate

Paré Pointer

Loaned money may not go as far as it used to, but it is still just as much trouble getting it back.

...MP CREOLE

Lots of good things for color such as green pepper, tomato, mushrooms and shrimp. Serve over rice.

Finely chopped onion	1 cup	250 mL
Chopped celery	½ cup	125 mL
Medium green pepper, chopped	1	1
Canned tomatoes, with juice, broken up	14 oz.	398 mL
Ketchup	2 tbsp.	30 mL
Canned sliced mushrooms, drained	10 oz.	284 mL
Salt	1 tsp.	5 mL
Pepper	¼ tsp.	1 mL
Garlic powder	¼ tsp.	1 mL
Cayenne pepper	¼ tsp.	1 mL
Lemon juice	1 tsp.	5 mL
Parsley flakes	1 tsp.	5 mL
Cooked fresh (or cooked frozen, thawed) shelled shrimp (or 2 cans, 4 oz., 114 g, each, drained)	1 lb.	454 g

Put onion, celery and green pepper into 3½ quart (3.5 L) slow cooker.

Combine next 9 ingredients in bowl. Stir. Pour over top. Cover. Cook on Low for 6 to 8 hours or on High for 3 to 4 hours.

Add shrimp. Stir. Cook on High for 20 to 30 minutes until shrimp is heated through. Stir before serving. Makes 4¼ cups (1 L).

1 cup (250 mL): 165 Calories; 1.7 g Total Fat; 1285 mg Sodium; 25 g Protein; 13 g Carbohydrate; good source of Dietary Fiber

TUNA CASSEROLE

Good combo and a good looking dish.

Chopped onion	½ cup	125 mL
Condensed cream of chicken soup	2 × 10 oz.	2 × 284 mL
Milk	1 cup	250 mL
Frozen peas	10 oz.	300 g
Uncooked medium egg noodles	8 oz.	225 g
Canned flaked tuna, drained	2 × 6½ oz.	2 × 184 g

(continued on next page)

Sprinkle onion in 3½ quart (3.5 L) slow cooker.

Mix soup and milk in large bowl. Add peas, egg noodles and tuna. Stir well. Turn into slow cooker. Smooth top with spoon. Cover. Cook on Low for 5 to 6 hours or on High for 2½ to 3 hours. Stir before serving. Makes 6⅔ cups (1.65 L).

1 cup (250 mL): 329 Calories; 7.5 g Total Fat; 952 mg Sodium; 25 g Protein; 40 g Carbohydrate; good source of Dietary Fiber

SHRIMP MARINARA

Delicious shrimp in an Italian spiced sauce. Serve over rice or pasta.

Canned tomatoes, with juice, broken up	14 oz.	398 mL
Finely chopped onion	1 cup	250 mL
Garlic cloves, minced (or ½ tsp., 2 mL, garlic powder)	2	2
Dried whole oregano	¾ tsp.	4 mL
Salt	1 tsp.	5 mL
Pepper	¼ tsp.	1 mL
Parsley flakes	½ tsp.	2 mL
Granulated sugar	½ tsp.	2 mL
Cooked fresh (or cooked frozen, thawed) shelled shrimp	1 lb.	454 g
Grated Parmesan cheese, sprinkle		

Combine first 8 ingredients in 3½ quart (3.5 L) slow cooker. Cover. Cook on Low for 6 to 7 hours or on High for 3 to 3½ hours until onion is cooked.

Add shrimp. Stir. Cook on High for about 15 minutes until heated through.

Serve over rice or pasta. Sprinkle with cheese. Makes 3⅓ cups (825 mL).

¾ cup (175 mL): 140 Calories; 1.4 g Total Fat; 992 mg Sodium; 23 g Protein; 8 g Carbohydrate

Pictured on page 89.

OOD CASSEROLE

food flavor with a golden cheese topping.

ensed cream of mushroom soup	10 oz.	284 mL
Water	1 cup	250 mL
Sherry (or alcohol-free sherry)	2 tbsp.	30 mL
Jars of chopped pimiento, drained	2 × 2 oz.	2 × 57 mL
Onion flakes	1 tbsp.	15 mL
Dill weed	1/2 tsp.	2 mL
Paprika	1/2 tsp.	2 mL
Parsley flakes	1 tsp.	5 mL
Cayenne pepper	1/8 tsp.	0.5 mL
Canned shrimp, drained	4 oz.	113 g
Canned crabmeat, drained, cartilage removed	4.2 oz.	120 g
Uncooked instant white rice	1 1/2 cups	375 mL
Grated medium Cheddar cheese	1 cup	250 mL

Mix first 9 ingredients in bowl.

Place shrimp, crabmeat and rice in 3 1/2 quart (3.5 L) slow cooker. Pour soup mixture over top. Stir lightly.

Sprinkle with cheese. Cover. Cook on Low for 3 to 4 hours or on High for 1 1/2 to 2 hours. Makes 5 cups (1.25 L).

1 cup (250 mL): 327 Calories; 13.3 g Total Fat; 832 mg Sodium; 18 g Protein; 33 g Carbohydrate

POACHED SALMON

Serve with lemon wedges or tartar sauce.

Salmon fillet	1 1/4 lbs.	560 g
Chopped chives	1 tsp.	5 mL
Chopped celery	1/2 cup	125 mL
Small bay leaf	1	1
Onion powder	1/4 tsp.	1 mL
Salt	1/2 tsp.	2 mL
Apple juice (or white wine)	1/2 cup	125 mL
Water	1/2 cup	125 mL
Lemon juice	1 tbsp.	15 mL

(continued on next page)

Lay salmon in 3½ quart (3.5 L) slow cooker.

Sprinkle chives, celery and bay leaf beside fillet.

Stir remaining 5 ingredients together in small bowl. Pour over salmon. Cover. Cook on Low for 3 to 4 hours or on High for 2 hours until salmon flakes when tested with fork. Discard bay leaf. Serves 4.

1 serving: 189 Calories; 6.5 g Total Fat; 458 mg Sodium; 28 g Protein; 5 g Carbohydrate

Pictured on page 71.

POACHED FISH: Substitute your favorite fish in place of salmon.

SALMON PATTIES

Crusty coated patties and condiments make good burgers.

Large eggs, fork-beaten	2	2
Canned salmon, drained, skin and round bones removed	2 × 7.5 oz.	2 × 213 g
Water	½ cup	125 mL
Soda cracker crumbs	1 cup	250 mL
Celery salt	½ tsp.	2 mL
Onion powder	½ tsp.	2 mL
Salt	¼ tsp.	1 mL
Dill weed	¼ tsp.	1 mL
Pepper	¹⁄₁₆ tsp.	0.5 mL
Corn flake crumbs	½ cup	125 mL

Combine first 9 ingredients in bowl. Mix well. Shape into 8 patties.

Coat with corn flake crumbs. Place 4 patties in bottom of 3½ quart (3.5 L) or 5 quart (5 L) slow cooker. Place remaining patties on top. Cover. Cook on Low for 4 to 5 hours or on High for 2 to 2½ hours. Makes 4 patties.

1 patty: 171 Calories; 7.7 g Total Fat; 578 mg Sodium; 11 g Protein; 13 g Carbohydrate

Pictured on page 143.

N LOAF

A very good salmon flavor to this loaf. Dense enough to slice thinly for sandwiches if desired.

Large eggs, fork-beaten	2	2
Reserved liquid from canned salmon		
Lemon juice	1½ tbsp.	25 mL
Onion flakes	1 tbsp.	15 mL
Salt	¾ tsp.	4 mL
Pepper	¼ tsp.	1 mL
Milk	½ cup	125 mL
Fine dry bread crumbs	1½ cups	375 mL
Canned salmon, drained, liquid reserved, skin and round bones removed (red salmon is best for color)	2 × 7.5 oz.	2 × 213 g
CREAM SAUCE		
All-purpose flour	2 tbsp.	30 mL
Parsley flakes	¼ tsp.	1 mL
Salt	½ tsp.	2 mL
Pepper	⅛ tsp.	0.5 mL
Onion powder	¼ tsp.	1 mL
Milk	1 cup	250 mL

Combine eggs, reserved liquid from salmon, lemon juice, onion flakes, salt, pepper and milk in bowl. Stir in bread crumbs.

Flake salmon. Stir into bread crumb mixture. Pack into greased 3½ quart (3.5 L) slow cooker. Pull sides in so it doesn't touch sides of slow cooker. Cover. Cook on Low for 4 to 5 hours or on High for 2 to 2½ hours. Loosen sides with knife. Cuts into 6 wedges. Serve with Cream Sauce.

Cream Sauce: Stir flour, parsley, salt, pepper and onion powder together in saucepan.

Whisk in milk gradually until no lumps remain. Heat and stir until boiling and thickened. Makes 1 cup (250 mL).

1 wedge with 2 tbsp. (30 mL) sauce: 295 Calories; 10.9 g Total Fat; 1125 mg Sodium; 20 g Protein; 28 g Carbohydrate

Pictured on page 35.

SHOULDER OF LAMB

A small economical cut of lamb.

Lamb shoulder roast (bone in)	2½ lbs.	1.1 kg
Liquid gravy browner	2 tsp.	10 mL
Salt, sprinkle		
Pepper, sprinkle		
Gravy, page 48		

Brush roast with gravy browner. Place in 3½ quart (3.5 L) slow cooker. Sprinkle with salt and pepper. Cover. Cook on Low for 8 to 9 hours or on High for 4 to 4½ hours.

Skim off any fat from remaining juice. Make gravy. Serves 4.

1 serving (with gravy): 331 Calories; 17.6 g Total Fat; 490 mg Sodium; 36 g Protein; 4 g Carbohydrate

LAMB LOAF

A moist firm loaf. Cuts well. Serve very hot or very cold as all lamb should be served.

Large eggs, fork-beaten	2	2
Minced onion	½ cup	125 mL
Beef bouillon powder	2 tsp.	10 mL
Quick-cooking rolled oats (not instant)	1 cup	250 mL
Lean ground lamb	2 lbs.	900 g
Ketchup (optional)	2 tbsp.	30 mL

Combine eggs, onion, bouillon powder and rolled oats in bowl. Stir.

Add ground lamb. Mix. Shape into round loaf and place in 3½ quart (3.5 L) slow cooker, not touching sides.

Spread ketchup over top. Cover. Cook on Low for 7 to 9 hours or on High for 3½ to 4½ hours. Cuts into 8 wedges.

1 wedge: 217 Calories; 7.9 g Total Fat; 239 mg Sodium; 26 g Protein; 8 g Carbohydrate

Paré Pointer

Looking for a job? Try the place with the sign asking for someone to work eight hours a day to replace someone who didn't.

RACK OF LAMB

The coating adds flavor and adds to the appearance. Luscious lamb.

Soda cracker (or fine dry bread) crumbs	¼ cup	60 mL
Dried rosemary, crushed	¼ tsp.	1 mL
Ground thyme	¼ tsp.	1 mL
Dried mint (optional)	¼ tsp.	1 mL
Garlic powder	¼ tsp.	1 mL
Parsley flakes	2 tsp.	10 mL
Salt	¼ tsp.	1 mL
Pepper	¼ tsp.	1 mL
Rack of lamb (or shoulder roast)	3¾ lbs.	1.7 kg
Cooking oil	1 tsp.	5 mL

Gravy, page 48

Combine first 8 ingredients in bowl. Mix well.

Rub rounded fat side of roast with cooking oil. Sprinkle with dry mixture. Press dry mixture against roast. Place in 5 quart (5 L) slow cooker, thin end at top. Cover. Cook on Low for 10 to 11 hours or on High for 5 to 5½ hours. Temperature should be 180°F (82°C) for well done.

Skim off any fat from remaining juice. Make gravy. Serves 4.

1 serving (with gravy): 502 Calories; 27.6 g Total Fat; 647 mg Sodium; 54 g Protein; 6 g Carbohydrate

1. Carrot Cake, page 66
2. Roast Chicken, page 115
3. Cranberry Sauce, page 128
4. Shrimp Marinara, page 83
5. Easy Bean Soup, page 138
6. Tomato Herb Bread, page 59

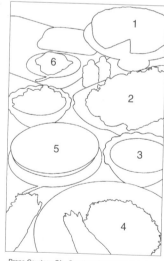

Props Courtesy Of: Creations By Design; Eaton's; Stokes; The Bay

RICE PORK CHOPS

Easy and quick to prepare. Looks great.

Pork loin chops, trimmed of fat	6	6
Liquid gravy browner	1 tsp.	5 mL
Condensed chicken and rice soup	10 oz.	284 mL

Brush both sides of pork chops with gravy browner. Place in 3½ quart (3.5 L) slow cooker.

Pour soup over top. Spread evenly. Cover. Cook on Low for 9 to 10 hours or on High for 4½ to 5 hours. Serves 6.

1 serving: 169 Calories; 6.5 g Total Fat; 417 mg Sodium; 23 g Protein; 3 g Carbohydrate

SWEET AND SOUR PORK

Good sauce, just asking to be spooned over rice. Even good on potatoes or noodles.

Lean pork, cubed	2¼ lbs.	1 kg
Brown sugar, packed	1 cup	250 mL
Water	1 cup	250 mL
White vinegar	½ cup	125 mL
Soy sauce	1 tbsp.	15 mL
Water	⅓ cup	75 mL
Cornstarch	¼ cup	60 mL

Place pork in 3½ quart (3.5 L) slow cooker.

Mix brown sugar and first amount of water in bowl. Add vinegar and soy sauce. Stir. Pour over pork. Cover. Cook on Low for 8 to 10 hours or on High for 4 to 5 hours. Tilt slow cooker and skim off any fat.

Stir second amount of water and cornstarch together in bowl. Add to slow cooker. Cook on High for 15 to 20 minutes to thicken or pour into large saucepan to thicken on burner. Serves 6 to 8.

⅙ recipe: 304 Calories; 3.9 g Total Fat; 240 mg Sodium; 23 g Protein; 44 g Carbohydrate

Paré Pointer

Love and concern for one another don't make the world go round, but they make the ride worth it all.

PORK LOIN ROAST

Serve slices of pork with this exquisite sauce and make gravy for potatoes from leftover juice. Sauce can be made ahead and reheated.

Boneless pork roast **Salt, sprinkle (optional)** **Pepper, sprinkle (optional)**	**3 lbs.**	**1.4 kg**
SPICY CRANBERRY SAUCE **Granulated sugar** **Cornstarch** **Dry mustard** **Ground cloves**	**½ cup** **2 tbsp.** **1 tsp.** **¼ tsp.**	**125 mL** **30 mL** **5 mL** **1 mL**
Cranberry cocktail	**2 cups**	**500 mL**
Gravy, page 48 (optional)		

Place roast in 3½ quart (3.5 L) slow cooker. Sprinkle with salt and pepper. Cover. Cook on Low for 8 to 10 hours or on High for 4 to 5 hours. Serves 6.

Spicy Cranberry Sauce: Measure first 4 ingredients into saucepan. Mix well.

Add cranberry cocktail. Heat and stir until boiling and thickened. Serve with pork. Makes 2 cups (500 mL).

Make gravy with remaining juice from roast to serve over potatoes if desired. Serves 6 to 8.

*⅙ **recipe:** 347 Calories; 8.7 g Total Fat; 96 mg Sodium; 32 g Protein; 33 g Carbohydrate*

Monsters will only drink ghoul-ade.

STUFFED PORK ROAST

A neat looking slice with a dark slice of prune in center of light-colored meat.

Dried pitted prunes, approximately	6-8	6-8
Boneless pork loins, tied together (about 3 lbs., 1.4 kg)	2	2
Liquid gravy browner	2 tsp.	10 mL
Gravy, page 48		

Push prunes down in between tied pork loins.

Brush roast with gravy browner. Place in 3½ quart (3.5 L) or 5 quart (5 L) slow cooker. Cover. Cook on Low for 8 to 10 hours or on High for 4 to 5 hours.

Make gravy with remaining juice from pork. Serves 6 to 8.

⅙ recipe: 641 Calories; 46.8 g Total Fat; 400 mg Sodium; 44 g Protein; 8 g Carbohydrate

Pictured on page 17.

PORK AND CABBAGE

With apple included, this is not only flavorful but an interesting dish.

Coarsely chopped cabbage (about 5 cups, 1.25 L)	1¼ lbs.	560 g
Sliced onion	1 cup	250 mL
Salt, sprinkle		
Pepper, sprinkle		
Medium cooking apples (such as McIntosh), peeled, cored and sliced	2	2
Granulated sugar	2 tbsp.	30 mL
Boneless lean pork shoulder, cubed	1½ lbs.	680 g

Layer first 6 ingredients in 3½ quart (3.5 L) slow cooker.

Place cubed pork on top. Cover. Cook on Low for 9 to 10 hours or on High for 4½ to 5 hours. Makes 6⅓ cups (1.6 L).

1 cup (250 mL): 213 Calories; 6 g Total Fat; 98 mg Sodium; 23 g Protein; 16 g Carbohydrate

CHERRY PORK CHOPS

Mildly spiced pie filling cooks with pork chops, giving them a different flavor and adding color.

Pork loin chops, trimmed of fat	6	6
Liquid gravy browner	1 tsp.	5 mL
Salt, sprinkle		
Pepper, sprinkle		
Cherry pie filling	1/2 x 19 oz.	1/2 x 540 mL
Cider vinegar	1 1/2 tsp.	7 mL
Prepared mustard	1 tsp.	5 mL
Ground cloves	1/16 tsp.	0.5 mL

Brush both sides of pork chops with gravy browner. Sprinkle with salt and pepper.

Stir pie filling, vinegar, mustard and cloves together in bowl. Layer pork chops with cherry sauce in 5 quart (5 L) slow cooker. Cover. Cook on Low for 9 to 10 hours or on High for 4 1/2 to 5 hours. Spoon juice over pork chops. Serves 6.

1 serving: 202 Calories; 5.9 g Total Fat; 102 mg Sodium; 22 g Protein; 15 g Carbohydrate

Pictured on page 107.

PORK CHOP CASSEROLE

Lots of onion rings over the chops. Ends up with some good gravy.

Pork loin chops, trimmed of fat	6	6
Liquid gravy browner	1 tsp.	5 mL
Medium onion, thinly sliced, separated into rings	1	1
Condensed cream of potato soup	10 oz.	284 mL
Non-fat sour cream	1 cup	250 mL
Ground thyme	1/4 tsp.	1 mL

Brush both sides of pork chops with gravy browner. Place in 3 1/2 quart (3.5 L) slow cooker.

Scatter onion rings over top.

Mix soup, sour cream and thyme in bowl. Spoon over top. Cover. Cook on Low for 9 to 10 hours or on High for 4 1/2 to 5 hours. Serves 6.

1 serving: 192 Calories; 6.7 g Total Fat; 508 mg Sodium; 24 g Protein; 8 g Carbohydrate

Serve pork mixture in buns, or serve open-faced. Dark red s

Lean pork roast, cubed	2 lbs.	900 g
Tomato sauce	7.5 oz.	213 mL
Ketchup	½ cup	125 mL
Chopped onion	1 cup	250 mL
White vinegar	⅓ cup	75 mL
Brown sugar, packed	⅓ cup	75 mL
Prepared mustard	1 tsp.	5 mL
Worcestershire sauce	1 tsp.	5 mL
Chili powder	1 tsp.	5 mL
Salt	¼ tsp.	1 mL
Molasses (not blackstrap)	2 tbsp.	30 mL
Water	⅔ cup	150 mL
Hamburger buns, split (buttered, optional)	8	8

Combine first 12 ingredients in 3½ quart (3.5 L) slow cooker. Cover. Cook on Low for 8 to 10 hours or on High for 4 to 5 hours.

Remove pork with slotted spoon to large bowl. Working with a few pieces at a time on plate, shred pork with 2 forks. Pork may be stirred into sauce and served over each bun half, or may be inserted into buns as a sandwich. Makes 16 open-faced buns or 8 sandwich buns.

1 open-faced bun (with sauce): 238 Calories; 7.9 g Total Fat; 397 mg Sodium; 18 g Protein; 23 g Carbohydrate

More and more electricians are driving Voltz Wagons.

PORK CHOPS

Colorful with tomato and french-cut green beans.

Canned tomatoes, with juice, cut up	14 oz.	398 mL
Canned french-cut green beans, drained	2 x 14 oz.	2 x 398 mL
Chopped onion	1 cup	250 mL
Garlic powder (or 1 clove, minced)	1/4 tsp.	1 mL
Granulated sugar	1 tsp.	5 mL
Pork chops, trimmed of fat	6	6
Liquid gravy browner	1 tsp.	5 mL

Place first 5 ingredients in 5 quart (5 L) slow cooker. Stir.

Brush both sides of pork chops with gravy browner. Layer over vegetables. Cover. Cook on Low for 10 to 12 hours or on High for 5 to 6 hours. Remove pork chops to platter. Use slotted spoon to remove vegetables or serve in sauce as is. Serves 6.

1 serving: 182 Calories; 5.9 g Total Fat; 318 mg Sodium; 23 g Protein; 9 g Carbohydrate

PORK CHOP DINNER

A complete dinner. A good mushroom gravy to serve over the pork chops.

Small bite-size pieces of carrot	1 1/2 cups	375 mL
Small bite-size pieces of potato	2 1/2 cups	625 mL
Small bite-size pieces of onion	1 cup	250 mL
Small bite-size pieces of parsnip	1 cup	250 mL
Pork loin chops, trimmed of fat	6	6
Liquid gravy browner	1 tsp.	5 mL
Condensed cream of mushroom soup	10 oz.	284 mL
Water	1/2 cup	125 mL

Put carrot in 5 quart (5 L) slow cooker. Layer potato, onion and parsnip over top.

Brush both sides of pork chops with gravy browner. Lay over parsnip.

Stir soup and water together in bowl. Pour over all. Cover. Cook on Low for 9 to 10 hours or on High for 4 1/2 to 5 hours. Serves 6.

1 serving: 291 Calories; 9.8 g Total Fat; 516 mg Sodium; 25 g Protein; 26 g Carbohydrate; good source of Dietary Fiber

SPICY PORK CHOPS

An excellent spicy sauce on these browned pork chops.

Pork loin chops, trimmed of fat	6	6
Liquid gravy browner	1 tsp.	5 mL
Ketchup	1/3 cup	75 mL
White vinegar	1/3 cup	75 mL
Water	2/3 cup	150 mL
Celery salt	1 tsp.	5 mL
Prepared mustard	1 tsp.	5 mL
Ground cloves	1/2 tsp.	2 mL
Granulated sugar	1 tsp.	5 mL

Brush both sides of pork chops with gravy browner. Arrange in 3¹/₂ quart (3.5 L) slow cooker.

Mix remaining 7 ingredients in bowl. Pour over pork chops, lifting pork chops to get a bit in between. Cover. Cook on Low for 9 to 10 hours or on High for 4¹/₂ to 5 hours. Serves 6.

1 serving: 168 Calories; 5.9 g Total Fat; 518 mg Sodium; 22 g Protein; 6 g Carbohydrate

PORK AND APPLES

Apples are a natural go-with. They taste great and aren't sweet when cooked. Some clear juice to pour over pork chops.

Pork loin chops, trimmed of fat, about 1 inch (2.5 cm) thick	4	4
Liquid gravy browner	1 tsp.	5 mL
Salt, sprinkle		
Pepper, sprinkle		
Medium cooking apples (such as McIntosh), peeled, cored and sliced	2	2
Granulated sugar	1/2 tsp.	2 mL

Brush both sides of pork chops with gravy browner. Arrange pork chops in 4¹/₂ quart (4.5 L) slow cooker. If cooker isn't big enough to hold in 1 layer, make 2 layers. Sprinkle with salt and pepper. Cover with apple slices.

Sprinkle with sugar. Cover. Cook on Low for 8 to 10 hours or on High for 4 to 5 hours. Serves 4.

1 serving: 185 Calories; 5.9 g Total Fat; 104 mg Sodium; 22 g Protein; 11 g Carbohydrate

STUFFED PORK CHOPS

Chops aren't served this way very often. Easy to prepare. A definite company dish.

STUFFING

Fine dry bread crumbs	⁷/₈ cup	200 mL
Finely chopped celery	1 tbsp.	15 mL
Finely chopped onion	¼ cup	60 mL
Poultry seasoning	¼ tsp.	1 mL
Parsley flakes	¼ tsp.	1 mL
Salt	¼ tsp.	1 mL
Pepper	¹/₁₆ tsp.	0.5 mL
Hot water	⅔ cup	150 mL
Chicken bouillon powder	½ tsp.	2 mL
Thick lean pork chops, slit horizontally to make pockets (see Note)	6	6

Stuffing: Mix first 7 ingredients in bowl.

Stir hot water and bouillon powder together in small cup. Pour over stuffing mixture. Toss, adding more water if needed to moisten.

Stuff pockets in pork chops. Arrange in slow cooker. Cover. Cook on Low for 8 to 10 hours or on High for 4 to 5 hours. Serves 6.

Note: Either you or your butcher can slit sides of chops to make pockets.

1 serving: 283 Calories; 9.3 g Total Fat; 383 mg Sodium; 34 g Protein; 13 g Carbohydrate

Most hairdressers take a short cut to their barbershops.

SWEET AND SOUR

Superb! Glazed well and delicious.

BROWN SUGAR SAUCE

Brown sugar, packed	2 cups	500 mL
All-purpose flour	¼ cup	60 mL
Water	⅓ cup	75 mL
White vinegar	½ cup	125 mL
Soy sauce	2 tbsp.	30 mL
Ketchup	2 tbsp.	30 mL
Ground ginger	¼ tsp.	1 mL
Garlic powder	¼ tsp.	1 mL
Meaty pork spareribs, cut into 2 or 3 rib sections	3 lbs.	1.4 kg

Brown Sugar Sauce: Mix brown sugar and flour in saucepan. Add water. Stir. Add next 5 ingredients. Heat and stir until boiling and thickened.

Layer ribs in a 5 quart (5 L) slow cooker, spooning sauce over each layer. Cover. Cook on Low for 10 to 12 hours or on High for 5 to 6 hours until ribs are very tender. Serves 6.

1 serving: 598 Calories; 20.8 g Total Fat; 516 mg Sodium; 22 g Protein; 82 g Carbohydrate

BARBECUED SPARERIBS

Reddish-brown ribs with a smoky barbecue flavor. Lots of sauce to spoon over rice, noodles or potatoes.

Meaty pork spareribs, cut into 2 or 3 rib sections	3 lbs.	1.4 kg
Chopped or sliced onion	1½ cups	375 mL
Smoky barbecue sauce	2 cups	500 mL

Place ½ of ribs in 3½ quart (3.5 L) slow cooker. Sprinkle ½ of onion over top. Spoon ½ of barbecue sauce over onion. Repeat layers with second ½ of ribs, onion and barbecue sauce. Cover. Cook on Low for 10 to 12 hours or on High for 5 to 6 hours. Serves 6.

1 serving: 358 Calories; 22.4 g Total Fat; 795 mg Sodium; 23 g Protein; 15 g Carbohydrate; excellent source of Dietary Fiber

POLYNESIAN RIBS

Sauce has a wonderful pineapple flavor. Lots of juice to use as gravy.

Brown sugar, packed	¼ cup	60 mL
All-purpose flour	⅓ cup	75 mL
White vinegar	¼ cup	60 mL
Ketchup	¼ cup	60 mL
Canned crushed pineapple, with juice	14 oz.	398 mL
Soy sauce	1 tbsp.	15 mL
Salt	½ tsp.	2 mL
Pepper	⅛ tsp.	0.5 mL
Pork spareribs, cut into 2 rib sections	3 lbs.	1.4 kg

Measure first 8 ingredients into saucepan. Heat and stir until boiling and thickened. Pour ⅓ of sauce into slow cooker.

Arrange ½ of ribs over top. Cover with second ⅓ of sauce followed by second ½ of ribs. Cover with remaining ⅓ of sauce. Cover. Cook on Low for 10 to 12 hours or on High for 5 to 6 hours. Serves 6.

1 serving: 397 Calories; 20.9 g Total Fat; 624 mg Sodium; 22 g Protein; 30 g Carbohydrate

RIBS 'N' STUFFING

Yummy ribs with stuffing as a bonus.

Box of stuffing mix, with seasoning	4½ oz.	120 g
Meaty pork spareribs, cut into 2 or 3 rib sections	3 lbs.	1.4 kg

Prepare stuffing according to package directions.

Place ribs in 6 quart (6 L) slow cooker. Ribs can be placed on trivet to allow fat to run to bottom if desired. Wrap prepared stuffing in foil leaving top partially open. Set on top of ribs. Cover. Cook on Low for 9 to 10 hours or on High for 4½ to 5 hours. Serves 6.

1 serving: 385 Calories; 25.4 g Total Fat; 388 mg Sodium; 23 g Protein; 15 g Carbohydrate

Paré Pointer

Mother worm to little worm, "Where in earth have you been?"

BASIC SPARER[

So easy to do; you end up with nicely browned ribs.

Meaty pork spareribs, cut into 2 or 3 rib sections	3 lbs.	1.4 kg
Liquid gravy browner	2 tsp.	10 mL

Brush ribs with gravy browner. Put into 3½ quart (3.5 L) slow cooker. Cover. Cook on Low for 9 to 10 hours or on High for 4½ to 5 hours. Serves 6.

1 serving: 280 Calories; 20.8 g Total Fat; 133 mg Sodium; 21 g Protein; 1 g Carbohydrate

RIBS AND KRAUT

A good combination to cook together. Tasty.

Chopped or sliced onion	1 cup	250 mL
Large cooking apple (such as McIntosh), peeled, cored and sliced	1	1
Canned sauerkraut, drained	14 oz.	398 mL
Meaty pork spareribs, cut into 2 or 3 rib sections	3 lbs.	1.4 kg
Salt, sprinkle		
Pepper, sprinkle		
Dill weed	1 tsp.	5 mL
Water	½ cup	125 mL

Put onion into 5 quart (5 L) slow cooker. Lay apple slices over top. Spoon sauerkraut over apple.

Sprinkle ribs with salt and pepper. Place over sauerkraut.

Combine dill weed and water in small cup. Stir. Pour over all. Cover. Cook on Low for 10 to 12 hours or on High for 5 to 6 hours. Serves 6.

1 serving: 312 Calories; 20.9 g Total Fat; 515 mg Sodium; 22 g Protein; 9 g Carbohydrate

Paré Pointer

Never lend money to a football player. Sometimes you get a quarterback and if you're lucky, a halfback.

GLAZED HAM

Such an easy way to cook a ham. Glaze is very tasty.

Boneless ham, trimmed of fat	5 lbs.	2.3 kg
Orange marmalade	1/4 cup	60 mL
Prepared mustard	1 tbsp.	15 mL
Prepared horseradish	1/2 tsp.	2 mL
Ground cloves	1/16 tsp.	0.5 mL
Gravy, page 48		

Place ham in 6 quart (6 L) slow cooker. Cut ham in half, if necessary, to fit in slow cooker.

Combine marmalade, mustard, horseradish and cloves in small bowl. Stir. Spread over ham. Cover. Cook on Low for 8 to 9 hours or on High for 4 to 4 1/2 hours.

Make gravy with remaining liquid. Serves 12.

1 serving: 273 Calories; 9.5 g Total Fat; 2827 mg Sodium; 37 g Protein; 8 g Carbohydrate

Pictured on page 71.

SCALLOPED HAM MEAL

Vegetables and ham cook while you do something else.

Medium potatoes, sliced 1/4 inch (6 mm) thick	4	4
Chopped onion	1 cup	250 mL
Salt, sprinkle		
Pepper, sprinkle		
Frozen peas	2 cups	500 mL
Smoked ham (or smoked pork shoulder piece), sliced 1/2 inch (12 mm) thick	2 lbs.	900 g
Condensed cream of chicken soup	10 oz.	284 mL
Water	1 cup	250 mL

Put potato into 3 1/2 quart (3.5 L) slow cooker. Scatter onion over top. Sprinkle with salt and pepper. Sprinkle with peas. Lay ham slices on top.

Stir soup and water together in bowl. Pour over ham. Cover. Cook on Low for 9 to 10 hours or on High for 4 1/2 to 5 hours. Serves 6.

1 serving: 352 Calories; 10.7 g Total Fat; 2600 mg Sodium; 35 g Protein; 28 g Carbohydrate; good source of Dietary Fiber

Pictured on page 143.

Pineapple slices and cranberries make these very showy and

Ham steak (about 1 inch, 2.5 cm, thick)	1½ lbs.	680 g
Pineapple slices	6	6
Brown sugar, packed	⅓ cup	75 mL
Fresh (or frozen) cranberries	¼ cup	60 mL
Ground cloves	⅛ tsp.	0.5 mL
Prepared orange juice	⅓ cup	75 mL

Place ham in 5 quart (5 L) slow cooker. Lay pineapple slices over top.

Mash brown sugar and cranberries together in small bowl. Add cloves and orange juice. Mix. Pour over pineapple. Cover. Cook on Low for 8 to 10 hours or on High for 4 to 5 hours. Cut ham into serving-size pieces. Serves 4.

1 serving: 320 Calories; 7.3 g Total Fat; 2164 mg Sodium; 34 g Protein; 29 g Carbohydrate

Pictured on page 53.

HAM LOAF

Use your leftover ham for this loaf. Easy to double recipe. Very tasty.

Ground ham	3 cups	750 mL
Quick-cooking rolled oats (not instant)	¾ cup	175 mL
Milk	¼ cup	60 mL
Large eggs	2	2
Prepared mustard	1 tbsp.	15 mL
Minced onion	2 tbsp.	30 mL
TOPPING		
Brown sugar, packed	⅓ cup	75 mL
Prepared mustard	2 tsp.	10 mL
Prepared orange juice	1 tbsp.	15 mL

Place first 6 ingredients in bowl. Mix well. Pack in 3½ quart (3.5 L) slow cooker.

Topping: Combine brown sugar, mustard and orange juice in small cup. Stir. Spread over loaf. Cover. Cook on Low for 6 to 7 hours or on High for 3 to 3½ hours. Serves 4.

1 serving: 302 Calories; 8.4 g Total Fat; 1395 mg Sodium; 24 g Protein; 33 g Carbohydrate

HAM POTATO BAKE

Color is fantastic with sweet potato and ham. A festive taste to be sure.

Small sweet potatoes, peeled, cut into bite-size pieces	2½ lbs.	1.1 kg
Boneless ham steak	1½ lbs.	680 g
Brown sugar, packed	⅓ cup	75 mL
Prepared mustard	1 tsp.	5 mL

Put sweet potato into 3½ quart (3.5 L) slow cooker. Place ham steak over top.

Mix brown sugar and mustard in small cup. Sprinkle over ham. Cover. Cook on Low for 7 to 8 hours or on High for 3½ to 4 hours. Cut ham into serving-size pieces. Serves 4.

1 serving: 580 Calories; 8.3 g Total Fat; 2250 mg Sodium; 38 g Protein; 88 g Carbohydrate; excellent source of Dietary Fiber

HAM AND NOODLES

In a delicious Parmesan cheese sauce with mushrooms.

Cubed cooked ham	1½ cups	375 mL
Canned whole or sliced mushrooms, drained	10 oz.	284 mL
Condensed cream of mushroom soup	10 oz.	284 mL
Water	½ cup	125 mL
Prepared horseradish	1½ tsp.	7 mL
Grated Parmesan cheese	¼ cup	60 mL
Sherry (or alcohol-free sherry)	2 tbsp.	30 mL
Uncooked broad egg noodles	2 cups	500 mL
Water	1 cup	250 mL

Place ham cubes and mushrooms in 3½ quart (3.5 L) slow cooker.

Combine soup and first amount of water in bowl. Add horseradish, cheese and sherry. Stir. Add to slow cooker. Cover. Cook on Low for 6 to 8 hours or on High for 3 to 4 hours.

Add noodles and second amount of water. Stir. Cover. Cook on High for 15 to 20 minutes until noodles are tender. Makes scant 4 cups (1 L).

1 cup (250 mL): 273 Calories; 11.5 g Total Fat; 1701 mg Sodium; 18 g Protein; 23 g Carbohydrate

HASH BROWN CASSER

Oniony, cheesy and yummy.

Condensed cream of mushroom soup	10 oz.	284 mL
Finely chopped onion	1/2 cup	125 mL
Non-fat sour cream	1 cup	250 mL
Salt	1 tsp.	5 mL
Pepper	1/4 tsp.	1 mL
Frozen hash brown potatoes	2 1/4 lbs.	1 kg
Grated sharp Cheddar cheese	1 cup	250 mL
TOPPING		
Hard margarine (or butter)	1 tbsp.	15 mL
Corn flake crumbs	1/4 cup	60 mL

Stir first 5 ingredients in large bowl.

Add potato and cheese. Turn into slow cooker. Cover. Cook on High for 3 to 4 hours.

Topping: Melt margarine in small saucepan. Stir in corn flake crumbs. Sauté until crisp. Scatter over top before serving. Makes 6 cups (1.5 L).

2/3 cup (150 mL): 212 Calories; 9 g Total Fat; 734 mg Sodium; 7 g Protein; 27 g Carbohydrate

JACKET POTATOES

Potatoes may be wrapped in foil, left dry or the skin greased. They all cook in the same time. Serve with sour cream, bacon bits and chives.

Medium baking potatoes, with peel	6	6

Poke potatoes with sharp knife. Wrap with foil if desired. Arrange, ends down, in a 5 quart (5 L) slow cooker. Cover. Cook on Low for 8 to 10 hours. Makes 6 potatoes.

1 potato: 111 Calories; 0.2 g Total Fat; 11 mg Sodium; 3 g Protein; 25 g Carbohydrate

Pare Pointer

Never play chess outside. Haven't you heard that squirrels eat chess-nuts?

SCALLOPED HAM POTATOES

Creamy sauce over vegetables and ham. Cheese adds extra flavor.

Water	1 cup	250 mL
Cream of tartar	½ tsp.	2 mL
Medium potatoes, thinly sliced	5	5
Chopped onion	1 cup	250 mL
Salt, sprinkle		
Pepper, sprinkle		
SAUCE		
All-purpose flour	¼ cup	60 mL
Salt	1 tsp.	5 mL
Pepper	⅛ tsp.	0.5 mL
Milk	2 cups	500 mL
Grated medium or sharp Cheddar cheese (optional)	1 cup	250 mL
Cubed boneless smoked ham	2 cups	500 mL

Combine water and cream of tartar in large bowl. Stir. Add potato. Stir well. This will help keep potato from darkening. Drain. Layer potato and onion in 5 quart (5 L) slow cooker. Sprinkle with salt and pepper.

Sauce: Stir flour, salt and pepper together in saucepan. Whisk in milk gradually until no lumps remain. Heat and stir until boiling. Pour ½ of sauce over vegetables.

Sprinkle with cheese and ham. Cover with remaining ½ of sauce. Cover. Cook on Low for 9 to 10 hours or on High for 4½ to 5 hours. Serves 6.

1 serving: 207 Calories; 3.6 g Total Fat; 1239 mg Sodium; 15 g Protein; 28 g Carbohydrate

1. Cherry Pork Chops, page 94
2. Lemonade Chicken, page 123
3. Sufferin' Succotash, page 23
4. Marbled Cheesecake, page 80
5. Spicy Spaghetti Sauce, page 28
6. Acorn Squash, page 149

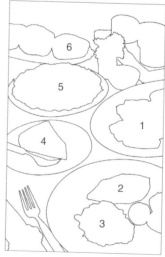

Props Courtesy Of: Eaton's; La Cache; Le Gnome; Stokes; The Bay; The Glasshouse; The Royal Doulton Store

STUFFED BAKED POTATOES

Arrive home to hot baked potatoes. Prepare stuffing while oven heats.

Medium baking potatoes	6	6
Water	2 tbsp.	30 mL
STUFFING		
Light cream cheese, softened	4 oz.	125 g
Non-fat sour cream	²/₃ cup	150 mL
Onion salt	1¹/₂ tsp.	7 mL
Chopped chives	1 tbsp.	15 mL
Salt	¹/₂ tsp.	2 mL
Pepper	¹/₈ tsp.	0.5 mL
Grated medium Cheddar cheese	¹/₃ cup	75 mL
Paprika, sprinkle		

Arrange potato in 3¹/₂ quart (3.5 L) slow cooker, stacking if necessary. Add water. Cover. Cook on Low for 8 to 10 hours.

Stuffing: Mash first 6 ingredients together in bowl. Cut lengthwise slice from top of each potato. Scoop hot potato into same bowl leaving shells intact. Mash well. Spoon back into shells.

Sprinkle with cheese and paprika. Arrange in single layer in 9 x 13 inch (22 x 33 cm) baking pan. Bake in 425°F (220°C) oven for about 15 minutes until hot. Makes 6 stuffed potatoes.

1 stuffed potato: 188 Calories; 5.8 g Total Fat; 827 mg Sodium; 8 g Protein; 27 g Carbohydrate

Pictured on page 125.

Little Mary thinks children grow in a kindergarden.

SCALLOPED POTATOES

A breeze to make. Creamy good.

Water	2 cups	500 mL
Cream of tartar	1 tsp.	5 mL
Medium potatoes, quartered lengthwise and thinly sliced	5	5
All-purpose flour	1/4 cup	60 mL
Salt	1 tsp.	5 mL
Pepper	1/8 tsp.	0.5 mL
Milk	1 1/2 cups	375 mL
Grated sharp Cheddar cheese	1/2 cup	125 mL

Combine water and cream of tartar in large bowl. Stir.

Add potato. Stir well. This will help keep potatoes from darkening. Drain. Turn potato into 4 quart (4 L) slow cooker.

Stir flour, salt and pepper together in saucepan.

Whisk in milk gradually until no lumps remain. Heat and stir until boiling and thickened.

Stir in cheese to melt. Pour over potato. Cover. Cook on Low for 6 to 8 hours. Makes 4 cups (1 L).

2/3 cup (150 mL): 161 Calories; 4.1 g Total Fat; 552 mg Sodium; 7 g Protein; 24 g Carbohydrate

Pictured on page 35.

STUFFED SWEET POTATOES

Delicious. Pineapple flavor comes through with pecans giving a nice crunch.

Medium sweet potatoes (or yams)	6	6
Canned crushed pineapple, with juice	1 cup	250 mL
Grated medium Cheddar cheese	1/4 cup	60 mL
Hard margarine (or butter), melted	1 tbsp.	15 mL
Salt	3/4 tsp.	4 mL
Pepper	1/8 tsp.	0.5 mL
Finely chopped pecans	2 tbsp.	30 mL
Paprika, sprinkle		

(continued on next page)

Place sweet potato, pointed ends up, in a 5 quart (5 L) slow cooker Cover. Cook on Low for 7 to 8 hours. Cut thick slice from top lengthwise. Scoop out pulp into bowl, leaving shell ¼ inch (6 mm) thick.

Add next 5 ingredients to potato pulp. Mash well. Spoon back into shells.

Sprinkle with pecans and paprika. Arrange on baking pan. Bake in 425°F (220°C) oven for 15 to 20 minutes until hot. Serves 6.

1 stuffed potato: 216 Calories; 5.6 g Total Fat; 409 mg Sodium; 4 g Protein; 39 g Carbohydrate; good source of Dietary Fiber

BEEFY MACARONI

One of the best looking casseroles from a slow cooker. Tastes great too!

Finely chopped onion	1 cup	250 mL
Uncooked elbow macaroni	2 cups	500 mL
Lean ground beef	1½ lbs.	680 g
All-purpose flour	¼ cup	60 mL
Salt	1 tsp.	5 mL
Pepper	¼ tsp.	1 mL
Milk	3 cups	750 mL
Canned sliced mushrooms, drained	10 oz.	284 mL
Frozen peas, thawed (2¼ cups, 560 mL)	10 oz.	300 g

Place onion and macaroni in 3½ quart (3.5 L) slow cooker.

Scramble-fry ground beef in non-stick frying pan until no longer pink. Drain. Add to slow cooker.

Stir flour, salt and pepper together in small saucepan. Whisk in milk gradually until no lumps remain. Heat, stirring constantly, until boiling and thickened. Pour over ground beef in slow cooker. Stir.

Sprinkle mushrooms and peas over top. Cover. Cook on Low for 3 to 4 hours or on High for 1½ to 2 hours. Makes 8½ cups (2.1 L).

1 cup (250 mL): 309 Calories; 8.3 g Total Fat; 507 mg Sodium; 23 g Protein; 34 g Carbohydrate; good source of Dietary Fiber

Pare Pointer

Little Johnny knows how to make an egg roll. Just push it.

CARONI AND CHEESE

nple one pot meal everyone will enjoy.

All-purpose flour	1/4 cup	60 mL
Salt	1 tsp.	5 mL
Pepper	1/4 tsp.	1 mL
Minced onion flakes	2 tbsp.	30 mL
Paprika	1/2 tsp.	2 mL
Milk	3 cups	750 mL
Grated medium or sharp Cheddar cheese	1 cup	250 mL
Uncooked elbow macaroni	2 cups	500 mL

Stir first 5 ingredients in saucepan.

Whisk in milk gradually until no lumps remain. Heat and stir until boiling and thickened.

Add cheese and macaroni. Stir. Turn into 3½ quart (3.5 L) slow cooker. Cover. Cook on Low for 2 to 2½ hours or on High for about 1 hour. Makes 4 cups (1 L).

1 cup (250 mL): 449 Calories; 13 g Total Fat; 965 mg Sodium; 22 g Protein; 60 g Carbohydrate

CHILI PASTA BAKE

Reddish color and a great taste.

Lean ground beef	1½ lbs.	680 g
Chopped onion	1 cup	250 mL
Canned tomatoes, with juice, mashed	2 x 14 oz.	2 x 398 mL
Chili powder	2 tsp.	10 mL
Dried whole oregano	1/2 tsp.	2 mL
Tomato sauce	7.5 oz.	213 mL
Salt	1 tsp.	5 mL
Pepper	1/4 tsp.	1 mL
Uncooked elbow macaroni	1¼ cups	300 mL
Grated Monterey Jack (or medium Cheddar) cheese	1 cup	250 mL

(continued on next page)

Scramble-fry ground beef in non-stick frying pan until browned. Drain well. Transfer to 3½ quart (3.5 L) slow cooker.

Add next 8 ingredients. Stir. Cover. Cook on Low for 5 to 7 hours or on High for 2½ to 3½ hours.

Sprinkle cheese over top. Cook on High for 10 to 15 minutes until cheese is melted. Makes 7 cups (1.75 L).

1 cup (250 mL): 329 Calories; 14 g Total Fat; 904 mg Sodium; 26 g Protein; 25 g Carbohydrate

BEEF AND PASTA

Large shaped pasta adds visual texture to this. Good flavor.

Canned tomatoes, with juice, broken up	2 x 14 oz.	2 x 398 mL
Water	1½ cups	375 mL
Parsley flakes	1 tsp.	5 mL
Garlic powder	¼ tsp.	1 mL
Onion powder	¼ tsp.	1 mL
Salt	1 tsp.	5 mL
Pepper	¼ tsp.	1 mL
Liquid gravy browner	1 tsp.	5 mL
Lean ground beef	1½ lbs.	680 g
Rotini pasta (scant 4 cups, 1 L)	8 oz.	250 g

Combine first 8 ingredients in large bowl. Stir well.

Add ground beef. Mix. Turn into 3½ quart (3.5 L) slow cooker. Cover. Cook on Low for 6 to 8 hours or on High for 3 to 4 hours.

Add pasta. Stir. Cook on High for 15 to 20 minutes until tender. Makes 8 cups (2 L).

1 cup (250 mL): 322 Calories; 13.6 g Total Fat; 584 mg Sodium; 21 g Protein; 28 g Carbohydrate

No one will ever steal this clock. The employees always watch it.

CHICKEN À LA KING

Good, mild and flavorful. Green pepper and pimiento add color. Serve in pastry cups for a company event.

Finely chopped celery	¼ cup	60 mL
Chopped onion	½ cup	125 mL
Medium green pepper, diced	1	1
Small fresh mushrooms, sliced	3 cups	750 mL
Jar of chopped pimiento, drained	2 oz.	57 mL
Boneless, skinless chicken breast halves, chopped	4	4
All-purpose flour	6 tbsp.	100 mL
Salt	1 tsp.	5 mL
Pepper	¼ tsp.	1 mL
Milk	1½ cups	375 mL
Sherry (or alcohol-free sherry)	¼ cup	60 mL

Put first 5 ingredients into 3½ quart (3.5 L) slow cooker. Stir.

Scatter chicken over top.

Combine flour, salt and pepper in saucepan. Stir. Whisk in milk gradually until no lumps remain. Heat and stir until boiling and thickened. Mixture will be quite thick.

Stir in sherry. Pour over chicken. Cover. Cook on Low for 6 to 8 hours or on High for 3 to 4 hours. Stir. If chicken pieces have stuck together, break apart before serving. Makes 6 cups (1.5 L).

1 cup (250 mL): 171 Calories; 2 g Total Fat; 544 mg Sodium; 22 g Protein; 14 g Carbohydrate

SNAPPY CHICKEN

A bit sweet, a bit sour. Cranberries add a great flavor. Makes a dark sauce.

Sliced onion	1 cup	250 mL
Skinless chicken thighs	12	12
Whole cranberry sauce	1 cup	250 mL
Beef bouillon powder	1 tbsp.	15 mL
Cider vinegar	1 tsp.	5 mL
Prepared mustard	1 tsp.	5 mL
Salt	1½ tsp.	7 mL

(continued on next page)

Place onion in 5 quart (5 L) slow cooker. Arrange chicken over onion.

Combine cranberry sauce, bouillon powder, vinegar, mustard and salt in bowl. Mix well. Spoon over chicken being sure to get some on every piece. Cover. Cook on Low for 6 to 8 hours or on High for 3 to 4 hours. Serves 4 to 6.

1 serving: 376 Calories; 8.6 g Total Fat; 1682 mg Sodium; 42 g Protein; 32 g Carbohydrate

ROAST CHICKEN

Final product is a tender, succulent chicken.

FRESH BREAD STUFFING		
Hard margarine (butter browns too fast)	2 tbsp.	30 mL
Chopped onion	1 cup	250 mL
Diced celery	½ cup	125 mL
Salt	1 tsp.	5 mL
Pepper	¼ tsp.	1 mL
Parsley flakes	1 tsp.	5 mL
Poultry seasoning	¼-½ tsp.	1-2 mL
Bread slices, cubed (about 4 cups,1 L)	5	5
CHICKEN		
Roasting chicken	3½ lbs.	1.6 kg
Liquid gravy browner	2 tsp.	10 mL

Gravy, page 48

Fresh Bread Stuffing: Melt margarine in frying pan. Add onion and celery. Sauté until soft. Remove from heat.

Mix in salt, pepper, parsley and poultry seasoning. Add bread cubes. Toss well. Wrap in foil, leaving an opening at top.

Chicken: Brush chicken with gravy browner. Place in 5 quart (5 L) slow cooker. Place foil pouch over chicken legs. Cover slow cooker. Cook on Low for 8 to 9 hours or on High for 4 to 4½ hours.

Make gravy with remaining juice from chicken. Stir stuffing before serving. Serves 6.

1 serving: 541 Calories; 35.4 g Total Fat; 1036 mg Sodium; 36 g Protein; 18 g Carbohydrate

Pictured on page 89.

CHICKEN STEW

Have this whole delicious meal ready and waiting. Juice may be left as is or it can be thickened.

Medium potatoes, cut bite size	4	4
Medium carrots, cut bite size	4	4
Chopped onion	1¼ cups	300 mL
Boneless, skinless chicken thighs (or drumsticks), cut bite size	1¼ lbs.	560 g
Hot water	2 cups	500 mL
Chicken bouillon powder	1 tbsp.	15 mL
Salt	1 tsp.	5 mL
Pepper	¼ tsp.	1 mL
Ground thyme	¼ tsp.	1 mL
Liquid gravy browner	½ tsp.	2 mL

Layer potato, carrot and onion in 5 quart (5 L) slow cooker. Lay chicken thighs on top.

Stir next 6 ingredients together in bowl. Pour over chicken. Cover. Cook on Low for 9 to 10 hours or on High for 4½ to 5 hours. Serves 6.

1 serving: *213 Calories; 4.2 g Total Fat; 896 mg Sodium; 21 g Protein; 23 g Carbohydrate; good source of Dietary Fiber*

CHICKEN IN SAUCE

Makes lots of sauce. A green salad is the only thing needed to complete this meal.

Peeled baby carrots	30	30
Medium potatoes, cut up	4	4
Canned whole mushrooms, drained	10 oz.	284 mL
Chopped or sliced onion	½ cup	125 mL
Boneless, skinless chicken breast halves	6	6
Condensed cream of mushroom soup	10 oz.	284 mL
Chicken (or beef) bouillon powder	1 tsp.	5 mL
White (or alcohol-free) wine	¼ cup	60 mL
Envelope dry onion soup mix	1 × 1½ oz.	1 × 42 g
Salt (optional)	¼ tsp.	1 mL
Pepper	⅛ tsp.	0.5 mL

(continued on next page)

Arrange vegetables in layers in 5 quart (5 L) slow cooker. Lay chicken pieces over top.

Stir remaining 6 ingredients together well in bowl. Mix well. Spoon over chicken. Cover. Cook on Low for 10 to 12 hours or on High for 5 to 6 hours. Serves 6.

1 serving: 465 Calories; 9.1 g Total Fat; 2021 mg Sodium; 48 g Protein; 45 g Carbohydrate; good source of Dietary Fiber

CHICKEN DIVAN

Broccoli adds color and the sauce is "icing on the cake."

Broccoli florets	3 cups	750 mL
Skinless chicken breast halves	4	4
SAUCE		
All-purpose flour	¼ cup	60 mL
Chicken bouillon powder	1 tbsp.	15 mL
Salt	½ tsp.	2 mL
Pepper	¼ tsp.	1 mL
Milk	2 cups	500 mL
Grated Parmesan cheese	¼ cup	60 mL

Place broccoli in 5 quart (5 L) slow cooker. Lay chicken over top.

Sauce: Stir together flour, bouillon powder, salt and pepper in saucepan. Gradually whisk in milk until no lumps remain. Heat and stir until boiling and thickened. Remove from heat.

Stir in cheese. Pour over chicken. Cover. Cook on Low for 6 to 8 hours or on High for 3 to 4 hours. Serves 4.

1 serving: 271 Calories; 5.5 g Total Fat; 1111 mg Sodium; 38 g Protein; 17 g Carbohydrate

Paré Pointer

Old actors never die—they just lose their parts.

SESAME CHICKEN

Toasted sesame seeds darken even more and add a great flavor to chicken.

Skinless chicken thighs	3 lbs.	1.4 kg
Soy sauce	1/2 cup	125 mL
Sherry	2 tbsp.	30 mL
Brown sugar, packed	1/3 cup	75 mL
Garlic powder	1/4 tsp.	1 mL
Ground ginger	1/4 tsp.	1 mL
Ketchup	2 tbsp.	30 mL
Toasted sesame seeds	2 tbsp.	30 mL

Place chicken thighs in 3½ quart (3.5 L) slow cooker.

Combine remaining 7 ingredients in bowl. Mix well. Pour over chicken, being sure to get some sauce on every piece. Cover. Cook on Low for 6 to 8 hours or on High for 3 to 4 hours. Serves 4 to 6.

1/4 recipe: 376 Calories; 10.1 g Total Fat; 2458 mg Sodium; 43 g Protein; 26 g Carbohydrate

COQ AU VIN

Wine flavor is evident in kohk-oh-VAHN. Served in fine restaurants.

Pearl onions, peeled (see Note)	24-36	24-36
Chicken parts, skin removed	3 lbs.	1.4 kg
Bacon slices, cooked crisp and crumbled	6	6
Small fresh mushrooms	2 cups	500 mL
Thinly sliced celery	1/2 cup	125 mL
Beef bouillon powder	2 tsp.	10 mL
Warm water	1½ cups	375 mL
Salt	1/2 tsp.	2 mL
Pepper	1/4 tsp.	1 mL
Garlic powder	1/4 tsp.	1 mL
Parsley flakes	1 tsp.	5 mL
Ground thyme	1/4 tsp.	1 mL
Bay leaf	1	1
Red (or alcohol-free) wine	2 cups	500 mL
Gravy, page 48		

(continued on next page)

Place onion in 5 quart (5 L) slow cooker. Arrange chicken pieces, bacon, mushrooms and celery in order given over top.

Stir bouillon powder and warm water together in small bowl. Add salt, pepper, garlic powder, parsley flakes, thyme and bay leaf. Stir. Pour over chicken.

Add wine. Cover. Cook on Low for 8 to 10 hours or on High for 4 to 5 hours. Discard bay leaf.

Make gravy with remaining liquid. Serves 6.

Note: Allow 6 onions per person. To peel pearl onions easily, blanch in boiling water for about 2 minutes. Rinse in cold water and simply peel away skin.

1 serving: 266 Calories; 6.7 g Total Fat; 852 mg Sodium; 28 g Protein; 9 g Carbohydrate

SWEET AND SOUR CHICKEN

This has lots of sauce to go over rice or noodles.

Ketchup	2 tbsp.	30 mL
Water	1 cup	250 mL
White vinegar	½ cup	125 mL
Soy sauce	1 tbsp.	15 mL
Brown sugar, packed	1 cup	250 mL
Boneless, skinless chicken breasts (or thighs), cut bite size	1½ lbs.	680 g
Cornstarch	2 tbsp.	30 mL
Water	2 tbsp.	30 mL

Combine first 5 ingredients in 3½ quart (3.5 L) slow cooker. Stir.

Add chicken. Stir. Cover. Cook on Low for 6 to 8 hours or on High for 3 to 4 hours.

Combine cornstarch and second amount of water in small bowl. Stir into slow cooker. Cook on High, stirring often, for 15 to 20 minutes until thickened. For faster cooking, pour into saucepan. Heat on stove, stirring often, until thickened. Serves 6.

1 serving: 290 Calories; 1.4 g Total Fat; 328 mg Sodium; 27 g Protein; 43 g Carbohydrate

GINGER CHICKEN

Good ginger flavor with a wee bit of a bite. Add more cayenne pepper if desired.

Chicken parts, skin removed	3 lbs.	1.4 kg
Canned diced tomatoes	19 oz.	540 mL
Grated gingerroot	1 tbsp.	15 mL
Minute tapioca	2 tbsp.	30 mL
Garlic powder	1 tsp.	5 mL
Parsley flakes	1 tsp.	5 mL
Brown sugar, packed	1 tbsp.	15 mL
Cayenne pepper	¼ tsp.	1 mL
Salt	½ tsp.	2 mL
Gravy, page 48		

Arrange chicken in 3½ quart (3.5 L) slow cooker.

Combine remaining 8 ingredients in bowl. Stir well. Pour over chicken. Cover. Cook on Low for 7 to 8 hours or on High for 3½ to 4 hours.

Spoon off any fat. Make gravy with remaining juice. Serves 4 to 6.

¼ **recipe:** *276 Calories; 5.4 g Total Fat; 1030 mg Sodium; 38 g Protein; 18 g Carbohydrate*

CHICKEN TETRAZZINI

A complete meal.

Chopped onion	1 cup	250 mL
Sliced fresh mushrooms	3 cups	750 mL
Chopped, boneless, skinless chicken (white or dark meat)	3 cups	750 mL
All-purpose flour	3 tbsp.	50 mL
Salt	1 tsp.	5 mL
Pepper	¼ tsp.	1 mL
Chicken bouillon powder	1 tbsp.	15 mL
Water	1½ cups	375 mL
Skim evaporated milk	1 cup	250 mL
Sherry (or alcohol-free sherry)	3 tbsp.	50 mL
Spaghetti noodles, broken into short pieces	8 oz.	250 g
Grated Parmesan cheese, sprinkle		

(continued on next page)

Combine first 7 ingredients in 5 quart (5 L) slow cooker. Stir well to coat chicken with flour.

Pour water, evaporated milk and sherry into bowl. Stir. Pour over top. Cover. Cook on Low for 6 to 8 hours or on High for 3 to 4 hours.

Add noodles. Stir well to avoid sticking together. Push under liquid. Sprinkle with cheese. Cook on High for 15 to 20 minutes until tender. Makes 7 cups (1.75 L).

1 cup (250 mL): 296 Calories; 3.4 g Total Fat; 780 mg Sodium; 26 g Protein; 38 g Carbohydrate

CHICKEN & RICE

Canned chicken makes this an easy dish to prepare.

Chopped onion	1 cup	250 mL
Chopped fresh mushrooms	1 cup	250 mL
Medium green pepper, chopped	1	1
Uncooked converted rice	¾ cup	175 mL
Canned flakes of chicken, with juice, broken up (or 2 cups, 500 mL, chopped cooked chicken)	2 × 6.5 oz.	2 × 184 g
Chicken bouillon powder	2 tsp.	10 mL
Warm water	1 cup	250 mL
Canned tomatoes, with juice, broken up	14 oz.	398 mL

Layer onion, mushrooms, green pepper, rice and chicken in 3½ quart (3.5 L) slow cooker.

Stir bouillon powder and warm water together in bowl. Add tomato. Stir. Pour over chicken. Cover. Cook on Low for 6 to 7 hours or on High for 3 to 3½ hours. Stir before serving. Makes 7 cups (1.75 L).

1 cup (250 mL): 185 Calories; 4.7 g Total Fat; 546 mg Sodium; 14 g Protein; 21 g Carbohydrate

Paré Pointer

One thing he can do better than anyone else is read his own handwriting.

...KEN CACCIATORE

...n color. Excellent choice. Tomato adds its own flavor.

~~Chopped~~ onion	1½ cups	375 mL
Chicken parts, skin removed	3 lbs.	1.4 kg
Canned tomatoes, with juice	14 oz.	398 mL
Tomato paste	5½ oz.	156 mL
Canned mushroom pieces, drained	10 oz.	284 mL
Bay leaf	1	1
Salt	1 tsp.	5 mL
Pepper	¼ tsp.	1 mL
Garlic powder	¼ tsp.	1 mL
Dried whole oregano	1 tsp.	5 mL
Dried sweet basil	½ tsp.	2 mL
White (or alcohol-free) wine	¼ cup	60 mL
Liquid gravy browner	½ tsp.	2 mL
Granulated sugar	1 tsp.	5 mL

Place onion and chicken in 3½ quart (3.5 L) slow cooker.

Combine next 12 ingredients in bowl. Stir. Pour over chicken. Cover. Cook on Low for 6 to 8 hours or on High for 3 to 4 hours. Discard bay leaf. Serves 4.

1 serving: 306 Calories; 5.7 g Total Fat; 1178 mg Sodium; 40 g Protein; 22 g Carbohydrate; excellent source of Dietary Fiber

Pictured on front cover.

QUICK FIX CHICKEN

A touch of sweetness with some onion flavor. Deep color with a nice glaze.

French dressing	½ cup	125 mL
Apricot jam	½ cup	125 mL
Envelope dry onion soup mix	1 × 1½ oz.	1 × 42 g
Chicken parts, skin removed	3 lbs.	1.4 kg

Mix first 3 ingredients in bowl.

Brush each piece of chicken with sauce. Arrange chicken in 3½ quart (3.5 L) slow cooker. Cover chicken with any remaining sauce. Cover. Cook on Low for 6 to 8 hours or on High 3 to 4 hours. Serves 6.

1 serving: 318 Calories; 12.4 g Total Fat; 1071 mg Sodium; 25 g Protein; 26 g Carbohydrate

It looks and tastes like fried chicken.

All-purpose flour	⅓ cup	75 mL
Salt	1 tsp.	5 mL
Pepper	¼ tsp.	1 mL
Paprika	1 tsp.	5 mL
Garlic powder (optional)	¼ tsp.	1 mL
Chicken parts, skin removed	3 lbs.	1.4 kg

Gravy, page 48

Stir first 5 ingredients together in bowl. Pour into plastic or paper bag.

Shake 2 or 3 pieces of chicken at a time in bag to coat. Repeat for all pieces of chicken. Arrange on broiler tray. Broil on top rack in oven to brown quickly, not to cook. Transfer to 3½ quart (3.5 L) slow cooker. Cover. Cook on Low for 8 to 10 hours or on High for 4 to 5 hours.

Make gravy with remaining juice. Serves 6.

1 serving: 171 Calories; 3.4 g Total Fat; 763 mg Sodium; 25 g Protein; 8 g Carbohydrate

LEMONADE CHICKEN

A sweet citrus flavor. Lots of liquid to make gravy with.

Frozen concentrated lemonade, thawed	½ × 12½ oz.	½ × 355 mL
Brown sugar, packed	3 tbsp.	50 mL
Ketchup	3 tbsp.	50 mL
White vinegar	1 tbsp.	15 mL
Liquid gravy browner	1 tsp.	5 mL
Boneless, skinless chicken breast halves	6	6

Gravy, page 48

Stir first 5 ingredients in bowl.

Arrange chicken pieces in bottom of 3½ quart (3.5 L) slow cooker, overlapping if necessary. Pour lemonade mixture over all. Cover. Cook on Low for 8 to 10 hours or on High for 4 to 5 hours.

Make gravy with remaining liquid. Serves 6.

1 serving: 244 Calories; 1.7 g Total Fat; 433 mg Sodium; 28 g Protein; 29 g Carbohydrate

Pictured on page 107.

CORNISH GAME HENS

Certainly a no-fuss way to cook these. Prepare commercial stuffing separately to serve along side.

SESAME COATING

Ketchup	1 tbsp.	15 mL
White vinegar	1½ tsp.	7 mL
Soy sauce	1½ tsp.	7 mL
Brown sugar, packed	1 tbsp.	15 mL
Ground ginger	⅛ tsp.	0.5 mL
Toasted sesame seeds	1 tbsp.	15 mL
Cornish hens (about 1¾ lbs., 790 g, each), see Note	2	2

Gravy, page 48

Sesame Coating: Stir first 6 ingredients together in small bowl.

Spread coating over each Cornish hen. Place side by side in 3½ quart (3.5 L) or 5 quart (5 L) slow cooker. Cover. Cook on Low for 7 to 8 hours or on High for 3½ to 4 hours.

Make gravy with remaining juice from Cornish hens. Serves 4.

1 serving: 664 Calories; 46.4 g Total Fat; 718 mg Sodium; 50 g Protein; 9 g Carbohydrate

Note: Double Sesame Coating to cook 4 Cornish hens. Place each Cornish hen in 5 quart (5 L) slow cooker, neck end touching bottom. To cook in 3½ quart (3.5 L) slow cooker, pile 2 Cornish hens on top of first 2. Bottom hens will cook faster so, if possible, reverse positions at half-time.

1. Beef In Wine, page 40
2. Stuffed Baked Potatoes, page 109
3. Chick Pea Stew, page 21
4. Chocolate Fondue, page 145
5. French Onion Soup, page 133
6. Apple Punch, page 51

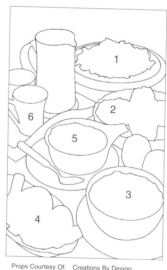

Props Courtesy Of: Creations By Design;
Sears Canada Inc; Stokes;
The Bay

CHICKEN MARENGO

Spaghetti sauce mix gives a flavor boost.

Canned sliced mushrooms, drained	10 oz.	284 mL
Sliced onion	1 cup	250 mL
Chicken parts, skin removed	3 lbs.	1.4 kg
Canned tomatoes, with juice, broken up	14 oz.	398 mL
Envelope spaghetti sauce mix	1 × 1½ oz.	1 × 43 g

Arrange mushrooms and onion in 5 quart (5 L) slow cooker. Lay chicken pieces over top.

Stir tomato and spaghetti sauce mix together in bowl. Pour over top of chicken. Cover. Cook on Low for 8 to 10 hours or on High for 4 to 5 hours. Serves 6.

1 serving: 179 Calories; 3.6 g Total Fat; 907 mg Sodium; 26 g Protein; 10 g Carbohydrate

DRUMSTICK BAKE

Browned drumsticks with nice gravy to spoon over mashed potato.

Chicken drumsticks, skin removed	12	12
Condensed cream of chicken soup	10 oz.	284 mL
Onion flakes	2 tbsp.	30 mL
Liquid gravy browner	½ tsp.	2 mL

Arrange drumsticks in 3½ quart (3.5 L) slow cooker.

Combine soup, onion flakes and gravy browner in bowl. Stir well. Spoon over chicken. Cover. Cook on Low for 6 to 7 hours or on High for 3 to 3½ hours. Serves 4 to 6.

¼ recipe: 303 Calories; 10.8 g Total Fat; 778 mg Sodium; 41 g Protein; 9 g Carbohydrate

Paré Pointer

Old bacteriologists never die—they go out to Pasteur.

CHICKEN CURRY

A pleasant curry flavor. You can adjust the amount of curry to make it milder or hotter. Lots of broth.

Chopped onion	1 cup	250 mL
Medium tomatoes, diced	2	2
Medium green pepper, chopped	1	1
Hot water	4 cups	1 L
Curry powder	3 tbsp.	50 mL
Chicken bouillon powder	4 tsp.	20 mL
Ketchup	1 tbsp.	15 mL
Salt	1 tsp.	5 mL
Boneless, skinless chicken breast halves (or thighs)	1½ lbs.	680 g

Put onion into 5 quart (5 L) slow cooker. Scatter tomato and green pepper over onion.

Stir next 5 ingredients together in bowl. Pour over vegetables.

Arrange chicken pieces over top. Cover. Cook on Low for 8 to 10 hours or on High for 4 to 5 hours. Transfer chicken to platter. Remove vegetables with slotted spoon and place beside chicken. Pour broth into gravy boat to serve over rice, noodles or mashed potatoes. Serves 6.

1 serving: 167 Calories; 2.4 g Total Fat; 1000 mg Sodium; 28 g Protein; 8 g Carbohydrate

CRANBERRY SAUCE

Gorgeous colored whole cranberry sauce. Needs no attention.

Granulated sugar	2 cups	500 mL
Boiling water	1 cup	250 mL
Fresh (or frozen) cranberries	4 cups	1 L

Stir sugar and boiling water together in 3½ quart (3.5 L) slow cooker.

Add cranberries. Cover. Cook on High for about 1½ hours until most of the berries have popped. Cool. Makes 3½ cups (875 mL).

2 tbsp. (30 mL): 62 Calories; trace Total Fat; trace Sodium; trace Protein; 16 g Carbohydrate

Pictured on page 89.

Golden chicken in golden sauce. Great with rice.

Large egg, fork-beaten	1	1
Salt	½ tsp.	2 mL
Pepper	¼ tsp.	1 mL
Fine dry bread crumbs	½ cup	125 mL
Chicken bouillon powder	2 tsp.	10 mL
Ground chicken	1½ lbs.	680 g
Canned pineapple tidbits, with juice	14 oz.	398 mL
White vinegar	⅓ cup	75 mL
Ketchup	2 tsp.	10 mL
Soy sauce	2 tsp.	10 mL
Chicken bouillon powder	1 tsp.	5 mL
Brown sugar, packed	⅓ cup	75 mL
Medium green pepper, diced into ¾ inch (2 cm) pieces	1	1
Chopped green onion	⅓ cup	75 mL
Water	⅔ cup	150 mL
Cornstarch	3 tbsp.	50 mL

Place first 5 ingredients in bowl. Stir well.

Add ground chicken. Mix. Shape into 1½ inch (3.8 cm) balls. Arrange on broiler tray. Broil, turning once, until browned. This will take about 4 to 5 minutes per side. Place meatballs in 3½ quart (3.5 L) slow cooker.

Combine next 8 ingredients in saucepan.

Mix water and cornstarch in small cup. Add to saucepan. Heat and stir until boiling and thickened. Pour over meatballs. (If preparing the evening before, cool sauce thoroughly before pouring over chicken and placing in the refrigerator.) Cover. Cook on Low for 4 to 5 hours or on High for 2 to 2½ hours. Makes 30 meatballs.

3 meatballs (with sauce and veggies): *178 Calories; 2.8 g Total Fat; 518 mg Sodium; 16 g protein; 22 g Carbohydrate*

Paré Pointer

One food strikes terror in Dracula's heart. Stake!

TURKEY DRUMS

Economical, moist and tasty.

Turkey drumsticks (about ¾ lbs., 340 g, each)	2	2
Beef bouillon powder	2 tsp.	10 mL
Onion powder	¼ tsp.	1 mL
Seasoning salt	½ tsp.	2 mL
Brown sugar, packed	¼ cup	60 mL
Ketchup	1 tbsp.	15 mL
Gravy, page 48		

Place drumsticks, meaty side down, in 3½ quart (3.5 L) slow cooker.

Combine next 5 ingredients in bowl. Mix well. Spread over top. Cover. Cook on Low for 7 to 9 hours or on High for 3½ to 4½ hours. Remove skin before serving if desired.

Make gravy with remaining juice from turkey. Serves 2.

1 serving: 438 Calories; 9.9 g Total Fat; 1889 mg Sodium; 47 g Protein; 38 g Carbohydrate

TURKEY ROLL

Makes any meal seem quite festive.

Boneless turkey roll	2½ lbs.	1.1 kg
Stuffing, page 131		
Gravy, page 48		

Place turkey roll in 3½ quart (3.5 L) slow cooker.

Prepare stuffing. Wrap in foil, leaving an opening at top. Place over turkey. Cover slow cooker. Cook on Low for 8 to 10 hours or on High for 4 to 5 hours.

Make gravy with remaining juice from turkey. Serves 6.

1 serving: 579 Calories; 14.8 g Total Fat; 1730 mg Sodium; 52 g Protein; 56 g Carbohydrate

The perfect solution when oven space is scarce.

Chopped celery	1 cup	250 mL
Chopped onion	1 cup	250 mL
Parsley flakes	1 tbsp.	15 mL
Poultry seasoning	2 tsp.	10 mL
Salt	1 tsp.	5 mL
Pepper	1/4 tsp.	1 mL
Dry bread cubes	10 cups	2.5 L
Hard margarine (or butter)	1/4 cup	60 mL
Chicken bouillon powder	1 tbsp.	15 mL
Hot water	1 1/2 cups	375 mL

Put first 6 ingredients into large bowl. Stir well.

Add bread cubes. Stir.

Combine margarine, bouillon powder and hot water in separate bowl. Stir to melt margarine and dissolve bouillon powder. Pour over bread cube mixture. Turn into 5 quart (5 L) slow cooker. Cover. Cook on Low for 5 to 6 hours. If you prefer a more moist stuffing, add a bit more hot water and stir. Makes 8 cups (2 L).

1/2 cup (125 mL): 135 Calories; 4.4 g Total Fat; 522 mg Sodium; 4 g Protein; 20 g Carbohydrate

Old taxis usually end up in the old cabb-age home.

TURKEY LOAF

Serve for supper and use leftovers for sandwiches. This loaf cuts so well for sandwiches.

Large egg, fork-beaten	1	1
Finely chopped onion	½ cup	125 mL
Salt	½ tsp.	2 mL
Pepper	¼ tsp.	1 mL
Ground thyme	¼ tsp.	1 mL
Prepared horseradish	1 tsp.	5 mL
Quick-cooking rolled oats (not instant)	½ cup	125 mL
Ground turkey	1½ lbs.	680 g
Ketchup	2 tbsp.	30 mL
Prepared mustard	1 tsp.	5 mL

Combine first 7 ingredients in bowl. Mix well.

Add ground turkey. Mix. Turn into greased 3½ quart (3.5 L) slow cooker.

Mix ketchup and mustard in small cup. Spread over top. Cover. Cook on Low for 5 to 6 hours or on High for 2½ to 3 hours. Serves 6.

1 serving: 177 Calories; 3.2 g Total Fat; 388 mg Sodium; 28 g Protein; 8 g Carbohydrate

TURKEY ROAST

Sliced white meat with an apple-flavored fruity sauce.

Medium cooking apples, peeled and sliced (such as McIntosh)	2	2
Whole cranberry sauce	½ cup	125 mL
Boneless, skinless turkey breast roast	2⅛ lbs.	1 kg
Liquid gravy browner	1 tsp.	5 mL

Arrange apple slices in 5 quart (5 L) slow cooker. Dot cranberry sauce here and there over apple.

Brush roast with gravy browner. Place on top of apple mixture. Cover. Cook on Low for 8 to 9 hours or on High for 4 to 4½ hours. Serve with remaining juice mixture. Serves 6.

1 serving: 242 Calories; 1.3 g Total Fat; 114 mg Sodium; 40 g Protein; 16 g Carbohydrate

It's easy to turn a meat soup recipe into a meatless soup recipe. Simply omit the meat and taste for seasoning. Chicken, beef or vegetable bouillon powder will add strength to the flavor. Taste for salt and pepper. Other popular spices are oregano, basil, garlic powder, onion powder and thyme. A touch of gravy browner or ketchup will add color.

FRENCH ONION SOUP

Simple and just like you would have when dining out.

Quartered and thinly sliced white onion (about 1½ lbs., 680 g)	4¼ cups	1 L
Water	4 cups	1 L
Beef bouillon powder	4 tsp.	20 mL
French bread slices, cut to fit	4	4
Grated mozzarella cheese	1 cup	250 mL
Grated Parmesan cheese, sprinkle		

Combine first 3 ingredients in 3½ quart (3.5 L) slow cooker. Cover. Cook on Low for 8 to 10 hours or on High for 4 to 5 hours.

Ladle soup into bowls. Place 1 slice of bread in each bowl. Divide mozzarella cheese and sprinkle over each slice. Sprinkle with Parmesan cheese. Broil until cheese is bubbly and golden brown. If preferred, bread with cheese may be broiled separately, then added to each bowl. Serves 4.

1 cup (250 mL): 211 Calories; 8.3 g Total Fat; 809 mg Sodium; 10 g Protein; 25 g Carbohydrate

Pictured on page 125.

Paré Pointer

Old lawyers never die—they just lose their appeal.

CHICKEN VEGETABLE SOUP

A colorful soup in a clear broth. Lots of chicken.

Boneless, skinless chicken breast halves, diced	3	3
Chopped onion	1 cup	250 mL
Thinly sliced carrot	1⅓ cups	325 mL
Diced celery	½ cup	125 mL
Diced turnip	½ cup	125 mL
Diced potato	2 cups	500 mL
Chicken bouillon powder	1 tbsp.	15 mL
Salt	1 tsp.	5 mL
Pepper	¼ tsp.	1 mL
Ground thyme	¼ tsp.	1 mL
Water	4 cups	1 L
Liquid gravy browner, to color slightly (optional)		

Place first 11 ingredients in 5 quart (5 L) slow cooker. Stir. Cover. Cook on Low for 8 to 10 hours or on High for 4 to 5 hours. If vegetables are large and not quite tender, turn heat to High for a few minutes.

Add gravy browner just before serving. Taste for salt and pepper, adding more if needed. Makes 8 cups (2 L).

1 cup (250 mL): 105 Calories; 0.9 g Total Fat; 635 mg Sodium; 12 g Protein; 12 g Carbohydrate

SPLIT PEA SOUP

Very attractive. Carrot adds color. A dandy green pea soup.

Dried split green peas	2 cups	500 mL
Canned flakes of ham, with liquid, broken up (or 1 cup, 250 mL, diced ham)	6.5 oz.	184 g
Medium carrot, thinly sliced or diced	1	1
Diced celery	½ cup	125 mL
Finely chopped onion	1 cup	250 mL
Salt	½ tsp.	2 mL
Pepper	¼ tsp.	1 mL
Parsley flakes	1 tsp.	5 mL
Chicken bouillon powder	1 tbsp.	15 mL
Ground thyme	¼ tsp.	1 mL
Water	5 cups	1.25 L

(continued on next page)

Combine all 11 ingredients in 3½ quart (3.5 L) slow cooker. Stir. Cover. Cook on Low for 8 to 10 hours or on High for 4 to 5 hours. Makes 7¾ cups (1.9 L).

1 cup (250 mL): 265 Calories; 5.4 g Total Fat; 771 mg Sodium; 18 g Protein; 37 g Carbohydrate; excellent source of Dietary Fiber

Pictured on page 143.

BEEF MINESTRONE

When your day away from home is long, this will be ready and waiting for your return.

Beef stew meat, diced small	½ lb.	225 g
Canned tomatoes, with juice, broken up	14 oz.	398 mL
Chopped onion	1 cup	250 mL
Grated cabbage	1 cup	250 mL
Medium carrot, diced or thinly sliced	1	1
Small zucchini with peel (about 7 inches, 18 cm), cubed	1	1
Medium potato, diced	1	1
Parsley flakes	1 tsp.	5 mL
Garlic powder	¼ tsp.	1 mL
Dried sweet basil	¼ tsp.	1 mL
Dried whole oregano	¼ tsp.	1 mL
Salt	1½ tsp.	7 mL
Pepper	¼ tsp.	1 mL
Water	4 cups	1 L
Canned kidney beans, drained	14 oz.	398 mL
Uncooked elbow macaroni	½ cup	125 mL
Grated Parmesan cheese, sprinkle		

Combine first 14 ingredients in 3½ quart (3.5 L) or 5 quart (5 L) slow cooker. Stir well. Cover. Cook on Low for 10 to 12 hours or on High for 5 to 6 hours.

Turn heat to High. Add kidney beans and macaroni. Cook for 15 to 20 minutes until macaroni is tender.

Sprinkle with cheese to serve. Makes 10½ cups (2.6 L).

1 cup (250 mL): 97 Calories; 1 g Total Fat; 514 mg Sodium; 7 g Protein; 15 g Carbohydrate; good source of Dietary Fiber

Pictured on front cover.

BEAN SOUP

Brownish color with tomato adding a bit of color. Thick soup with a good flavor. Contains canned ham. Simple to make.

Dried navy beans (1 lb., 454 g)	2⅓ cups	575 mL
Chopped onion	1¼ cups	300 mL
Garlic clove, minced (or ¼ tsp.,1 mL, powder)	1	1
Canned flakes of ham, with liquid, broken up (or 1 cup, 250 mL, diced ham)	6.5 oz.	184 g
Canned tomatoes, with juice, broken up	14 oz.	398 mL
Water	6 cups	1.5 L
Salt	1 tsp.	5 mL
Pepper	¼ tsp.	1 mL

Measure all 8 ingredients into 5 quart (5 L) slow cooker. Stir well. Cover. Cook on Low for 8 to 10 hours or on High for 4 to 5 hours. Taste for salt and pepper, adding more if needed. Makes 9⅔ cups (2.4 L).

1 cup (250 mL): 232 Calories; 4.4 g Total Fat; 616 mg Sodium; 15 g Protein; 35 g Carbohydrate; good source of Dietary Fiber

BEEF BARLEY SOUP

A hearty soup.

Beef stew meat, diced small	1 lb.	454 g
Sliced or chopped carrot	1¼ cups	300 mL
Chopped onion	1¼ cups	300 mL
Chopped celery	¾ cup	175 mL
Water	5 cups	1.25 L
Parsley flakes	1 tsp.	5 mL
Pepper	¼ tsp.	1 mL
Granulated sugar	1 tsp.	5 mL
Beef bouillon powder	2 tbsp.	30 mL
Pearl barley	½ cup	125 mL
Tomato sauce	2 × 7.5 oz.	2 × 213 mL

Place all 11 ingredients in 5 quart (5 L) slow cooker. Stir. Cover. Cook on Low for 8 to 10 hours or on High for 4 to 5 hours. Makes 10¼ cups (2.5 L).

1 cup (250 mL): 113 Calories; 1.8 g Total Fat; 637 mg Sodium; 9 g Protein; 16 g Carbohydrate; good source of Dietary Fiber

BEEF VEGETABLE SOUP

Rich color and a full-meal soup. Serve with garlic bread or crusty rolls.

Lean ground beef	1 lb.	454 g
Canned diced tomatoes	14 oz.	398 mL
Chopped onion	1 cup	250 mL
Frozen mixed vegetables	10 oz.	300 g
Thinly sliced or diced carrot	1 cup	250 mL
Diced potato	1½ cups	375 mL
Diced celery	½ cup	125 mL
Condensed tomato soup	10 oz.	284 mL
Water	3 cups	750 mL
Granulated sugar	1 tsp.	5 mL
Salt	½ tsp.	2 mL
Pepper	¼ tsp.	1 mL
Liquid gravy browner	1 tsp.	5 mL

Scramble-fry ground beef in non-stick frying pan until no longer pink. Drain well.

Combine ground beef and remaining 12 ingredients in 5 quart (5 L) slow cooker. Stir well. Cover. Cook on Low for 9 to 10 hours or on High for 4½ to 5 hours. Makes 10⅔ cups (2.68 L).

1 cup (250 mL): 141 Calories; 4.2 g Total Fat; 439 mg Sodium; 10 g Protein; 17 g Carbohydrate

SIMPLE BEAN SOUP

A good soup born of convenience food you can have ready in record time.

Canned navy beans	2 × 14 oz.	2 × 398 mL
Canned flakes of ham, with liquid, broken up (or 1 cup, 250 mL, diced ham)	6.5 oz.	184 g
Chopped onion	1½ cups	375 mL
Beef bouillon powder	1 tbsp.	15 mL
Warm water	2½ cups	625 mL
Ketchup	1 tbsp.	15 mL

Combine all 6 ingredients in 3½ quart (3.5 L) slow cooker. Stir. Cover. Cook on Low for 8 to 10 hours or on High for 4 to 5 hours. Makes 7 cups (1.75 L).

1 cup (250 mL): 225 Calories; 5.7 g Total Fat; 1208 mg Sodium; 14 g Protein; 30 g Carbohydrate; good source of Dietary Fiber

EASY BEAN SOUP

Excellent and easy-to-make soup. Vegetables add color.

Canned brown beans with molasses	2 x 14 oz.	2 x 398 mL
Canned flakes of ham, with liquid, broken up (or 1 cup, 250 mL, diced ham)	6.5 oz.	184 g
Chopped onion	3/4 cup	175 mL
Chopped celery	1/2 cup	125 mL
Medium carrots, thinly sliced or diced	2	2
Medium tomatoes, diced	2	2
Garlic powder	1/4 tsp.	1 mL
Chicken bouillon powder	2 tbsp.	30 mL
Water	4 cups	1 L
Dried sweet basil	1/4 tsp.	1 mL
Granulated sugar	1 tsp.	5 mL

Combine all 11 ingredients in 3½ quart (3.5 L) slow cooker. Stir. Cover. Cook on Low for 8 to 10 hours or on High for 4 to 5 hours. Makes 9 cups (2.25 L).

1 cup (250 mL): 165 Calories; 4.8 g Total Fat; 1104 mg Sodium; 9 g Protein; 25 g Carbohydrate; excellent source of Dietary Fiber

Pictured on page 89.

CHICKEN STOCK

Easy to make soup from scratch, beginning with stock. No need to keep an eye on this.

Chicken drumsticks (or meaty backs and necks), see Note	1 lb.	454 g
Medium onion, chopped	1	1
Medium carrot, chopped	1	1
Chopped celery	1 cup	250 mL
Small bay leaf	1	1
Parsley flakes	1 tsp.	5 mL
Whole cloves	4	4
Salt	2 tsp.	10 mL
Pepper	1/2 tsp.	2 mL
Ground thyme	1/4 tsp.	1 mL
Liquid gravy browner (optional)	1/2 tsp.	2 mL
Water, to cover		

(continued on next page)

Place drumsticks in 3½ quart (3.5 L) slow cooker. Add next 10 ingredients.

Pour water over all. Cover. Cook on Low for 8 to 10 hours or on High for 4 to 5 hours. Skim if needed. Remove chicken and take off skin. Chop chicken and reserve for soup. Strain broth. Chill. Spoon off fat from top. Makes 4⅓ cups (1 L) stock.

1 cup (250 mL): 9 Calories; 0.2 g Total Fat; 1367 mg Sodium; trace Protein; 2 g Carbohydrate

Note: To strengthen flavor, chicken bouillon cubes or powder may be added. If using bones to make soup, browning bones before placing in slow cooker also adds to the flavor. You may choose to cook bones without the vegetables.

BEEF STOCK

The slow cooker is ideal for getting all the flavor from soup bones. Takes no minding.

Meaty beef soup bone, cut into pieces (see Note)	3 lbs.	1.4 kg
Medium carrots, chopped	2	2
Medium onion, chopped	1	1
Celery ribs, chopped	2	2
Parsley flakes (or ⅓ cup, 75 mL, fresh)	4 tsp.	20 mL
Whole peppercorns	6	6
Bay leaf	1	1
Salt	1 tsp.	5 mL
Ground thyme	⅛ tsp.	0.5 mL
Water, to cover (approximately)	7 cups	1.75 L

Roast bones in small uncovered roaster in 350°F (175°C) oven for about 1 hour until brown. Transfer to slow cooker.

Add remaining 9 ingredients. Stir. Cover. Cook on Low for 10 to 12 hours or on High for 5 to 6 hours. Remove bones. Cut off beef. Chop and reserve to use in soup. Discard bones. Strain stock into container. Chill. Spoon off fat from top. Discard vegetables. Use in any beef soup recipe. Makes 5¼ cups (1.3 L).

Note: For a more flavorful stock, have your butcher saw beef bone into pieces.

1 cup (250 mL): 7 Calories; trace Total Fat; 524 mg Sodium; trace Protein; 2 g Carbohydrate

BEEF AND SPLIT PEA SOUP

Makes a large batch. Make half the recipe for a small slow cooker.
Chunky, colorful and thick. Freezes well.

Lean ground beef	1 lb.	454 g
Chopped onion	1 cup	250 mL
Yellow split peas	1/2 cup	125 mL
Pearl barley	1/2 cup	125 mL
Uncooked long grain converted rice	1/2 cup	125 mL
Parsley flakes	1 tsp.	5 mL
Liquid gravy browner	1/2 tsp.	2 mL
Canned tomatoes, with juice, broken up	2 x 14 oz.	2 x 398 mL
Condensed tomato soup	10 oz.	284 mL
Beef bouillon powder	1 tbsp.	15 mL
Salt	2 tsp.	10 mL
Pepper	1/2 tsp.	2 mL
Water	12 cups	3 L
Ground thyme	1/4 tsp.	1 mL
Uncooked tiny shell pasta	2 cups	500 mL

Scramble-fry ground beef in non-stick frying pan until no longer pink.
Drain well.

Combine next 13 ingredients in 5 quart (5 L) slow cooker. Add ground
beef. Stir. Cover. Cook on Low for 9 to 11 hours or on High for 4 1/2 to
5 1/2 hours.

Add pasta. Stir. Cover. Cook on High for 15 to 20 minutes until pasta
is tender. Makes 17 1/3 cups (4.3 L).

1 cup (250 mL): 177 Calories; 3 g Total Fat; 631 mg Sodium; 10 g Protein; 28 g Carbohydrate

One worm to another: "I saw my first robin today—and just in time too!"

Meaty, colorful and a meal in itself. Sour cream makes it authentic.

Medium beets, peeled and cut into thin strips	2	2
Medium carrot, chopped	1	1
Medium onion, chopped	1	1
Coarsely shredded cabbage, packed	1 cup	250 mL
Medium potato, chopped	1	1
Chopped celery	1/2 cup	125 mL
Water, to cover (approximately), see Note	6 cups	1.5 L
Beef bouillon powder	2 tbsp.	30 mL
Boiling water	1/2 cup	125 mL
Lemon juice	2 tsp.	10 mL
Dill weed	1/2 tsp.	2 mL
Salt	2 tsp.	10 mL
Pepper	1/2 tsp.	2 mL
Lean ground beef	1 lb.	454 g
Frozen peas	1 cup	250 mL
Canned cut green beans, drained	14 oz.	398 mL
Light sour cream, dollop for each bowl (optional, but good)		

Place first 7 ingredients in 5 quart (5 L) slow cooker.

Stir bouillon powder into boiling water in bowl. Add lemon juice, dill weed, salt and pepper. Stir. Pour into slow cooker. Stir.

Scramble-fry ground beef in non-stick frying pan until no longer pink. Drain. Add to slow cooker.

Sprinkle peas and green beans over top. Cover. Cook on Low for 10 to 12 hours or on High for 5 to 6 hours.

Stir before serving. Add a dollop of sour cream to each bowl. Makes 13 cups (3.25 L).

Note: To shorten cooking time by at least 1 hour on Low, use boiling water.

1 cup (250 mL): 86 Calories; 3.2 g Total Fat; 763 mg Sodium; 8 g Protein; 7 g Carbohydrate

Pictured on page 71.

SIMMERING POTPOURRI

To add a subtle aroma in your home, start potpourri simmering one hour before your guests arrive and continue throughout the evening.

Dried lavender leaves	1 cup	250 mL
Dried rose petals	4 cups	1 L
Anise seed	1 tsp.	5 mL
Ground nutmeg	1 tbsp.	15 mL
Whole cloves	1 tbsp.	15 mL
Cinnamon stick (2 inches, 5 cm, in length), broken up and crushed in plastic bag	1	1
Crushed benzoin fixative	1 tbsp.	15 mL
Drops of jasmine oil	5	5
Drops of patchouli oil	5	5
Drops of rose geranium oil	5	5
Drops of rosemary oil	5	5

Mix all ingredients in a large bowl. Place in a large opaque container, or in a glass container in a dark cupboard. Let stand for 1 month to season before using. Makes about 5 cups (1.25 L). To use, fill slow cooker half full with water. Add 1 to 2 cups (250 to 500 mL) potpourri. Heat on Low with the lid off.

1. Split Pea Soup, page 134
2. Stuffed Peppers, page 147
3. Scalloped Ham Meal, page 102
4. Polynesian Steak Strips, page 47
5. Salmon Patties, page 85

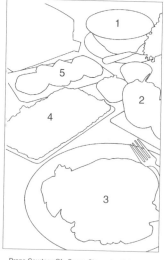

Props Courtesy Of: Scona Clayworks; Stokes; The Bay; Wicker World

Specialty

CHOCOLATE FONDUE

The ultimate! Smooth and delicious. A favorite to be sure. Use fondue forks to spear and dip maraschino cherries, whole strawberries, banana chunks, large marshmallows, or cake cubes.

Semisweet chocolate chips	2½ cups	625 mL
Skim evaporated milk	½ cup	125 mL
Jar of marshmallow cream	7 oz.	200 g

Put first 3 ingredients into 3½ quart (3.5 L) slow cooker. Cover. Cook on Low for 1 hour until quite warm. Stir well at half-time. Makes a generous 2⅓ cups (575 mL).

2 tbsp. (30 mL) fondue: 156 Calories; 8.3 g Total Fat; 20 mg Sodium; 2 g Protein; 22 g Carbohydrate

Pictured on page 125.

CHOCOLATE SUNDAE: Spoon hot Chocolate Fondue sauce over scoops of vanilla, strawberry or chocolate ice cream. Also excellent used as a topping for Marbled Cheesecake, page 80.

CHEESE FONDUE

Take your slow cooker and a loaf of French bread on a trip to the mountains and enjoy this in your hotel room or cabin. Cook on Low to avoid cheese going stringy. At home, dip broccoli florets or cauliflower florets (cooked tender crisp), or warmed wiener chunks into sauce.

Condensed Cheddar cheese soup	10 oz.	284 mL
Grated Monterey Jack cheese	1 cup	250 mL
Grated Parmesan cheese	2 tbsp.	30 mL
Chopped chives	2 tbsp.	30 mL
Garlic powder	⅛ tsp.	0.5 mL
Cayenne pepper	⅛ tsp.	0.5 mL
White wine (or alcohol-free wine or milk)	¼ cup	60 mL

Place all ingredients in 3½ quart (3.5 L) slow cooker. Stir well. Cover. Cook on Low for 2 to 2½ hours until quite warm. Makes 1¾ cups (425 mL).

2 tbsp. (30 mL) fondue: 63 Calories; 4.4 g Total Fat; 215 mg Sodium; 3 g Protein; 2 g Carbohydrate

RATATOUILLE

This ra-tuh-TOO-ee is made up of six different vegetables.

Canned tomatoes, with juice, broken up (or 4 fresh medium tomatoes, diced)	19 oz.	540 mL
Small eggplant, with peel, cut into ¹/₂ inch (12 mm) cubes	1	1
Finely chopped onion	1 cup	250 mL
Chopped celery	1 cup	250 mL
Medium green or red pepper, chopped	1	1
Ketchup (or chili sauce)	¹/₄ cup	60 mL
Granulated sugar	2 tsp.	10 mL
Sliced zucchini, with peel (¹/₄ inch, 6 mm, thick)	3 cups	750 mL
Parsley flakes	1 tsp.	5 mL
Salt	¹/₂ tsp.	2 mL
Pepper	¹/₈ tsp.	0.5 mL
Garlic powder	¹/₄ tsp.	1 mL
Dried whole oregano	¹/₂ tsp.	2 mL
Dried sweet basil	¹/₂ tsp.	2 mL

Measure all 14 ingredients into a 5 quart (5 L) slow cooker. Stir. Cover. Cook on Low for 8 to 9 hours or on High for 4 to 4¹/₂ hours. Makes 6¹/₂ cups (1.6 L).

1 cup (250 mL): 64 Calories; 0.5 g Total Fat; 500 mg Sodium; 2 g Protein; 15 g Carbohydrate

CREAMED CABBAGE

In a delicious cream sauce.

Medium cabbage, finely chopped	1	1
Finely chopped onion	¹/₂ cup	125 mL
Water	¹/₄ cup	60 mL
All-purpose flour	3 tbsp.	50 mL
Chicken bouillon powder	¹/₂ tsp.	2 mL
Salt	¹/₂ tsp.	2 mL
Pepper	¹/₈ tsp.	0.5 mL
Milk	2 cups	500 mL
TOPPING		
Hard margarine (or butter)	1 tbsp.	15 mL
Fine dry bread crumbs	¹/₄ cup	60 mL

(continued on next page)

Place cabbage, onion and water in 5 quart (5 L) slow cooker. Cove Cook on Low for 4 to 6 hours or on High for 2 to 3 hours. Drain.

Stir next 4 ingredients in saucepan. Whisk in milk gradually until no lumps remain. Heat and stir until boiling and thickened. Pour over cabbage. Stir.

Topping: Melt margarine in saucepan. Stir in bread crumbs. Heat and stir until browned. Sprinkle over cabbage mixture before serving. Makes 4 cups (1 L).

½ cup (125 mL): 104 Calories; 2.8 g Total Fat; 317 mg Sodium; 5 g Protein; 17 g Carbohydrate; good source of Dietary Fiber

STUFFED PEPPERS

Green peppers with red soup topping. Filling is mild and very delicious.

Boiling water	¼ cup	60 mL
Instant white rice	¼ cup	60 mL
Finely chopped onion	¼ cup	60 mL
Grated carrot	¼ cup	60 mL
Kernel corn, frozen or canned	¼ cup	60 mL
Worcestershire sauce	½ tsp.	2 mL
Prepared horseradish	½ tsp.	2 mL
Salt	½ tsp.	2 mL
Pepper	⅛ tsp.	0.5 mL
Lean ground beef	½ lb.	225 g
Medium green peppers, tops cut off, ribs and seeds removed	4	4
Condensed tomato soup	10 oz.	284 mL

Pour boiling water over rice in bowl. Cover. Let stand for 5 minutes.

Add next 8 ingredients. Mix well.

Stuff peppers with rice mixture. Place in 5 quart (5 L) slow cooker.

Spoon soup over top and around peppers. Cover. Cook on Low for 7 to 9 hours or on High for 3½ to 4½ hours. Serves 4.

1 serving: 234 Calories; 9.9 g Total Fat; 915 mg Sodium; 14 g Protein; 24 g Carbohydrate

Pictured on page 143.

ASPARAGUS BAKE

Retains shape and color.

Fresh asparagus	1 lb.	454 g
All-purpose flour	1 1/2 tbsp.	25 mL
Salt	1/4 tsp.	1 mL
Pepper	1/16 tsp.	0.5 mL
Skim evaporated milk	3/4 cup	175 mL
Grated sharp Cheddar cheese	1/4 cup	60 mL

Cut off any tough ends of asparagus. Lay spears in 5 quart (5 L) slow cooker.

Stir flour, salt and pepper together in saucepan. Whisk in evaporated milk gradually until no lumps remain. Heat and stir until boiling and thickened.

Stir in cheese to melt. Pour over asparagus. Cover. Cook on Low for 3 to 4 hours. If you like your asparagus crunchy, check for doneness at 2 to 2 1/2 hours. Remove asparagus with slotted spoon. Serves 6.

1 serving: 71 Calories; 1.9 g Total Fat; 185 mg Sodium; 6 g Protein; 8 g Carbohydrate

Pictured on page 71.

RED CABBAGE

It does lose its brightness but keeps the good taste.

Small red cabbage, quartered, cored and thinly sliced (about 2 lbs., 900 g)	1	1
Chopped onion	1 1/2 cups	375 mL
Medium cooking apples (such as McIntosh), peeled, cored and chopped	3	3
Brown sugar, packed	1/4 cup	60 mL
Water	1/2 cup	125 mL
White vinegar	1/4 cup	60 mL
Hard margarine (or butter), melted	1 tbsp.	15 mL
Salt	1 tsp.	5 mL
Pepper	1/4 tsp.	1 mL

Place all 9 ingredients in 5 quart (5 L) slow cooker. Stir to coat all with liquid. Cover. Cook on Low for 5 to 6 hours or on High for 2 1/2 to 3 hours. Makes 7 cups (1.75 L).

1/2 cup (125 mL): 64 Calories; 1.1 g Total Fat; 213 mg Sodium; 1 g Protein; 14 g Carbohydrate

ACORN SQUASH

Glazing just before serving gives this a hint of sweetness.

Small whole acorn squash	3	3
Water	1/4 cup	60 mL
TOPPING		
Liquid honey	3 tbsp.	50 mL
Hard margarine (or butter), softened	2 tbsp.	30 mL
Salt	1/2 tsp.	2 mL
Pepper	1/8 tsp.	0.5 mL

Place squash in 5 quart (5 L) slow cooker. Pour water over top. Cover. Cook on Low for 8 hours.

Topping: Mix all 4 ingredients well. Cut each squash in half lengthwise. Scoop out seeds. Brush cavities and edges with honey mixture. Serves 6.

1 serving: 132 Calories; 4.3 g Total Fat; 279 mg Sodium; 3 g Protein; 24 g Carbohydrate; good source of Dietary Fiber

Pictured on page 107.

GLAZED CARROTS

These are best cooked on High to keep the great taste of carrot. Nicely glazed.

Peeled baby carrots	2 lbs.	900 g
Water	1/4 cup	60 mL
Cornstarch	1 tbsp.	15 mL
Brown sugar, packed	1/2 cup	125 mL
Hard margarine (or butter), melted	1 tbsp.	15 mL

Place carrot in 3 1/2 quart (3.5 L) slow cooker.

Stir water, cornstarch, brown sugar and margarine together in small bowl. Pour over carrot. Cover. Cook on High for 3 to 4 hours. Stir before serving. Makes 5 cups (1.25 L).

1/2 cup (125 mL): 95 Calories; 1.2 g Total Fat; 48 mg Sodium; 1 g Protein; 21 g Carbohydrate

CARROT ONION CASSEROLE

The slow cooking really brings out the carrot and onion flavors.

Diagonally sliced carrot	6 cups	1.5 L
Sliced onion	1½ cups	375 mL
Salt	½ tsp.	2 mL
Water	½ cup	125 mL
SAUCE		
All-purpose flour	1 tbsp.	15 mL
Salt, sprinkle		
Pepper, sprinkle		
Milk	½ cup	125 mL
Grated medium or sharp Cheddar cheese	½ cup	125 mL
TOPPING		
Hard margarine (or butter)	1 tbsp.	15 mL
Fine dry bread crumbs	¼ cup	60 mL

Place carrot, onion, salt and water in 3½ quart (3.5 L) slow cooker. Stir. Cover. Cook on High for 4 to 5 hours. Drain. Place in serving bowl.

Sauce: Stir flour, salt and pepper together in small saucepan. Whisk in milk gradually until no lumps remain. Heat and stir until boiling and thickened.

Add cheese. Stir to melt. Pour over vegetables. Stir.

Topping: Melt margarine in saucepan. Stir in bread crumbs. Heat and stir until browned. Sprinkle over vegetables before serving. Makes 6 cups (1.5 L).

*½ **cup (125 mL):** 92 Calories; 3.1 g Total Fat; 177 mg Sodium; 3 g Protein; 14 g Carbohydrate*

Pictured on page 17.

Patience is yours if you can count down before you blast off.

Throughout this book measurements are given in Conventional and Metric measure. To compensate for differences between the two measurements due to rounding, a full metric measure is not always used. The cup used is the standard 8 fluid ounce. Temperature is given in degrees Fahrenheit and Celsius. Baking pan measurements are in inches and centimetres as well as quarts and litres. An exact metric conversion is given below as well as the working equivalent (Standard Measure).

OVEN TEMPERATURES

Fahrenheit (°F)	Celsius (°C)
175°	80°
200°	95°
225°	110°
250°	120°
275°	140°
300°	150°
325°	160°
350°	175°
375°	190°
400°	205°
425°	220°
450°	230°
475°	240°
500°	260°

SPOONS

Conventional Measure	Metric Exact Conversion Millilitre (mL)	Metric Standard Measure Millilitre (mL)
1/8 teaspoon (tsp.)	0.6 mL	0.5 mL
1/4 teaspoon (tsp.)	1.2 mL	1 mL
1/2 teaspoon (tsp.)	2.4 mL	2 mL
1 teaspoon (tsp.)	4.7 mL	5 mL
2 teaspoons (tsp.)	9.4 mL	10 mL
1 tablespoon (tbsp.)	14.2 mL	15 mL

CUPS

	Metric Exact Conversion Millilitre (mL)	Metric Standard Measure Millilitre (mL)
1/4 cup (4 tbsp.)	56.8 mL	60 mL
1/3 cup (5 1/3 tbsp.)	75.6 mL	75 mL
1/2 cup (8 tbsp.)	113.7 mL	125 mL
2/3 cup (10 2/3 tbsp.)	151.2 mL	150 mL
3/4 cup (12 tbsp.)	170.5 mL	175 mL
1 cup (16 tbsp.)	227.3 mL	250 mL
4 1/2 cups	1022.9 mL	1000 mL (1 L)

PANS

Conventional Inches	Metric Centimetres
8x8 inch	20x20 cm
9x9 inch	22x22 cm
9x13 inch	22x33 cm
10x15 inch	25x38 cm
11x17 inch	28x43 cm
8x2 inch round	20x5 cm
9x2 inch round	22x5 cm
10x4 1/2 inch tube	25x11 cm
8x4x3 inch loaf	20x10x7.5 cm
9x5x3 inch loaf	22x12.5x7.5 cm

DRY MEASUREMENTS

Conventional Measure Ounces (oz.)	Metric Exact Conversion Grams (g)	Metric Standard Measure Grams (g)
1 oz.	28.3 g	28 g
2 oz.	56.7 g	57 g
3 oz.	85.0 g	85 g
4 oz.	113.4 g	125 g
5 oz.	141.7 g	140 g
6 oz.	170.1 g	170 g
7 oz.	198.4 g	200 g
8 oz.	226.8 g	250 g
16 oz.	453.6 g	500 g
32 oz.	907.2 g	1000 g (1 kg)

CASSEROLES (Canada & Britain)

Standard Size Casserole	Exact Metric Measure
1 qt. (5 cups)	1.13 L
1 1/2 qts. (7 1/2 cups)	1.69 L
2 qts. (10 cups)	2.25 L
2 1/2 qts. (12 1/2 cups)	2.81 L
3 qts. (15 cups)	3.38 L
4 qts. (20 cups)	4.5 L
5 qts. (25 cups)	5.63 L

CASSEROLES (United States)

Standard Size Casserole	Exact Metric Measure
1 qt. (4 cups)	900 mL
1 1/2 qts. (6 cups)	1.35 L
2 qts. (8 cups)	1.8 L
2 1/2 qts. (10 cups)	2.25 L
3 qts. (12 cups)	2.7 L
4 qts. (16 cups)	3.6 L
5 qts. (20 cups)	4.5 L

INDEX

RECIPE NOTES

RECIPE NOTES

Company's Coming®

ONE-DISH MEALS

Jean Paré

ONE-DISH MEALS

by
Jean Paré

companyscoming.com
visit our web-site

Dedication

One-dish meals . . .
All for one, and one for all!

Cover Photo

1. Chicken Vinaigrette, page 105

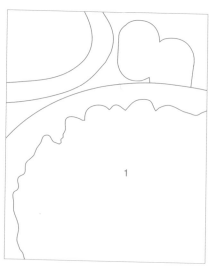

Props Courtesy Of: C C on Whyte, Dansk Gifts,
Handworks Gallery,
La Cache, The Bay

Want to learn our secrets?

Check out our website
for **_hints, tips_** and
timesaving shortcuts
that have made our
recipes so popular.

Visit us at **_companyscoming.com_**

table of Contents

Foreword

One-Dish Meals features a variety of recipes that can be prepared in a casserole dish, roaster, Dutch oven, slow cooker, large saucepan, electric or other frying pan, or even a large salad bowl. Oven cooking as well as stove top cooking offers you more choice in how you would like to prepare your dish. Some recipes are prepared completely in one container, while others require more than one to prepare but are served in one dish.

Cooking in one dish saves time, uses less fuel, and cleanup is a breeze. Even with recipes that are prepared in several steps, cleanup can be done as you go. Here is the perfect opportunity to double your favorite recipe and put half into the freezer.

To complete these meals, try adding a salad, dinner rolls and dessert. If a recipe is very hearty, you may choose to skip either the salad or the rolls. On the other hand, if extra people turn up at mealtime you can stretch any recipe by serving not only a salad but also an extra vegetable to complement your main dish. The

addition of garlic toast or baking powder biscuits goes particularly well with a lighter one-dish meal.

Want to keep it simple? One-Dish Meals is a helpful collection of easy-to-serve mealtime ideas—perfect for when company's coming!

Jean Paré

E ach recipe has been analyzed using the most up-to-date version of the Canadian Nutrient File from Health Canada, which is based on the United States Department of Agriculture (USDA) Nutrient Data Base. If more that one ingredient is listed (such as "hard margarine or butter"), then the first ingredient is used in the analysis. Where an ingredient reads "sprinkle," "optional," or "for garnish," it is not included as part of the nutrition information.

Margaret Ng, B.Sc. (Hon), M.A.
Registered Dietitian

SAUCY SKILLET DINNER

This is a very easy all-in-one dish. Rich tasting and thick.

Lean ground beef	1 lb.	454 g
Chopped onion	1 cup	250 mL
Garlic clove, minced (or ¼ tsp., 1 mL, powder)	1	1
Medium zucchini, with peel, halved lengthwise and sliced	1	1
Chopped fresh mushrooms	1 cup	250 mL
Water	1 cup	250 mL
Spaghetti sauce	2 cups	500 mL
Dried sweet basil	½ tsp.	2 mL
Granulated sugar	½ tsp.	2 mL
Dried whole oregano, just a pinch		
Uncooked spaghetti, broken into 1-2 inch (2.5-5 cm) lengths	6 oz.	170 g
Grated part-skim mozzarella cheese	½ cup	125 mL

Scramble-fry ground beef, onion and garlic in large non-stick frying pan for 3 to 4 minutes.

Add zucchini and mushrooms. Cook for 6 to 7 minutes, stirring occasionally, until beef is no longer pink. Drain.

Add water, spaghetti sauce, basil, sugar and oregano. Heat until boiling. Add pasta. Reduce heat. Cover. Simmer for 20 minutes until pasta is tender but firm and liquid is mostly absorbed.

Add mozzarella cheese. Stir until melted. Serves 4.

1 serving: 451 Calories; 13.7 g Total Fat; 825 mg Sodium; 32 g Protein; 50 g Carbohydrate; 5 g Dietary Fiber

There is no question as to what dinosaurs eat. They eat anything they want.

This has the popular taco seasoning with a touch of chili powder which may easily be increased. Very tasty.

Lean ground beef	1 lb.	454 g
Finely chopped onion	1 cup	250 mL
Chopped green pepper	1 cup	250 mL
Garlic salt	1 tsp.	5 mL
Pepper	1/8 tsp.	0.5 mL
Canned stewed tomatoes, with juice, broken up	2 x 14 oz.	2 x 398 mL
Canned kernel corn, with liquid	12 oz.	341 mL
Envelope taco seasoning mix	1 x 1 1/4 oz.	1 x 35 g
Granulated sugar	1 tsp.	5 mL
Chili powder (or more to taste)	1/2 tsp.	2 mL
Water	1/2 cup	125 mL
Uncooked long grain white rice	2/3 cup	150 mL
Grated medium Cheddar cheese	1/2 cup	125 mL
Light sour cream	3/4 cup	175 mL
Sliced pitted ripe olives	1/4 cup	60 mL
Corn chips, for garnish (optional)	1 cup	250 mL

Scramble-fry first 5 ingredients in large non-stick frying pan until onion is soft and beef is no longer pink. Drain.

Stir in next 7 ingredients. Cover. Simmer for about 20 minutes, stirring occasionally, until rice is tender and liquid is absorbed. Turn into serving dish.

Sprinkle with cheese. Dab sour cream over top. Sprinkle with olives. Add corn chips here and there. Serves 4.

1 serving: 566 Calories; 19.6 g Total Fat; 2289 mg Sodium; 33 g Protein; 69 g Carbohydrate; 6 g Dietary Fiber

Pictured on page 17.

There weren't nearly so many accidents when horsepower was with the horses.

...AT AND POTATOES

...ow cooker is required for this ground beef stew.

Medium potatoes, thinly sliced	4	4
Sliced carrot	2 cups	500 mL
Chopped onion	2 cups	500 mL
Frozen peas (about 10 oz., 285 g)	2 cups	500 mL
Salt, sprinkle		
Pepper, sprinkle		
Condensed cream of chicken soup	10 oz.	284 mL
Water	1 cup	250 mL
Liquid gravy browner	$1/4$-$1/2$ tsp.	1-2 mL
Lean ground beef	$1^1/_2$ lbs.	680 g

Layer first 4 ingredients in order given in 5 quart (5 L) slow cooker, sprinkling each layer with salt and pepper.

Mix soup, water and gravy browner in medium bowl.

Add ground beef. Mix well. Place over vegetables. Cover. Cook on Low for 10 to 12 hours or on High for 5 to 6 hours. Makes 13 cups (3.25 L).

$1^1/_2$ cups (375 mL): 296 Calories; 14.2 g Total Fat; 383 mg Sodium; 19 g Protein; 23 g Carbohydrate; 4 g Dietary Fiber

COMFORT CHILI

This is more beany than meaty. Even better flavor when reheated the next day. Very nutritious.

Lean ground beef	1 lb.	454 g
Chopped onion	1 cup	250 mL
Chopped celery	1 cup	250 mL
Small green pepper, chopped	1	1
Canned diced tomatoes, drained	14 oz.	398 mL
Canned kidney beans, drained	3 × 14 oz.	3 × 398 mL
Condensed cream of mushroom soup	10 oz.	284 mL
Chili powder	1 tbsp.	15 mL
Garlic salt	1 tsp.	5 mL
Pepper	$1/2$ tsp.	2 mL

(continued on next page)

Scramble-fry ground beef, onion, celery and green pepper in large pot or Dutch oven until beef is no longer pink. Drain.

Add remaining 6 ingredients. Bring to a boil. Reduce heat. Simmer, uncovered, for 1 hour, stirring often to prevent burning. Makes 8 cups (2 L).

1¹/₂ cups (375 mL): 388 Calories; 12.5 g Total Fat; 1205 mg Sodium; 29 g Protein; 42 g Carbohydrate; 12 g Dietary Fiber

EASY TACO SUPPER

Fast, easy and so good.

Lean ground beef	1 lb.	454 g
Chopped onion	¹/₂ cup	125 mL
Chopped green pepper	¹/₂ cup	125 mL
Hot water	2¹/₂ cups	625 mL
Envelope taco seasoning mix	1 × 1¹/₄ oz.	1 × 35 g
Package macaroni and cheese dinner, cheese-flavored packet reserved	6¹/₂ oz.	200 g
Reserved cheese-flavored packet Diced tomato	1 cup	250 mL
Non-fat sour cream (optional)	¹/₂ cup	125 mL
Thinly sliced green onion (optional)	¹/₄ cup	60 mL
Shredded lettuce (optional)	2 cups	500 mL

Scramble-fry ground beef, onion and green pepper in large non-stick frying pan for about 5 minutes until onion is soft and beef is no longer pink. Drain.

Stir in hot water and taco seasoning mix. Bring to a boil. Stir in macaroni from package. Cover. Simmer, stirring occasionally, for 7 to 8 minutes until macaroni is tender.

Add reserved cheese-flavored packet and tomato. Stir together well.

Serve immediately with sour cream, green onion and lettuce. Serves 6.

1 serving: 275 Calories; 8.1 g Total Fat; 691 mg Sodium; 20 g Protein; 31 g Carbohydrate; 1 g Dietary Fiber

͵sting mix. Rich looking and full of beans. Goes well with the
ni. Very flavorful.

Leͣ, ground beef	1 lb.	454 g
Chopped onion	1 cup	250 mL
Chopped green pepper	1/4 cup	60 mL
Elbow macaroni	1 1/2 cups	375 mL
Boiling water	2 1/2 qts.	2.5 L
Cooking oil (optional)	2 tsp.	10 mL
Salt	1 tsp.	5 mL
Tomato sauce	2 x 7 1/2 oz.	2 x 213 mL
Chili powder (or more to taste)	1 1/2 tsp.	7 mL
Salt	1 tsp.	5 mL
Canned kidney beans, drained	14 oz.	398 mL
Frozen kernel corn	1 cup	250 mL
Grated medium Cheddar cheese	1 cup	250 mL

Combine ground beef, onion and green pepper in large non-stick frying pan. Sauté until onion is soft and beef is no longer pink. Drain.

Cook pasta in boiling water, cooking oil and salt in large uncovered pot or Dutch oven for 5 to 7 minutes, stirring occasionally, until tender but firm. Drain. Return pasta to pot.

Add tomato sauce, chili powder and salt to beef mixture. Cook, uncovered, for 10 to 12 minutes until thickened.

Add kidney beans. Stir together. Turn into ungreased 2 quart (2 L) casserole.

Sprinkle with corn. Spread macaroni over corn.

Sprinkle cheese over macaroni. Cover. Bake in 350°F (175°C) oven for 25 minutes. Remove cover. Bake for 5 minutes until cheese is melted. Serves 6.

1 serving: 407 Calories; 14 g Total Fat; 1149 mg Sodium; 28 g Protein; 44 g Carbohydrate; 6 g Dietary Fiber

Pictured on page 53.

A homemade TV dinner.

BEEF PATTIES

Non-fat sour cream	²/₃ cup	150 mL
Finely chopped onion	¹/₃ cup	75 mL
Coarsely crushed corn flakes cereal	²/₃ cup	150 mL
Pepper	¹/₄ tsp.	1 mL
Beef bouillon powder	1 tsp.	5 mL
Lean ground beef	1 lb.	454 g
Cooking oil	1 tsp.	5 mL
Frozen green beans	2¹/₄ cups	560 mL
Elbow macaroni	1¹/₂ cups	375 mL
Boiling water	2 qts.	2 L
Salt	1 tsp.	5 mL
Condensed tomato soup	10 oz.	284 mL
Beef bouillon powder	1 tbsp.	15 mL
Water	¹/₂ cup	125 mL
Pepper	¹/₄ tsp.	1 mL
Onion powder	¹/₄ tsp.	1 mL

Beef Patties: Mix first 5 ingredients in medium bowl. Add ground beef. Mix. Let stand for 15 minutes. Shape into 8 patties. Remove patties and blot on paper towel.

Heat cooking oil in large frying pan. Add patties. Cook both sides until browned and no longer pink inside.

Cook green beans and pasta in boiling water and salt in large uncovered saucepan for 5 to 7 minutes, stirring occasionally, until pasta is tender but firm. Drain. Turn into ungreased 9 x 13 inch (22 x 33 cm) pan or casserole large enough to hold beef patties in single layer. Arrange patties over top.

Mix remaining 5 ingredients in small bowl. Pour over top. Cover. Bake in 350°F (175°C) oven for 20 to 30 minutes until bubbly hot. Serves 4.

1 serving: 500 Calories; 12.9 g Total Fat; 1347 mg Sodium; 31 g Protein; 65 g Carbohydrate; 3 g Dietary Fiber

Pictured on page 53.

ORIENTAL BEEF DINNER

This lends itself to variations. Sliced water chestnuts or bamboo shoots can be added.

Lean ground beef	½ lb.	225 g
Chopped onion	½ cup	125 mL
Sliced celery	½ cup	125 mL
Uncooked long grain white rice	½ cup	125 mL
Canned sliced mushrooms, with liquid	10 oz.	284 mL
Soy sauce	2 tbsp.	30 mL
Beef bouillon powder	1 tsp.	5 mL
Garlic powder	⅛ tsp.	0.5 mL
Pepper, sprinkle		
Hot water	1 cup	250 mL
Frozen pea pods	6 oz.	170 g
Fresh bean sprouts (about 2 large handfuls), coarsely chopped	2 cups	500 mL
Cornstarch	1 tsp.	5 mL
Water	1 tbsp.	15 mL
Chili sauce	1 tbsp.	15 mL

Scramble-fry ground beef and onion in large non-stick frying pan until onion is soft and beef is no longer pink. Drain.

Add next 8 ingredients. Stir together. Cover. Simmer for 15 minutes.

Add pea pods and bean sprouts. Stir together.

Mix cornstarch and water in small cup. Add chili sauce. Stir into beef mixture until boiling. Makes 6 cups (1.5 L).

1½ cups (375 mL): 244 Calories; 5.3 g Total Fat; 920 mg Sodium; 17 g Protein; 33 g Carbohydrate; 4 g Dietary Fiber

Pare Pointer

Golfers never starve; they live on the greens.

An all-in-one meal. Spices add pizzazz to the taste.

Lean ground beef	1 lb.	454 g
Chopped onion	½ cup	125 mL
Chopped celery	½ cup	125 mL
Seasoning salt	1¼ tsp.	6 mL
Pepper, sprinkle		
All-purpose flour	1 tbsp.	15 mL
Uncooked elbow macaroni	1¾ cups	425 mL
Thinly sliced zucchini, with peel	2 cups	500 mL
Canned stewed tomatoes, with juice, blended	28 oz.	796 mL
Dried whole oregano	1 tsp.	5 mL
Granulated sugar	½ tsp.	2 mL
Hot pepper sauce	½ tsp.	2 mL
Salt	¼ tsp.	1 mL
Pepper, sprinkle		
Bread slices, processed into crumbs (about 1½ cups, 375 mL)	2	2
Grated light medium Cheddar cheese	½ cup	125 mL

Scramble-fry ground beef, onion and celery in medium non-stick frying pan until onion is soft and beef is no longer pink. Drain.

Sprinkle with seasoning salt, pepper and flour. Mix well. Place beef mixture in bottom of lightly greased 3 quart (3 L) casserole.

Cover with pasta. Layer zucchini over pasta.

Combine tomatoes with juice, oregano, sugar, hot pepper sauce, salt and pepper in small bowl. Pour over zucchini.

Combine bread crumbs and cheese in small bowl. Sprinkle over surface of casserole. Bake, uncovered, in 350°F (175°C) oven for 50 to 55 minutes until pasta is tender and casserole is bubbling and browned. Cover with piece of foil if bread crumbs become too brown before pasta is cooked. Let stand for 10 minutes to absorb any excess liquid. Serves 6.

1 serving: 348 Calories; 9.4 g Total Fat; 914 mg Sodium; 23 g Protein; 43 g Carbohydrate; 4 g Dietary Fiber

CABBAGE ROLL CASSEROLE

flavor without all the work.

Bacon slices, diced	4	4
Lean ground beef	1½ lbs.	680 g
Chopped onion	1 cup	250 mL
Condensed tomato soup	10 oz.	284 mL
Canned tomato juice	10 oz.	284 mL
Salt	½ tsp.	2 mL
Pepper	¼ tsp.	1 mL
Coarsely shredded cabbage	8 cups	2 L
Uncooked long grain white rice	⅓ cup	75 mL

Cook bacon in large frying pan until browned. Drain. Remove to plate.

Scramble-fry ground beef and onion in same frying pan until onion is soft and beef is no longer pink. Drain.

Add soup, tomato juice, salt and pepper. Stir.

Layer cabbage in ungreased 9 x 13 inch (22 x 33 cm) pan. Pack down. Sprinkle with rice. Scatter bacon over rice. Spoon beef mixture over top. Cover. Bake in 350°F (175°C) oven for about 1½ hours. Serves 6.

1 serving: 312 Calories; 12.6 g Total Fat; 876 mg Sodium; 25 g Protein; 25 g Carbohydrate; 3 g Dietary Fiber

1. Tamale Rice Dish, page 9
2. Tuna Frills, page 46
3. Spicy Sausage And Pasta, page 79
4. Stove Top Pot Pie, page 26

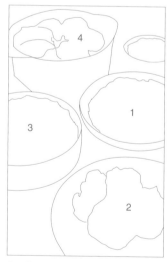

Props Courtesy Of: Dansk Gifts, Eaton's,
Handworks Gallery,
The Bay, X/S Wares

CAPPELLETTI CASSEROLE

Additional helpers added to the ground beef. Good dish. This pasta looks like little hats.

Lean ground beef	1½ lbs.	680 g
Chopped onion	1½ cups	375 mL
Chopped celery	½ cup	125 mL
Cooking oil	1 tsp.	5 mL
Uncooked cappelletti pasta (8 oz., 225 g)	2⅔ cups	650 mL
Frozen peas (about 10 oz., 285 g)	2 cups	500 mL
Beef bouillon powder	2 tsp.	10 mL
Worcestershire sauce	1 tsp.	5 mL
Condensed cream of mushroom soup	10 oz.	284 mL
Condensed tomato soup	10 oz.	284 mL
Water	½ cup	125 mL
Grated medium Cheddar cheese	1 cup	250 mL

Scramble-fry ground beef, onion and celery in cooking oil in large non-stick frying pan until onion is soft and beef is no longer pink. Drain. Turn into ungreased 3 quart (3 L) casserole.

Add next 4 ingredients. Stir together.

Mix both soups and water in small bowl. Add to pasta mixture. Mix well, making sure pasta is covered.

Sprinkle with cheese. Cover. Bake in 350°F (175°C) oven for about 1½ hours. Makes 8 cups (2 L).

1½ cups (375 mL): 579 Calories; 26.6 g Total Fat; 1521 mg Sodium; 40 g Protein; 45 g Carbohydrate; 4 g Dietary Fiber

Sign on an optician's window: If you don't see what you want, you need my help.

MEATLOAF CASSEROLE

Mellow and flavorful as well as a very different presentation.

Large egg, fork-beaten	1	1
Milk	½ cup	125 mL
Rolled oats (not instant)	½ cup	125 mL
Finely chopped onion	1 cup	250 mL
Grated Parmesan cheese	2 tbsp.	30 mL
Beef bouillon powder	2 tsp.	10 mL
Worcestershire sauce	1 tsp.	5 mL
Salt	½ tsp.	2 mL
Pepper	¼ tsp.	1 mL
Lean ground beef	1½ lbs.	680 g
Ketchup	2 tbsp.	30 mL
Medium carrots, cut bite size	6	6
Medium potatoes	6	6
Water, to cover		
Hot milk	½ cup	125 mL
Salt, sprinkle		
Pepper, sprinkle		
Frozen peas	2 cups	500 mL
Water, to cover		
Grated medium Cheddar cheese	½ cup	125 mL

Combine first 9 ingredients in medium bowl. Stir together.

Mix in ground beef. Shape into loaf. Place in center of ungreased 9 x 13 inch (22 x 33 cm) pan.

Spread ketchup over top of loaf.

Arrange carrot around loaf. Bake, uncovered, in 350°F (175°C) oven for 1½ hours. Drain off any liquid.

Cook potatoes in water until tender. Drain.

Mash potatoes, adding hot milk, salt and pepper.

Cook peas in water for about 3 minutes. Drain. Spoon over carrot. Spoon mashed potato over vegetables around meatloaf.

(continued on next page)

Sprinkle potato with cheese. Return to oven for about 10 minut
cheese is melted. Serves 6.

1 serving: 464 Calories; 15.5 g Total Fat; 779 mg Sodium; 34 g Protein; 48 g Carboh
7 g Dietary Fiber

MEXICAN CORN CHIP CASSEROLE

Use less jalapeño pepper or omit altogether if you need to keep the
"heat" down.

Lean ground beef	1 lb.	454 g
Garlic clove, minced	1	1
Chopped onion	1/2 cup	125 mL
Chopped green pepper	1/2 cup	125 mL
Chopped fresh parsley	1/2 cup	125 mL
Medium tomatoes, diced	3	3
Tomato sauce	7 1/2 oz.	213 mL
Fresh (or canned) jalapeño pepper, finely diced (wear rubber gloves)	1	1
Ground cumin	1 tsp.	5 mL
Chili powder	1/4 tsp.	1 mL
Canned pinto beans, drained	14 oz.	398 mL
Broken corn chips	2 cups	500 mL
Grated Monterey Jack cheese	1/2 cup	125 mL
Grated medium Cheddar cheese	1/2 cup	125 mL

Scramble-fry ground beef, garlic, onion, green pepper and parsley in large non-stick frying pan for about 5 minutes until beef is no longer pink. Drain.

Add tomato, tomato sauce and jalapeño pepper. Sauté until jalapeño pepper is soft and mixture is simmering.

Add cumin and chili powder. Stir together well. Simmer for 10 minutes. Remove from heat.

Add pinto beans. Stir. Pour into lightly greased 2 quart (2 L) casserole.

Sprinkle corn chips and both cheeses over top. Bake, uncovered, in 350°F (175°C) oven for 30 minutes. Serves 6.

1 serving: 387 Calories; 19.5 g Total Fat; 618 mg Sodium; 24 g Protein; 30 g Carbohydrate;
4 g Dietary Fiber

AUTUMN BAKE

Very attractive and appetizing.

Medium potatoes, quartered lengthwise	4-5	4-5
Water, to cover		
Salt	¾ tsp.	4 mL
Pepper	¼ tsp.	1 mL
All-purpose flour	¼ cup	60 mL
Beef sirloin steak, cut into paper-thin strips	1¼ lbs.	568 g
Cooking oil	2 tsp.	10 mL
Salt, sprinkle		
Pepper, sprinkle		
Small zucchini, with peel, sliced to cover	1	1
Large tomatoes, sliced to cover	2	2
Dried whole oregano	½ tsp.	2 mL
Dried sweet basil	½ tsp.	2 mL
Onion powder	½ tsp.	2 mL
Hard margarine (or butter)	4 tsp.	20 mL
Dry bread crumbs	½ cup	125 mL
Grated part-skim mozzarella cheese	1 cup	250 mL

Cook potato in water in medium saucepan for 5 minutes. Drain. When cool enough to handle, slice.

Mix salt and pepper and flour in medium bowl. Add sliced potato. Toss together to coat. Place potato in greased 3 quart (3 L) casserole.

Brown steak strips in cooking oil in medium frying pan. Sprinkle with salt and pepper. Layer over potato.

Add layers of zucchini and tomato.

Mix oregano, basil and onion powder in small cup. Sprinkle over top.

Melt margarine in small saucepan. Stir in bread crumbs and cheese. Sprinkle over all. Cover. Bake in 350°F (175°C) oven for about 1 hour. Serves 4.

1 serving: 511 Calories; 17.7 g Total Fat; 907 mg Sodium; 44 g Protein; 44 g Carbohydrate; 4 g Dietary Fiber

Take this to the next potluck. Good for a barbecue too.

Lean ground beef	1 lb.	454 g
Chopped onion	1½ cups	375 mL
Cooking oil	2 tsp.	10 mL
Canned kidney beans, drained	14 oz.	398 mL
Canned beans in tomato sauce	2 × 14 oz.	2 × 398 mL
Canned chick peas (garbanzo beans), drained	19 oz.	540 mL
Hickory smoked barbecue sauce	½ cup	125 mL
Brown sugar, packed	¼ cup	60 mL
White vinegar	1 tbsp.	15 mL
Prepared mustard	2 tsp.	10 mL
Salt	½ tsp.	2 mL
Pepper	⅛ tsp.	0.5 mL

Scramble-fry ground beef and onion in cooking oil in large frying pan until onion is soft and beef is no longer pink. Drain. Turn into ungreased 3 quart (3 L) casserole.

Add next 3 ingredients.

Stir remaining 6 ingredients together in small bowl. Add to casserole. Stir together lightly. Cover. Bake in 350°F (175°C) oven for about 1 hour until bubbling and browning around edge, stirring at half-time. Makes about 10 cups (2.5 L).

1½ cups (375 mL): 399 Calories; 9.2 g Total Fat; 1092 mg Sodium; 25 g Protein; 58 g Carbohydrate; 16 g Dietary Fiber

Sign over teller's window: Deposits welcomed, withdrawals tolerated.

DILLY BEEF DINNER

A slow cooker is required for this recipe. Long slow cooking tenderizes steak. A touch of dill adds to the flavor of this full meal.

Diced potato (about ½ inch, 12 mm)	4 cups	1 L
Thinly sliced carrot	3 cups	750 mL
Thinly sliced celery	¾ cup	175 mL
Sliced or chopped onion	1½ cups	375 mL
Beef flank steak (or brisket), cut into 6 serving pieces	2 lbs.	900 g
Canned tomatoes, with juice, broken up	14 oz.	398 mL
Dill weed	1½ tsp.	7 mL
Salt	1 tsp.	5 mL
Pepper	¼ tsp.	1 mL

Place potato, carrot, celery and onion in 5 quart (5 L) slow cooker.

Lay steak pieces over top.

Stir remaining 4 ingredients together in small bowl. Pour over beef. Cover. Cook on Low for 12 to 14 hours or on High for 6 to 7 hours. Serves 6.

1 serving: 324 Calories; 13.7 g Total Fat; 695 mg Sodium; 36 g Protein; 32 g Carbohydrate; 5 g Dietary Fiber

BEEFY RICE CASSEROLE

A slow cooker is required for this recipe. A mild chili flavor. Good mixture.

Cooking oil	1 tsp.	5 mL
Lean ground beef	1½ lbs.	680 g
Canned tomatoes, with juice	28 oz.	796 mL
Chopped onion	1½ cups	375 mL
Chopped green pepper	¼ cup	60 mL
Uncooked converted long grain rice	1 cup	250 mL
Salt	1½ tsp.	7 mL
Chili powder	1 tsp.	5 mL
Water	1 cup	250 mL

(continued on next page)

Heat cooking oil in medium non-stick frying pan. Add ground beef. Scramble-fry until beef is no longer pink. Drain. Turn into 3½ quart (3.5 L) slow cooker.

Add remaining 7 ingredients. Stir together. Cover. Cook on Low for 6 to 8 hours or on High for 3 to 4 hours. Makes 7½ cups (1.8 L).

1½ cups (375 mL): 414 Calories; 13 g Total Fat; 1138 mg Sodium; 29 g Protein; 44 g Carbohydrate; 3 g Dietary Fiber

VEGGIE BEEF CASSEROLE

Mild tomato flavor. Good creamy sauce.

Diced bacon	1 cup	250 mL
Lean ground beef	1½ lbs.	680 g
Medium onions, chopped	2	2
Thinly sliced potato	1½ cups	375 mL
Thinly sliced carrot	1½ cups	375 mL
Thinly sliced celery	½ cup	125 mL
Thinly sliced zucchini, with peel	1 cup	250 mL
Frozen cut green beans	1½ cups	375 mL
Uncooked broad noodles (about 6 oz., 170 g)	3 cups	750 mL
Salt	½ tsp.	2 mL
Condensed cream of mushroom soup	2 × 10 oz.	2 × 284 mL
Water	½ cup	125 mL
Condensed tomato soup	2 × 10 oz.	2 × 284 mL

Scramble-fry bacon, ground beef and onion in large frying pan until onion is soft and beef is no longer pink. Drain. Turn into ungreased 4 quart (4 L) casserole or small roaster.

Add next 7 ingredients. Stir together.

Stir mushroom soup and water together in small bowl. Add to beef mixture. Stir.

Empty tomato soup into small bowl. Stir vigorously. Spoon over all. Make sure pasta is underneath soup. Cover. Bake in 350°F (175°C) oven for 1½ to 2 hours until vegetables are tender. Serves 8.

1 serving: 436 Calories; 20.5 g Total Fat; 1558 mg Sodium; 25 g Protein; 38 g Carbohydrate; 3 g Dietary Fiber

STOVE TOP POT PIE

This not only tastes wonderful, it has a cozy look to it. Biscuit topping cooks on the top of the stove, not in the oven.

Medium carrots, cut into ¼ inch (6 mm) slices	4	4
Medium potatoes, cut into 1 inch (2.5 cm) cubes	4	4
Medium onion, cut into wedges	1	1
Large celery rib, coarsely chopped	1	1
Sliced fresh mushrooms	1 cup	250 mL
Diced zucchini, with peel	1 cup	250 mL
Boiling water	2 cups	500 mL
Canned stewed tomatoes, with juice, processed in blender	14 oz.	398 mL
Beef bouillon powder	2 tbsp.	30 mL
Worcestershire sauce	1 tsp.	5 mL
Pepper	⅛ tsp.	0.5 mL
Cooked roast beef, cut into ½ inch (12 mm) cubes	2 cups	500 mL
Instant potato flakes	2 tbsp.	30 mL
BISCUIT TOPPING		
Biscuit mix	1½ cups	375 mL
Milk	⅓ cup	75 mL

Combine first 11 ingredients in large pot or Dutch oven. Stir. Cover. Simmer for about 20 minutes until carrots are tender-crisp.

Add beef and potato flakes. Cook until hot and simmering.

Biscuit Topping: Stir biscuit mix and milk together in medium bowl to form soft ball. Knead on lightly floured surface 6 to 8 times. Roll out into ½ inch (12 mm) thick circle. Cut into 6 wedges. Position wedges on top of casserole. Cover. Cook for 12 to 15 minutes until biscuit wedges have risen and are cooked. Serves 6.

1 serving: 361 Calories; 7.7 g Total Fat; 1297 mg Sodium; 21 g Protein; 52 g Carbohydrate; 5 g Dietary Fiber

Pictured on page 17.

Meatballs, vegetables and beans. It's all here.

Large egg, fork-beaten	1	1
Dry bread crumbs	1/3 cup	75 mL
Finely minced onion	1/4 cup	60 mL
Parsley flakes	1 tbsp.	15 mL
Seasoning salt	1 tsp.	5 mL
Lean ground beef	1 lb.	454 g
Cooking oil	2 tsp.	10 mL
Medium onion, halved and sliced	1	1
Medium green pepper, slivered	1	1
Canned diced tomatoes, with juice	19 oz.	540 mL
Medium carrot, grated	1	1
Granulated sugar	1/2 tsp.	2 mL
Dried whole oregano	1/4 tsp.	1 mL
Dried sweet basil	1/4 tsp.	1 mL
Bay leaf	1	1
Canned red kidney beans, drained	14 oz.	398 mL
Canned white kidney beans, drained	19 oz.	540 mL
Romano (or black) beans, drained	14 oz.	398 mL
Grated medium Cheddar cheese	3/4 cup	175 mL

Stir first 5 ingredients together in medium bowl.

Add ground beef. Mix. Shape into 1 inch (2.5 cm) balls. You should get about 40.

Heat cooking oil in large pot or Dutch oven. Add meatballs. Cook until browned, removing to paper towel-lined plate as they brown. Drain all but 1 tsp. (5 mL) fat from pot.

Add onion and green pepper to pot. Sauté until onion is soft.

Add next 9 ingredients. Stir together. Add meatballs. Stir together gently. Simmer, uncovered, for about 30 minutes. Discard bay leaf.

Sprinkle cheese over each serving. Serves 6.

1 serving: 418 Calories; 14.1 g Total Fat; 844 mg Sodium; 31 g Protein; 43 g Carbohydrate; 8 g Dietary Fiber

EF STEWED IN WINE ▬▬▬

d hearty flavor. Full-bodied with a hint of bacon.

Bacon slices	4	4
All-purpose flour	3 tbsp.	50 mL
Salt	³/₄ tsp.	4 mL
Pepper	¹/₂ tsp.	2 mL
Garlic powder	¹/₂ tsp.	2 mL
Beef top round steak, trimmed of fat, cut into 1 inch (2.5 cm) cubes	2 lbs.	900 g
Large onion, sliced	1	1
Small (or medium, halved) fresh mushrooms	¹/₂ lb.	225 g
Sliced carrot	2 cups	500 mL
Dry red (or alcohol-free red) wine	¹/₄ cup	60 mL
Dry red (or alcohol-free red) wine	³/₄ cup	175 mL
Condensed beef broth	10 oz.	284 mL
Water	1 cup	250 mL
Bay leaves	2	2
Uncooked medium egg noodles	3 cups	750 mL

Cook bacon in large frying pan until browned. Remove to plate. Cut into 1 inch (2.5 cm) pieces. Drain all but 1 tbsp. (15 mL) fat from pan.

Combine flour, salt, pepper and garlic powder in bag or small bowl.

Add steak cubes, a few at a time, and shake to coat. Brown well in reserved bacon drippings in same frying pan, removing cubes to medium bowl as they brown. You will need to do this in 2 batches.

Add onion, mushrooms, carrot and first amount of wine to same frying pan. Stir to loosen any browned bits in pan. Return beef to pan.

Add second amount of wine, beef broth, water and bay leaves. Cover. Simmer for about 1¹/₂ hours until beef is very tender. Discard bay leaves.

Add noodles. Stir together. Noodles must be covered completely with vegetables or liquid. Cover. Boil gently for about 15 minutes until noodles are tender but firm. Add bacon. Stir together. Serves 6.

1 serving: 380 Calories; 11.3 g Total Fat; 788 mg Sodium; 35 g Protein; 26 g Carbohydrate; 3 g Dietary Fiber

Just place this in the oven before doing errands a incredible meal that awaits you when you get home.

Beef stew meat, cut into ³/₄ inch (2 cm) cubes	1¹/₂ lbs.	680 g
Cooking oil	1 tsp.	5 mL
Medium potatoes, cut up	4	4
Medium carrots, cut up	5	5
Medium onions, cut up	2	2
Sliced celery	1 cup	250 mL
Diced yellow turnip (rutabaga)	1¹/₂ cups	375 mL
Condensed onion soup	10 oz.	284 mL
Condensed tomato soup	10 oz.	284 mL
Salt	¹/₂ tsp.	2 mL
Pepper	¹/₈ tsp.	0.5 mL

Brown beef in cooking oil in large frying pan. Turn into small roaster.

Add next 5 ingredients.

Pour both soups, salt and pepper into same frying pan. Stir together well to loosen all browned bits in pan. Pour over vegetables. Cover. Bake in 300°F (150°C) oven for 3¹/₂ to 4 hours until tender. Makes 9 cups (2.25 L).

1¹/₂ cups (375 mL): 371 Calories; 12.3 g Total Fat; 1136 mg Sodium; 30 g Protein; 36 g Carbohydrate; 5 g Dietary Fiber

Politicians love ribbons, especially red tape.

BORSCHT STEW

Rich looking with a delicious beet flavor.

Boneless beef short ribs	2¹/₂ lbs.	1.1 kg
Sliced carrot	2 cups	500 mL
Sliced onion	1 cup	250 mL
Sliced celery	1 cup	250 mL
Tomato sauce	3 × 7¹/₂ oz.	3 × 213 mL
Water	1 cup	250 mL
Beef bouillon powder	2 tsp.	10 mL
Salt	2 tsp.	10 mL
Pepper	¹/₄ tsp.	1 mL
Dill weed	¹/₂ tsp.	2 mL
White vinegar	1 tbsp.	15 mL
Granulated sugar	2 tsp.	10 mL
Shredded cabbage	5 cups	1.25 L
Medium beets, peeled and cut into ¹/₄ inch (6 mm) thick matchsticks	3	3

Place ribs on rack in broiling tray. Broil each side for about 5 minutes until browned. Place in small roaster.

Add carrot, onion and celery.

Combine next 6 ingredients in medium bowl. Stir together. Pour over all. Cover. Bake in 325°F (160°C) oven for 2¹/₂ hours. Tilt roaster to skim off fat. Blot remaining fat with paper toweling.

Stir vinegar and sugar together in small cup. Pour over beef and vegetables.

Add cabbage and beets. Stir together as much as you can. Cover. Bake for about 1 hour until all vegetables and beef are tender. Serves 6.

1 serving: 440 Calories; 19.9 g Total Fat; 1987 mg Sodium; 42 g Protein; 24 g Carbohydrate; 4 g Dietary Fiber

Pictured on page 71.

A good beef and gravy dish with light, fluffy dumplings.

Beef stew meat, cut into ¾ inch (2 cm) cubes	1½ lbs.	680 g
Sliced onion	1 cup	250 mL
Beef bouillon powder	2 tsp.	10 mL
Salt	1 tsp.	5 mL
Pepper	¼ tsp.	1 mL
Water	1½ cups	375 mL
Water	¼ cup	60 mL
All-purpose flour	2 tbsp.	30 mL
Frozen peas (about 10 oz., 285 g)	2 cups	500 mL

BISCUIT DUMPLINGS

All-purpose flour	2 cups	500 mL
Baking powder	4 tsp.	20 mL
Granulated sugar	1 tbsp.	15 mL
Salt	¾ tsp.	4 mL
Cooking oil	⅓ cup	75 mL
Milk	¾ cup	175 mL
Hard margarine (or butter), melted (optional)	2 tsp.	10 mL

Put first 6 ingredients into ungreased 2 quart (2 L) casserole. Cover. Bake in 325°F (160°C) oven for about 3 hours, stirring each hour until beef is very tender. Remove from oven.

Whisk second amount of water and flour together in small bowl until smooth. Stir into casserole. Add peas. Stir. Cover to keep hot. Increase oven temperature to 400°F (205°C).

Biscuit Dumplings: Stir flour, baking powder, sugar and salt together in medium bowl.

Add cooking oil and milk. Stir together to make a ball. Knead on lightly floured surface 6 to 8 times. Roll out or press ¾ inch (2 cm) thick. Cut into 2 inch (5 cm) rounds. Arrange over top of beef mixture. Bake, uncovered, for about 20 minutes until lightly browned.

Brush hot dumplings with margarine. Serves 6.

1 serving: 551 Calories; 23.6 g Total Fat; 1139 mg Sodium; 33 g Protein; 50 g Carbohydrate; 4 g Dietary Fiber

Pictured on page 71.

POT ROAST

A sure way to get tender beef. A bit of nostalgia here. Makes lots of gravy.

Cooking oil	1 tsp.	5 mL
Boneless beef chuck (or blade or eye of round) roast	3 lbs.	1.4 kg
Boiling water	½ cup	125 mL
Beef bouillon powder	2 tsp.	10 mL
Canned tomatoes, with juice	14 oz.	398 mL
Brown sugar, packed	2 tbsp.	30 mL
Ground thyme	¼ tsp.	1 mL
Worcestershire sauce	1 tsp.	5 mL
Bay leaf	1	1
Medium potatoes, cut bite size	5	5
Medium carrots, cut bite size	6	6
Medium onions, cut into wedges	2	2
Salt	1 tsp.	5 mL
Pepper	¼ tsp.	1 mL
GRAVY		
All-purpose flour	¼ cup	60 mL
Water	½ cup	125 mL
Liquid gravy browner (optional)		
Salt, sprinkle (optional)		
Pepper, sprinkle (optional)		

Heat cooking oil in heavy pot or Dutch oven. Add roast. Brown both sides.

Stir boiling water and bouillon powder together in small cup. Add to beef.

Add next 5 ingredients. Stir around beef. Bring to a boil. Cover. Simmer gently for about 2½ hours until beef is tender. Turn beef 2 or 3 times while cooking. Add more liquid if needed to keep 1½ to 2 inches (3.8 to 5 cm) deep.

Add potato, carrot, onion, salt and pepper around beef. Cover. Simmer for 30 to 40 minutes until vegetables are tender. Discard bay leaf. Strain juice into measuring cup. Add water, if necessary, to make 2 cups (500 mL).

(continued on next page)

Beef

Gravy: Pour juice into small saucepan. Skim off fat. M___
water in small cup until no lumps remain. Gradually add f___
until boiling and thickened. Add a bit of gravy browner for___
for salt and pepper, adding if needed. Makes 3½ cup___
Serves 6.

1 serving: 497 Calories; 14.3 g Total Fat; 992 mg Sodium; 51 g Protein; 40 g Carbohydrate, 5 g Dietary Fiber

DINTY'S SPECIAL

Mild, satisfying and easy to make.

Shredded cabbage	4 cups	1 L
Chopped onion	½ cup	125 mL
Water	1½ cups	375 mL
Canned corned beef, cut into ½ inch (12 mm) cubes	12 oz.	340 g
Diced medium Cheddar cheese	1 cup	250 mL
Milk	1½ cups	375 mL
All-purpose flour	3 tbsp.	50 mL
Salt	½ tsp.	2 mL
Pepper	⅛ tsp.	0.5 mL
Jar of chopped pimiento, drained	2 oz.	57 mL
TOPPING		
Hard margarine (or butter)	¼ cup	60 mL
Dry bread crumbs	1 cup	250 mL

Cook cabbage and onion in water in large saucepan until tender. Drain. Turn into ungreased 2 quart (2 L) casserole. Cool.

Add corned beef and cheese. Stir together.

Gradually whisk milk into flour in small saucepan until no lumps remain. Heat and stir until boiling and thickened. Stir in salt, pepper and pimiento. Pour into casserole. Stir.

Topping: Melt margarine in small saucepan. Stir in bread crumbs. Sprinkle over top. Bake, uncovered, in 350°F (175°C) oven for about 30 minutes. Serves 6.

1 serving: 431 Calories; 25 g Total Fat; 1200 mg Sodium; 26 g Protein; 25 g Carbohydrate; 2 g Dietary Fiber

ꞈEAK IN FOIL

An autumn mix of colors. Cooking in foil means no pan to wash.

Beef chuck steak	1½ lbs.	680 g
Envelope dry onion soup mix	1 x 1½ oz.	1 x 42 g
Condensed cream of mushroom soup	10 oz.	284 mL
Medium sweet potatoes (size of medium potatoes)	4	4
Medium parsnips, quartered	4	4
Medium onions, quartered	2	2

Place large piece of foil in small roaster, leaving ends hanging outside roaster. Lay steak on foil.

Combine dry soup mix and mushroom soup in small bowl. Spread over beef.

Arrange sweet potatoes, parsnip and onion over top. Fold foil and seal. Cover. Bake in 300°F (150°C) oven for 2½ to 3 hours. Carefully open foil to test for doneness with fork. Steak should be very tender. Serves 4.

1 serving: 530 Calories; 16.7 g Total Fat; 1712 mg Sodium; 40 g Protein; 55 g Carbohydrate; 8 g Dietary Fiber

Variation: Omit sweet potatoes and parsnips. Add potatoes and carrots.

1. Red-Topped Frittata, page 41
2. Ham Stratawich, page 42
3. Egg Scramble Deluxe, page 44
4. Zucchini Frittata, page 40
5. Breakfast Strata, page 45

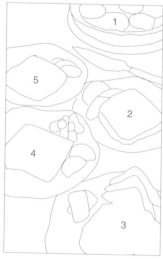

Props Courtesy Of: C C on Whyte, Dansk Gifts,
Eaton's, Handworks Gallery,
Stokes, The Bay

A tender and juicy dinner.

Beef short ribs, cut up	3½ lbs.	1.6 kg
White vinegar	3 tbsp.	50 mL
Brown sugar, packed	3 tbsp.	50 mL
Salt	1½ tsp.	7 mL
Pepper	½ tsp.	2 mL
Beef bouillon powder	2 tsp.	10 mL
Garlic powder	¼ tsp.	1 mL
Prepared horseradish	1 tbsp.	15 mL
Water, to cover		
Medium potatoes, quartered	4	4
Sliced onion	1 cup	250 mL
Peeled baby carrots	24	24
GRAVY		
All-purpose flour	¼ cup	60 mL
Salt	½ tsp.	2 mL
Liquid gravy browner (optional)		

Place ribs on rack in broiling tray. Broil each side for 5 minutes until browned. Place in small roaster.

Mix next 7 ingredients in small bowl. Pour over short ribs.

Add enough water to barely cover beef. Cover. Bake in 325°F (160°C) oven for 1½ to 2 hours until almost tender.

Add potato, onion and carrots. Cover. Bake for 1 hour until beef is very tender and vegetables are cooked. Strain liquid into measuring cup. Add water to make 2 cups (500 mL).

Gravy: Gradually whisk strained liquid into flour and salt in small saucepan until smooth. Heat and stir until boiling and thickened. Add bit of gravy browner for color. Makes 2 cups (500 mL). Serves 4.

1 serving: 920 Calories; 41.1 g Total Fat; 1999 mg Sodium; 84 g Protein; 50 g Carbohydrate; 5 g Dietary Fiber

CORNY BEEF ENCHILADAS

You can make these as spicy as you like by adjusting the kind of salsa you use as well as adding jalapeño peppers.

Chopped cooked roast beef	2 cups	500 mL
Cooked kernel corn	1 cup	250 mL
Canned chopped green chilies, drained	4 oz.	114 mL
Mild or medium salsa	⅔ cup	150 mL
Ground cumin	½ tsp.	2 mL
Salt	½ tsp.	2 mL
Mild or medium salsa	⅔ cup	150 mL
Corn tortillas (6 inches, 15 cm)	8	8
Mild or medium salsa	⅔ cup	150 mL
Grated sharp Cheddar cheese	1 cup	250 mL
Chopped pitted ripe olives (optional)	2 tbsp.	30 mL
Chopped jalapeño peppers (optional)	2 tbsp.	30 mL

Combine first 6 ingredients in medium bowl.

Spread second amount of salsa in greased casserole large enough to hold 8 enchiladas in single layer.

Place 1 tortilla on working surface. Cover remaining tortillas with damp tea towel to keep from drying out. Place about ⅓ cup (75 mL) beef mixture on tortilla. Fold sides over center. Lay, folded side up, over salsa in casserole. Repeat with remaining tortillas.

Drizzle third amount of salsa over enchiladas. Sprinkle with cheese, olives and jalapeño peppers. Cover. Bake in 350°F (175°C) oven for 45 minutes. Remove cover. Bake for about 15 minutes until very hot. Makes 8 enchiladas. Serves 4.

1 serving: 529 Calories; 16.7 g Total Fat; 2665 mg Sodium; 38 g Protein; 62 g Carbohydrate; 6 g Dietary Fiber

Variation: Scramble-fry 1 lb. (454 g) lean ground beef to use instead of roast beef.

Taste of corned beef comes through. Mellow and flavorful.

Chopped onion	¹/₂ cup	125 mL
Cooking oil	1 tsp.	5 mL
Canned corned beef, cut into ¹/₂ inch (12 mm) cubes	12 oz.	340 g
Frozen peas	2 cups	500 mL
Fettuccine, broken up	8 oz.	225 g
Boiling water	3 qts.	3 L
Cooking oil (optional)	1 tbsp.	15 mL
Salt	2 tsp.	10 mL
Condensed cream of mushroom soup	10 oz.	284 mL
Milk	¹/₄ cup	60 mL
TOPPING		
Hard margarine (or butter)	2 tbsp.	30 mL
Soda cracker crumbs	¹/₂ cup	125 mL

Sauté onion in first amount of cooking oil in small frying pan until soft. Turn into ungreased 2¹/₂ quart (2.5 L) casserole.

Add corned beef and peas. Stir together.

Cook pasta in boiling water, second amount of cooking oil and salt in large uncovered pot or Dutch oven for 5 to 7 minutes, stirring occasionally, until tender but firm. Drain. Add to casserole. Stir as best you can.

Mix soup and milk in small bowl. Pour over casserole. Poke with knife in several places to allow soup to run through.

Topping: Melt margarine in small saucepan. Stir in cracker crumbs. Sprinkle over top. Bake, uncovered, in 350°F (175°C) oven for 20 to 30 minutes until bubbly hot. Serves 6.

1 serving: 451 Calories; 18.7 g Total Fat; 1157 mg Sodium; 25 g Protein; 45 g Carbohydrate; 4 g Dietary Fiber

FRITTATA

Zucchini fits right into this tasty concoction.

Cooking oil	1 tbsp.	15 mL
Medium onion, chopped	1	1
Medium potato, diced small	1	1
Medium zucchini, with peel, thinly sliced	2	2
Large eggs	8	8
Grated Parmesan cheese	2½ tbsp.	37 mL
Salt	½ tsp.	2 mL
Dried sweet basil, sprinkle		
Dried whole oregano, sprinkle		
Pepper, sprinkle		
Grated medium Cheddar cheese	½ cup	125 mL

Heat cooking oil in large non-stick frying pan. Add onion, potato and zucchini. Sauté until potato is almost cooked and onion and zucchini are soft.

Beat eggs in medium bowl until smooth. Add next 5 ingredients. Beat together well. Pour over zucchini mixture. Cover. Cook over medium-low for 13 to 15 minutes until eggs are set.

Remove from heat. Sprinkle with Cheddar cheese. Cover. Let stand for 2 to 4 minutes until cheese is melted. Serves 4.

1 serving: *299 Calories; 19.6 g Total Fat; 622 mg Sodium; 19 g Protein; 12 g Carbohydrate; 2 g Dietary Fiber*

Note: Stove top temperatures may affect cooking time. If cooked too low, top eggs won't set. If cooked too high, bottom eggs burn.

Pictured on page 35.

They are trying their best to budget so that they can live beyond their yearnings.

RED-TOPPED FRITTATA

Tomatoes nesting in a poofy egg pie. Serve at your next brunch.

Hard margarine (or butter)	2 tsp.	10 mL
Chopped onion	1/2 cup	125 mL
Diced green, red or yellow pepper	1/3 cup	75 mL
Chopped cooked ham (5 oz., 140 g)	1 cup	250 mL
Grated Edam (or Gouda) cheese	1/2 cup	125 mL
Large eggs, fork-beaten	6	6
Salt	1 tsp.	5 mL
Pepper, sprinkle		
Cayenne pepper, sprinkle		
Medium tomatoes, sliced	2	2

Heat margarine in large frying pan. Add onion. Sauté until onion is beginning to soften.

Add green pepper and ham. Sauté for 2 to 3 minutes. Turn into greased 10 inch (25 cm) glass pie plate or shallow 9 × 9 inch (22 × 22 cm) casserole.

Sprinkle with cheese.

Stir eggs, salt, pepper and cayenne pepper together in medium bowl. Pour over cheese.

Arrange tomato slices over top, overlapping if necessary. Bake, uncovered, in 350°F (175°C) oven for about 30 minutes until set. Serves 4.

1 serving: 289 Calories; 20.4 g Total Fat; 1422 mg Sodium; 20 g Protein; 7 g Carbohydrate; 1 g Dietary Fiber

Pictured on page 35.

Paré Pointer

Sergeants in the army must suffer from headaches. They are always shouting "Tension."

HAM STRATAWICH

Very tasty and very showy with an evenly browned top. A handy make-ahead breakfast or brunch. Cuts nicely into "sandwiches."

Sliced onion	1 cup	250 mL
Cooking oil	1 tsp.	5 mL
Bread slices, with crusts	6	6
Frozen chopped broccoli, thawed (chop larger pieces smaller)	2½ cups	625 mL
Diced cooked ham	2 cups	500 mL
Grated medium Cheddar cheese	2 cups	500 mL
Bread slices, with crusts	6	6
Large eggs	5	5
Milk	2½ cups	625 mL
Dry mustard	½ tsp.	2 mL
Salt	½ tsp.	2 mL
Pepper	¼ tsp.	1 mL
Garlic powder	¼ tsp.	1 mL
Onion powder	¼ tsp.	1 mL
TOPPING		
Hard margarine (or butter)	2 tbsp.	30 mL
Coarsely crushed corn flakes cereal	½ cup	125 mL

Sauté onion in cooking oil in medium frying pan until soft.

Line greased 9 x 13 inch (22 x 33 cm) pan with first amount of bread slices. Spread onion over top. Layer with broccoli, ham, cheese and second amount of bread slices.

Beat eggs in medium bowl until smooth. Add next 6 ingredients. Mix. Pour over all.

Topping: Melt margarine in small saucepan. Stir in corn flake crumbs. Sprinkle over egg mixture. Cover. Refrigerate overnight. Remove cover. Bake in 325°F (160°C) oven for about 1 hour. Serves 6.

1 serving: 612 Calories; 30.6 g Total Fat; 1666 mg Sodium; 35 g Protein; 49 g Carbohydrate; 4 g Dietary Fiber

Pictured on page 35.

SPINACH ONION Q|

Nicely browned. Attractive and good flavor combination.

Pastry (your own or a mix), for 10 inch (25 cm) pie		
Frozen chopped spinach, thawed and squeezed dry	**10 oz.**	**300 g**
Canned french-fried onions	**$1/2 \times 2^3/4$ oz.**	**$1/2 \times 79$ g**
Crumbled feta cheese	**$1^1/2$ cups**	**375 mL**
Grated sharp Cheddar cheese	**$2/3$ cup**	**150 mL**
Large eggs	**4**	**4**
Skim evaporated milk	**$13^1/2$ oz.**	**385 mL**
Pepper	**$1/4$ tsp.**	**1 mL**
Ground nutmeg	**$1/16$ tsp.**	**0.5 mL**
Canned french-fried onions	**$1/2 \times 2^3/4$ oz.**	**$1/2 \times 79$ g**
Parsley flakes	**1 tsp.**	**5 mL**

Roll out pastry on lightly floured surface. Fit into ungreased 10 inch (25 cm) glass pie plate. Glass will ensure a browned bottom crust. Trim and crimp edge.

Scatter spinach in pie shell. Sprinkle first amount of onion rings over spinach. Sprinkle with both cheeses.

Beat eggs in medium bowl until smooth. Add next 3 ingredients. Beat together. Pour over cheese.

Scatter second amount of onion rings and parsley over top. Bake, uncovered, on bottom rack in 375°F (190°C) oven for about 45 minutes until knife inserted in center comes out clean. Let stand for 5 to 10 minutes before cutting. Cuts into 8 wedges.

1 wedge: 341 Calories; 21.2 g Total Fat; 666 mg Sodium; 16 g Protein; 22 g Carbohydrate; 1 g Dietary Fiber

Pictured on page 71.

Paré Pointer

She thought a filling station was a dentist's office.

EGG SCRAMBLE DELUXE

A fast and easy dish to prepare for the whole family.

Large eggs	8	8
Water	3 tbsp.	50 mL
Grated sharp Cheddar cheese	½ cup	125 mL
Worcestershire sauce	¼ tsp.	1 mL
Canned flakes of ham, with liquid, broken up	6½ oz.	184 g
Salt, sprinkle		
Pepper, sprinkle		
Hard margarine (or butter)	1 tsp.	5 mL

Beat eggs and water together in medium bowl.

Add cheese, Worcestershire sauce, ham flakes with liquid, salt and pepper. Stir together well.

Melt margarine in large non-stick frying pan. Add egg mixture. Scramble-fry constantly until softly set. Serves 8.

1 serving: 164 Calories; 12.3 g Total Fat; 431 mg Sodium; 12 g Protein; 1 g Carbohydrate; 0 g Dietary Fiber

Pictured on page 35.

Phantoms always pick up their mail at the ghost office.

Sausage always adds a good taste to anything for breakfast as it does in this strata. A great make-ahead.

Bread slices, crusts removed	8	8
Grated medium Cheddar cheese	2 cups	500 mL
Small pork sausages, browned and each cut into 4 or 5 pieces	1½ lbs.	680 g
Large eggs	5	5
Milk	2¼ cups	560 mL
Dry mustard	½ tsp.	2 mL
Onion salt	¼ tsp.	1 mL
Pepper	⅛ tsp.	0.5 mL
Condensed cream of mushroom soup	10 oz.	284 mL
Milk	½ cup	125 mL
TOPPING		
Hard margarine (or butter)	2 tbsp.	30 mL
Dry bread crumbs	½ cup	125 mL

Line greased 9 x 13 inch (22 x 33 cm) pan with bread slices, trimming to fit. Sprinkle with cheese. Scatter sausage over cheese.

Beat eggs in medium bowl until smooth. Add next 4 ingredients. Stir together. Pour over sausage. Cover. Refrigerate overnight.

About 45 minutes before serving, mix soup and second amount of milk in small bowl. Pour over all. Let stand for 30 to 45 minutes.

Topping: Melt margarine in small saucepan. Stir in bread crumbs. Sprinkle over top. Bake, uncovered, in 350°F (175°C) oven for about 1½ hours. Let stand for 10 to 15 minutes before serving. Serves 8.

1 serving: 521 Calories; 33.5 g Total Fat; 1365 mg Sodium; 26 g Protein; 28 g Carbohydrate; 1 g Dietary Fiber

Pictured on page 35.

Paré Pointer

They call their kitten "Penny" because it has a head on one side and a tail on the other.

TUNA FRILLS

Perky little rolls filled with tuna, spinach and different kinds of cheese.

Lasagne noodles	8	8
Boiling water	3 qts.	3 L
Cooking oil (optional)	1 tbsp.	15 mL
Salt	2 tsp.	10 mL
SAUCE		
Hard margarine (or butter)	1 tbsp.	15 mL
Medium onion, finely chopped	1	1
All-purpose flour	1 tbsp.	15 mL
Chicken bouillon powder	1 tsp.	5 mL
Garlic salt	½ tsp.	2 mL
Dill weed	½ tsp.	2 mL
Dry mustard	½ tsp.	2 mL
Cayenne pepper, sprinkle		
Milk	2 cups	500 mL
Canned flaked tuna, drained	6 oz.	170 g
Large egg, fork-beaten	1	1
Part-skim ricotta cheese	16 oz.	500 g
Frozen chopped spinach, thawed and squeezed dry	10 oz.	300 g
Grated part-skim mozzarella cheese	1 cup	250 mL
Grated Parmesan cheese	⅓ cup	75 mL
Parsley flakes	1 tbsp.	15 mL
Dried sweet basil	1 tsp.	5 mL
Garlic salt	½ tsp.	2 mL
Pepper	¼ tsp.	1 mL
Fresh dill, sprinkle (optional)		

Cook pasta in boiling water, cooking oil and salt in large uncovered pot or Dutch oven for 10 to 12 minutes, stirring occasionally, until tender but firm. Drain. Rinse with cold water. Drain.

Sauce: Melt margarine in large frying pan. Add onion. Sauté until soft.

Mix in next 6 ingredients. Stir in milk until boiling and thickened.

Add tuna. Mix well. Pour ½ of sauce into greased 9 x 9 inch (22 x 22 cm) pan or casserole.

(continued on next page)

Combine next 9 ingredients in medium bowl. Spread about ½ cup (125 mL) spinach mixture down length of each noodle. Roll up. Cut each roll in half crosswise. Set in pan, frill side up. Pour remaining ½ of sauce over and around noodles. Cover. Bake in 350°F (175°C) oven for 1 to 1½ hours until bubbly hot.

Garnish with dill. Makes 16 frills, enough for 4 large servings.

1 serving: 622 Calories; 24.9 g Total Fat; 1254 mg Sodium; 48 g Protein; 51 g Carbohydrate; 3 g Dietary Fiber

Pictured on page 17.

TUNA POTATO GRIDDLE

It takes many adjectives such as colorful, moist and perfectly seasoned to describe this meal. This is similar to fried onion and potato.

Hard margarine (or butter)	1 tbsp.	15 mL
Finely chopped onion	½ cup	125 mL
Diced green or red pepper	½ cup	125 mL
Frozen hash brown potatoes	4 cups	1 L
Seasoning salt	1 tsp.	5 mL
Pepper, sprinkle		
Frozen mixed vegetables	1 cup	250 mL
Canned flaked tuna, drained	6 oz.	170 g
Grated medium Cheddar cheese	1 cup	250 mL

Melt margarine in large frying pan. Add onion and green pepper. Sauté until onion is soft.

Add potatoes, seasoning salt and pepper. Stir together. Cover. Cook for about 5 minutes until potatoes are soft.

Stir in vegetables and tuna. Cover. Cook for about 5 minutes until hot.

Sprinkle with cheese. Cover. Let stand for 2 to 3 minutes until cheese is melted. Makes 5 cups (1.25 L).

1 cup (250 mL): 332 Calories; 12.2 g Total Fat; 611 mg Sodium; 19 g Protein; 39 g Carbohydrate; 5 g Dietary Fiber

STANDBY TUNA CASSEROLE

Can be prepared ahead of time and baked when needed. Delicious.

Small shell pasta	1 cup	250 mL
Boiling water	6 cups	1.5 L
Cooking oil (optional)	2 tsp.	10 mL
Salt	1 tsp.	5 mL
Chopped onion	1/2 cup	125 mL
Chopped red pepper	1/2 cup	125 mL
Hard margarine (or butter)	2 tsp.	10 mL
Chopped fresh mushrooms	1 cup	250 mL
All-purpose flour	2 tbsp.	30 mL
Skim evaporated milk	13 1/2 oz.	385 mL
Beef bouillon powder	2 tsp.	10 mL
Celery seed	1/2 tsp.	2 mL
Pepper, sprinkle		
Light process Cheddar (or mozzarella) cheese slices	4	4
Canned solid white tuna, drained and broken into chunks	6 1/2 oz.	184 g
Grated medium Cheddar cheese	1/2 cup	125 mL

Cook pasta in boiling water, cooking oil and salt in large uncovered saucepan for 8 to 10 minutes, stirring occasionally, until tender but firm. Drain. Return to saucepan.

Sauté onion and red pepper in margarine in separate large saucepan until onion is soft. Add mushrooms. Sauté until liquid is evaporated.

Whisk flour and evaporated milk together in small bowl until smooth. Add to onion mixture, stirring often, until boiling and thickened.

Add bouillon powder, celery seed, pepper and cheese slices. Stir until cheese is melted.

Add tuna and pasta. Stir. Pour into greased 2 quart (2 L) casserole.

Sprinkle with cheese. Bake, uncovered, in 350°F (175°C) oven for about 35 minutes. Serves 4.

1 serving: 375 Calories; 10.1 g Total Fat; 997 mg Sodium; 31 g Protein; 40 g Carbohydrate; 2 g Dietary Fiber

Kids will discover this in a hurry.

Condensed cream of mushroom soup	10 oz.	284 mL
Milk	³/₄ cup	175 mL
Salt	¹/₂ tsp.	2 mL
Pepper	¹/₄ tsp.	1 mL
Dried whole oregano (optional)	¹/₂ tsp.	2 mL
Uncooked instant white rice	2 cups	500 mL
Frozen peas and carrots	2 cups	500 mL
Onion flakes	1 tbsp.	15 mL
Canned solid white tuna, drained and flaked	6¹/₂ oz.	184 g

TOPPING

Hard margarine (or butter)	2 tbsp.	30 mL
Dry bread crumbs	¹/₂ cup	125 mL

Mix first 5 ingredients in large bowl.

Add next 4 ingredients. Stir. Turn into ungreased 2 quart (2 L) casserole.

Topping: Melt margarine in small saucepan. Stir in bread crumbs. Sprinkle over top. Bake, uncovered, in 350°F (175°C) oven for about 30 minutes. Serves 4.

1 serving: 490 Calories; 14.1 g Total Fat; 1350 mg Sodium; 21 g Protein; 70 g Carbohydrate; 4 g Dietary Fiber

Tennis players have to be satisfied with net profits.

MUSHROOM AND CRAB CASSEROLE

Assemble ahead of time, cover and refrigerate. Bake when ready.

Sliced fresh mushrooms	2 cups	500 mL
White (or alcohol-free white) wine	1 tbsp.	15 mL
All-purpose flour	2 tbsp.	30 mL
Skim milk	2 cups	500 mL
Light spreadable cream cheese	2 tbsp.	30 mL
Canned crabmeat, drained and cartilage removed (or 2 cups, 500 mL, chopped imitation crabmeat)	2 x 4 oz.	2 x 113 g
Seafood (or vegetable) bouillon powder	1/2 tsp.	2 mL
Salt	1/2 tsp.	2 mL
Dried sweet basil	1/4 tsp.	1 mL
Cayenne pepper, sprinkle		
Freshly ground pepper, sprinkle		
Ground nutmeg, sprinkle		
Jar of sliced pimiento, drained (optional)	2 oz.	57 mL
Small shell pasta (about 8 oz., 225 g)	2 1/3 cups	575 mL
Boiling water	2 qts.	2 L
Cooking oil (optional)	1 tbsp.	15 mL
Salt	2 tsp.	10 mL
Grated light Monterey Jack cheese	1/2 cup	125 mL
Grated light Parmesan cheese product	1 tbsp.	15 mL

Sauté mushrooms in large non-stick frying pan for 7 to 8 minutes until liquid is evaporated.

Add wine. Simmer for about 1 minute until liquid is almost evaporated.

Measure flour into small bowl. Gradually whisk in milk until smooth. Add to mushrooms, stirring constantly, until boiling and thickened. Stir in cream cheese until melted.

Stir in next 8 ingredients. Remove from heat.

(continued on next page)

Cook pasta in boiling water, cooking oil and second amount of salt in large uncovered pot or Dutch oven for 4 minutes, stirring occasionally. Pasta will still be slightly firm. Drain. Rinse with cold water. Drain. Add to crab sauce. Mix. Pour into greased 1½ quart (1.5 L) casserole.

Sprinkle with Monterey Jack cheese and Parmesan cheese. Cover. Bake in 350°F (175°C) oven for 30 minutes until hot and bubbling. Serves 4.

1 serving: 385 Calories; 5.8 g Total Fat; 1065 mg Sodium; 27 g Protein; 55 g Carbohydrate; 2 g Dietary Fiber

NEPTUNE'S PIE

If shepherds can have a pie, so can Neptune.

Medium potatoes, cut up (about 1½ lbs., 680 g)	6	6
Water, to cover		
Hot milk	⅔ cup	150 mL
Hard margarine (or butter)	2 tbsp.	30 mL
Salt	¼ tsp.	1 mL
Pepper	¹⁄₁₆ tsp.	0.5 mL
Fine dry bread crumbs	½ cup	125 mL
Salt	½ tsp.	2 mL
Onion powder	½ tsp.	2 mL
Poultry seasoning	¾ tsp.	4 mL
Fish fillets (your choice)	1¼ lbs.	568 g
Frozen peas and carrots	2 cups	500 mL
Paprika, sprinkle		

Cook potato in water in large saucepan until tender. Drain.

Add milk, margarine, first amount of salt and pepper. Mash together well. Keep warm.

Mix next 4 ingredients in small bowl.

Dip fish into crumb mixture to coat. Arrange in greased 9 x 9 inch (22 x 22 cm) pan. Spread peas and carrots over top. Spoon dabs of potato here and there. Smooth out as best you can. Sprinkle with paprika. Bake, uncovered, in 400°F (205°C) oven for 30 minutes. Serves 4.

1 serving: 415 Calories; 8.5 g Total Fat; 1107 mg Sodium; 34 g Protein; 51 g Carbohydrate; 5 g Dietary Fiber

⁓ate, rich, tart, sweet and scrumptious.

Long grain white rice	³/₄ cup	175 mL
Water	1¹/₂ cups	375 mL
Salt	¹/₂ tsp.	2 mL
Condensed cream of mushroom soup	10 oz.	284 mL
Light salad dressing (or mayonnaise)	¹/₂ cup	125 mL
Milk	¹/₂ cup	125 mL
Lemon juice	1 tsp.	5 mL
Onion flakes	1 tbsp.	15 mL
Curry powder	¹/₂ tsp.	2 mL
Frozen chopped broccoli, thawed and drained	2¹/₄ cups	560 mL
Fish fillets (your choice), cut bite size	1 lb.	454 g

Cook rice in water and salt in covered medium saucepan for 15 to 20 minutes until tender and water is absorbed. Transfer to ungreased 9 x 9 inch (22 x 22 cm) pan.

Mix next 6 ingredients in medium bowl until fairly smooth.

Add broccoli and fish. Stir lightly. Pour over rice. Cover. Bake in 350°F (175°C) oven for 30 to 40 minutes until fish flakes when tested with fork. Serves 4.

1 serving: 438 Calories; 15.3 g Total Fat; 1291 mg Sodium; 28 g Protein; 47 g Carbohydrate; 4 g Dietary Fiber

1. Minestrone, page 141
2. Macaroni Hash, page 12
3. Rice And Broccoli Chicken, page 111
4. Patty Bake, page 13

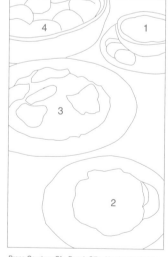

CREAMED RICE AND SALMON

Cheesy with a hint of dill.

Hard margarine (or butter)	1 tbsp.	15 mL
Chopped onion	½ cup	125 mL
Chopped celery	1 cup	250 mL
Chopped green or red pepper	⅔ cup	150 mL
Uncooked converted long grain rice	1¼ cups	300 mL
Water	1½ cups	375 mL
Condensed Cheddar cheese soup	10 oz.	284 mL
Milk	⅔ cup	150 mL
Light cream cheese, cut up	4 oz.	125 g
Canned salmon, drained, skin and round bones removed, flaked	7½ oz.	213 g
Frozen baby peas, thawed	1 cup	250 mL
Chopped fresh dill (or ½ tsp., 2 mL, dill weed)	2 tsp.	10 mL

Melt margarine in large non-stick frying pan. Add onion, celery and green pepper. Sauté until soft.

Add rice, water, soup and milk. Stir together. Bring to a boil. Cover. Simmer for 30 to 40 minutes until rice is tender.

Add cream cheese. Stir until melted.

Add salmon and peas. Stir. Heat through.

Garnish with dill. Makes 8 cups (2 L).

1½ cups (375 mL): 412 Calories; 13.7 g Total Fat; 937 mg Sodium; 19 g Protein; 52 g Carbohydrate; 3 g Dietary Fiber

Paré Pointer

That fellow made a fortune from operating a flea circus. He started from scratch.

SCALLOPED SALMON

Fabulous fare for company as well as family. Red salmon is best for color.

Box of au gratin scalloped potatoes with sauce packet	5½ oz.	155 g
Water	2¼ cups	560 mL
Milk	1 cup	250 mL
Dill weed	¼ tsp.	1 mL
Onion salt	¼ tsp.	1 mL
Onion flakes	1 tbsp.	15 mL
Frozen peas	2 cups	500 mL
Canned salmon, drained, skin and round bones removed, flaked	7½ oz.	213 g
TOPPING		
Hard margarine (or butter)	2 tbsp.	30 mL
Dry bread crumbs	½ cup	125 mL

Combine potatoes and sauce packet in ungreased 2 quart (2 L) casserole.

Heat water, milk, dill weed and onion salt in medium saucepan until boiling. Pour over potatoes. Stir. Cover. Bake in 350°F (175°C) oven for 20 to 30 minutes until potato is tender.

Sprinkle with onion flakes. Scatter peas over onion flakes. Spread salmon over peas.

Topping: Melt margarine in small saucepan. Stir in bread crumbs. Sprinkle over all. Bake, uncovered, in 350°F (175°C) oven for about 30 minutes. Serves 4.

1 serving: 446 Calories; 18.5 g Total Fat; 1272 mg Sodium; 21 g Protein; 52 g Carbohydrate; 6 g Dietary Fiber

Those farm kids couldn't stand milking so they sat down.

SALMON STEW

A slow cooker is required for this recipe. A full meal with fish as the cornerstone rather than beef. Red salmon is best for color.

Medium potatoes, thinly sliced	4	4
Thinly sliced carrot	1 cup	250 mL
Chopped onion	1 cup	250 mL
All-purpose flour	2 tbsp.	30 mL
Salt	1 tsp.	5 mL
Pepper	1/8 tsp.	0.5 mL
Canned salmon, drained, skin and round bones removed, flaked	2 x 7 1/2 oz.	2 x 213 g
Condensed cream of mushroom soup	10 oz.	284 mL
Water	1/4 cup	60 mL
Parsley flakes	1/2 tsp.	2 mL
Paprika	1/4 tsp.	1 mL

Place first 6 ingredients in 5 quart (5 L) slow cooker. Stir together well to coat with flour.

Scatter salmon over top.

Stir remaining 4 ingredients together in small bowl. Pour over all. Cover. Cook on Low for 9 to 11 hours or on High for 4 1/2 to 5 1/2 hours. Makes 5 1/4 cups (1.3 L).

1 1/2 cups (375 mL): 407 Calories; 13.2 g Total Fat; 2051 mg Sodium; 30 g Protein; 42 g Carbohydrate; 4 g Dietary Fiber

That small piece of land is like a bad tooth. It's an acre.

SHRIMP SUPREME

A bit reminiscent of shrimp cocktail. Flavor is great.

Long grain white rice	1 cup	250 mL
Water	2 cups	500 mL
Salt	½ tsp.	2 mL
Cooking oil	1 tsp.	5 mL
Chopped onion	½ cup	125 mL
Finely chopped green pepper	¼ cup	60 mL
Chopped fresh mushrooms	1 cup	250 mL
Condensed tomato soup	10 oz.	284 mL
Skim evaporated milk	1 cup	250 mL
Salt	1 tsp.	5 mL
Pepper	¼ tsp.	1 mL
Ground nutmeg, just a pinch		
Sherry (or alcohol-free sherry)	3 tbsp.	50 mL
Worcestershire sauce	½ tsp.	2 mL
Cooked medium fresh (or frozen, thawed) shrimp	1 lb.	454 g
Lemon juice	1 tbsp.	15 mL
Sliced almonds, toasted	2 tbsp.	30 mL

Cook rice in water and first amount of salt in covered medium saucepan for 15 to 20 minutes until tender and water is absorbed. Transfer to ungreased 2 quart (2 L) casserole.

Heat cooking oil in medium frying pan. Add onion, green pepper and mushrooms. Sauté until soft. Add to rice. Stir.

Stir next 7 ingredients together well in medium bowl. Pour over rice mixture.

Put shrimp into medium bowl. Drain well. Blot dry with paper towels. Drizzle with lemon juice. Toss to coat. Let stand for 10 minutes. Add to casserole. Toss lightly to distribute shrimp evenly.

Sprinkle with almonds. Bake, uncovered, in 350°F (175°C) oven for 45 to 60 minutes until heated through. Let stand for 10 minutes before serving. Makes 8 cups (2 L).

*1½ **cups (375 mL):** 335 Calories; 4.3 g Total Fat; 1414 mg Sodium; 26 g Protein; 46 g Carbohydrate; 2 g Dietary Fiber*

SHRIMP FETTUCCINE

Fresh or frozen shrimp give this a nice fresh taste.

Cooking oil	2 tsp.	10 mL
Chopped onion	1 cup	250 mL
Chopped celery	¾ cup	175 mL
Chopped green pepper	⅓ cup	75 mL
Fettuccine, broken	8 oz.	225 g
Boiling water	3 qts.	3 L
Cooking oil (optional)	1 tbsp.	15 mL
Salt	2 tsp.	10 mL
Condensed cream of mushroom soup	10 oz.	284 mL
Parsley flakes	2 tsp.	10 mL
Milk	½ cup	125 mL
Lemon pepper	½-1 tsp.	2-5 mL
Cooked medium fresh (or frozen, thawed) shrimp	½ lb.	225 g
Chow mein noodles	½ cup	125 mL

Heat first amount of cooking oil in medium frying pan. Add onion, celery and green pepper. Sauté until soft.

Cook pasta in boiling water, second amount of cooking oil and salt in large uncovered pot or Dutch oven for 5 to 7 minutes, stirring occasionally, until tender but firm. Drain. Return pasta to pot.

Stir soup, parsley, milk and lemon pepper together vigorously in large bowl. Add onion mixture and pasta.

Add shrimp. Stir together lightly. Turn into ungreased 2 quart (2 L) casserole.

Top with chow mein noodles. Cover. Bake in 350°F (175°C) oven for 30 minutes until hot. Serves 4.

1 serving: 431 Calories; 11.8 g Total Fat; 806 mg Sodium; 23 g Protein; 58 g Carbohydrate; 3 g Dietary Fiber

SPICY FISH STEWP

Stewp is part stew and part soup. Crusty bread is perfect for dunking.

Cooking oil	2 tsp.	10 mL
Medium onions, halved lengthwise and thinly sliced	2	2
Garlic cloves, minced (or ½ tsp., 2 mL, powder)	2	2
Chopped celery	1½ cups	375 mL
Medium carrots, sliced	2	2
Medium green pepper, diced	1	1
Canned diced tomatoes, with juice	14 oz.	398 mL
Reserved liquid from clams, plus water to make	1 cup	250 mL
White (or alcohol-free white) wine	¼ cup	60 mL
Parsley flakes	1 tbsp.	15 mL
Dried sweet basil	½ tsp.	2 mL
Thyme leaves	½ tsp.	2 mL
Bay leaves	2	2
Hot red chili peppers, chopped (or ½-1 tsp., 2-5 mL, dried crushed chilies)	1-2	1-2
Firm white fish fillets, cut into 1½ inch (3.8 cm) squares	½ lb.	225 g
Salt	½ tsp.	2 mL
Pepper, sprinkle		
Very small (bay) scallops	4 oz.	113 g
Canned baby clams, drained and liquid reserved	5 oz.	142 g

Heat cooking oil in large pot or Dutch oven. Add onion and garlic. Sauté until soft. Do not brown.

Add next 11 ingredients. Stir together. Cover. Simmer for 20 minutes.

Add fish pieces, salt and pepper. Stir gently. Cover. Cook for 5 minutes.

Add scallops and clams. Cover. Cook for 5 minutes until scallops are opaque. Discard bay leaves. Makes 7 cups (1.75 L), enough to serve 4.

1 serving: 214 Calories; 3.9 g Total Fat; 746 mg Sodium; 23 g Protein; 20 g Carbohydrate; 4 g Dietary Fiber

Pictured on page 143.

Delicious herbed vegetables.

Garlic clove, minced	1	1
Coarsely chopped onion	1 cup	250 mL
Olive (or cooking) oil	1 tbsp.	15 mL
Medium zucchini, with peel, diced	1	1
Diced green, red, orange or yellow pepper	1 cup	250 mL
Sliced fresh mushrooms	1 cup	250 mL
Canned diced tomatoes, drained	28 oz.	796 mL
Salt	1/2 tsp.	2 mL
Dried sweet basil	1 tsp.	5 mL
Granulated sugar	1 tsp.	5 mL
Dried whole oregano	1/4 tsp.	1 mL
Ground thyme	1/4 tsp.	1 mL
Large (not jumbo) shell pasta (about 8 oz., 225 g)	3 cups	750 mL
Boiling water	2 1/2 qts.	2.5 L
Cooking oil (optional)	1 tbsp.	15 mL
Salt	2 tsp.	10 mL
Grated Parmesan cheese, sprinkle (optional)	2 tbsp.	30 mL

Sauté garlic and onion in olive oil in large non-stick frying pan for 4 minutes until onion is soft.

Add next 9 ingredients. Stir together well. Cover. Simmer for 15 minutes.

Cook pasta in boiling water, cooking oil and second amount of salt in large uncovered pot or Dutch oven for 10 to 12 minutes, stirring occasionally, until tender but firm. Drain. Return pasta to pot. Pour vegetable mixture over top. Toss together well to coat.

Sprinkle with Parmesan cheese. Serves 4 to 6.

1 serving: 359 Calories; 5.3 g Total Fat; 677 mg Sodium; 12 g Protein; 68 g Carbohydrate; 6 g Dietary Fiber

MEATLESS CHILI

This long list of ingredients looks intimidating but persevere and you will have a great spicy meal. Tender vegetables and full of beans. Serve with a hearty bread.

Cooking oil	1 tbsp.	15 mL
Garlic cloves, minced (or ½ tsp., 2 mL, powder)	2	2
Sliced celery	1½ cups	375 mL
Chopped onion	1 cup	250 mL
Sliced fresh mushrooms	2 cups	500 mL
Medium red pepper, diced	1	1
Medium green pepper, diced	1	1
Diced (½ inch, 12 mm) zucchini, with peel	3 cups	750 mL
Finely diced or grated carrot	¾ cup	175 mL
Canned stewed tomatoes, with juice, chopped	2 × 14 oz.	2 × 398 mL
Canned chopped green chilies, with liquid	4 oz.	114 mL
Canned mixed beans, drained	2 × 19 oz.	2 × 540 mL
Canned pinto (or romano) beans, drained	14 oz.	398 mL
Frozen kernel corn (or 1 can, 12 oz., 341 mL, drained)	1½ cups	375 mL
Beer (or water)	1 cup	250 mL
Canned green lentils, drained	19 oz.	540 mL
Prepared mustard	1 tbsp.	15 mL
Chili powder	1-2 tsp.	5-10 mL
Ground cumin	1 tsp.	5 mL
Salt	1 tsp.	5 mL
Dried whole oregano	½ tsp.	2 mL
Pepper	¼ tsp.	1 mL

Heat cooking oil in large pot or Dutch oven. Add garlic, celery and onion. Sauté until onion is soft.

Add mushrooms, red and green peppers, zucchini and carrot. Cook, stirring often, for 3 to 4 minutes until mushrooms and zucchini begin to soften.

(continued on next page)

Stir in remaining 13 ingredients. Bring to a slow boil. Cover. Simmer for 15 minutes to blend flavors. Remove cover. Boil slowly for 15 minutes to reduce liquid. Makes 13 cups (3.25 L), enough to serve 6.

1 serving: 379 Calories; 4.7 g Total Fat; 1418 mg Sodium; 19 g Protein; 69 g Carbohydrate; 16 g Dietary Fiber

Pictured on page 89.

MACARONI SPECIAL

Has a crunchy topping. Good combinations.

Chopped onion	½ cup	125 mL
Hard margarine (or butter)	2 tsp.	10 mL
Condensed tomato soup	10 oz.	284 mL
Water	½ cup	125 mL
Grated medium Cheddar cheese	1 cup	250 mL
Elbow macaroni	2 cups	500 mL
Boiling water	3 qts.	3 L
Cooking oil (optional)	1 tbsp.	15 mL
Salt	2 tsp.	10 mL
TOPPING		
Hard margarine (or butter)	2 tbsp.	30 mL
Dry bread crumbs	½ cup	125 mL

Sauté onion in margarine in large frying pan until soft.

Add soup, water and cheese. Stir together until cheese is melted. Remove from heat.

Cook pasta in boiling water, cooking oil and salt in large uncovered pot or Dutch oven for 5 to 7 minutes, stirring occasionally, until tender but firm. Drain. Return pasta to pot. Add tomato soup mixture to pasta. Stir. Turn into ungreased 2 quart (2 L) casserole.

Topping: Melt margarine in small saucepan. Stir in bread crumbs. Sprinkle over all. Bake, uncovered, in 350°F (175°C) oven for 30 minutes. Makes 8 cups (2 L).

1½ cups (375 mL): 386 Calories; 15.3 g Total Fat; 684 mg Sodium; 13 g Protein; 49 g Carbohydrate; 2 g Dietary Fiber

BEAN DISH

A bit of a pleasant nip. Good eating.

Canned beans in tomato sauce	14 oz.	398 mL
Canned chick peas (garbanzo beans), drained	19 oz.	540 mL
Canned kidney beans, drained	14 oz.	398 mL
Chopped onion	1½ cups	375 mL
Cooking oil	2 tsp.	10 mL
All-purpose flour	2 tbsp.	30 mL
Tomato sauce	7½ oz.	213 mL
Ketchup	½ cup	125 mL
Brown sugar, packed	¼ cup	60 mL
White vinegar	2 tbsp.	30 mL
Hot pepper sauce	½-¾ tsp.	2-4 mL

Combine all 3 beans in ungreased 2 quart (2 L) casserole.

Sauté onion in cooking oil in medium frying pan until soft.

Mix in flour. Stir in tomato sauce until boiling and thickened. Add ketchup, brown sugar, vinegar and hot pepper sauce. Stir together. Add to casserole. Stir lightly. Bake, uncovered, in 350°F (175°C) oven for about 45 minutes. Makes 6 cups (1.5 L).

1½ cups (375 mL): 436 Calories; 5 g Total Fat; 1469 mg Sodium; 18 g Protein; 88 g Carbohydrate; 17 g Dietary Fiber

That very noisy green animal is a frog horn.

CHEESY RICE CASSEROLE

Colorful surprises await you in this rice dish.

Long grain white rice	2 cups	500 mL
Water	4 cups	1 L
Salt	1 tsp.	5 mL
Canned chopped green chilies, drained	2 x 4 oz.	2 x 114 mL
Medium tomatoes, sliced	2	2
Salt, sprinkle		
Pepper, sprinkle		
Dried sweet basil, sprinkle		
Grated part-skim mozzarella cheese	³/₄ cup	175 mL
Milk	²/₃ cup	150 mL
Grated medium Cheddar cheese	1 cup	250 mL

Cook rice in water and salt in covered medium saucepan for 15 to 20 minutes until tender and water is absorbed. Spoon ½ of rice into greased 3 quart (3 L) casserole.

Cover rice with green chilies. Arrange tomato slices over green chilies, overlapping if needed. Sprinkle with salt, pepper and basil. Scatter mozzarella cheese over top. Pour milk around edge.

Cover with remaining ½ of rice. Sprinkle with Cheddar cheese. Cover. Bake in 325°F (160°C) oven for about 40 minutes. Remove cover. Bake for 15 minutes. Makes 9 cups (2.25 L).

1½ cups (375 mL): 381 Calories; 9.9 g Total Fat; 669 mg Sodium; 15 g Protein; 57 g Carbohydrate; 1 g Dietary Fiber

Paré Pointer

The best coal miners are hippies. They dig.

PORK STEW WITH ROTINI

Quite colorful. Cooking pasta separately keeps it firmer.

Cooking oil	2 tsp.	10 mL
Pork roast, trimmed of fat, cut into 1 inch (2.5 cm) cubes	1 lb.	454 g
Salt	½ tsp.	2 mL
Pepper	¼ tsp.	1 mL
Garlic cloves, minced (or ½ tsp., 2 mL powder)	2	2
Sliced carrot, ½ inch (12 mm) thick	2 cups	500 mL
Canned diced tomatoes, with juice	28 oz.	796 mL
Tomato (or vegetable) juice	1 cup	250 mL
Dried whole oregano, crushed	1 tsp.	5 mL
Granulated sugar	1 tsp.	5 mL
Medium zucchini, halved lengthwise and sliced ½ inch (12 mm) thick	2	2
Rotini (spiral pasta)	3 cups	750 mL
Boiling water	3 qts.	3 L
Cooking oil (optional)	1 tbsp.	15 mL
Salt	2 tsp.	10 mL

Heat first amount of cooking oil in large non-stick frying pan. Add pork. Sauté for about 4 minutes.

Add first amount of salt, pepper, garlic and carrot. Cook for 3 to 4 minutes until carrot is bright colored and pork is browned.

Stir in next 4 ingredients. Cover. Simmer for 30 to 35 minutes, stirring occasionally, until carrot is tender-crisp.

Stir in zucchini. Cook, uncovered, for 10 to 15 minutes until zucchini is tender-crisp.

Cook pasta in boiling water, second amounts of cooking oil and salt in large uncovered pot or Dutch oven for 10 to 12 minutes, stirring occasionally, until tender but firm. Drain. Add to stew. Stir together well. Serves 4.

1 serving: 528 Calories; 10.7 g Total Fat; 993 mg Sodium; 37 g Protein; 71 g Carbohydrate; 7 g Dietary Fiber

Pictured on page 107.

You will need a large, deep frying pan for this tasty meal.

Pork chops (½ inch, 12 mm, thick), trimmed of fat	**1½ lbs.**	**680 g**
Garlic powder	**⅛ tsp.**	**0.5 mL**
Pepper	**⅛ tsp.**	**0.5 mL**
Cooking oil	**1 tsp.**	**5 mL**
Frozen hash brown potatoes (or shredded potato)	**4 cups**	**1 L**
Diced carrot	**1 cup**	**250 mL**
Sliced fresh mushrooms	**1 cup**	**250 mL**
Onion slices (¼ inch, 6 mm, thick)	**4-6**	**4-6**
Condensed cream of mushroom soup	**10 oz.**	**284 mL**
Milk	**½ cup**	**125 mL**
Salt, sprinkle (optional)		
Pepper, sprinkle		

Sprinkle pork chops with garlic powder and pepper. Brown both sides well in cooking oil in large frying pan. Transfer to plate. Drain any fat from pan.

Combine potatoes, carrot and mushrooms in same frying pan. Arrange pork chops over top.

Lay 1 onion slice on each pork chop.

Stir soup, milk, salt and pepper together in small bowl. Pour over top, being sure to get some on each pork chop. Cover. Cook for 30 minutes. Move pork chops aside to stir potato mixture gently. Replace chops. Cover. Cook for about 15 minutes until vegetables are tender. Serves 4.

1 serving: 495 Calories; 18.4 g Total Fat; 743 mg Sodium; 31 g Protein; 52 g Carbohydrate; 6 g Dietary Fiber

This is a non profit store. We didn't intend it to be but we are.

PORK AND RICE DISH

Appetizing cheesy topping covers the chops.

Pork chops (¾ inch, 2 cm, thick), trimmed of fat	6	6
Cooking oil	2 tsp.	10 mL
Salt, sprinkle		
Pepper, sprinkle		
Boiling water	½ cup	125 mL
Beef bouillon powder	1 tbsp.	15 mL
Granulated sugar	1 tsp.	5 mL
Pepper	¼ tsp.	1 mL
Onion flakes	1 tbsp.	15 mL
Uncooked long grain white rice	1 cup	250 mL
Canned stewed tomatoes, with juice, broken up	2 × 14 oz.	2 × 398 mL
TOPPING		
Hard margarine (or butter)	2 tbsp.	30 mL
Dry bread crumbs	½ cup	125 mL
Grated medium Cheddar cheese	¾ cup	175 mL

Brown pork chops on both sides in cooking oil in large frying pan. Sprinkle with salt and pepper.

Pour boiling water into large bowl. Add bouillon powder, sugar, pepper and onion flakes. Stir together well.

Add rice and tomatoes with juice. Stir. Pour into ungreased 9 x 13 inch (22 x 33 cm) pan. Arrange pork chops over top. Cover with foil. Bake in 350°F (175°C) oven for 45 to 60 minutes.

Topping: Melt margarine in small saucepan. Add bread crumbs and cheese. Stir. Sprinkle over all. Cover. Return to oven for about 15 minutes until pork is very tender and rice is cooked. Serves 6.

1 serving: 456 Calories; 17.1 g Total Fat; 933 mg Sodium; 30 g Protein; 45 g Carbohydrate; 2 g Dietary Fiber

Very fresh looking with pea pods over top. Complete meal with pork, vegetables and rice.

Cooking oil	2 tsp.	10 mL
Boneless pork shoulder steak, cut into ¾ inch (2 cm) cubes	1 lb.	454 g
Salt, sprinkle		
Pepper, sprinkle		
Medium carrots, cut into strips	2	2
Medium onion, sliced	1	1
Canned whole mushrooms, drained	10 oz.	284 mL
Uncooked instant white rice	2 cups	500 mL
Chicken bouillon powder	1 tbsp.	15 mL
Boiling water	2 cups	500 mL
Soy sauce	2 tbsp.	30 mL
Frozen pea pods, thawed	10 oz.	285 g
Green onions, chopped	1-2	1-2
Medium green pepper, cut into strips	1	1

Heat cooking oil in large frying pan. Add pork. Brown all sides. Turn into ungreased 2 quart (2 L) casserole. Sprinkle with salt and pepper.

Add carrot, onion, mushrooms and rice. Stir together.

Stir bouillon powder and boiling water together in small bowl. Add soy sauce. Stir. Pour over all. Cover. Bake in 350°F (175°C) oven for about 1½ hours until pork is very tender.

Stir in pea pods, green onion and green pepper. Cover. Bake for 10 to 15 minutes. Serves 4.

1 serving: 539 Calories; 21.9 g Total Fat; 1240 mg Sodium; 27 g Protein; 58 g Carbohydrate; 6 g Dietary Fiber

Paré Pointer

The best way to catch a squirrel is to act like a nut.

Only a bit more time if you brown chops first. Good either way.

Pork chops (¾ inch, 2 cm, thick), trimmed of fat	4	4
Medium potatoes, thickly sliced	3	3
Medium parsnips, quartered	2	2
Frozen kernel corn	1 cup	250 mL
Medium onion, sliced	1	1
Canned tomatoes, with juice, cut up	14 oz.	398 mL
Envelope dry onion soup mix	1 × 1½ oz.	1 × 42 g

Layer pork chops in ungreased baking dish large enough to hold in single layer. Cover pork with potato. Add layers of parsnip, corn and onion.

Stir tomatoes with juice and dry soup mix together in small bowl. Pour over top. Cover. Bake in 350°F (175°C) oven for 1½ to 2 hours until pork is very tender. Serves 4.

1 serving: *341 Calories; 7.1 g Total Fat; 1178 mg Sodium; 27 g Protein; 44 g Carbohydrate; 6 g Dietary Fiber*

Variation: For an extra touch brown pork chops in 2 tsp. (10 mL) cooking oil before layering in casserole.

1. Spinach Onion Quiche, page 43
2. Sausage Hash, page 78
3. Chef's Salad, page 130
4. Borscht Stew, page 30
5. Beef And Dumplings, page 31

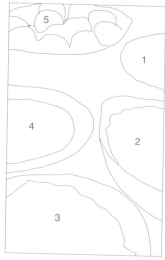

Props Courtesy Of: C C on Whyte, Dansk Gifts, La Cache, Le Gnome, The Bay, X/S Wares

PINEAPPLE PORK AND RICE

Peachy-red color with a sweet and sour flavor.

Cornstarch	2 tbsp.	30 mL
Ground ginger	2 tsp.	10 mL
Garlic salt	1 tsp.	5 mL
Pepper	1/4 tsp.	1 mL
Lean pork loin, cut into 1 inch (2.5 cm) pieces	1 lb.	454 g
Cooking oil	1 tbsp.	15 mL
Canned pineapple tidbits, with juice	14 oz.	398 mL
Brown sugar, packed	1/3 cup	75 mL
White vinegar	2 tbsp.	30 mL
Ketchup	2 tbsp.	30 mL
Soy sauce	1 tbsp.	15 mL
Canned tomato juice	10 oz.	284 mL
Water	1 cup	250 mL
Uncooked long grain white rice	1¼ cups	300 mL

Combine cornstarch, ginger, garlic salt and pepper in plastic bag. Add pork pieces, a few at a time, and shake to coat.

Heat cooking oil in large frying pan. Sauté pork until browned.

Add next 5 ingredients. Stir together. Cover. Simmer for 20 minutes.

Stir in tomato juice, water and rice. Cover. Simmer for 35 to 40 minutes, stirring after 20 minutes, until rice is cooked and pork is tender. Serves 4.

1 serving: 561 Calories; 6.9 g Total Fat; 1026 mg Sodium; 30 g Protein; 95 g Carbohydrate; 2 g Dietary Fiber

The favorite piece of clothing for an octopus on a cold day is a coat of arms.

*⟩ noodles, vegetables and bean sprouts round out this dish. The
eat flavor of this stir-fry comes from the sauce.*

Soy sauce	2 tbsp.	30 mL
Lemon juice	2 tsp.	10 mL
Cooking oil	2 tsp.	10 mL
Grated fresh gingerroot	1 tsp.	5 mL
Garlic cloves, minced (or ½ tsp., 2 mL, powder)	2	2
Dried crushed chilies, finely crushed	¼ tsp.	1 mL
Pork tenderloin, cut into 1 × 2 inch (2.5 × 5 cm) strips	¾ lb.	340 g
Rice stick noodles, broken up	2 cups	500 mL
Warm water	6 cups	1.5 L
Thin diagonally sliced carrot	½ cup	125 mL
Thin diagonally sliced celery	½ cup	125 mL
Coarsely chopped onion	½ cup	125 mL
Coarsely shredded cabbage	2 cups	500 mL
Fresh bean sprouts (small handful)	½ cup	125 mL
Cornstarch	1½ tbsp.	25 mL
Cold water	¾ cup	175 mL
Soy sauce	1 tbsp.	15 mL
Chili sauce (or ketchup)	1 tbsp.	15 mL
Granulated sugar	½ tsp.	2 mL

Stir first 6 ingredients together in medium bowl. Add pork strips. Press
down to coat. Let stand for 15 minutes.

Place noodles in separate medium bowl. Pour warm water over top.
Let stand for 15 minutes. Drain.

Turn pork and marinade into hot non-stick wok or large frying pan.
Stir-fry for about 3 minutes until pork is no longer pink.

Stir in carrot, celery, onion and cabbage. Cover. Cook for about
3 minutes until vegetables are tender-crisp.

Stir in bean sprouts.

(continued on next page)

Stir cornstarch and cold water together in small cup. Add s
amount of soy sauce, chili sauce and sugar. Stir together well. A
wok. Stir until boiling and slightly thickened. Mix in rice noo
Cover. Cook for 1 minute until heated through. Serves 4.

*1 serving: 461 Calories; 5.3 g Total Fat; 913 mg Sodium; 26 g Protein; 77 g Carbohydrate;
4 g Dietary Fiber*

GREEK PIZZA

Greek favorites—spinach and feta cheese.

Commercial partially baked 12 inch (30 cm) pizza crust	1	1
Bacon slices, cut into ½ inch (12 mm) pieces	8	8
Thinly sliced onion, separated into rings	2 cups	500 mL
Commercial pizza sauce	½ cup	125 mL
Frozen chopped spinach, thawed and squeezed dry	10 oz.	300 g
Grated part-skim mozzarella cheese	1 cup	250 mL
Crumbled feta cheese	½ cup	125 mL

Place crust on greased 12 inch (30 cm) pizza pan.

Cook bacon in medium frying pan until partially cooked. Drain.

Add onion rings. Sauté until onion is soft and bacon is cooked.

Spread pizza sauce over crust. Arrange spinach over top. Spread with
bacon and onion. Scatter mozzarella cheese and feta cheese over
top. Bake on bottom rack in 425°F (220°C) oven for 8 to 12 minutes.
Cuts into 8 wedges.

*1 wedge: 276 Calories; 11.6 g Total Fat; 451 mg Sodium; 12 g Protein; 31 g Carbohydrate;
3 g Dietary Fiber*

Pictured on page 107.

CURRIED PORK AND MANGO SAUCE

The sauce has a nice bite to it. Delicious!

Pork tenderloin, cut into ½ inch (12 mm) thick medallions	1 lb.	454 g
Chili powder, sprinkle		
Cooking oil	1 tsp.	5 mL
MANGO SAUCE		
Chopped onion	1 cup	250 mL
Cooking oil	1 tsp.	5 mL
Curry paste (available in ethnic section of grocery stores)	2 tsp.	10 mL
Canned mangoes, diced, juice reserved	14 oz.	398 mL
Small red chili pepper, finely chopped (or ¼ tsp., 1 mL, dried crushed chilies), optional	1	1
Diced zucchini, with peel	2 cups	500 mL
Diced red pepper	1 cup	250 mL
Lime juice	1 tbsp.	15 mL
Paprika	1 tsp.	5 mL
Skim evaporated milk	½ cup	125 mL
Coconut flavoring	½ tsp.	2 mL
Cornstarch	1 tbsp.	15 mL
Fresh pea pods (or frozen, thawed), about 6 oz. (170 g), sliced diagonally	2½ cups	625 mL
Angel hair pasta	10 oz.	285 g
Boiling water	3 qts.	3 L
Cooking oil (optional)	1 tbsp.	15 mL
Salt	1 tbsp.	15 mL
Flake coconut, toasted	2 tsp.	10 mL

Sprinkle both sides of each pork medallion with chili powder. Sauté pork in cooking oil in large non-stick frying pan until browned on both sides. Remove to plate. Keep warm.

Mango Sauce: Sauté onion in first cooking oil and curry paste in same frying pan for about 2 minutes until onion is soft.

Stir in next 6 ingredients. Cover. Cook for 4 minutes.

(continued on next page)

Combine evaporated milk, coconut flavoring and cornstarch in small cup. Mix well. Stir into zucchini mixture until boiling and thickened. Stir in ½ cup (125 mL) reserved mango juice, if needed, to thin sauce. Add pork. Simmer, uncovered, for about 8 minutes until cooked. Add pea pods. Cook for 3 to 4 minutes until tender-crisp.

Cook pasta in boiling water, second amount of cooking oil and salt in large uncovered pot or Dutch oven for 5 to 6 minutes, stirring occasionally, until tender but firm. Drain. Serve pork and mango sauce over pasta.

Sprinkle with coconut. Serves 4.

1 serving: 581 Calories; 8.2 g Total Fat; 110 mg Sodium; 40 g Protein; 87 g Carbohydrate; 8 g Dietary Fiber

Pictured on page 89.

PORK STEW

Pork is tender and flavorful. Good meal.

Lean pork, cut into ¾ inch (2 cm) cubes	1 lb.	454 g
Cooking oil	2 tsp.	10 mL
Boiling water, to cover	¾ cup	175 mL
Salt	1 tsp.	5 mL
Pepper	¼ tsp.	1 mL
Medium potatoes, diced	2	2
Medium carrots, sliced	2	2
Medium onion, sliced	1	1
Light sour cream	1 cup	250 mL
All-purpose flour	3 tbsp.	50 mL
Liquid gravy browner, for color	½ tsp.	2 mL

Sauté pork in cooking oil in large frying pan until browned. Put into ungreased 3 quart (3 L) casserole. Add boiling water. Sprinkle with salt and pepper. Cover. Bake in 350°F (175°C) oven for 45 minutes.

Add potato, carrot and onion. Cover. Bake for 45 minutes. Drain stock into measuring cup. Add water, if needed, to make 1 cup (250 mL).

Gradually whisk sour cream into flour in medium bowl. Add gravy browner. Add stock. Stir together well. Pour over pork mixture. Bake for 20 minutes. Serves 4.

1 serving: 298 Calories; 9.6 g Total Fat; 799 mg Sodium; 28 g Protein; 24 g Carbohydrate; 2 g Dietary Fiber

SAGE HASH

good. Cabbage and rice are moist. Slices of rye bread go well
his.

Chopped onion	1½ cups	375 mL
Cooking oil	2 tsp.	10 mL
Ukrainian (or ham) sausage, diced	¾ lb.	340 g
Chopped cabbage	4 cups	1 L
Condensed onion soup	10 oz.	284 mL
Tomato sauce	7½ oz.	213 mL
Water	⅔ cup	150 mL
Uncooked long grain white rice	1 cup	250 mL
Salt	½ tsp.	2 mL
Pepper	¼ tsp.	1 mL
Diced tomato	1 cup	250 mL
Chopped fresh parsley, sprinkle (optional)		

Sauté onion in cooking oil in large frying pan until soft.

Add sausage and cabbage. Cover. Cook for about 5 minutes until cabbage is soft.

Stir in next 6 ingredients. Boil slowly, stirring once or twice, for about 30 minutes until rice is tender and liquid is absorbed.

Stir in tomato. Sprinkle with parsley. Makes 8 cups (2 L).

1½ cups (375 mL): 422 Calories; 20.4 g Total Fat; 1684 mg Sodium; 15 g Protein; 46 g Carbohydrate; 3 g Dietary Fiber

Pictured on page 71.

The first comment from firemen when they arrived at the burning church was "Holy Smoke."

SPICY SAUSAGE AND PASTA

If you prefer less spice, simply use sweet sausage rather than hot. Hot pepper sauce may also be omitted.

Spicy Italian sausage, cut into ½ inch (12 mm) slices	1 lb.	454 g
Chopped onion	½ cup	125 mL
Chopped green pepper	½ cup	125 mL
Diced zucchini, with peel	2 cups	500 mL
Canned stewed tomatoes, with juice, chopped	14 oz.	398 mL
Granulated sugar	½ tsp.	2 mL
Drops of hot pepper sauce (optional)	2-4	2-4
Vermicelli	8 oz.	225 g
Boiling water	2 qts.	2 L
Cooking oil (optional)	1 tbsp.	15 mL
Salt	2 tsp.	10 mL

Cook sausage in large non-stick frying pan on both sides until browned. With slotted spoon, remove to paper towel-lined plate to drain. Drain all but 2 tsp. (10 mL) fat from pan.

Add onion, green pepper and zucchini to same frying pan. Sauté until soft.

Stir in tomatoes with juice, sugar and hot pepper sauce. Add sausage. Cover. Simmer for 15 minutes.

Cook pasta in boiling water, cooking oil and salt in large uncovered pot or Dutch oven for 6 to 7 minutes until tender but firm. Drain. Return pasta to pot. Add sausage mixture. Stir together. Makes 8 cups (2 L).

1½ cups (375 mL): 339 Calories; 12.9 g Total Fat; 579 mg Sodium; 15 g Protein; 41 g Carbohydrate; 3 g Dietary Fiber

Pictured on page 17.

ITALIAN PASTA SKILLET

Sausage, tomatoes and pasta say Italian. Use hot sausage if you like more spice.

Italian sausages, cut into 1/2 inch (12 mm) pieces	3/4 lb.	340 g
Large onion, chopped	1	1
Garlic clove, minced (or 1/4 tsp., 1 mL, powder)	1	1
Chopped fresh mushrooms	1 cup	250 mL
Medium green pepper, diced	1	1
Canned diced tomatoes, with juice	28 oz.	796 mL
Tomato (or vegetable) juice	1 cup	250 mL
Water	1 cup	250 mL
Dried sweet basil	2 tsp.	10 mL
Granulated sugar	1/2 tsp.	2 mL
Dried whole oregano	1/4 tsp.	1 mL
Uncooked penne (about 6 oz., 170 g)	2 cups	500 mL
Grated Parmesan cheese	2 tbsp.	30 mL
Chopped fresh parsley (or 1 1/2 tsp., 7 mL, flakes)	2 tbsp.	30 mL

Sauté sausage, onion and garlic in large frying pan until onion is soft.

Add mushrooms and green pepper. Sauté until onion and sausage are lightly browned. Drain.

Add next 7 ingredients. Stir together. Cover. Boil gently for 30 to 35 minutes until pasta is tender.

Serve with Parmesan cheese and parsley sprinkled over top. Serves 6.

1 serving: 257 Calories; 8.3 g Total Fat; 651 mg Sodium; 12 g Protein; 34 g Carbohydrate; 3 g Dietary Fiber

The first nudist convention was given very little coverage.

SIMPLE CASSOULET

Pronounced ka-soo-LAY. Really good. Lots of flavor from sausage and bacon.

Sliced carrot	1½ cups	375 mL
Medium or large onion, chopped	1	1
Sliced celery	½ cup	125 mL
Water	2 cups	500 mL
Small zucchini, with peel, diced	1	1
Instant potato flakes	2 tbsp.	30 mL
Canned small white beans (or white kidney beans), drained	19 oz.	540 mL
Small link sausages	1 lb.	454 g
Bacon slices, diced	6	6
Canned stewed tomatoes, with juice, broken up	14 oz.	398 mL
Garlic powder	¼ tsp.	1 mL
TOPPING		
Hard margarine (or butter)	2 tbsp.	30 mL
Dry bread crumbs	½ cup	125 mL

Combine carrot, onion, celery and water in large frying pan. Cover. Cook until almost tender.

Add zucchini. Cook for 5 minutes. Drain. Sprinkle with potato flakes. Stir. Turn into ungreased 2 quart (2 L) casserole.

Layer beans over top.

Poke holes in sausages with tip of knife. Cook sausages and bacon in medium frying pan. Drain on paper towels. Cut sausages in half crosswise. Place sausage and bacon over beans.

Mix tomatoes with juice and garlic powder in small bowl. Pour over all.

Topping: Melt margarine in small saucepan. Stir in bread crumbs. Sprinkle over top. Bake, uncovered, in 350°F (175°C) oven for about 45 minutes. Makes 7 cups (1.75 L).

1½ cups (375 mL): 460 Calories; 26.8 g Total Fat; 1040 mg Sodium; 17 g Protein; 39 g Carbohydrate; 6 g Dietary Fiber

CHEESY WIENERS AND POTATOES

A great dish for any age.

Chopped onion	⅔ cup	150 mL
Hard margarine (or butter)	2 tsp.	10 mL
Diced potato	3 cups	750 mL
Water	⅓ cup	75 mL
Salt	½ tsp.	2 mL
Wieners, cut into ½ inch (12 mm) slices	1 lb.	454 g
All-purpose flour	3 tbsp.	50 mL
Seasoned salt	1 tsp.	5 mL
Pepper, sprinkle		
Cayenne pepper, sprinkle (optional)		
Milk	1½ cups	375 mL
Grated medium Cheddar cheese	1 cup	250 mL
Canned kernel corn, drained	12 oz.	341 mL

Sauté onion in margarine in medium saucepan until soft.

Add potato, water and salt. Cover. Cook gently for about 15 minutes, stirring occasionally, until tender and water is evaporated.

Add wieners. Stir often as wieners get plump and start to brown. This will take about 5 minutes.

Stir flour, seasoned salt, pepper and cayenne pepper together in small saucepan. Gradually whisk in milk until smooth. Add to wiener mixture. Stir until boiling and thickened.

Add cheese and corn. Stir until cheese is melted and corn is heated through. Serves 4.

1 serving: 712 Calories; 46.5 g Total Fat; 2365 mg Sodium; 28 g Protein; 47 g Carbohydrate; 4 g Dietary Fiber

Paré Pointer

Those holes in the wood are knotholes. If they're not holes, what are they?

Hard to say who likes this best—kids, moms or dads.

Chopped onion	½ cup	125 mL
Hard margarine (or butter)	1 tsp.	5 mL
Canned beans in tomato sauce	2 × 14 oz.	2 × 398 mL
Canned kidney beans, drained	14 oz.	398 mL
Wieners, cut crosswise into bite-size pieces	1 lb.	454 g
Fancy molasses	2 tbsp.	30 mL
Ketchup	¼ cup	60 mL
Brown sugar, packed	2 tbsp.	30 mL
Prepared mustard	1 tsp.	5 mL
Apple cider vinegar	1 tsp.	5 mL
Worcestershire sauce	1 tsp.	5 mL
Dry mustard	½ tsp.	2 mL

Sauté onion in margarine in small frying pan until soft. Transfer to ungreased 2 quart (2 L) casserole.

Add next 3 ingredients. Stir.

Stir remaining 7 ingredients together in small bowl. Add to casserole. Stir well. Cover. Bake in 350°F (175°C) oven for 40 to 50 minutes, stirring at half-time. Serves 6.

1 serving: 483 Calories; 23.7 g Total Fat; 1679 mg Sodium; 19 g Protein; 53 g Carbohydrate; 14 g Dietary Fiber

Variation: Use tofu wieners to make this meatless.

The first one to take a bath is the ringleader.

PINEAPPLE HAM BAKE

If you have never tried baked beans with pineapple, this is where to start. So easy. So good.

Medium red onion, chopped (see Note)	1	1
Diced or chopped cooked ham	2 cups	500 mL
Canned beans in tomato sauce	2 × 14 oz.	2 × 398 mL
Canned pineapple tidbits, drained	19 oz.	540 mL
White vinegar	1 tbsp.	15 mL
Brown sugar, packed	3 tbsp.	50 mL
Prepared mustard	1½ tsp.	7 mL

Combine red onion, ham, beans and pineapple in ungreased 2 quart (2 L) casserole.

Mix vinegar, brown sugar and mustard in small cup. Add to casserole. Stir together well. Bake, uncovered, in 350°F (175°C) oven for 30 to 40 minutes until very hot. Makes 8 cups (2 L).

1½ cups (375 mL): 291 Calories; 3.3 g Total Fat; 1383 mg Sodium; 20 g Protein; 51 g Carbohydrate; 14 g Dietary Fiber

Note: Red onions are mild. If using a stronger onion, sauté in 1 tsp. (5 mL) margarine first.

HAM AND POTATOES

A slow cooker is required for this recipe. Very tasty. Good cheese flavor. Good brunch or luncheon dish.

Frozen hash brown potatoes	1 lb.	454 g
Minced onion flakes	1 tbsp.	15 mL
Canned flakes of ham, with liquid, broken up	2 × 6½ oz.	2 × 184 g
Jar of chopped pimiento	2 oz.	57 mL
Condensed Cheddar cheese soup	10 oz.	284 mL
Milk	¾ cup	175 mL

Combine potatoes, onion flakes, ham with liquid and pimiento in 3.5 quart (3.5 L) slow cooker. Mix well.

Stir soup and milk together in small bowl. Pour over top. Cover. Cook on Low for 7 to 9 hours or on High for 3½ to 4½ hours. Makes 4⅔ cups (1.15 L).

1½ cups (375 mL): 560 Calories; 32 g Total Fat; 2423 mg Sodium; 29 g Protein; 40 g Carbohydrate; 3 g Dietary Fiber

HAM AND CABBAGE CASSEF

All the flavors come through in this crunchy casserole.

Skim evaporated milk	13½ oz.	385 mL
All-purpose flour	¼ cup	60 mL
Dijon mustard	2 tsp.	10 mL
Salt	½ tsp.	2 mL
Pepper	¼ tsp.	1 mL
Ground nutmeg, sprinkle		
Coarsely chopped cabbage	5 cups	1.25 L
Chopped onion	1 cup	250 mL
Hard margarine (or butter)	1 tbsp.	15 mL
Chopped cooked ham	2 cups	500 mL
Whole wheat macaroni	⅔ cup	150 mL
Boiling water	1½ qts.	1.5 L
Cooking oil (optional)	2 tsp.	10 mL
Salt	1½ tsp.	7 mL
Bread slice, processed into crumbs	1	1
Grated medium Cheddar cheese	¼ cup	60 mL

Gradually whisk evaporated milk into flour in small saucepan until smooth. Heat, stirring constantly, until sauce is boiling and thickened. Stir in mustard, first amount of salt, pepper and nutmeg. Set aside.

Sauté cabbage and onion in margarine in large non-stick frying pan for about 6 minutes until cabbage is soft. Stir sauce into cabbage mixture. Pour ½ into greased 2 quart (2 L) casserole.

Cover with ham.

Cook pasta in boiling water, cooking oil and second amount of salt in large uncovered saucepan for 6 minutes, stirring occasionally, until just tender but still slightly undercooked. Drain. Layer over ham. Cover with remaining creamed cabbage mixture.

Combine bread crumbs and cheese in small bowl. Sprinkle over surface of casserole. Bake, uncovered, in 350°F (175°C) oven for 35 minutes until bubbly and topping is browned. Makes about 5½ cups (1.4 L), enough to serve 4.

1 serving: 385 Calories; 9.9 g Total Fat; 1596 mg Sodium; 31 g Protein; 45 g Carbohydrate; 5 g Dietary Fiber

◢ BROCCOLI HAM ROLLS ▬▬▬▬

Excellent dish. Sauce has a french-fried onion flavor.

Lasagne noodles	6	6
Boiling water	2 qts.	2 L
Salt	2 tsp.	10 mL
Condensed cream of chicken soup	10 oz.	284 mL
Light sour cream	1/2 cup	125 mL
Milk	1/2 cup	125 mL
Grated medium Cheddar cheese	1/2 cup	125 mL
Large egg	1	1
All-purpose flour	1 tsp.	5 mL
Grated Parmesan cheese	1/4 cup	60 mL
Frozen chopped broccoli, thawed and very finely chopped	2 1/2 cups	625 mL
Onion powder	1/4 tsp.	1 mL
Thin slices of cooked ham, halved lengthwise	6	6
Grated medium Cheddar cheese	1/2 cup	125 mL
Canned french-fried onions (add more if desired)	1/2 × 2 3/4 oz.	1/2 × 79 g

Cook lasagne noodles in boiling water and salt in large uncovered saucepan for 14 to 16 minutes until tender but firm. Drain. Rinse with cold water. Drain. Return pasta to saucepan.

Mix soup, sour cream, milk and first amount of Cheddar cheese in medium bowl. Pour about 1/3 to 1/2 into ungreased 9 × 9 inch (22 × 22 cm) pan.

Beat egg and flour together in small bowl. Stir in Parmesan cheese, broccoli and onion powder.

Lay out lasagne noodles on working surface. Place 2 pieces of ham on each noodle. Spread 1/6 of broccoli mixture over each ham slice. Roll up tightly. Cut in half crosswise. Place cut side down in pan. Pour remaining soup mixture over top.

Sprinkle with second amount of Cheddar cheese. Scatter onions over top. Cover. Bake in 350°F (175°C) oven for about 1 1/4 hours. Remove cover. Bake for 5 minutes. Serves 4.

1 serving: 550 Calories; 28.3 g Total Fat; 1724 mg Sodium; 32 g Protein; 43 g Carbohydrate; 4 g Dietary Fiber

A good home-cooked taste. Topping adds a great finish.

MUSHROOM CREAM SAUCE

Chopped fresh mushrooms	1 cup	250 mL
Finely chopped onion	1/4 cup	60 mL
Hard margarine (or butter)	1 tsp.	5 mL
All-purpose flour	1/4 cup	60 mL
Chicken bouillon powder	2 tsp.	10 mL
Paprika	1/2 tsp.	2 mL
Salt	1 tsp.	5 mL
Pepper	1/4 tsp.	1 mL
Milk	2 cups	500 mL
Thin center ham slice (bone-in), diced	1 lb.	454 g
Medium potatoes, thinly sliced	4	4
Medium carrots, thinly sliced	4	4
Medium onion, sliced or chopped	1	1
Frozen peas, thawed	1 1/2 cups	375 mL

TOPPING

Hard margarine (or butter)	2 tbsp.	30 mL
Dry bread crumbs	1/2 cup	125 mL
Grated Cheddar cheese	1/4 cup	60 mL

Mushroom Cream Sauce: Sauté mushrooms and onion in margarine in medium frying pan until soft.

Stir next 5 ingredients together in medium saucepan. Gradually whisk in milk until no lumps remain. Heat and stir until boiling and thickened. Stir in mushroom mixture.

Place ham in greased 3 quart (3 L) casserole. Layer potato, carrot and onion over top. Pour sauce over all. Cover. Bake in 350°F (175°C) oven for about 1 1/4 hours.

Add peas. Push down so all peas are covered with sauce.

Topping: Melt margarine in small saucepan. Stir in bread crumbs and cheese. Sprinkle over casserole. Return to oven. Bake, uncovered, for 15 minutes until potato and carrot are tender. Serves 6.

1 serving: 375 Calories; 11.5 g Total Fat; 1895 mg Sodium; 26 g Protein; 43 g Carbohydrate; 5 g Dietary Fiber

LAMB STEW

Probably not Irish but delicious just the same.

Boneless leg of lamb, cut into ¾ inch (2 cm) cubes	1½ lbs.	680 g
Medium potatoes, cut into 1 inch (2.5 cm) cubes	4	4
Medium carrots, cut into bite-size pieces	4	4
Coarsely chopped onion	1 cup	250 mL
Cubed yellow turnip (rutabaga)	1½ cups	375 mL
Canned tomatoes, with juice, broken up	14 oz.	398 mL
Salt	1½ tsp.	7 mL
Pepper, generous measure	¼ tsp.	1 mL
Granulated sugar	1 tsp.	5 mL
Ground rosemary	½ tsp.	2 mL
Garlic powder (or 1 clove, minced)	¼ tsp.	1 mL
Minute tapioca	1 tbsp.	15 mL
Water	½ cup	125 mL

Combine first 5 ingredients in small roaster.

Mix remaining 8 ingredients in medium bowl. Pour over top. Cover. Bake in 300°F (150°C) oven for about 2½ to 3 hours. Makes 8 cups (2 L).

1½ cups (375 mL): 310 Calories; 7.2 g Total Fat; 994 mg Sodium; 30 g Protein; 32 g Carbohydrate; 5 g Dietary Fiber

1. Taco Salad, page 135
2. Curried Pork And Mango Sauce, page 76
3. Corn Chowder, page 146
4. Meatless Chili, page 62

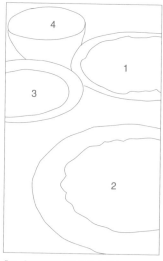

Props Courtesy Of: C C on Whyte, Stokes, The Bay

Surprise! This uses potatoes rather than eggplant. Great flavor.

Medium potatoes, sliced lengthwise $\frac{1}{2}$ **inch (12 mm) thick**	9	9
Water, to cover		
Cooking oil	2 tsp.	10 mL
Lean ground lamb (or beef)	1$\frac{1}{2}$ lbs.	680 g
Chopped onion	1 cup	250 mL
Tomato sauce	2 × 7$\frac{1}{2}$ oz.	2 × 213 mL
Beef bouillon powder	1 tbsp.	15 mL
Granulated sugar	1 tsp.	5 mL
Parsley flakes	1 tsp.	5 mL
Ground marjoram	$\frac{1}{4}$ tsp.	1 mL
Garlic powder	$\frac{1}{4}$ tsp.	1 mL
Salt	1 tsp.	5 mL
Pepper	$\frac{1}{2}$ tsp.	2 mL
Grated Parmesan cheese	$\frac{1}{4}$ cup	60 mL
Grated part-skim mozzarella cheese	1$\frac{1}{2}$ cups	375 mL

Cook potato in water in large pot or Dutch oven until just tender. Potato will cook further in oven. Drain. Cool enough to handle.

Heat cooking oil in large frying pan. Add ground lamb and onion. Scramble-fry until lamb is no longer pink.

Add next 9 ingredients. Stir together. Simmer for 2 minutes. Layer in greased 9 x 13 inch (22 x 33 cm) pan as follows:

1. $\frac{1}{2}$ of potato slices

2. $\frac{1}{2}$ of meat sauce

3. $\frac{1}{2}$ of potato slices

4. $\frac{1}{2}$ of meat sauce

Sprinkle with mozzarella cheese. Bake, uncovered, in 350°F (175°C) oven for about 30 minutes until very hot. Cuts into 8 large pieces, enough to serve 8.

1 serving: 380 Calories; 17.7 g Total Fat; 1121 mg Sodium; 25 g Protein; 30 g Carbohydrate; 3 g Dietary Fiber

QUICK CHICKEN STROGANOFF

Lots of chicken in this creamy dish. Mushrooms are an added bonus.

Lean ground chicken	1 lb.	454 g
Finely chopped onion	1 cup	250 mL
Salt	1 tsp.	5 mL
Pepper	¼ tsp.	1 mL
Garlic powder	¼ tsp.	1 mL
Ground thyme	⅛ tsp.	0.5 mL
Sliced fresh mushrooms	2 cups	500 mL
Soy sauce	2 tbsp.	30 mL
Chicken bouillon powder	1 tbsp.	15 mL
Uncooked medium egg noodles (about 4 oz., 113 g)	2 cups	500 mL
Hot water	3 cups	750 mL
All-purpose flour	3 tbsp.	50 mL
Light sour cream	1 cup	250 mL
Sherry (or alcohol-free sherry)	2 tbsp.	30 mL

Spray large non-stick frying pan with no-stick cooking spray. Add first 6 ingredients. Scramble-fry for about 5 minutes.

Add mushrooms, soy sauce, bouillon powder, noodles and hot water. Make sure noodles are covered. Cover. Boil slowly for about 12 minutes until noodles are cooked.

Combine flour and sour cream in small bowl. Stir together well. Stir into chicken mixture. Stir for 2 to 3 minutes until boiling and thickened.

Stir in sherry. Makes 7 cups (1.75 L).

1½ cups (375 mL): 276 Calories; 6.1 g Total Fat; 1538 mg Sodium; 29 g Protein; 24 g Carbohydrate; 2 g Dietary Fiber

Paré Pointer

The main difference between lightning and electricity is that we have to pay for electricity.

This deep dish pie has a thick rich filling.

Lean ground chicken	1 lb.	454 g
Finely chopped onion	1/4 cup	60 mL
Finely chopped celery	1/4 cup	60 mL
All-purpose flour	2 tbsp.	30 mL
Salt	1/2 tsp.	2 mL
Pepper	1/8 tsp.	0.5 mL
Garlic powder	1/8 tsp.	0.5 mL
Milk	1 1/4 cups	300 mL
Herb-flavored non-fat spreadable cream cheese	1/2 cup	125 mL
Large egg, fork-beaten	1	1
Chopped fresh (or frozen) broccoli, cooked and drained	4 cups	1 L
Grated Edam (or Gouda or Monterey Jack) cheese	1 cup	250 mL
Pastry for 10 inch (25 cm) double crust pie		
Milk (optional)	1 tbsp.	15 mL

Scramble-fry ground chicken, onion and celery in large non-stick frying pan until onion is soft and chicken is no longer pink.

Mix in flour, salt, pepper and garlic powder. Stir in milk until boiling and thickened. Remove from heat.

Stir in cream cheese until melted.

Mix in egg, broccoli and Edam cheese.

Roll out pastry on lightly floured surface. Fit into ungreased 10 inch (25 cm) glass pie plate or 9 inch (22 cm) deep dish pie plate. Add broccoli mixture. Roll out second crust. Moisten edges of bottom crust. Put second crust in place. Trim and crimp around edge. Cut slits in top.

Brush with milk if desired. Bake on bottom rack in 350°F (175°C) oven for 45 to 50 minutes until golden. Cuts into 8 wedges.

1 wedge: 411 Calories; 21.2 g Total Fat; 676 mg Sodium; 25 g Protein; 30 g Carbohydrate; 4 g Dietary Fiber

CHICKEN VERONIQUE

The addition of grapes makes this a French pot pie.

Lean ground chicken	1 lb.	454 g
Chopped onion	²/₃ cup	150 mL
Chopped celery	¹/₂ cup	125 mL
Cooking oil	2 tsp.	10 mL
White (or alcohol-free white) wine	¹/₄ cup	60 mL
Skim evaporated milk	1 cup	250 mL
All-purpose flour	¹/₄ cup	60 mL
Light salad dressing (or mayonnaise)	¹/₄ cup	60 mL
Salt	1 tsp.	5 mL
Granulated sugar	1 tsp.	5 mL
Ground cinnamon (optional)	¹/₁₆ tsp.	0.5 mL
Pepper	¹/₈ tsp.	0.5 mL
Halved seedless green grapes	1 cup	250 mL

LATTICE TOPPING		
Whole wheat flour	²/₃ cup	150 mL
All-purpose flour	²/₃ cup	150 mL
Granulated sugar	2 tsp.	10 mL
Baking powder	2 tsp.	10 mL
Salt	¹/₂ tsp.	2 mL
Milk	¹/₃ cup	75 mL
Hard margarine (or butter), melted	¹/₄ cup	60 mL

Scramble-fry ground chicken, onion and celery in cooking oil in large frying pan until onion is soft and chicken is no longer pink. Stir in wine. Cook for 1 minute.

Gradually whisk evaporated milk into flour in medium bowl until smooth. Add next 5 ingredients. Stir together. Stir into chicken mixture until boiling and thickened. Stir in grapes. Pour into greased 10 inch (25 cm) glass pie plate or shallow 2 quart (2 L) casserole.

Lattice Topping: Combine first 5 ingredients in medium bowl.

Add milk and margarine. Stir to form soft ball. Knead on lightly floured surface about 8 times. Roll to same size as pie plate. Cut ¹/₂ inch (12 mm) wide strips. Make lattice design over chicken mixture. Bake, uncovered, in 450°F (230°C) oven for about 15 minutes until bubbling and browned. Serves 4.

1 serving: 595 Calories; 21 g Total Fat; 1453 mg Sodium; 39 g Protein; 60 g Carbohydrate; 5 g Dietary Fiber

TURKEY VERONIQUE: Substitute ground turkey for ground chicken.

A flavorful and pleasant meal. Parmesan cheese adds great flavor.

Cooking oil	2 tsp.	10 mL
Boneless, skinless chicken breast halves (about 4), cut into thin strips	1 lb.	454 g
Chopped onion	1/2 cup	125 mL
Thinly sliced fresh mushrooms	2 cups	500 mL
Salt, sprinkle		
Pepper, sprinkle		
Spaghetti	8 oz.	225 g
Boiling water	3 qts.	3 L
Cooking oil (optional)	1 tbsp.	15 mL
Salt	2 tsp.	10 mL
Condensed cream of mushroom soup	10 oz.	284 mL
Skim evaporated milk	1 cup	250 mL
Sherry (or alcohol-free sherry)	3 tbsp.	50 mL
Grated Parmesan cheese	1/3 cup	75 mL
Grated nutmeg, just a pinch		
Chicken bouillon powder	2 tsp.	10 mL
TOPPING		
Hard margarine (or butter)	1 tbsp.	15 mL
Dry bread crumbs	1/2 cup	125 mL
Grated Parmesan cheese	1/4 cup	60 mL

Heat first amount of cooking oil in large frying pan. Add chicken, onion and mushrooms. Sauté until chicken is no longer pink. Sprinkle with salt and pepper. Transfer to ungreased 3 quart (3 L) casserole.

Cook pasta in boiling water, second amount of cooking oil and salt in large uncovered pot or Dutch oven for 11 to 13 minutes, stirring occasionally, until tender but firm. Drain. Add pasta to chicken.

Stir next 6 ingredients together in small bowl. Pour over pasta. Poke holes to allow some to reach bottom.

Topping: Melt margarine in small saucepan. Stir in bread crumbs and cheese. Sprinkle over all. Bake, uncovered, in 350°F (175°C) oven for 25 to 30 minutes until hot and golden. Serves 6.

1 serving: 445 Calories; 12.7 g Total Fat; 1014 mg Sodium; 33 g Protein; 47 g Carbohydrate; 2 g Dietary Fiber

CHICKEN FAJITA DINNER

Everyone in the family will like this one. A very child-friendly meal.

Lime juice	2 tbsp.	30 mL
Garlic cloves, minced (or ½ tsp., 2 mL, powder)	2	2
Dried crushed chilies, finely crushed	¼ tsp.	1 mL
Salt	¼ tsp.	1 mL
Pepper, sprinkle		
Boneless, skinless chicken breast halves (about 4), cut into thin strips	1 lb.	454 g
Cooking oil	2 tsp.	10 mL
Small or medium mild red or white onions, sliced and separated into rings	2	2
Medium red pepper, slivered	1	1
Medium green or yellow pepper, slivered	1	1
Frozen kernel corn, thawed	1 cup	250 mL
Medium chunky salsa	1 cup	250 mL
Water	2 tsp.	10 mL
Cornstarch	1 tsp.	5 mL
Corn chips (optional)	8½ oz.	240 g

Put first 5 ingredients into medium bowl. Stir together well. Add chicken strips. Stir. Cover. Marinate in refrigerator for 1 to 2 hours.

Heat cooking oil in large frying pan. Add chicken and marinade. Stir-fry for about 3 minutes.

Add red onion and red and green peppers. Stir together. Cover. Cook, stirring occasionally, for about 4 minutes.

Add corn and salsa. Stir. Cook, uncovered, stirring occasionally, until hot and bubbling.

Mix water and cornstarch in small cup. Stir into boiling mixture until thickened.

Sprinkle with corn chips or stir them in. They will stay crisp for about 15 minutes if stirred in. Makes 6½ cups (1.6 L).

*1½ **cups** (375 mL): 219 Calories; 3.9 g Total Fat; 1128 mg Sodium; 27 g Protein; 23 g Carbohydrate; 3 g Dietary Fiber*

Tender-crisp veggies with slivers of chicken.

Cooking oil	2 tsp.	10 mL
Boneless, skinless chicken breast halves (about 4), cut into slivers	1 lb.	454 g
Garlic clove, minced (or 1/4 tsp., 1 mL, powder)	1	1
Ground ginger	1/4 tsp.	1 mL
Medium onion, halved lengthwise and cut into wedges	1	1
Thinly sliced carrot	1/2 cup	125 mL
Thinly sliced celery	1 cup	250 mL
Small broccoli florets	2 cups	500 mL
Water	1 cup	250 mL
Package Oriental dry noodle soup (original flavor), flavor packet reserved	3 oz.	85 g
Fresh bean sprouts (1 large handful)	1 cup	250 mL
Soy sauce	1/4 cup	60 mL
Cornstarch	2 tsp.	10 mL
Reserved flavor packet		
Steam fried (or chow mein) noodles	1/2 cup	125 mL

Heat cooking oil in large frying pan. Add chicken, garlic and ginger. Stir-fry for about 3 minutes.

Add next 5 ingredients. Break up Oriental noodles and add. Cover. Cook for 2 to 3 minutes until vegetables are tender-crisp and noodles are almost cooked.

Stir in bean sprouts.

Whisk soy sauce, cornstarch and reserved flavor packet together in small bowl. Add to center of vegetable mixture. Stir until boiling and thickened.

Sprinkle with steam fried noodles. Makes 7 cups (1.75 L).

1 1/2 cups (375 mL): 270 Calories; 8.4 g Total Fat; 1391 mg Sodium; 29 g Protein; 21 g Carbohydrate; 3 g Dietary Fiber

SWEET AND SOUR SKILLET

A favorite flavor to be sure!

Soy sauce	2 tsp.	10 mL
Garlic cloves, minced (or ½ tsp., 2 mL, powder)	2	2
Boneless, skinless chicken breast halves (about 4), cut into 1 inch (2.5 cm) pieces	1 lb.	454 g
Cooking oil	2 tsp.	10 mL
Medium onion, cut into 8 wedges	1	1
Sliced celery	1 cup	250 mL
Medium green or red pepper, cut into slivers	1	1
Coarsely shredded cabbage, packed	2 cups	500 mL
Canned tomatoes, with juice, broken up	14 oz.	398 mL
Water	¾ cup	175 mL
White vinegar	3 tbsp.	50 mL
Brown sugar, packed	2 tbsp.	30 mL
Soy sauce	1 tbsp.	15 mL
Uncooked long grain white rice	1 cup	250 mL

Stir first amount of soy sauce and garlic together in medium bowl. Add chicken. Stir well. Cover. Let stand for 15 minutes.

Heat cooking oil in large frying pan. Add chicken. Sauté until slightly browned. Remove to plate.

Put onion, celery, green pepper and cabbage into same frying pan. Cook, stirring occasionally, for 4 to 5 minutes until cabbage is soft.

Add tomatoes with juice, water, vinegar, brown sugar and second amount of soy sauce. Stir together.

Add rice and chicken. Mix. Bring to a boil. Cover. Boil slowly for 20 to 25 minutes, stirring after 15 minutes, until rice is tender. Makes 8 cups (2 L).

1½ cups (375 mL): 306 Calories; 3.4 g Total Fat; 536 mg Sodium; 24 g Protein; 44 g Carbohydrate; 3 g Dietary Fiber

CURRIED PEANUT CHICKEN

Wonderful curry flavor that isn't too strong. Serve with pita bread, yogurt and perhaps a salad.

Boneless, skinless chicken breast halves (about 4), cut into 1 inch (2.5 cm) pieces	1 lb.	454 g
Diced onion	½ cup	125 mL
Curry paste (available in ethnic section of grocery stores)	1 tbsp.	15 mL
Cooking oil	1 tsp.	5 mL
Diced red pepper	½ cup	125 mL
Finely diced carrot	½ cup	125 mL
Dark raisins	¼ cup	60 mL
Condensed chicken broth	10 oz.	284 mL
Water	1 cup	250 mL
Smooth peanut butter	3 tbsp.	50 mL
Dried crushed chilies	⅛ tsp.	0.5 mL
Uncooked long grain white rice	1 cup	250 mL
Green onion, thinly sliced (optional)	1	1
Whole or coarsely chopped salted peanuts	¼ cup	60 mL

Sauté chicken, onion and curry paste in cooking oil in large non-stick frying pan until onion is soft.

Add next 8 ingredients. Stir together. Bring to a boil. Cover. Cook slowly for about 20 minutes, stirring once or twice, until rice is tender and liquid is absorbed.

Sprinkle with green onion and peanuts. Serves 4.

1 serving: 525 Calories; 15.7 g Total Fat; 695 mg Sodium; 39 g Protein; 57 g Carbohydrate; 4 g Dietary Fiber

Paré Pointer

The man who rows the boat generally doesn't have time to rock it.

CHICKEN AND BLACK BEAN STEW

Colorful and very nutritious. Has a slight bite but not overpowering.

Boneless, skinless chicken breast halves (about 4), cut into ¾ inch (2 cm) cubes	1 lb.	454 g
Chopped onion	1½ cups	375 mL
Garlic cloves, minced (or ½ tsp., 2 mL, powder)	2	2
Cooking oil	1 tsp.	5 mL
Canned stewed tomatoes, with juice, chopped	2 × 14 oz.	2 × 398 mL
Diced carrot	1 cup	250 mL
Chopped red or orange pepper	1 cup	250 mL
Frozen kernel corn	1 cup	250 mL
Bay leaves	2	2
Ground cumin	1 tsp.	5 mL
Salt	1 tsp.	5 mL
Ground coriander	¼ tsp.	1 mL
Cayenne pepper	¹⁄₁₆ tsp.	0.5 mL
Canned black beans, drained	19 oz.	540 mL
Canned chopped green chilies, drained	4 oz.	114 mL
Lemon juice	1 tbsp.	15 mL

Sauté chicken, onion and garlic in cooking oil in large frying pan until onion is soft.

Add next 9 ingredients. Stir together. Bring to a boil. Boil gently, uncovered, for about 30 minutes until vegetables are soft.

Stir in beans, green chilies and lemon juice. Cover. Cook slowly for 10 minutes. Discard bay leaves. Makes 6 cups (1.5 L), enough to serve 4.

1 serving: 373 Calories; 4 g Total Fat; 1470 mg Sodium; 37 g Protein; 51 g Carbohydrate; 9 g Dietary Fiber

Pictured on page 107.

Poh-toh-FEUH is French for "Pot on fire." Makes an attractive full platter. A comfort food meal. If you don't have a stockpot, use a roaster on the burner.

Medium onions	2	2
Garlic cloves	3	3
Whole chicken, skin removed	3 lbs.	1.4 kg
Medium carrots, cut in half crosswise	5	5
Medium cabbage, into wedges	1/2	1/2
Medium yellow turnip (rutabaga), cut into six 1/2 inch (12 mm) thick slices	1	1
Celery ribs, cut into 4 inch (10 mm) lengths	2	2
Water	2 cups	500 mL
Couscous (or instant white rice), same amount as drained liquid (about 2 cups, 500 mL)		
Salt	1 tsp.	5 mL
Pepper (optional)	1/8 tsp.	0.5 mL

Place onions and garlic in cavity of chicken. Set chicken in center of stockpot.

Put next 5 ingredients around chicken. Simmer for about 1½ hours until vegetables are tender. Gently remove vegetables around chicken with slotted spoon to large platter. Transfer chicken to platter. Discard onion and cloves. Cover to keep warm. Measure remaining liquid (should be about 2 cups, 500 mL) and pour into medium saucepan.

Add same amount of couscous, salt and pepper to saucepan. Stir together. Bring to a boil. Cover. Remove from heat. Let stand for 5 minutes. Fluff with fork. Add to platter or serving bowl. Serves 6.

1 serving: 445 Calories; 4 g Total Fat; 606 mg Sodium; 35 g Protein; 66 g Carbohydrate; 7 g Dietary Fiber

ROAST CHICKEN DINNER

Chicken surrounded with vegetables.

SAUSAGE STUFFING

Sausage meat	½ lb.	225 g
Chopped onion	½ cup	125 mL
Fine dry bread crumbs	4 cups	1 L
Poultry seasoning	1½ tsp.	7 mL
Salt	¾ tsp.	4 mL
Pepper	¼ tsp.	1 mL
Parsley flakes	1 tsp.	5 mL
Water, approximately	1 cup	250 mL
Chicken bouillon powder	1 tsp.	5 mL
Roasting chicken	5 lbs.	2.3 kg
Medium potatoes, halved	4	4
Medium carrots, cut bite size	6	6
Small zucchini, with peel, cut in half crosswise	3	3
Small yellow turnip, (rutabaga), cut bite size	1	1
Hot water	1 cup	250 mL
Chicken bouillon powder	1 tsp.	5 mL

GRAVY

All-purpose flour	¼ cup	60 mL
Salt	½ tsp.	2 mL
Pepper	¼ tsp.	1 mL
Liquid gravy browner (optional)		

Sausage Stuffing: Scramble-fry sausage meat and onion in large frying pan until browned.

Add next 5 ingredients. Stir together well.

Whisk first amounts of water and bouillon powder together in small bowl. Add more or less water mixture to stuffing until damp enough to form a ball when squeezed.

Spoon stuffing into chicken. Close with skewers. Place in large roaster.

Add potato, carrot, zucchini and turnip.

(continued on next page)

Whisk second amounts of water and bouillon powder together in small bowl. Add to roaster. Cover. Bake in 325°F (160°C) oven for 1½ to 2 hours until chicken is cooked. Thermometer should read 190°F (90°C). Remove cover last few minutes to brown if desired. Strain juice into measuring cup. Skim off any fat. Add water, if needed, to make 2 cups (500 mL). Pour into small bowl.

Gravy: Whisk flour, salt, pepper and gravy browner into reserved juice. Pour into small saucepan. Heat and stir until boiling and thickened. Makes 2 cups (500 mL). Serves 6.

1 serving: 1199 Calories; 55.2 g Total Fat; 1851 mg Sodium; 83 g Protein; 89 g Carbohydrate; 6 g Dietary Fiber

SIMPLE CHICKEN BAKE

A cacciatore-type dish.

Ingredient	Imperial	Metric
Chicken parts, skin removed	3 lbs.	1.4 kg
Cooking oil	1 tsp.	5 mL
Chopped onion	1 cup	250 mL
Penne pasta	8 oz.	225 g
Boiling water	3 qts.	3 L
Cooking oil (optional)	1 tbsp.	15 mL
Salt	2 tsp.	10 mL
Spaghetti sauce	2 cups	500 mL
Canned sliced mushrooms, drained	10 oz.	284 mL
Dried whole oregano	½ tsp.	2 mL
Salt	½ tsp.	2 mL
Pepper	¼ tsp.	1 mL

Cook chicken on both sides in cooking oil in large non-stick frying pan until no longer pink inside. Turn into ungreased 3 quart (3 L) casserole or small roaster.

Add onion to same frying pan. Sauté until soft. Add to chicken.

Cook pasta in boiling water, cooking oil and first amount of salt in large uncovered pot or Dutch oven for 8 to 10 minutes until tender but firm. Drain. Return pasta to pot.

Add remaining 5 ingredients. Stir together well. Pour over chicken. Cover. Bake in 350°F (175°C) oven for about 30 minutes until hot. Serves 4.

1 serving: 591 Calories; 13.4 g Total Fat; 1374 mg Sodium; 47 g Protein; 70 g Carbohydrate; 6 g Dietary Fiber

JAMBALAYA

Very flavorful. A mild spicy taste.

Cooking oil	2 tsp.	10 mL
Skinless chicken thighs	1½ lbs.	680 g
Salt, sprinkle		
Pepper, sprinkle		
Chopped onion	1 cup	250 mL
Garlic cloves, minced (or ½ tsp., 2 mL, powder)	2	2
Medium green pepper, chopped	1	1
Uncooked long grain white rice	1½ cups	375 mL
Diced cooked ham (½ lb., 225 g)	1¼ cups	300 mL
Canned stewed tomatoes, with juice, broken up	14 oz.	398 mL
Water	1½ cups	375 mL
White (or alcohol-free white) wine	¼ cup	60 mL
Chicken bouillon powder	2 tsp.	10 mL
Salt	1 tsp.	5 mL
Ground coriander	½ tsp.	2 mL
Cayenne pepper	⅛ tsp.	0.5 mL
Pepper	¹⁄₁₆ tsp.	0.5 mL
Bay leaf	1	1
Fresh medium shrimp, peeled and deveined	12	12

Heat cooking oil in large non-stick frying pan. Add chicken. Sprinkle with salt and pepper. Sauté for about 5 minutes. Remove to plate.

Combine onion, garlic and green pepper in same frying pan. Sauté until onion is soft.

Add next 11 ingredients. Stir together well. Add chicken. Cover. Simmer for 20 to 25 minutes until rice is tender. Discard bay leaf.

Add shrimp. Stir. Cook for about 5 minutes until shrimp curl and turn pink. Makes 8 cups (2 L).

1½ cups (375 mL): 411 Calories; 7.4 g Total Fat; 1501 mg Sodium; 30 g Protein; 52 g Carbohydrate; 2 g Dietary Fiber

Balsamic vinegar gives the wonderful flavor.

Cooking oil	1 tsp.	5 mL
Chicken parts, skin removed	3 lbs.	1.4 kg
Salt, sprinkle		
Pepper, sprinkle		
Large onion, chopped	1	1
Garlic clove, minced (or 1/4 tsp., 1 mL, powder)	1	1
Medium carrots, sliced into 1/4 inch (6 mm) coins	4	4
Medium red potatoes, cut into eighths	4	4
Water	1/2 cup	125 mL
Parsley flakes	1 tbsp.	15 mL
Dried sweet basil	1 tsp.	5 mL
Chicken bouillon powder	1/2 tsp.	2 mL
Ground thyme	1/16 tsp.	0.5 mL
Small green or red pepper, diced	1	1
Green onions, sliced	2	2
Balsamic vinegar	1/4 cup	60 mL

Heat cooking oil in large non-stick frying pan. Add chicken. Brown both sides well. Sprinkle with salt and pepper. Transfer chicken to plate.

Add onion and garlic to same frying pan. Sauté until soft.

Add next 7 ingredients. Stir. Add chicken. Cover. Simmer for 25 minutes, stirring once or twice. Add more water if needed.

Add green pepper and green onion. Cover. Cook for 5 to 10 minutes until chicken and vegetables are tender.

Add vinegar. Stir. Heat through. Serves 4.

1 serving: 358 Calories; 6.4 g Total Fat; 252 mg Sodium; 40 g Protein; 35 g Carbohydrate; 5 g Dietary Fiber

Pictured on front cover.

ARROZ CON POLLO

Pronounced ah-ROHS con POH-yoh and literally means "rice with chicken." A Spanish and Mexican dish.

Chicken parts, skin removed	3½ lbs.	1.6 kg
Uncooked long grain white rice	1½ cups	375 mL
Finely chopped onion	½ cup	125 mL
Frozen peas, thawed	2 cups	500 mL
Chicken bouillon powder	1 tbsp.	15 mL
Salt	1 tsp.	5 mL
Pepper	¼ tsp.	1 mL
Saffron (or turmeric)	¼ tsp.	1 mL
Jar of chopped pimiento, drained	2 oz.	57 mL
Boiling water	3 cups	750 mL
Canned tomatoes, with juice, broken up	14 oz.	398 mL
Dried sweet basil	½ tsp.	2 mL
Garlic powder	¼ tsp.	1 mL

Arrange chicken in greased 9 x 13 inch (22 x 33 cm) pan. Bake, uncovered, in 350°F (175°C) oven for 30 minutes. Transfer chicken to plate.

Stir remaining 12 ingredients together in same pan. Place chicken over rice mixture. Cover. Return to oven. Bake for 35 to 45 minutes until rice and chicken are tender. Serves 6.

1 serving: 395 Calories; 4.7 g Total Fat; 1050 mg Sodium; 35 g Protein; 51 g Carbohydrate; 4 g Dietary Fiber

1. Tuna Penne Salad, page 123
2. Chicken And Black Bean Stew, page 100
3. Greek Pizza, page 75
4. Whiskey Stew, page 115
5. Pork Stew With Rotini, page 66

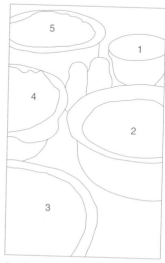

Props Courtesy Of: Dansk Gifts, Le Gnome, Scona Clayworks, Stokes, The Bay

Pronounced pi-AY-yuh. A popular mixture of shrimp, chicken and of course, rice.

Chicken parts, skin removed	3 lbs.	1.4 kg
Cooking oil	1 tbsp.	15 mL
Chopped onion	1 cup	250 mL
Chopped fresh mushrooms	1 cup	250 mL
Medium red or yellow pepper, chopped	1	1
Condensed chicken broth	10 oz.	284 mL
Water	1 cup	250 mL
Uncooked long grain white rice	1⅓ cups	325 mL
Frozen peas, thawed	1 cup	250 mL
Cooked fresh (or frozen, thawed) shrimp	4 oz.	113 g
Paprika, sprinkle		

Brown both sides of chicken in cooking oil in large frying pan. Transfer to greased 3 quart (3 L) casserole.

Add onion, mushrooms and red pepper to same frying pan. Sauté until soft.

Add chicken broth, water and rice. Bring to a boil.

Add peas and shrimp. Stir together. Pour over chicken. Cover. Bake in 350°F (175°C) oven for 30 minutes. Stir.

Sprinkle with paprika. Cover. Bake for 30 minutes until chicken and rice are tender. Serves 4.

1 serving: 567 Calories; 10 g Total Fat; 717 mg Sodium; 53 g Protein; 62 g Carbohydrate; 4 g Dietary Fiber

Paré Pointer

Mother flea was very upset. Her children had gone to the dogs.

CHICKEN AND DUMPLINGS

Old-fashioned to be sure. Just as yummy today as then.

Chicken parts, skin removed	3½ lbs.	1.6 kg
Water	7 cups	1.75 L
Chopped celery leaves and white center ribs	1 cup	250 mL
Medium onion, quartered	1	1
Bay leaf	1	1
Salt	2 tsp.	10 mL
Whole peppercorns	1 tsp.	5 mL
Diced celery	1½ cups	375 mL
Chopped onion	1½ cups	375 mL
Cooking oil	2 tsp.	10 mL
Diced carrot	1½ cups	375 mL
Chopped fresh parsley (or 2 tsp., 10 mL, flakes)	2 tbsp.	30 mL
Frozen peas	1½ cups	375 mL
Skim evaporated milk	1 cup	250 mL
All-purpose flour	¼ cup	60 mL
DUMPLINGS		
All-purpose flour	2 cups	500 mL
Baking powder	4 tsp.	20 mL
Granulated sugar	2 tsp.	10 mL
Salt	1 tsp.	5 mL
Chopped fresh parsley (or 4 tsp., 20 mL, flakes)	¼ cup	60 mL
Hard margarine (or butter)	6 tbsp.	100 mL
Milk	¾ cup	175 mL

Combine first 7 ingredients in large pot or Dutch oven. Cover. Cook for about 1½ hours. Remove chicken with slotted spoon or tongs to medium bowl. Strain broth. Skim off fat. Reserve 4 cups (1 L) broth. Remainder may be frozen for another use. Remove bones from chicken. Coarsely chop chicken.

Sauté second amounts of celery and onion in cooking oil in same pot until soft. Add carrot, parsley and reserved chicken stock. Simmer for 15 minutes until carrot is tender.

Stir in peas and chicken.

Gradually whisk evaporated milk into flour in small bowl. Stir into simmering mixture until boiling and thickened.

(continued on next page)

Dumplings: Measure first 6 ingredients into medium bowl. Cut in margarine until crumbly.

Stir in milk until moistened. Drop 12 to 14 large spoonfuls of dough over bubbling stew. Cover. Simmer for about 20 minutes until dumplings have risen. Wooden pick inserted in center of dumplings should come out clean. Serves 6.

1 serving: 681 Calories; 24.6 g Total Fat; 1781 mg Sodium; 51 g Protein; 61 g Carbohydrate; 6 g Dietary Fiber

RICE AND BROCCOLI CHICKEN

An attractive combination.

Cooking oil	1 tbsp.	15 mL
Chicken parts, skin removed	3 lbs.	1.4 kg
Garlic salt	1/2 tsp.	2 mL
Paprika	1/2 tsp.	2 mL
Pepper, sprinkle		
Medium onion, sliced	1	1
Condensed cream of mushroom soup	10 oz.	284 mL
Water	1²/₃ cups	400 mL
White (or alcohol-free white) wine	1/3 cup	75 mL
Uncooked long grain white rice	1 cup	250 mL
Frozen cut broccoli, thawed	1 lb.	500 g

Heat cooking oil in large frying pan. Add chicken. Sprinkle with garlic salt, paprika and pepper. Brown both sides. Remove to medium bowl.

Add onion to same frying pan. Sauté until soft.

Stir soup vigorously in small bowl. Gradually whisk in water and wine until smooth. Add to onion. Stir together. Bring to a boil.

Add rice. Stir together well. Arrange chicken over top. Cover. Cook slowly for 15 minutes.

Add broccoli around and on top of chicken. Cover. Cook slowly for 20 to 25 minutes, stirring occasionally, to loosen any stuck rice, until chicken is cooked. Serves 4.

1 serving: 543 Calories; 14.8 g Total Fat; 948 mg Sodium; 45 g Protein; 54 g Carbohydrate; 5 g Dietary Fiber

Pictured on page 53.

VEGETABLE CHICKEN

Old-fashioned creamy chicken.

Hard margarine (or butter)	1 tbsp.	15 mL
Chicken parts, skin removed	3 lbs.	1.4 kg
Garlic salt	1/2 tsp.	2 mL
Pepper, sprinkle		
Water	1/2 cup	125 mL
White (or alcohol-free white) wine	1/4 cup	60 mL
Chicken bouillon powder	1 tsp.	5 mL
Medium potatoes, cut bite size	3	3
Parsley flakes	1 tbsp.	15 mL
Salt	1/2 tsp.	2 mL
Ground thyme	1/16 tsp.	0.5 mL
Ground rosemary	1/16 tsp.	0.5 mL
Frozen peas, thawed	10 oz.	284 mL
Green onions, sliced	3	3
All-purpose flour	2 tbsp.	30 mL
Light sour cream	1 cup	250 mL
Granulated sugar	1 tsp.	5 mL

Melt margarine in large frying pan. Add chicken. Brown both sides. Sprinkle with garlic salt and pepper. Turn into large pot or Dutch oven.

Stir next 8 ingredients together in small bowl. Add to chicken. Cover. Simmer for about 25 minutes until potato is tender.

Add peas and green onion. Stir. Cover. Cook for 2 to 3 minutes until peas are cooked. Using slotted spoon, remove vegetables and chicken to serving platter. Cover to keep warm.

Whisk flour and sour cream together in small bowl until smooth. Add to pot. Heat and stir until just boiling and thickened. Drizzle over chicken and vegetables. Serves 4.

1 serving: 414 Calories; 12.4 g Total Fat; 923 mg Sodium; 43 g Protein; 29 g Carbohydrate; 4 g Dietary Fiber

The easiest dumplings going.

Cooking oil	1 tbsp.	15 mL
Boneless, skinless chicken breast halves (about 6), cut bite size	1½ lbs.	680 g
Seasoned salt	1½ tsp.	7 mL
Pepper	⅛-¼ tsp.	0.5-1 mL
Chopped onion	1¼ cups	300 mL
Chopped celery	1¼ cups	300 mL
Diced carrot	2½ cups	625 mL
Condensed chicken broth	10 oz.	284 mL
Water	1¾ cups	425 mL
Chicken bouillon powder	4 tsp.	20 mL
Parsley flakes	1 tbsp.	15 mL
Ground thyme	⅛ tsp.	0.5 mL
Evaporated milk (small can)	⅔ cup	150 mL
All-purpose flour	¼ cup	60 mL
Refrigerator country-style biscuits (10 per tube)	12 oz.	340 g

Heat cooking oil in large frying pan. Add chicken. Sprinkle with seasoned salt and pepper. Stir-fry to brown quickly. Remove to medium bowl.

Add next 8 ingredients to same frying pan. Stir together. Cover. Cook slowly until vegetables are tender.

Gradually whisk milk into flour in small bowl until no lumps remain. Stir into vegetables until boiling and thickened. Add chicken. Stir.

Cut each biscuit into 2 layers. Arrange over top. Cover. Simmer slowly for about 20 minutes until biscuits are cooked. They will be puffy and white. Serves 6.

1 serving: 407 Calories; 8.5 g Total Fat; 1730 mg Sodium; 37 g Protein; 44 g Carbohydrate; 3 g Dietary Fiber

BRUNSWICK STEW

A tasty hearty stew. A good chance to try okra if you never have.

Bacon slices, diced	2	2
Chicken thighs (about 12), skin removed	3½ lbs.	1.6 kg
Garlic salt, sprinkle		
Pepper, sprinkle		
Large onion, coarsely chopped	1	1
Condensed chicken broth	10 oz.	284 mL
Water	1 cup	250 mL
Canned diced tomatoes, with juice	14 oz.	398 mL
Granulated sugar	2 tsp.	10 mL
Dried rosemary, crushed	½ tsp.	2 mL
Thyme leaves	½ tsp.	2 mL
Bay leaf	1	1
Medium potatoes, cut into 1½ inch (3.8 cm) chunks	3	3
Frozen lima beans	2 cups	500 mL
Frozen baby okra, each cut into 2-3 pieces	8 oz.	250 g
Frozen kernel corn	2 cups	500 mL
Medium red pepper, diced	1	1
Worcestershire sauce	2 tsp.	10 mL
Salt	½ tsp.	2 mL

Cook bacon in large frying pan. Remove with slotted spoon to paper towel to drain.

Brown both sides of chicken in bacon fat in same frying pan. Sprinkle with garlic salt and pepper. Transfer to large pot or Dutch oven.

Sauté onion in same frying pan until soft. Add to pot.

Add next 7 ingredients. Stir together. Cover. Simmer for 30 minutes, stirring occasionally.

Add remaining 7 ingredients. Add bacon. Stir. Simmer, uncovered, for 30 to 40 minutes until potato is tender and stew is thickened. Discard bay leaf. Makes 8 cups (2 L) vegetables and 12 pieces of chicken, enough to serve 6.

1 serving: 423 Calories; 11.3 g Total Fat; 885 mg Sodium; 38 g Protein; 44 g Carbohydrate; 7 g Dietary Fiber

Tender chicken with a slight hint of caramel. Wonderful aroma.

All-purpose flour	¼ cup	60 mL
Garlic salt (or salt)	1 tsp.	5 mL
Pepper	⅛ tsp.	0.5 mL
Cayenne pepper, sprinkle		
Chicken parts, skin removed	8	8
Cooking oil	1 tbsp.	15 mL
Cooking oil	1 tsp.	5 mL
Chopped onion	1 cup	250 mL
Chopped celery	1 cup	250 mL
Rye whiskey	3 tbsp.	50 mL
Brown sugar, packed	1 tbsp.	15 mL
Condensed chicken broth	10 oz.	284 mL
Water	1 cup	250 mL
Diced carrot	1½ cups	375 mL
Fresh (or frozen) green beans, cut or frenched	1½ cups	375 mL
Whole new baby potatoes, with skin (or large red potatoes, cut into chunks)	1½ lbs.	680 g
Water	1 tbsp.	15 mL
Cornstarch	1 tbsp.	15 mL

Stir first 4 ingredients together in pie plate or shallow dish.

Dip chicken into flour mixture to coat. Brown both sides in first amount of cooking oil in large frying pan. Transfer to large pot or Dutch oven.

Add second amount of cooking oil to same frying pan. Add onion and celery. Sauté until golden. Add to chicken.

Add next 7 ingredients to pot. Stir together. Cover. Simmer for about 30 minutes until potato and carrot are tender. Drain liquid into small saucepan.

Mix second amount of water and cornstarch in small cup. Stir into liquid. Heat and stir until boiling and thickened. Pour over stew. Serves 4.

1 serving: 541 Calories; 9.6 g Total Fat; 980 mg Sodium; 40 g Protein; 68 g Carbohydrate; 7 g Dietary Fiber

Pictured on page 107.

KEN STRATA

n be made ahead and refrigerated overnight or can be made three hours ahead.

Ground chicken	1½ lbs.	680 g
Finely chopped onion	½ cup	125 mL
Finely chopped green pepper	¼ cup	60 mL
Cooking oil	2 tsp.	10 mL
Salt, sprinkle		
Pepper, sprinkle		
Bread slices, crusts removed	6-8	6-8
Frozen peas, thawed	10 oz.	284 mL
Non-fat process Cheddar cheese slices	6	6
Bread slices, crusts removed	6	6
Large eggs	5	5
Condensed cream of mushroom soup	10 oz.	284 mL
Milk	1¾ cups	425 mL
Poultry seasoning	¼ tsp.	1 mL

Scramble-fry ground chicken, onion and green pepper in cooking oil in large frying pan until no longer pink. Drain. Sprinkle with salt and pepper.

Cover bottom of greased 9 x 13 inch (22 x 33 cm) pan with first amount of bread slices, cutting to fit. Spoon chicken mixture over bread. Scatter peas over top. Lay cheese slices over peas. Cover with second amount of bread slices.

Beat eggs in medium bowl until smooth. Add remaining 3 ingredients. Mix. Pour over all. Cover and chill for 3 hours or overnight. Bake, uncovered, in 350°F (175°C) oven for about 1 hour until knife inserted in center comes out clean. Serves 6.

1 serving: 495 Calories; 13.9 g Total Fat; 1161 mg Sodium; 47 g Protein; 44 g Carbohydrate; 3 g Dietary Fiber

TURKEY STRATA: Use ground turkey instead of ground chicken.

Vegetables in a stuffing crust. Excellent.

Hard margarine (or butter)	2 tbsp.	30 mL
Finely chopped onion	⅔ cup	150 mL
Finely chopped celery	⅔ cup	150 mL
Fine dry bread crumbs	2 cups	500 mL
Parsley flakes	1 tbsp.	15 mL
Ground sage	¼-½ tsp.	1-2 mL
Pepper	¼ tsp.	1 mL
Hot water	¼ cup	60 mL
Milk	¼ cup	60 mL
Condensed chicken broth	10 oz.	284 mL
All-purpose flour	⅓ cup	75 mL
Frozen mixed vegetables	2 cups	500 mL
Celery salt	¼ tsp.	1 mL
Onion powder	⅛ tsp.	0.5 mL
Pepper, sprinkle		
Diced cooked turkey (or chicken)	2 cups	500 mL

Melt margarine in large frying pan. Add onion and celery. Sauté until very soft. Remove from heat.

Stir in next 4 ingredients. Gradually mix in hot water and milk. You should be able to squeeze some in your hand and it will hold its shape. Reserve ½ cup (125 mL) crumb mixture. Press remaining crumb mixture in bottom and up sides of greased 9 inch (22 cm) pie plate.

Gradually whisk chicken broth into flour in small saucepan until smooth. Heat and stir until boiling and thickened.

Add remaining 5 ingredients. Stir. Pour into stuffing crust. Sprinkle with reserved crumb mixture. Bake, uncovered, in 350°F (175°C) oven for 30 minutes until heated through. Let stand for 10 minutes. Cuts into 6 wedges.

1 wedge: 351 Calories; 7.2 g Total Fat; 777 mg Sodium; 26 g Protein; 46 g Carbohydrate; 1 g Dietary Fiber

TURKEY WITH CRANBERRY RICE

Nice combination of flavors.

Cooking oil	2 tsp.	10 mL
Thin turkey cutlets, cut into thin strips	1 lb.	454 g
Diced onion	1 cup	250 mL
Thinly sliced celery	1 cup	250 mL
Water	1½ cups	375 mL
Grated peel and juice of 1 large orange	¾ cup	175 mL
Jalapeño pepper jelly	½ cup	125 mL
Garlic salt	½ tsp.	2 mL
Pepper, sprinkle		
Package long grain and wild rice mix, with seasoning packet	6½ oz.	180 g
Fresh (or frozen) cranberries	1 cup	250 mL
Chopped toasted almonds (or pecans)	2 tbsp.	30 mL
Chopped fresh parsley	2 tbsp.	30 mL

Heat cooking oil in large frying pan. Add turkey strips, onion and celery. Sauté until onion is soft.

Add next 6 ingredients. Stir together. Cover. Simmer for 30 minutes.

Stir in cranberries. Cover. Cook for 5 to 10 minutes until rice is tender. Stir.

Sprinkle with almonds and parsley just before serving. Makes 6 cups (1.5 L).

1½ cups (375 mL): 487 Calories; 7.7 g Total Fat; 1255 mg Sodium; 32 g Protein; 76 g Carbohydrate; 6 g Dietary Fiber

The ocean should be clean—it uses tide morning and night.

TURKEY STROGANOFF

Good texture and flavor. Mushrooms are tasty.

Cooking oil	1 tsp.	5 mL
Ground turkey	1 lb.	454 g
Finely chopped onion	½ cup	125 mL
Sliced fresh mushrooms	1 cup	250 mL
Salt	½ tsp.	2 mL
Pepper	¼ tsp.	1 mL
Condensed cream of chicken soup	10 oz.	284 mL
Condensed beef broth	10 oz.	284 mL
Light sour cream	1 cup	250 mL
Lemon juice	1 tsp.	5 mL
Uncooked broad egg noodles (about 4 cups, 1 L)	8 oz.	225 g
Frozen peas (or green beans)	2 cups	500 mL

Heat cooking oil in large frying pan. Add ground turkey, onion and mushrooms. Scramble-fry until lightly browned. Sprinkle with salt and pepper.

Add soup, beef broth, sour cream and lemon juice. Heat and stir until very hot.

Place noodles and peas in bottom of ungreased 3 quart (3 L) casserole. Gently pour turkey mixture over top. Do not stir. Cover. Bake in 350°F (175°C) oven for 40 to 45 minutes until noodles are tender but firm. Makes 7 cups (1.75 L).

1½ cups (375 mL): 476 Calories; 12.6 g Total Fat; 1366 mg Sodium; 37 g Protein; 53 g Carbohydrate; 5 g Dietary Fiber

CHICKEN STROGANOFF: Substitute ground chicken for ground turkey.

BEEF STROGANOFF: Substitute ground beef for ground turkey.

Paré Pointer

The only way he ever says a mouthful is to talk while he's eating.

CRAB SALAD

Delicious luncheon salad. Prepare ahead and assemble at the last minute.

Cooked fresh (or frozen or imitation) crabmeat, cartilage removed, broken up	2 cups	500 mL
Large hard-boiled eggs, chopped	3	3
Thinly sliced celery	½ cup	125 mL
Chopped pimiento	1 tbsp.	15 mL
Salt, sprinkle		
Pepper, sprinkle		
Chopped lettuce	6 cups	1.5 L
DRESSING		
Light salad dressing (or mayonnaise)	¾ cup	175 mL
Milk	3 tbsp.	50 mL
Granulated sugar	½ tsp.	2 mL
Seasoned salt	½ tsp.	2 mL
Paprika	½ tsp.	2 mL

Combine first 6 ingredients in medium bowl.

Put lettuce into large bowl.

Dressing: Stir salad dressing, milk, sugar, seasoned salt and paprika together in small bowl. Reserve ⅓ of dressing. Pour ⅔ of dressing over lettuce just before serving. Toss together. Divide among 4 plates. Divide crabmeat mixture over lettuce. Drizzle with remaining ⅓ of dressing. Serves 4.

1 serving: 282 Calories; 17.1 g Total Fat; 1370 mg Sodium; 20 g Protein; 11 g Carbohydrate; 1 g Dietary Fiber

There is no harm in taking a stand providing you are facing the right way.

Also contains tuna and shrimp. A new spin on coleslaw.

Small shell pasta	1½ cups	375 mL
Boiling water	2 qts.	2 L
Cooking oil (optional)	2 tsp.	10 mL
Salt	1½ tsp.	7 mL
Grated cabbage, lightly packed	3 cups	750 mL
Grated carrot	½ cup	125 mL
Thinly sliced celery	½ cup	125 mL
Chopped green onion	½ cup	125 mL
Canned solid white tuna, drained and broken up	6½ oz.	184 g

DRESSING

Light salad dressing (or mayonnaise)	½ cup	125 mL
Milk	2 tbsp.	30 mL
White vinegar	1 tsp.	5 mL
Granulated sugar	½ tsp.	2 mL
Onion powder	¼ tsp.	1 mL
Celery salt	⅛ tsp.	0.5 mL
Cooked small fresh (or frozen, thawed) shrimp	¼ lb.	113 g

Cook pasta in boiling water, cooking oil and salt in large uncovered pot or Dutch oven for 8 to 11 minutes, stirring occasionally, until tender but firm. Drain. Rinse with cold water. Drain well. Return pasta to pot.

Add cabbage, carrot, celery, green onion and tuna. Toss together.

Dressing: Measure all 6 ingredients into small bowl. Stir together. Pour over pasta mixture. Toss to coat. Divide among 6 plates or serve in large bowl.

Sprinkle shrimp over top. Serves 6.

1 serving: 223 Calories; 6.6 g Total Fat; 348 mg Sodium; 14 g Protein; 26 g Carbohydrate; 2 g Dietary Fiber

PASTA HAM SALAD

Sweet with a slight tang. The ham adds flavor as well.

Elbow macaroni	2 cups	500 mL
Boiling water	3 qts.	3 L
Cooking oil (optional)	1 tbsp.	15 mL
Salt	2 tsp.	10 mL
Diced cooked ham	2 cups	500 mL
Thinly sliced celery	³⁄₄ cup	175 mL
Grated carrot	¹⁄₃ cup	75 mL
Chopped green onion	¹⁄₃ cup	75 mL
DRESSING		
Light salad dressing (or mayonnaise)	1 cup	250 mL
White vinegar	1 tbsp.	15 mL
Granulated sugar	1 tbsp.	15 mL
Sweet pickle relish	¹⁄₄ cup	60 mL
Shredded lettuce	6 cups	1.5 L

Cook pasta in boiling water, cooking oil and salt in large uncovered pot or Dutch oven for 5 to 7 minutes, stirring occasionally, until tender but firm. Drain. Rinse with cold water. Drain. Turn into large bowl.

Add ham, celery, carrot and green onion. Stir together.

Dressing: Stir all 4 ingredients together in small bowl. Pour over salad. Toss to coat.

Scatter lettuce on 6 plates or on 1 large platter. Divide salad over top. Serves 6.

1 serving: 350 Calories; 13.5 g Total Fat; 1030 mg Sodium; 16 g Protein; 41 g Carbohydrate; 2 g Dietary Fiber

The only way he will keep a check on his waist would be to wear a gingham jacket.

TUNA PENNE SAL

*Pronounced PEH-nay. Salad and dressing complement each oth\
Leftovers keep well in the refrigerator for lunch the next day.*

DRESSING

Cooking oil	¼ cup	60 mL
White vinegar	⅓ cup	75 mL
Granulated sugar	3 tbsp.	50 mL
Dried sweet basil	1½ tsp.	7 mL
Dried whole oregano	½ tsp.	2 mL
Garlic powder	¼ tsp.	1 mL
Salt	½ tsp.	2 mL
Pepper	¼ tsp.	1 mL
Penne pasta	3½ cups	875 mL
Boiling water	3 qts.	3 L
Cooking oil (optional)	1 tbsp.	15 mL
Salt	1 tbsp.	15 mL
Frozen peas	2 cups	500 mL
Water	½ cup	125 mL
Canned solid white tuna, drained and broken up	2 × 6½ oz.	2 × 184 g
Grated cabbage, lightly packed	2 cups	500 mL
Medium tomatoes, diced	2	2
Frozen kernel corn, thawed	½ cup	125 mL
Grated Parmesan cheese (optional)	2 tbsp.	30 mL
Chopped green onion	¼ cup	60 mL

Dressing: Measure first 8 ingredients into small bowl. Stir together well. Let stand for about 30 minutes to blend flavors. Makes ¾ cup (175 mL).

Cook pasta in boiling water, cooking oil and salt in large uncovered pot or Dutch oven for 10 to 12 minutes, stirring occasionally, until tender but firm. Drain. Rinse with cold water. Drain well. Turn into large bowl.

Cook peas in second amount of water in small saucepan for about 3 minutes. Drain. Rinse with cold water. Drain well. Add to pasta.

Add tuna, cabbage, tomato, corn, Parmesan cheese and green onion. Stir lightly. Add dressing. Toss together. Serves 6.

1 serving: 438 Calories; 12.2 g Total Fat; 483 mg Sodium; 23 g Protein; 60 g Carbohydrate; 5 g Dietary Fiber

Pictured on page 107.

TUNA BAKE SALAD

Just the right tang from the salad dressing.

Water	1 cup	250 mL
Skim evaporated milk	13½ oz.	385 mL
Light salad dressing (or mayonnaise)	¾ cup	175 mL
White vinegar	1 tbsp.	15 mL
Worcestershire sauce	1½ tsp.	7 mL
Cayenne pepper	⅛ tsp.	0.5 mL
Salt	1 tsp.	5 mL
Pepper	¼ tsp.	1 mL
Uncooked ditali (or elbow macaroni)	2 cups	500 mL
Finely chopped onion	½ cup	125 mL
Diced celery	¾ cup	175 mL
Grated carrot	½ cup	125 mL
Canned solid white tuna, drained and flaked	6½ oz.	184 g
Hard margarine (or butter)	2 tbsp.	30 mL
Dry bread crumbs	½ cup	125 mL

Whisk first 8 ingredients together in large bowl.

Add next 5 ingredients. Stir. Turn into ungreased 3 quart (3 L) casserole, making sure pasta is covered. Bake, uncovered, in 350°F (175°C) oven for 45 minutes. Stir well.

Melt margarine in small saucepan. Stir in bread crumbs. Sprinkle over top. Return to oven. Bake, uncovered, for 15 minutes until browned and pasta is tender but firm. Makes 7 cups (1.75 L).

1½ cups (375 mL): 517 Calories; 17.6 g Total Fat; 1309 mg Sodium; 23 g Protein; 66 g Carbohydrate; 2 g Dietary Fiber

1. Chicken Caesar Salad, page 131
2. Sandwich Salad, page 132
3. Spicy Beef Salad, page 134
4. Rice And Bean Salad, page 132
5. Chicken Salad Pizza, page 129

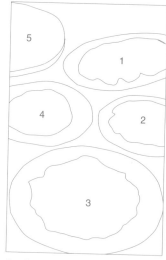

Props Courtesy Of: Eaton's, La Cache, Le Gnome, The Basket House, The Royal Doulton Store, X/S Wares

Makes a light summer lunch or supper.

Hard margarine (or butter)	2 tsp.	10 mL
Boneless, skinless chicken breast halves (about 2), pounded flat	1/2 lb.	225 g
Reserved flavor packet		
Grated cabbage, lightly packed	4 cups	1 L
Package chicken-flavored instant noodles, flavor packet reserved	3 oz.	85 g
Toasted sesame seed	1/4 cup	60 mL
Chopped green onion	1/4 cup	60 mL
Grated carrot	1/2 cup	125 mL
DRESSING		
Water	1/2 cup	125 mL
Cornstarch	1 tbsp.	15 mL
Granulated sugar	2 tbsp.	30 mL
Salt	1 tsp.	5 mL
Pepper	1/4 tsp.	1 mL
White vinegar	3 tbsp.	50 mL
Cooking oil	1 tbsp.	15 mL

Melt margarine in large frying pan. Brown 1 side of chicken in margarine. Turn. Sprinkle with contents of flavor packet. Brown second side until no longer pink. Cut into small cubes. Cool.

Place next 5 ingredients in large bowl. Add chicken.

Dressing: Combine water and cornstarch in small saucepan. Heat and stir until boiling and thickened. Remove from heat.

Add sugar, salt, pepper, vinegar and cooking oil. Stir until sugar is dissolved. Cool thoroughly. Pour over salad. Toss to coat. Chill. Serves 4.

1 serving: 294 Calories; 15 g Total Fat; 1139 mg Sodium; 17 g Protein; 24 g Carbohydrate; 4 g Dietary Fiber

CHICKEN AND RICE SALAD

Makes a very tasty light lunch or supper.

Boneless, skinless chicken breast halves (about 2), pounded flat	½ lb.	225 g
Cooking oil	1 tsp.	5 mL
Salt, sprinkle		
Pepper, sprinkle		
Uncooked long grain white rice	¾ cup	175 mL
Chopped onion	½ cup	125 mL
Chicken bouillon powder	2 tsp.	10 mL
Water	1½ cups	375 mL
Frozen peas	2 cups	500 mL
Water	½ cup	125 mL
Light salad dressing (or mayonnaise)	⅔ cup	150 mL
Milk	3 tbsp.	50 mL
White vinegar	1 tsp.	5 mL
Prepared mustard	½ tsp.	2 mL
Granulated sugar	½ tsp.	2 mL
Jar of chopped pimiento, drained	2 oz.	57 mL
Green onions, chopped	2	2
Small head of iceberg lettuce, cut or torn	1	1

Brown both sides of chicken in cooking oil in large frying pan. Sprinkle with salt and pepper. Cook until no longer pink. Cool. Cut into bite-size pieces.

Combine rice, onion, bouillon powder and first amount of water in medium saucepan. Cover. Simmer for 15 to 20 minutes until rice is tender and water is absorbed. Set saucepan, uncovered, in cold water in sink, stirring often, until cooled.

Cook peas in second amount of water in small saucepan until barely cooked. Drain. Rinse in cold water. Drain well. Put chicken, rice mixture and peas into large bowl.

Stir next 7 ingredients together in small bowl. Add to chicken mixture. Toss to coat.

Divide lettuce among 6 plates. Spoon chicken mixture over each. Serves 6.

1 serving: 287 Calories; 9.1 g Total Fat; 524 mg Sodium; 15 g Protein; 36 g Carbohydrate; 4 g Dietary Fiber

Wonderful fresh flavor. Serve with a knife and fork for easier eating. Assemble shortly before serving to prevent sogginess.

Partially baked commercial (12 inch, 30 cm) pizza crust	1	1
Light salad dressing (or mayonnaise)	½ cup	125 mL
Granulated sugar	½ tsp.	2 mL
Prepared mustard	½ tsp.	2 mL
Diced cooked chicken	1 cup	250 mL
Large hard-boiled eggs, chopped	2	2
Small red onion, thinly sliced (raw or cooked)	1	1
Sweet pickle relish	1 tbsp.	15 mL
Chopped celery	½ cup	125 mL
Salt	¼ tsp.	1 mL
Finely chopped lettuce, lightly packed	1½ cups	375 mL

Place crust on greased 12 inch (30 cm) pizza pan. Bake on bottom rack in 425°F (220°C) oven for 8 to 10 minutes until crisp. Cool.

Stir next 3 ingredients together in small bowl. Spread over crust.

Stir next 6 ingredients together in medium bowl.

Spread lettuce over salad dressing mixture on crust. Spoon dabs of chicken mixture here and there to cover. Cuts into 8 wedges.

1 wedge: 256 Calories; 9.8 g Total Fat; 340 mg Sodium; 11 g Protein; 30 g Carbohydrate; 2 g Dietary Fiber

Pictured on page 125.

Timbuktu can be found between Timbuk-one and Timbuk-three.

CHEF'S SALAD

Variation of an old standby. Yummy two ingredient dressing.

Cut or torn romaine lettuce	3 cups	750 mL
Cut or torn iceberg lettuce	3 cups	750 mL
Julienned cooked turkey (or chicken)	1 cup	250 mL
Chopped green onion	½ cup	125 mL
Julienned cooked beef (or ham)	1 cup	250 mL
Medium green pepper, cut julienne	½	½
Julienned Swiss (or your favorite) cheese	1 cup	250 mL
Pitted ripe (or pimiento-stuffed green) olives (1 or 2 per serving), optional	6-12	6-12
Large hard-boiled eggs, sliced	3	3
Medium tomatoes, diced	2	2
Large fresh mushrooms, sliced	6	6
DRESSING		
Light salad dressing (or mayonnaise)	⅔ cup	150 mL
Chili sauce	2 tbsp.	30 mL

Combine first 7 ingredients in large bowl. Divide among 6 plates.

Arrange olives, egg slices, tomato and mushrooms over each.

Dressing: Mix salad dressing and chili sauce in small cup. Drizzle over salad. Makes ¾ cup (175 mL). Serves 6.

1 serving: 298 Calories; 16.8 g Total Fat; 411 mg Sodium; 25 g Protein; 12 g Carbohydrate; 2 g Dietary Fiber

Pictured on page 71.

Paré Pointer

The pen is still mightier than the sword. No one has invented a ball point sword yet.

CHICKEN CAESAR SALAD

Chicken can be cooked ahead and served cold, or can be warmed before serving. Try the variation.

Large head of romaine lettuce, cut or torn	1	1
Croutons	½ cup	125 mL
Grated Parmesan cheese	2 tbsp.	30 mL
Hard margarine (or butter)	1 tsp.	5 mL
Boneless, skinless chicken breast halves (about 1 lb., 454 g), pounded flat	4	4
Salt, sprinkle		
Pepper, sprinkle		
Commercial light Creamy Caesar dressing	½ cup	125 mL
Granulated sugar (optional)	¼ tsp.	1 mL

Toss lettuce, croutons and cheese together in large bowl.

Melt margarine in large frying pan. Add chicken. Brown both sides. Sprinkle with salt and pepper. Cook until no longer pink.

Mix Caesar dressing and sugar in small cup. Pour over lettuce mixture. Toss together to coat. Divide among 4 plates. Cut each chicken breast into pieces or leave whole. Divide among salads, either over top or along side. Serves 4.

1 serving: 282 Calories; 13.2 g Total Fat; 389 mg Sodium; 31 g Protein; 9 g Carbohydrate; 2 g Dietary Fiber

Pictured on page 125.

Variation: Sprinkle chicken with seasoned salt, no-salt spice mix or lemon pepper.

Paré Pointer

The robot went berserk. They found he had a screw loose.

WICH SALAD

...avor and lots of variety. A sandwich in a bowl.

...ss, skinless chicken breast halves (about 2)	½ lb.	225 g
Cooking oil	1 tsp.	5 mL
Small head of lettuce, cut or torn	1	1
Chopped cooked ham	1 cup	250 mL
Green onions, chopped	2	2
Medium tomatoes, seeded and cut bite size	2	2
Large hard-boiled eggs, cut up	2	2
Cooked peas	1 cup	250 mL
Sliced cucumber (or sliced fresh mushrooms, pea pods, bean sprouts or chopped green or red pepper)	¾ cup	175 mL
Light salad dressing (or mayonnaise)	⅓ cup	75 mL
Chili sauce	1 tbsp.	15 mL

Cook chicken in cooking oil in large frying pan until no longer pink. Cut into bite-size pieces. Place in large bowl.

Add lettuce, ham, green onion, tomato, egg, peas and cucumber.

Stir salad dressing and chili sauce together in small cup. Pour over salad. Toss to coat. Makes 10 cups (2.5 L).

2 cups (500 mL): 233 Calories; 9.9 g Total Fat; 657 mg Sodium; 22 g Protein; 13 g Carbohydrate; 3 g Dietary Fiber

Pictured on page 125.

RICE AND BEAN SALAD

Makes lots of colorful salad.

Long grain white rice	1¼ cups	300 mL
Chopped onion	½ cup	125 mL
Boiling water	2½ cups	625 mL
Frozen kernel corn, thawed	1¼ cups	300 mL
Canned kidney beans, drained	14 oz.	398 mL
Chopped green onion	¼ cup	60 mL
Large tomato, seeded and diced	1	1
Light Italian dressing	1 cup	250 mL
Chili powder	1 tsp.	5 mL

(continued on next page)

Combine rice, onion and boiling water in medium saucepan. Cover. Simmer for about 15 to 20 minutes until rice is tender and water is absorbed. Cool.

Combine corn, beans, green onion and tomato in large bowl. Add rice mixture. Stir together.

Add Italian dressing. Sprinkle with chili powder. Stir well. Makes 9 cups (2.25 L).

1½ cups (375 mL): 258 Calories; 2.2 g Total Fat; 696 mg Sodium; 8 g Protein; 53 g Carbohydrate; 5 g Dietary Fiber

Pictured on page 125.

BEEF SALAD

Fresh tasting, dilly and creamy.

Julienned cooked roast beef	2 cups	500 mL
Chopped peeled cucumber	1 cup	250 mL
Radishes, sliced or diced	6	6
Chopped celery	½ cup	125 mL
Cooked peas	1 cup	250 mL
Cut or torn lettuce, lightly packed	4 cups	1 L
DRESSING		
Fat-free sour cream	1 cup	250 mL
Dill weed	1 tsp.	5 mL
Salt	½ tsp.	2 mL
Milk	1 tbsp.	15 mL
Granulated sugar	½ tsp.	2 mL

Combine first 6 ingredients in large bowl.

Dressing: Combine all 5 ingredients in small bowl. Chill for at least 30 minutes. Pour over salad just before serving. Toss to coat. Serves 4.

1 serving: 195 Calories; 4.3 g Total Fat; 476 mg Sodium; 26 g Protein; 13 g Carbohydrate; 3 g Dietary Fiber

SPICY BEEF SALAD

Apt to remind you of Szechuan beef. Delicious salad.

SUPREME DRESSING

Light salad dressing (or mayonnaise)	½ cup	125 mL
Milk	¼ cup	60 mL
Prepared horseradish	1 tbsp.	15 mL
Chili sauce (or ketchup)	2 tsp.	10 mL
Granulated sugar	1 tsp.	5 mL
Onion powder	¼ tsp.	1 mL

MARINADE

Soy sauce	2 tbsp.	30 mL
Water	2 tbsp.	30 mL
White vinegar	2 tbsp.	30 mL
Brown sugar, packed	3 tbsp.	50 mL
Worcestershire sauce	1 tsp.	5 mL
Dry mustard	½ tsp.	2 mL
Dried crushed chilies	½ tsp.	2 mL
Ground ginger	¼ tsp.	1 mL
Garlic powder	¼ tsp.	1 mL
Pepper	¼ tsp.	1 mL
Beef sirloin steak (partially frozen for easier slicing), cut into thin slices	1 lb.	454 g
Cooking oil	2 tsp.	10 mL
Cut or torn lettuce, lightly packed	5 cups	1.25 L
Chopped fresh mushrooms	1 cup	250 mL
Green onions, chopped	3	3
Thin green, red or orange pepper strips	½ cup	125 mL
Paper-thin red onion slices	⅓ cup	75 mL

Supreme Dressing: Stir all 6 ingredients together in small bowl. Makes ¾ cup (175 mL).

Marinade: Stir all 10 ingredients together in medium bowl.

Add beef to marinade. Stir to coat. Cover. Refrigerate for 2 to 3 hours.

Heat cooking oil in large frying pan. Drain beef well. Add to frying pan. Stir-fry until desired doneness.

(continued on next page)

Combine lettuce, mushrooms, green onion, green pepper strips and red onion in large bowl. Add 1 tbsp. (15 mL) dressing. Toss to coat. Divide among 4 plates. Spoon beef over each. Drizzle with remaining dressing or serve on the side. Serves 4.

1 serving: 323 Calories; 13.9 g Total Fat; 892 mg Sodium; 26 g Protein; 24 g Carbohydrate; 2 g Dietary Fiber

Pictured on page 125.

TACO SALAD

Quick and easy. Most can be prepared ahead to assemble just before serving. An interesting salad. Sour cream makes the perfect garnish.

Cooking oil	2 tsp.	10 mL
Lean ground beef	1 lb.	454 g
Chopped onion	1 cup	250 mL
Envelope taco seasoning mix	1 x 1¼ oz.	1 x 35 g
Canned tomatoes, with juice, broken up	14 oz.	398 mL
Grated light sharp Cheddar cheese	1 cup	250 mL
Cut or torn lettuce	6 cups	1.5 L
Medium tomatoes, diced	2	2
Grated light medium or sharp Cheddar cheese	½ cup	125 mL
Green onions, chopped	2	2
Tortilla chips, broken up	½ cup	125 mL

Heat cooking oil in large frying pan. Add ground beef and onion. Scramble-fry until onion is soft and beef is no longer pink. Drain.

Add taco seasoning mix, tomatoes with juice and first amount of cheese. Heat and stir until cheese is melted. Can prepare ahead to this point. Reheat before serving.

Divide lettuce among 6 plates. Scatter diced tomato over each. Spoon hot beef mixture over top. Sprinkle with second amount of cheese. Scatter green onion and tortilla chips over top. Serve immediately. Serves 6.

1 serving: 304 Calories; 16.5 g Total Fat; 997 mg Sodium; 24 g Protein; 16 g Carbohydrate; 3 g Dietary Fiber

Pictured on page 89.

TERIYAKI BEEF AND RICE SALAD

They're all here—hot, cold, sweet and sour.

Water	3 cups	750 mL
Lemon juice	¼ cup	60 mL
Soy sauce	2 tbsp.	30 mL
Brown sugar, packed	¼ cup	60 mL
Vegetable bouillon powder	2 tsp.	10 mL
Ground ginger	1 tsp.	5 mL
Pepper	¼ tsp.	1 mL
Garlic cloves, minced (or ½ tsp., 2 mL, powder)	2	2
Uncooked converted long grain white rice	1⅔ cups	400 mL
Sliced fresh mushrooms	2 cups	500 mL
Broccoli florets and thinly sliced stems	3 cups	750 mL
Cooked leftover (or deli) roast beef, cut into thin strips (about ½ lb., 225 g)	2 cups	500 mL
Cherry tomatoes, halved	12	12
Shredded lettuce	6 cups	1.5 L
Green onions, sliced	2	2

Measure first 10 ingredients into large saucepan. Stir together. Cover. Cook for about 15 minutes.

Stir in broccoli. Cover. Cook for 5 to 10 minutes until rice and broccoli are tender.

Stir in beef and tomato. Heat through.

Serve over lettuce. Sprinkle with green onion. Serves 6.

1 serving: 346 Calories; 2.9 g Total Fat; 599 mg Sodium; 18 g Protein; 62 g Carbohydrate; 4 g Dietary Fiber

Paré Pointer

To know how many feet are in a yard you have to find out how many people are standing in it.

Making this attractive soup is time-consuming but worth it. The tiny meatballs look really nice in the soup.

Canned tomatoes, with juice, broken up	14 oz.	398 mL
Chopped celery	½ cup	125 mL
Chopped onion	1¼ cups	300 mL
Medium potato, peeled and diced	1	1
Beef bouillon powder	2 tbsp.	30 mL
Water	6 cups	1.5 L
Garlic powder	¼ tsp.	1 mL
Parsley flakes	1 tsp.	5 mL
Salt	½ tsp.	2 mL
Granulated sugar	½ tsp.	2 mL
Dried sweet basil	½ tsp.	2 mL
Pepper	⅛ tsp.	0.5 mL
MEATBALLS		
Dry bread crumbs	¼ cup	60 mL
Salt	¼ tsp.	1 mL
Pepper	⅛ tsp.	0.5 mL
Seasoned salt	¼ tsp.	1 mL
Lean ground beef	½ lb.	225 g

Combine first 12 ingredients in large pot or Dutch oven. Stir together. Bring to a boil. Simmer, uncovered, for 30 minutes.

Meatballs: Mix bread crumbs, salt, pepper and seasoned salt in medium bowl. Add ground beef. Mix well. Shape into ½ inch (12 mm) balls. Arrange on greased baking sheet. Bake in 375°F (190°C) oven for 5 to 7 minutes. Add to pot. Simmer for 15 minutes. Makes 10½ cups (2.6 L).

2 cups (500 mL): 176 Calories; 7.4 g Total Fat; 1342 mg Sodium; 11 g Protein; 17 g Carbohydrate; 2 g Dietary Fiber

Paré Pointer

The toughest part of dieting is watching what your friends eat.

CHICKEN NOODLE SOUP

Flavorful with lots of noodles.

Cooking oil	2 tsp.	10 mL
Boneless, skinless chicken breast halves (about 3), pounded flat and cut bite size	¾ lb.	340 g
Cooking oil	2 tsp.	10 mL
Chopped onion	1½ cups	375 mL
Chopped celery	½ cup	125 mL
Thinly sliced carrot	1½ cups	375 mL
Salt	½ tsp.	2 mL
Pepper	¼ tsp.	1 mL
Ground thyme	⅛ tsp.	0.5 mL
Chicken bouillon powder	2 tbsp.	30 mL
Bay leaf	1	1
Parsley flakes	1 tsp.	5 mL
Water	6 cups	1.5 L
Uncooked broad egg noodles	3 cups	750 mL

Heat first amount of cooking oil in large frying pan. Add chicken. Brown and cook until no longer pink. Remove to large saucepan or pot.

Heat second amount of cooking oil in same frying pan. Add onion, celery and carrot. Stir-fry until tender-crisp. Add to saucepan.

Add remaining 8 ingredients. Bring to a boil. Boil gently for 8 to 9 minutes until pasta is tender but firm. Discard bay leaf. Makes 7½ cups (1.8 L).

2 cups (500 mL): 268 Calories; 7.7 g Total Fat; 1498 mg Sodium; 26 g Protein; 24 g Carbohydrate; 3 g Dietary Fiber

SPLIT PEA SOUP

Try this different version containing hot Italian sausage and potato.

Water	8 cups	2 L
Dried green split peas	2 cups	500 mL
Hot Italian sausages	½ lb.	225 g
Diced potato	1½ cups	375 mL
Diced or sliced carrot	1 cup	250 mL
Chopped onion	1 cup	250 mL
Chopped celery	½ cup	125 mL

(continued on next page)

Measure water and split peas into large pot or Dutch oven. Bring to a boil. Simmer, uncovered, stirring occasionally, for 1 hour.

Cook sausages in medium frying pan until well browned. Drain. Slice each sausage lengthwise into quarters. Cut into ¼ inch (6 mm) pieces. Add sausage pieces to pea mixture.

Add potato, carrot, onion and celery. Stir. Simmer, uncovered, stirring occasionally, for 40 minutes. Makes about 10 cups (2.5 L).

2 cups (500 mL): 426 Calories; 6.6 g Total Fat; 231 mg Sodium; 27 g Protein; 67 g Carbohydrate; 13 g Dietary Fiber

BEEF AND BARLEY SOUP

A meaty and filling soup.

Beef stew meat, trimmed of fat, diced into ¼ inch (6 mm) pieces	¾ lb.	340 g
Pearl (or pot) barley	⅓ cup	75 mL
Canned tomatoes, with juice, broken up	14 oz.	398 mL
Liquid gravy browner	1 tsp.	5 mL
Water	7 cups	1.75 L
Finely shredded cabbage	1 cup	250 mL
Thinly sliced carrot	½ cup	125 mL
Thinly sliced celery	½ cup	125 mL
Chopped onion	1 cup	250 mL
Diced yellow turnip (rutabaga)	½ cup	125 mL
Beef bouillon powder	1 tbsp.	15 mL
Salt	½ tsp.	2 mL
Pepper	¼ tsp.	1 mL
Parsley flakes	½ tsp.	2 mL
Dried sweet basil	½ tsp.	2 mL

Combine beef, barley, tomatoes with juice, gravy browner and water in large pot or Dutch oven. Simmer, uncovered, for 1 hour. Skim off foam as needed.

Add remaining 10 ingredients. Stir. Simmer, uncovered, stirring occasionally, for about 40 minutes. Makes 6½ cups (1.6 L).

2 cups (500 mL): 254 Calories; 4.3 g Total Fat; 1299 mg Sodium; 22 g Protein; 33 g Carbohydrate; 7 g Dietary Fiber

Pictured on page 143.

BLACK BEAN SOUP

Mild and so healthy. A sticks-to-the ribs soup.

Dried black beans	2 cups	500 mL
Water	12 cups	3 L
Chopped onion	2 cups	500 mL
Medium carrots, diced	2	2
Chopped celery	⅔ cup	150 mL
Lean ground beef	½ lb.	225 g
Chopped cooked ham	1¼ cups	300 mL
Garlic powder	¼ tsp.	1 mL
Brown sugar, packed	1 tbsp.	15 mL
Salt	1½ tsp.	7 mL
Pepper	¼ tsp.	1 mL
Dried sweet basil	1 tsp.	5 mL
Sherry (or alcohol-free sherry)	½ cup	125 mL
Chopped green onion	¼ cup	60 mL
Large hard-boiled eggs, grated	2	2
Freshly ground pepper, sprinkle		

Put beans into large pot or Dutch oven. Add water. Bring to a boil. Cover. Boil gently, stirring occasionally, for about 1¼ hours. Beans should be almost tender.

Add onion, carrot and celery. Cover. Boil gently for 30 minutes until tender.

Scramble-fry ground beef in medium non-stick frying pan until no longer pink. Drain. Add to beans.

Add next 6 ingredients. Stir. Run through blender to purée. Return to pot.

Add sherry. Stir. Heat through.

Sprinkle each serving with green onion and egg. Sprinkle pepper over top. Makes 14 cups (3.5 L).

2 cups (500 mL): 206 Calories; 5.7 g Total Fat; 1066 mg Sodium; 17 g Protein; 19 g Carbohydrate; 3 g Dietary Fiber

Pictured on page 143.

Pictured on page 143.

A good substantial soup. Easy to make for a rainy day meal—or any day.

Cooking oil	1 tbsp.	15 mL
Lean ground beef	1 lb.	454 g
Chopped onion	1½ cups	375 mL
Chopped celery	1½ cups	375 mL
Grated carrot	¾ cup	175 mL
Canned kidney beans, with liquid	14 oz.	398 mL
Canned tomatoes, with juice, broken up	14 oz.	398 mL
Water	4 cups	1 L
Beef bouillon powder	4 tsp.	20 mL
Salt	1 tsp.	5 mL
Pepper	¼ tsp.	1 mL
Garlic powder	¼ tsp.	1 mL
Dried whole oregano	½ tsp.	2 mL
Dried sweet basil	½ tsp.	2 mL
Coarsely grated cabbage	3 cups	750 mL
Uncooked tiny shell pasta	¾ cup	175 mL
Grated Parmesan cheese, sprinkle		

Heat cooking oil in large frying pan. Add ground beef, onion, celery and carrot. Sauté until beef is no longer pink. Drain. Turn into large pot or Dutch oven.

Add next 9 ingredients. Stir together. Heat until boiling.

Add cabbage and pasta. Boil slowly, uncovered, stirring occasionally, for 20 minutes.

Serve with a sprinkle of cheese. Makes 12 cups (3 L).

2 cups (500 mL): 274 Calories; 8.3 g Total Fat; 1117 mg Sodium; 21 g Protein; 30 g Carbohydrate; 6 g Dietary Fiber

Pictured on page 53.

Paré Pointer

To make a sandcastle in a hurry, use quick sand.

HAM AND BEAN SOUP

A wonderful warm, comforting soup.

Dried navy beans	2 cups	500 mL
Lean meaty ham bone (or 2 smoked pork hocks)	1	1
Water	11 cups	2.75 L
Diced carrot	1 cup	250 mL
Chopped onion	1¼ cups	300 mL
Chopped celery	½ cup	125 mL
Salt	1½ tsp.	7 mL
Pepper	¼ tsp.	1 mL

Combine beans and ham bone in water in large pot or Dutch oven. Simmer, covered, for 1 hour until beans are almost tender. Remove ham bone. Skim off fat. Dice ham and return to pot.

Add remaining 5 ingredients. Stir together. Simmer for about 20 minutes until vegetables are tender. Makes 11 cups (2.75 L).

2 cups (500 mL): 316 Calories; 2.2 g Total Fat; 1118 mg Sodium; 24 g Protein; 52 g Carbohydrate; 8 g Dietary Fiber

Variation: Omit ham bone or pork hocks. Add 1 cup (250 mL) chopped cooked ham after beans have been cooked for 1 hour.

1. Chicken Rice Soup, page 145
2. Bouillabaisse, page 148
3. Spicy Fish Stewp, page 60
4. Beef And Barley Soup, page 139
5. Black Bean Soup, page 140

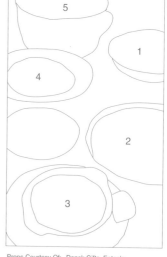

Props Courtesy Of: Dansk Gifts, Eaton's,
Handworks Gallery, Le Gnome,
Scona Clayworks, X/S Wares

At last, chicken soup with lots of chicken.

Boneless, skinless chicken breast halves (about 2)	½ lb.	225 g
Whole chicken legs (drumstick and thigh each), skin removed	2	2
Small bay leaf	1	1
Vegetable bouillon powder	1 tbsp.	15 mL
Water	6 cups	1.5 L
Chopped celery	1 cup	250 mL
Medium carrot, diced	1	1
Chopped onion	1½ cups	375 mL
Canned tomatoes, with juice, broken up	2 × 14 oz.	2 × 398 mL
Salt	½ tsp.	2 mL
Pepper, sprinkle		
Uncooked long grain white rice	½ cup	125 mL
Parsley flakes	1 tsp.	5 mL

Combine chicken, bay leaf and bouillon powder in water in large pot or Dutch oven. Bring to a boil. Skim off foam. Cook, uncovered, for about 30 minutes until chicken is tender. Remove chicken. Discard bones and bay leaf. Cut chicken into bite-size pieces. Return to pot.

Add next 6 ingredients. Cook, uncovered, for 20 minutes.

Add rice and parsley. Cook for 15 to 20 minutes until rice is tender. Makes 8½ cups (2.1 L).

2 cups (500 mL): 295 Calories; 4 g Total Fat; 1171 mg Sodium; 29 g Protein; 35 g Carbohydrate; 4 g Dietary Fiber

Pictured on page 143.

Paré Pointer

Their teacher is a regular bird. He watches them like a hawk.

CORN CHOWDER

Serve this for rave reviews.

Diced potato	3 cups	750 mL
Chopped celery	1 cup	250 mL
Grated carrot	1 cup	250 mL
Chopped onion	1 cup	250 mL
Water	1 cup	250 mL
Diced bacon	1 cup	250 mL
Milk	2¼ cups	560 mL
All-purpose flour	¼ cup	60 mL
Skim evaporated milk	13½ oz.	385 mL
Salt	1 tsp.	5 mL
Pepper	½ tsp.	2 mL
Canned cream-style corn	14 oz.	398 mL

Cook potato, celery, carrot and onion slowly in water in large pot or Dutch oven until tender. Add a bit more water, if necessary, to keep from burning. Remove to large bowl.

Cook bacon in medium frying pan until crispy. Drain. Add to cooked vegetables.

Gradually whisk both milks together into flour, salt and pepper in small bowl. Add to pot. Heat and stir until boiling and thickened.

Add corn and vegetable mixture. Stir. Heat through. Makes 10 cups (2.5 L).

2 cups (500 mL): 419 Calories; 12 g Total Fat; 1303 mg Sodium; 21 g Protein; 59 g Carbohydrate; 4 g Dietary Fiber

Pictured on page 89.

There is no better or more blessed bondage than to be a prisoner of hope.

This has a mild curry flavor. If you're into the real thing you will want to double the curry powder.

Boneless, skinless chicken breast halves (about 2)	½ lb.	225 g
Dried yellow split peas	⅓ cup	75 mL
Boiling water	8 cups	2 L
Hard margarine (or butter)	2 tbsp.	30 mL
Chopped onion	1½ cups	375 mL
Large cooking apple, peeled and diced (McIntosh is good)	1	1
Curry powder	1 tbsp.	15 mL
All-purpose flour	¼ cup	60 mL
Salt	½ tsp.	2 mL
Pepper	⅛ tsp.	0.5 mL
Diced carrot	⅔ cup	150 mL
Diced celery	⅔ cup	150 mL
Ground mace	⅛ tsp.	0.5 mL
Ground cloves	⅛ tsp.	0.5 mL
Canned tomatoes, with juice, broken up	14 oz.	398 mL
Skim evaporated milk	1 cup	250 mL
Cooked long grain white rice (optional), allow ¼ cup (60 mL) per bowl		

Combine chicken and split peas in boiling water in large pot or Dutch oven. Cover. Boil gently for about 10 minutes until chicken is tender. Skim off foam. Remove chicken to plate. Dice. Return to pot.

Melt margarine in large frying pan. Add onion, apple and curry powder. Sauté for about 5 minutes until onion is soft.

Mix in flour, salt and pepper. Stir into chicken mixture.

Add carrot, celery, mace, cloves and tomatoes with juice. Simmer, uncovered, for 30 to 40 minutes until carrot is tender.

Stir in evaporated milk. Heat through.

Scoop ¼ cup (60 mL) of rice into each soup bowl. Fill with soup. Makes 9 cups (2.25 L).

2 cups (500 mL): 301 Calories; 6.9 g Total Fat; 638 mg Sodium; 23 g Protein; 38 g Carbohydrate; 6 g Dietary Fiber

BOUILLABAISSE

Pronounced BOOL-yuh-BAYZ. Very well-known fish and seafood soup.

Olive (or cooking) oil	2 tsp.	10 mL
Garlic cloves, minced (or ½ tsp., 2 mL, powder)	2	2
Finely diced onion	½ cup	125 mL
Chopped celery, with leaves	1 cup	250 mL
Water	1 cup	250 mL
White (or alcohol-free white) wine	½ cup	125 mL
Canned stewed tomatoes, with juice, blended	14 oz.	398 mL
Medium green or yellow pepper, diced	1	1
Sweet potatoes, diced	12 oz.	341 mL
Granulated sugar	1 tsp.	5 mL
Salt	½ tsp.	2 mL
Dried sweet basil	1 tsp.	5 mL
Thyme leaves	½ tsp.	2 mL
Dried crushed chilies, finely crushed	⅛ tsp.	0.5 mL
Hot pepper sauce, just a dash		
Skim evaporated milk	1 cup	250 mL
All-purpose flour	1 tbsp.	15 mL
Seafood (or chicken) bouillon powder	2 tsp.	10 mL
Fresh (or frozen, partially thawed) cod fillets, cut into 1½ inch (3.8 cm) squares	1 lb.	454 g
Uncooked fresh (or frozen, thawed) medium shrimp, peeled and deveined	4 oz.	113 g
Frozen tiny (bay) scallops	4 oz.	113 g
Chopped fresh parsley, for garnish	2 tbsp.	30 mL

Heat olive oil in large pot or Dutch oven. Add garlic, onion and celery. Sauté until onion is soft.

Stir in next 11 ingredients. Bring to a boil. Cover. Simmer for 30 minutes until vegetables are tender.

Gradually whisk evaporated milk into flour and bouillon powder in small bowl. Stir into simmering mixture until boiling and thickened.

(continued on next page)

Add fish, shrimp and scallops. Cover. Cook gently for 6 to 10 minutes until fish flakes, shrimp curl and turn pink and scallops are opaque.

Garnish with parsley. Makes 9 cups (2.25 L).

2 cups (500 mL): 309 Calories; 3.9 g Total Fat; 1037 mg Sodium; 33 g Protein; 32 g Carbohydrate; 4 g Dietary Fiber

Pictured on page 143.

TUNA CORN CHOWDER

Depending on what you serve with this, you may want to double the recipe.

Bacon slices, diced	4	4
Chopped onion	1 cup	250 mL
Chopped green pepper	1/4 cup	60 mL
Medium carrot, diced	1	1
Medium potato, diced	1	1
Frozen kernel corn	1 cup	250 mL
All-purpose flour	1/4 cup	60 mL
Chicken bouillon powder	1 tsp.	5 mL
Salt	1/4 tsp.	1 mL
Pepper	1/4 tsp.	1 mL
Parsley flakes	1/2 tsp.	2 mL
Milk	5 cups	1.25 L
Instant potato flakes	1/4-1/2 cup	60-125 mL
Canned solid white tuna, drained and flaked	6 1/2 oz.	184 g

Put first 6 ingredients into large frying pan. Sauté until bacon is crispy. Cover most of the time so vegetables cook.

Mix in flour, bouillon powder, salt, pepper and parsley.

Stir in milk until boiling and thickened. Add potato flakes. Stir together until thickened.

Add tuna. Stir together. Heat through. Makes 6 cups (1.5 L).

2 cups (500 mL): 588 Calories; 24.1 g Total Fat; 1085 mg Sodium; 35 g Protein; 60 g Carbohydrate; 4 g Dietary Fiber

CREAMY FISH CHOWDER

Creamy with mild garlic flavor. A delicious hearty soup.

Hard margarine (or butter)	2 tsp.	10 mL
Finely chopped onion	½ cup	125 mL
Water	3 cups	750 mL
Seafood (or vegetable) bouillon powder	3 tbsp.	50 mL
Diced celery	1½ cups	375 mL
Small carrots, thinly sliced	1½ cups	375 mL
Medium potatoes, diced	2	2
Pepper	¼ tsp.	1 mL
Thyme leaves	¼ tsp.	1 mL
Bay leaves	2	2
Fresh (or frozen, thawed) cod fillets, cut into 1½ inch (3.8 cm) squares	1 lb.	454 g
Skim evaporated milk	⅔ cup	150 mL
All-purpose flour	¼ cup	60 mL
Chopped fresh parsley, for garnish		

Melt margarine in large pot or Dutch oven. Add onion. Sauté until soft.

Add next 8 ingredients. Stir together. Bring to a boil. Simmer, uncovered, for about 15 minutes until potato is tender. Discard bay leaves.

Gently stir in fish. Cover. Cook for about 5 minutes until fish flakes.

Gradually whisk evaporated milk into flour in small bowl until smooth. Stir slowly into chowder until boiling and thickened.

Sprinkle with parsley. Makes 8 cups (2 L).

2 cups (500 mL): 274 Calories; 3.8 g Total Fat; 1534 mg Sodium; 28 g Protein; 32 g Carbohydrate; 3 g Dietary Fiber

Paré Pointer

Turkeys don't eat much because they're always stuffed.

MEASUREMENT TABLES

Throughout this book measurements are given in Conventional and Metric measure. To compensate for differences between the two measurements due to rounding, a full metric measure is not always used. The cup used is the standard 8 fluid ounce. Temperature is given in degrees Fahrenheit and Celsius. Baking pan measurements are in inches and centimetres as well as quarts and litres. An exact metric conversion is given below as well as the working equivalent (Standard Measure).

OVEN TEMPERATURES

Fahrenheit (°F)	Celsius (°C)
175°	80°
200°	95°
225°	110°
250°	120°
275°	140°
300°	150°
325°	160°
350°	175°
375°	190°
400°	205°
425°	220°
450°	230°
475°	240°
500°	260°

SPOONS

Conventional Measure	Metric Exact Conversion Millilitre (mL)	Metric Standard Measure Millilitre (mL)
1/8 teaspoon (tsp.)	0.6 mL	0.5 mL
1/4 teaspoon (tsp.)	1.2 mL	1 mL
1/2 teaspoon (tsp.)	2.4 mL	2 mL
1 teaspoon (tsp.)	4.7 mL	5 mL
2 teaspoons (tsp.)	9.4 mL	10 mL
1 tablespoon (tbsp.)	14.2 mL	15 mL

CUPS

1/4 cup (4 tbsp.)	56.8 mL	60 mL
1/3 cup (5 1/3 tbsp.)	75.6 mL	75 mL
1/2 cup (8 tbsp.)	113.7 mL	125 mL
2/3 cup (10 2/3 tbsp.)	151.2 mL	150 mL
3/4 cup (12 tbsp.)	170.5 mL	175 mL
1 cup (16 tbsp.)	227.3 mL	250 mL
4 1/2 cups	1022.9 mL	1000 mL (1 L)

PANS

Conventional Inches	Metric Centimetres
8x8 inch	20x20 cm
9x9 inch	22x22 cm
9x13 inch	22x33 cm
10x15 inch	25x38 cm
11x17 inch	28x43 cm
8x2 inch round	20x5 cm
9x2 inch round	22x5 cm
10x4 1/2 inch tube	25x11 cm
8x4x3 inch loaf	20x10x7.5 cm
9x5x3 inch loaf	22x12.5x7.5 cm

DRY MEASUREMENTS

Conventional Measure Ounces (oz.)	Metric Exact Conversion Grams (g)	Metric Standard Measure Grams (g)
1 oz.	28.3 g	28 g
2 oz.	56.7 g	57 g
3 oz.	85.0 g	85 g
4 oz.	113.4 g	125 g
5 oz.	141.7 g	140 g
6 oz.	170.1 g	170 g
7 oz.	198.4 g	200 g
8 oz.	226.8 g	250 g
16 oz.	453.6 g	500 g
32 oz.	907.2 g	1000 g (1 kg)

CASSEROLES (Canada & Britain)

Standard Size Casserole	Exact Metric Measure
1 qt. (5 cups)	1.13 L
1 1/2 qts. (7 1/2 cups)	1.69 L
2 qts. (10 cups)	2.25 L
2 1/2 qts. (12 1/2 cups)	2.81 L
3 qts. (15 cups)	3.38 L
4 qts. (20 cups)	4.5 L
5 qts. (25 cups)	5.63 L

CASSEROLES (United States)

Standard Size Casserole	Exact Metric Measure
1 qt. (4 cups)	900 mL
1 1/2 qts. (6 cups)	1.35 L
2 qts. (8 cups)	1.8 L
2 1/2 qts. (10 cups)	2.25 L
3 qts. (12 cups)	2.7 L
4 qts. (16 cups)	3.6 L
5 qts. (20 cups)	4.5 L

INDEX

RECIPE NOTES

RECIPE NOTES

Company's Coming®

Everyday **recipes** trusted by **millions**

LIGHT CASSEROLES

Jean Paré

LIGHT CASSEROLES

by
Jean Paré

companyscoming.com
visit our ↑ web-site

Dedication

The light side of comfort food.

Cover Photo

1. A Meal In One, page 109
2. Chicken In Wine, page 69
3. Salmon Rolls, page 85

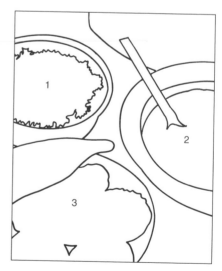

Props Courtesy Of: Chintz & Company, Le Gnome,
Scona Clayworks, The Bay

Want to talk recipes?

Our on-line **question and answer bulletin board** connects you with cooks from around the world.

Visit us at **companyscoming.com**

table of Contents

Foreword

Cooking an all-in-one dish has always been a convenient and popular way to prepare a meal. In Light Casseroles, you will find new and familiar recipes that are trimmed of calories, cholesterol, sodium and fat. Although this is not a diet or medical reference book, the recipes do contain alternative ingredients for healthy, tasty meals. When planning your daily menus, select ingredients from all food groups to ensure balanced nutrition. Choose from the many low-fat and sodium-reduced ingredients found on grocery shelves.

All recipes may be frozen before or after cooking. Allow up to twice as long if cooking from the frozen state, and be sure to use freezer-to-oven cookware.

A teflon-lined frying pan coated with no-stick cooking spray is ideal for browning meats or sautéing vegetables. You will be amazed how tasty the recipes can be!

Chicken Linguini Bake is sure to please everyone at your table. Teener's Dish has always been a hit with the

younger crowd. Try Tuna Divan for family or company as an easy, economical and delicious dish.

Once again, company's coming for casseroles — Light Casseroles.

Jean Paré

Healthy eating and cooking are essential to a healthy lifestyle. The casserole recipes in this cookbook are lower in fat and offer many ideas for simple, one-dish meals. Many of the recipes can be complemented with a green salad, a roll and perhaps a glass of milk. Canned soups and vegetables are quick and handy, not necessarily unhealthy as long as they are used in moderation. The nutrition guide providing the contents of calories, cholesterol, sodium and fat for each portion or serving can help you keep things in perspective.

E ach recipe has been analyzed using the most up-to-date version of the Canadian Nutrient File from Health Canada, which is based on the United States Department of Agriculture (USDA) Nutrient Data Base. If more that one ingredient is listed (such as "hard margarine or butter"), then the first ingredient is used in the analysis. Where an ingredient reads "sprinkle," "optional," or "for garnish," it is not included as part of the nutrition information.

Margaret Ng, B.Sc. (Hon), M.A.
Registered Dietitian

Calorie: A unit measure of energy which is required for healthy living. To determine the number of Calories needed to maintain the current weight of an average person, multiply the weight in pounds by 15.

Formula	Weight	x	15 Calories	=	Average Requirement of Calories per Day
Example	140 lbs.	x	15	=	2,100

Cholesterol: Only found in animal, fish and shellfish sources of food, not in plant foods. Guidelines for cholesterol intake generally suggest 300 mg or less per day. Cholesterol count per serving is given in each recipe to make you aware of your intake.

Egg Substitute: To use the frozen egg products on the market rather than eggs, allow one quarter cup of egg product to one large egg.

Fat: The recommended total fat intake of all foods eaten in one day should not be more than 30% of total calories, 20% is better. Be sure to include everything you eat in a day when calculating the total calories from fat. To determine the maximum fat grams for your total daily intake, the following chart will help. Remember, 1 gram of fat gives approximately 9 Calories.

Total Daily Calorie Intake	Percentage of Total Daily Calories From Fat in Grams	
	20%	**30%**
1200	26 grams	40 grams
1500	33 grams	50 grams
1800	40 grams	60 grams
2100	46 grams	70 grams
2400	53 grams	80 grams
2700	60 grams	90 grams
3000	66 grams	100 grams

Formula	Total Daily Calories	x	Percent	Divide By 9	=	Total Grams Of Fat Per Day
Example	2100	x	30%	÷ 9	=	70 g of fat

Fresh Versus Canned: Fresh food is always the wisest choice but not always the most convenient. Use canned ingredients in moderation for tasty results.

Labels: Do not be confused with % MF (milk fat) or % BF (butter fat) as seen on labels of dairy products. This percentage refers to weight of fat in the product not percentage of fat calories. For example, a cheese with 31% MF (or BF) may have 75% of its calories resulting from the fat content. Choose skim or 1% milk and low-fat dairy products.

New Products: There are new products showing up on grocery-store shelves everyday. Watch for alternatives which help you reduce your fat and sodium intake. Learn how to read manufacturer's labels so you can make wise nutritional choices.

Pepper: A pepper grinder is a great utensil. Fresh pepper will perk up any food which is on the bland side without jeopardizing the nutritional value.

Salt and Sodium: It is recommended to limit the intake of sodium to between 2000 and 3000 mg per day. Sodium is abundant in packaged and processed foods. Salt consists of 40% sodium. A teaspoon (5 mL) of salt has approximately 2000 mg of sodium. Sodium is also found in a variety of foods including dairy products, meat, poultry and vegetables. If conscientious about your sodium intake, watch for sodium-reduced versions of packaged foods, omit salt or use a salt alternative.

Salt Alternatives: Use sodium-free herbs and spices to enhance flavors of foods. For fish, try a sprinkle of basil, dill, curry or tarragon. For fruit, try allspice, cinnamon, ginger or nutmeg. For meat or poultry, cook with bay leaf, chili powder, curry, garlic, oregano, basil, thyme, hot pepper sauce, cayenne pepper or wine. For salads and vegetables, try freshly ground pepper, basil, celery seed, chives, dill, garlic, oregano, tarragon, thyme or fresh lemon juice.

Servings: As a guide to determine servings of meat, a rule of thumb is to use 4 oz. (113 g) of boneless fresh meat per person, which equals 3 oz. (84 g) of cooked meat. This is approximately the size of a deck of playing cards. A kitchen scale is a big asset.

Soup: Canned soups are wonderful convenience foods for using in preparation of many recipes. If you are on a sodium restricted diet, substitute traditional canned soups with the lower-sodium soups. There are also fat reduced soups available. Ask your grocer.

Sweetener: A liquid sugar substitute has been used for testing some of the recipes in this book. Sugar may be used if you prefer. However, to create the same degree of sweetness you will need to use about 4 times more sugar than the substitute. Total calories will also increase. One teaspoon (5 mL) of sugar has 15 Calories.

GREEN PEPPER STEAK

The tomato and green pepper adds color to this tasty dish.

Lean boneless round steak, cut into thin strips	1½ lbs.	680 g
Condensed onion soup	10 oz.	284 mL
Canned tomatoes	14 oz.	398 mL
Thinly sliced onion	½ cup	125mL
Large green pepper, seeded, cut in thin strips	1	1
Sliced fresh mushrooms	2 cups	500 mL
Light soy sauce (40% less salt)	1 tbsp.	15 mL
Pepper	⅛ tsp.	0.5 mL

Spray frying pan with no-stick cooking spray. Add steak strips. Sauté until browned. Turn into 2 quart (2 L) casserole.

Stir remaining ingredients together in bowl. Pour over meat. Stir. Cover. Bake in 350°F (175°C) oven for 1½ to 2 hours until very tender. Makes 5 cups (1.13 L).

Pictured on page 71.

NUTRITION GUIDE	1 cup (225 mL) contains:	
	Energy	221 Calories (924 kJ)
	Cholesterol	63 mg
	Sodium	808 mg
	Fat	6 g

BURGER SPROUT SPECIAL

Let the good times roll. This will be ready for the finale.

Lean ground beef	1 lb.	454 g
Chopped onion	2 cups	500 mL
Sliced celery	1 cup	250 mL
Long grain rice, uncooked	½ cup	125 mL
Fresh bean sprouts, packed	2 cups	500 mL
Condensed cream of mushroom soup	2 × 10 oz.	2 × 284 mL
Water	1½ cups	375 mL
Light soy sauce (40% less salt)	3 tbsp.	50 mL
Pepper	¼ tsp.	1 mL

(continued on next page)

Spray frying pan with no-stick cooking spray. Add ground beef. Scramble-fry to brown. Transfer to 3 quart (3 L) casserole.

Add next 4 ingredients. Stir.

Combine remaining 4 ingredients in bowl. Stir until smooth. Pour over top. Stir lightly. Cover. Bake in 350°F (175°C) oven for 1¼ hours. Stir. Bake, uncovered, for 15 minutes more until rice is cooked. Makes 7⅓ cups (1.65 L).

NUTRITION GUIDE	1 cup (225 mL) contains:	
	Energy	251 Calories (1051 kJ)
	Cholesterol	33 mg
	Sodium	967 mg
	Fat	11.5 g

RUSTIC MEATLOAF

A mixture of beef and turkey makes up this good loaf. Good choice.

Lean ground beef	¾ lb.	375 g
Ground skinless turkey breast	¾ lb.	375 g
Finely chopped onion	¾ cup	175 mL
Dry bread crumbs	⅓ cup	75 mL
Water	⅓ cup	75 mL
Ketchup, page 99	⅓ cup	75 mL
Large egg, beaten	1	1
Light soy sauce (40% less salt)	2 tbsp.	30 mL
Beef bouillon powder (35% less salt)	1 tsp.	5 mL
Pepper	¼ tsp.	1 mL
Garlic powder	¼ tsp.	1 mL
Gravy browner	¼ tsp.	1 mL

Mix first 11 ingredients in large bowl. Shape into loaf about 8 x 4 inches (20 x 10 cm). Place on foil lined baking sheet. Bake, uncovered, in 350°F (175°C) oven for about 1 hour.

Using damp brush, dip in gravy browner and brush over loaf before serving. Makes 8 servings.

NUTRITION GUIDE	1 serving contains:	
	Energy	170 Calories (710 kJ)
	Cholesterol	81 mg
	Sodium	347 mg
	Fat	5 g

BAKED CHOP SUEY

The no-fuss way to do this dish.

Boneless sirloin steak, fat removed, cut in short thin strips	**1 lb.**	**454 g**
Chopped onion	**1 cup**	**250 mL**
Chopped celery	**1 cup**	**250 mL**
Fresh bean sprouts, packed	**2 cups**	**500 mL**
Sliced fresh mushrooms	**2 cups**	**500 mL**
Condensed cream of mushroom soup	**10 oz.**	**284 mL**
Grated low-fat sharp Cheddar cheese (less than 21% MF)	**½ cup**	**125 mL**
Chow mein noodles	**⅓ cup**	**75 mL**
Red pepper rings, for garnish		

Spray frying pan with no-stick cooking spray. Add steak strips. Sauté until browned.

Stir in next 5 ingredients. Turn into 2 quart (2 L) casserole. It will be quite full but will cook down. Cover. Bake in 350°F (175°C) oven for 60 minutes or until meat is tender.

Sprinkle with cheese and noodles. Arrange pepper rings down center. Bake, uncovered, about 15 minutes more. Makes 5 servings.

Pictured on page 35.

NUTRITION GUIDE	1 serving contains:	
	Energy	259 Calories (1083 kJ)
	Cholesterol	50 mg
	Sodium	648 mg
	Fat	11.5 g

Did you hear about the glass blower who inhaled? He had a pane in his stomach.

Add a green salad and you're ready.

Lean round steak	1 lb.	454 g
Salt, sprinkle (optional)		
Pepper, sprinkle		
Paprika, sprinkle		
Sliced onion	1 cup	250 mL
Frozen cut green beans	2 cups	500 mL
Peeled, sliced potato	3 cups	750 mL
Canned tomatoes, mashed	1 cup	250 mL
Ketchup, page 99	1 tbsp.	15 mL
Salt	½ tsp.	2 mL
Granulated sugar	½ tsp.	2 mL

Spray frying pan with no-stick cooking spray. Add steak. Brown both sides well. Sprinkle with salt, pepper and paprika. Cut into 4 pieces. Place in 3 quart (3 L) casserole.

Add onion layer, then beans and potato.

Place next 4 ingredients in frying pan. Stir to loosen brown bits. Pour into casserole. Cover. Bake in 350°F (175°C) oven for 1¾ to 2 hours until meat is tender. Add a bit of water if it dries. Makes 4 servings.

NUTRITION GUIDE	1 serving contains:	
	Energy	276 Calories (1155 kJ)
	Cholesterol	53 mg
	Sodium	519 mg
	Fat	4.7 g

Television has opened many doors, mostly refrigerator.

CROWD PLEASING CHILI

So simple to increase to feed large numbers. Chili powder may be increased to suit your taste.

Lean ground beef	**1 lb.**	**454 g**
Chopped onion	**1¼ cups**	**275 mL**
Chopped celery	**1¼ cups**	**275 mL**
Chopped green pepper	**1 cup**	**250 mL**
Diced fresh tomatoes (see Note)	**2½ cups**	**575 mL**
Condensed tomato soup	**10 oz.**	**284 mL**
Kidney beans with juice	**14 oz.**	**398 mL**
Chili powder	**1 tsp.**	**5 mL**
Prepared mustard	**1 tsp.**	**5 mL**
Pepper	**¼ tsp.**	**1 mL**
Granulated sugar	**1 tsp.**	**5 mL**

Spray large Dutch oven with no-stick cooking spray. Add ground beef. Brown, stirring often to break up.

Add remaining ingredients. Stir. Bring to a boil. Simmer, covered, for about 30 minutes to cook vegetables and to blend flavors. Makes 6⅔ cups (1.5 L).

Pictured on page 71.

NUTRITION GUIDE	1 cup (225 mL) contains:	
	Energy	224 Calories (936 kJ)
	Cholesterol	35 mg
	Sodium	604 mg
	Fat	7 g

Note: One 14 oz. (398 mL) can of tomatoes can be substituted for fresh tomatoes, but sodium content will be higher.

Pare Pointer

The son told his dad he was quitting his studies to drive big machinery. His dad said he wouldn't stand in his way.

QUICK TAMALE CASSEROLE

Get the tamale flavor the easy way.

Lean ground beef	1 lb.	454 g
Chopped onion	1 cup	250 mL
Canned tomatoes	14 oz.	398 mL
Yellow cornmeal	½ cup	125 mL
Kernel corn, fresh or frozen	1½ cups	325 mL
Chili powder	1 tsp.	5 mL
Salt	½ tsp.	2 mL
Pepper	¼ tsp.	1 mL

Spray frying pan with no-stick cooking spray. Add ground beef and onion. Sauté until onions are soft and no pink remains in meat. Remove from heat.

Combine tomatoes and cornmeal in saucepan. Bring to a boil and simmer for 5 minutes, stirring occasionally.

Add remaining ingredients along with meat mixture. Stir. Turn into 2 quart (2 L) casserole. Bake, uncovered, in 350°F (175°C) oven for about 30 minutes. Makes 6 servings.

Pictured on page 53.

NUTRITION GUIDE	1 serving contains:	
	Energy	223 Calories (934 kJ)
	Cholesterol	39 mg
	Sodium	376 mg
	Fat	7 g

Steady. Try not to lose your grip. Especially when you are catching a train.

STEWED BEEF CHUNKS

Tender beef in a rich brown gravy.

Lean beef stew meat	**2 lbs.**	**900 g**
Onion flakes	**3 tbsp.**	**50 mL**
Beef bouillon powder (35% less salt)	**1 tbsp.**	**15 mL**
Condensed golden mushroom soup	**10 oz.**	**284 mL**
Sherry (or alcohol-free sherry)	**½ cup**	**125 mL**

Lay meat in small roaster.

In small bowl, stir onion flakes, bouillon powder, soup and sherry together well. Pour over meat. Cover. Bake in 325°F (160°C) oven for 2½ to 3 hours until tender. Makes 8 servings.

NUTRITION GUIDE	**1 serving contains:**	
	Energy	140 Calories (585 kJ)
	Cholesterol	46 mg
	Sodium	436 mg
	Fat	4.4 g

1. Bannock Biscuits Modern, page 100
2. Potato Biscuits, page 102
3. Oriental Tuna Casserole, page 83
4. Wiener Pasta Bake, page 124
5. Ham Rolls, page 129

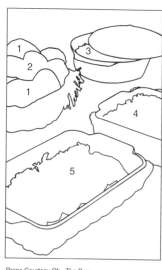

Props Courtesy Of: The Bay

Pasta is added raw to this casserole. A real time saver in prep

Lean ground beef	1 lb.	454 g
Chopped onion	1 cup	250 mL
Green pepper, seeded and slivered	1	1
Frozen kernel corn	1½ cups	375 mL
Salt	¾ tsp.	4 mL
Pepper	¼ tsp.	1 mL
Dry colored fusilli (or other pasta)	2⅔ cups	600 mL
Tomato juice	2¾ cups	675 mL
Grated low-fat sharp Cheddar cheese (less than 21% MF)	1 cup	250 mL

Spray frying pan with no-stick cooking spray. Add ground beef, onion and green pepper. Sauté until no pink remains in beef and onion is soft.

Add corn, salt and pepper. Stir.

Layer ½ dry fusilli in 3 quart (3 L) casserole followed by ½ beef mixture, second ½ fusilli and second ½ beef.

Pour tomato juice over all. Cover. Bake in 350°F (175°C) oven for 50 to 60 minutes until noodles are tender.

Sprinkle with cheese. Bake, uncovered, for 5 minutes more. Makes 6⅔ cups (1.5 L).

Pictured on page 125.

NUTRITION GUIDE	1 cup (225 mL) contains:	
	Energy	351 Calories (1468 kJ)
	Cholesterol	46 mg
	Sodium	820 mg
	Fat	9.5 g

PORCUPINES

Carrot and green pepper sticks make this a colorful casserole.

Lean ground beef	1 lb.	454 g
Long grain rice, uncooked	½ cup	125 mL
Finely chopped onion	¼ cup	50 mL
Salt	½ tsp.	2 mL
Pepper	¼ tsp.	1 mL
Sliced onion	1 cup	250 mL
Green pepper, seeded, cut in strips	½	½
Strips of carrot	½ cup	125 mL
Tomato juice	3 cups	750 mL

Put first 5 ingredients in bowl. Mix. Shape into 25 balls. Arrange in 9 x 9 inch (22 x 22 cm) pan, or 3 quart (3 L) casserole, in single layer.

Lay onion slices, green pepper strips and carrot strips among meatballs.

Pour tomato juice over top. Cover. Bake in 350°F (175°C) oven for about 1 hour until rice is cooked. Makes 25 meatballs.

Pictured on page 143.

NUTRITION GUIDE	1 meatball contains:	
	Energy	49 Calories (206 kJ)
	Cholesterol	9 mg
	Sodium	172 mg
	Fat	1.5 g

Experience enables you to recognize a mistake when you make it again.

BEEF CABBAGE

Similar to an extra-meaty lazy cabbage roll casserole.

Small head of cabbage, coarsely grated	1½ lbs.	68_ g
Dry elbow macaroni	½ cup	125 mL
Lean ground beef	1 lb.	454 g
Chopped onion	1 cup	250 mL
Salt	½ tsp.	2 mL
Pepper	¼ tsp.	1 mL
Condensed tomato soup	10 oz.	284 mL
Water	1 cup	250 mL

Layer ½ cabbage in 2 quart (2 L) casserole. Spread macaroni over top.

Spray frying pan with no-stick cooking spray. Add ground beef, onion, salt and pepper. Scramble-fry until brown and onion is soft. Layer over macaroni. Add second layer of cabbage over top.

Stir soup and water together in small bowl. Pour over all. Do not stir. Cover. Bake in 350°F (175°C) oven for 1 to 1½ hours until cabbage and macaroni are tender. Makes 6 servings.

N U T R I T I O N G U I D E	**1 serving contains:**	
	Energy	229 Calories (959 kJ)
	Cholesterol	39 mg
	Sodium	635 mg
	Fat	7.6 g

When the grape got stepped on it didn't cry out. It just let out a wine.

BEEFY CHEESE BAKE ━━━━━━

With low-fat yogurt and cream cheese, you're way ahead on fat savings with this good casserole.

Dry tiny shells (or other pasta)	2 cups	500 mL
Boiling water	3 qts.	3 L
Lean ground beef	1 lb.	454 g
Canned tomatoes, mashed	14 oz.	398 mL
Salt	½ tsp.	2 mL
Garlic powder (or 2 cloves minced)	¼ tsp.	1 mL
Granulated sugar	½ tsp.	2 mL
Low-fat plain yogurt (less than 1% MF)	1 cup	250 mL
All-purpose flour	2 tbsp.	30 mL
Low-fat cream cheese (less than 20% MF), softened	4 oz.	125 g
Green onions, sliced	6	6
Grated low-fat sharp Cheddar cheese (less than 21% MF)	½ cup	125 mL

Cook shells in boiling water in large uncovered pot about 8 to 11 minutes, until tender but firm. Drain. Pour into 3 quart (3 L) casserole.

Scramble-fry ground beef in frying pan that has been sprayed with no-stick cooking spray, until no pink remains in meat.

Add tomatoes, salt, garlic powder and sugar. Stir. Pour over pasta shells.

Stir yogurt and flour together well in bowl. Add cream cheese. Mash together. Stir in onion. Spoon over meat layer.

Bake, uncovered, in 350°F (175°C) oven for 25 minutes. Sprinkle with cheese. Continue to bake for about 5 minutes more. Makes 7¾ cups (1.74 L).

NUTRITION GUIDE	1 cup (225 mL) contains:	
	Energy	275 Calories (1149 kJ)
	Cholesterol	46 mg
	Sodium	469 mg
	Fat	8 g

SWEET AND SOUR MEATBALLS

Sugar-free grape jelly is used to make this good sauce. Make meatballs smaller to use as an appetizer.

MEATBALLS

Dry bread crumbs	½ cup	125 mL
All-purpose flour	2 tbsp.	30 mL
Salt	½ tsp.	2 mL
Pepper	¼ tsp.	1 mL
Garlic powder	¼ tsp.	1 mL
Parsley flakes	½ tsp.	2 mL
Water	½ cup	125 mL
Finely chopped onion	⅓ cup	75 mL
Lean ground beef	1 lb.	454 g

SWEET AND SOUR SAUCE

Boiling water	1 cup	250 mL
Low-calorie grape jelly	½ cup	125 mL
Ketchup, page 99	¼ cup	60 mL
Cornstarch	2 tbsp.	30 mL
Water	2 tbsp.	30 mL

Meatballs: Combine first 8 ingredients in bowl. Stir well.

Add ground beef. Mix. Shape into 30 balls. Arrange on baking sheet with sides. Cook in 375°F (190°C) oven for 15 to 20 minutes.

Sweet And Sour Sauce: Stir boiling water and jelly together in saucepan. Add ketchup. Stir. Bring to a boil stirring occasionally.

Mix cornstarch and second amount of water together in small cup. Stir into boiling liquid until it boils and thickens. Pour over meatballs. Cover. Bake in 350°F (175°C) oven for 20 minutes or until hot. Makes 30 meatballs with 1¼ cups (275 mL) sauce.

NUTRITION GUIDE	1 meatball with 2 tsp. (10 mL) sauce contains:	
	Energy	42 Calories (175 kJ)
	Cholesterol	8 mg
	Sodium	80 mg
	Fat	1.4 g

MOCK RAVIOLI

A simple way to make ravioli. The pasta layers are sandwiched with a dark vegetable-meat filling. Just spicy enough.

Frozen chopped spinach	2 × 10 oz.	2 × 284 g
Sliced fresh mushrooms	2 cups	500 mL
Canned tomatoes, mashed	28 oz.	796 mL
Chopped onion	3 cups	750 mL
Parsley flakes	1 tsp.	5 mL
Ground rosemary	1 tsp.	5 mL
Thyme	1 tsp.	5 mL
Oregano	1 tsp.	5 mL
Granulated sugar	1 tsp.	5 mL
Lean ground beef	1 lb.	454 g
Salt	½ tsp.	2 mL
Pepper	¼ tsp.	1 mL
Garlic powder	¼ tsp.	1 mL
Lasagne noodles	9	9
Boiling water	4 qts.	4 L
Grated low-fat sharp Cheddar cheese (less than 21% MF)	1 cup	250 mL

Combine first 9 ingredients in large saucepan. Bring to a boil. Simmer about 30 minutes, stirring occasionally.

Spray frying pan with no-stick cooking spray. Add ground beef. Brown well, breaking up chunks. Add salt, pepper and garlic powder. Stir into spinach mixture.

In large uncovered Dutch oven, cook noodles in boiling water until tender but firm, about 14 to 16 minutes. Drain. Rinse with cold water. Drain. Line bottom of 9 x 13 inch (22 x 33 cm) pan with 3 long noodles. Spread ⅓ meat mixture over top. Repeat twice. Bake, uncovered, in 350°F (175°C) oven for about 20 minutes until hot.

Sprinkle with cheese. Bake for 5 minutes more. Cuts into 12 pieces.

NUTRITION GUIDE

1 piece contains:

Energy	194 Calories (814 kJ)
Cholesterol	25 mg
Sodium	344 mg
Fat	6 g

POT ROAST

Once this is in the oven, your mind will be at ease. One-pot cooking at its best.

Beef roast, fat removed, cheaper cut	3 lbs.	1.36 kg
Water	1 cup	250 mL
Medium potatoes, peeled and quartered	6	6
Medium carrots, halved	12	12
Medium onions, quartered	4	4
Celery ribs, quartered	6	6

Place beef in roaster. Add water. Cover. Bake in 300°F (150°C) oven for 2½ hours.

Pile all 4 vegetables around meat. Cover. Continue to bake for about 1¼ hours or until vegetables are tender. Remove vegetables and keep warm while you make gravy if desired. Makes 12 servings.

NUTRITION GUIDE

1 serving contains:

Energy	251 Calories (1051 kJ)
Cholesterol	45 mg
Sodium	124 mg
Fat	4 g

GRAVY

Juice left in roaster plus water to make	2 cups	500 mL
All-purpose flour	¼ cup	60 mL
Water	¼ cup	60 mL
Beef bouillon powder (35% less salt)	2 tsp.	10 mL
Pepper	⅛ tsp.	0.5 mL
Gravy browning sauce, if needed		

Gravy: Juice may be left in roaster or poured into smaller saucepan. Bring to a boil.

Mix flour with second amount of water until no lumps remain. Stir into boiling liquid, along with remaining ingredients, until it boils and thickens. Add more water to thin if desired. Makes 2 cups (450 mL).

NUTRITION GUIDE

2 tbsp. (30 mL) contains:

Energy	9 Calories (37 kJ)
Cholesterol	trace
Sodium	39 mg
Fat	trace

BEANS AND MEATBALL DISH

A great team. Meatballs are covered with beans followed by a tasty sauce. Dark and delicious.

Large egg	1	1
Skim milk	½ cup	125 mL
Regular or quick rolled oats (not instant)	½ cup	125 mL
Salt	½ tsp.	2 mL
Pepper	¼ tsp	1 mL
Lean ground beef	1 lb.	454 g
Canned beans in tomato sauce	14 oz.	398 mL
Chopped onions	1 cup	250 mL
Water		
Ketchup, page 99	½ cup	125 mL
White vinegar	2 tbsp.	30 mL
Worcestershire sauce	1 tbsp.	15 mL
Liquid sweetener (or 2 tbsp., 30 mL, brown sugar)	1½ tsp.	7 mL

Beat egg in bowl. Add milk, rolled oats, salt and pepper. Stir.

Mix in ground beef. Shape into 20 meatballs. Arrange on baking sheet with sides. Bake in 375°F (190°C) oven for 20 minutes. Turn into 3 quart (3 L) casserole in single layer.

Spoon beans over meatballs.

Cook onion in some water until tender. Drain.

Add remaining ingredients to onion. Stir. Pour over beans. Bake, uncovered, in 350°F (175°F) oven for 20 to 30 minutes until hot and bubbly. Makes 8 servings.

NUTRITION GUIDE	1 serving contains:	
	Energy	205 Calories (858 kJ)
	Cholesterol	60 mg
	Sodium	587 mg
	Fat	6.3 g

TOMATO NOODLE CASSEROLE

Layers of noodles and meat with melted cheese on top. Family size without the richer fat content of regular cheese.

Dry fettuccine	8 oz.	250 g
Boiling water	3 qts.	3 L
Chopped onion	1 cup	250 mL
Lean ground beef	1 lb.	454 g
Canned tomatoes, mashed	2 × 14 oz.	2 × 398 mL
Oregano	2 tsp.	10 mL
Granulated sugar	1 tsp.	5 mL
Salt	1 tsp.	5 mL
Grated part-skim mozzarella cheese (35% less fat)	2 cups	500 mL

Cook fettuccine in boiling water in large uncovered saucepan about 9 to 11 minutes until tender but firm. Drain. Pour into 3 quart (3 L) casserole.

Spray frying pan with no-stick cooking spray. Add onion and ground beef. Scramble-fry until brown and onion is soft.

Add tomatoes, oregano, sugar, and salt. Stir. Pour over fettuccine. Bake, uncovered, in 350°F (175°C) oven for 30 minutes.

Sprinkle cheese over top. Bake for 5 to 10 minutes more until cheese melts. Makes 8½ cups (1.91 L).

NUTRITION GUIDE	1 cup (225 mL) contains:	
	Energy	294 Calories (1230 kJ)
	Cholesterol	44 mg
	Sodium	631 mg
	Fat	9.7 g

PATTIES IN GRAVY

This has lots of gravy to serve over rice or mashed potatoes.

PATTIES

Dry bread crumbs	**²/₃ cup**	**150 mL**
All-purpose flour	**2 tbsp.**	**30 mL**
Allspice	**1 tsp.**	**5 mL**
Pepper	**¼ tsp.**	**1 mL**
Skim milk	**½ cup**	**125 mL**
Lean ground beef	**1 lb.**	**454 g**

GRAVY

Condensed tomato soup	**10 oz.**	**284 mL**
Beef bouillon powder (35% less salt)	**2 tsp.**	**10 mL**
Onion flakes	**2 tbsp.**	**30 mL**
Water	**1¼ cups**	**275 mL**

Patties: Combine first 4 ingredients in bowl. Stir.

Mix in milk, then ground beef. Shape into 8 patties. Brown both sides under broiler. Turn into 2 quart (2 L) casserole.

Gravy: Stir all 4 ingredients together. Pour over patties. Cover. Bake in 350°F (175°C) oven for about 1 hour. Makes 8 patties and 1²/₃ cups (375 mL) gravy.

N U T R I T I O N G U I D E	**1 patty plus 3¹/₃ tbsp. (50 mL) gravy contains:**
	Energy 166 Calories (695 kJ)
	Cholesterol 30 mg
	Sodium 428 mg
	Fat 5.8 g

A doctor tries hard to keep his temper. He doesn't want to lose patients.

SWISS STEAK IN GRAVY

Carrots and celery add color as does the gravy. An economical way to serve steak.

Lean boneless round steak, fat removed, cut in 8 pieces	2 lbs.	900 g
All-purpose flour	¼ cup	60 mL
Water	1½ cups	375 mL
Canned tomatoes	14 oz.	398 mL
Chopped onion	1 cup	250 mL
Sliced celery	¾ cup	175 mL
Sliced carrots	¾ cup	175 mL
Salt	1 tsp.	5 mL
Pepper	¼ tsp.	1 mL

Spray frying pan with no-stick cooking spray. Add steak. Brown both sides. Transfer to small roaster or 3 quart (3 L) casserole.

Place flour in small bowl. Add water gradually, mixing until no lumps remain. Pour into frying pan. Stir, loosening brown bits, until it boils and thickens.

Add remaining ingredients. Stir. Pour over steak. Cover. Bake in 350°F (175°C) oven for about 1½ to 2 hours until meat is tender. Makes 8 servings.

NUTRITION GUIDE	1 serving contains:	
	Energy	171 Calories (715 kJ)
	Cholesterol	52 mg
	Sodium	476 mg
	Fat	4.4 g

Paré Pointer

The best way to eat a grapefruit is by yourself.

SWISS STEAK

Served with good brown gravy. A slight hint of horseradish.

Boneless round steak, fat removed, cut into 8 pieces	**2 lbs.**	**900 g**
All-purpose flour	**¼ cup**	**60 mL**
Water	**2 cups**	**450 mL**
Sliced onion	**2 cups**	**500 mL**
Low-fat plain yogurt (less than 1% MF)	**½ cup**	**125 mL**
Prepared horseradish	**1 tbsp.**	**15 mL**
Salt	**½ tsp.**	**2 mL**
Pepper	**¼ tsp.**	**1 mL**
Paprika	**⅛ tsp.**	**0.5 mL**

Spray frying pan with no-stick cooking spray. Add steak. Brown both sides. Transfer to 3 quart (3 L) casserole.

Place flour in small bowl. Add water gradually, mixing until no lumps remain. Pour into frying pan, stirring until it boils and thickens. Loosen all brown bits in pan.

Stir in remaining ingredients. Pour over steak. Cover. Bake in 350°F (175°C) oven for 1½ to 2 hours until meat is fork tender. Makes 8 servings.

NUTRITION GUIDE	**1 serving contains:**	
	Energy	171 Calories (714 kJ)
	Cholesterol	53 mg
	Sodium	219 mg
	Fat	4.3 g

A piano and a fish are quite different. You can't tuna fish.

Pretty as a picture. Mild flavored. Excellent choice.

Lean ground beef	1 lb.	454 g
Tomato sauce	7½ oz.	213 mL
Dry colored fusilli (or other pasta)	2⅔ cup	600 mL
Boiling water	2½ qts.	3 L
Low-fat cottage cheese (less than 1% MF)	1 cup	250 mL
Low-fat plain yogurt (less than 1% MF)	1 cup	250 mL
All-purpose flour	2 tbsp.	30 mL
Green onions, chopped	6	6
Salt	½ tsp.	2 mL
Pepper	⅛ tsp.	0.5 mL
Garlic powder	¼ tsp.	1 mL
Grated low-fat sharp Cheddar cheese (less than 21% MF)	¼ cup	60 mL

Scramble-fry ground beef in frying pan that has been sprayed with no-stick cooking spray.

Add tomato sauce. Stir. Simmer 5 minutes.

In large uncovered saucepan, cook fusilli in boiling water about 8 minutes until tender but firm. Drain.

Add next 7 ingredients to pasta. Stir well. Using 2 quart (2 L) casserole, alternate 2 layers of beef mixture with 2 layers pasta, making beef the first layer. Bake, uncovered, in 350°F (175°C) oven for about 30 minutes until hot.

Sprinkle with cheese. Bake about 5 minutes more or until cheese is melted. Makes 6¾ cups (1.53 L).

NUTRITION GUIDE	1 cup (225 mL) contains:	
	Energy	324 Calories (1354 kJ)
	Cholesterol	42 mg
	Sodium	663 mg
	Fat	8 g

SAUERKRAUT CASSEROLE

With a shiny golden topping. Includes meat and potatoes.

Potatoes, peeled and quartered	2 lbs.	900 g
Water		
Lean ground beef	1½ lbs.	680 g
Finely chopped onion	½ cup	125 mL
White vinegar	3 tbsp.	50 mL
Chili powder	1 tbsp.	15 mL
Oregano	1 tsp.	5 mL
Salt	½ tsp.	2 mL
Pepper	¼ tsp.	1 mL
Garlic powder	¼ tsp.	1 mL
Water	¼ cup	50 mL
Sauerkraut, rinsed and drained	28 oz.	796 mL
Grated Parmesan cheese	1½ tbsp.	25 mL

Cook potatoes in some water until tender. Drain. Mash.

Spray frying pan with no-stick cooking spray. Add ground beef and onion. Scramble-fry until no pink remains in meat.

Add next 7 ingredients. Stir.

Spread sauerkraut in bottom of 3 quart (3 L) casserole. Cover with meat mixture. Place potato over top. Smooth.

Sprinkle with Parmesan cheese. Bake, uncovered, in 350°F (175°C) oven for about 35 minutes. Makes 8¾ cups (2 L).

NUTRITION GUIDE	1 cup (225 mL) contains:	
	Energy	236 Calories (986 kJ)
	Cholesterol	41 mg
	Sodium	635 mg
	Fat	7.1 g

Soft and moist.

Tomato sauce	7¹/₂ oz.	213 mL
Corn syrup	¹/₄ cup	60 mL
Prepared mustard	2 tbsp.	30 mL
Egg whites (large)	2	2
Finely chopped peeled apple	1 cup	250 mL
Chopped onion	¹/₂ cup	125 mL
Tomato mixture		
Fine dry bread crumbs	³/₄ cup	175 mL
Worcestershire sauce	1 tsp.	5 mL
Salt	1 tsp.	5 mL
Nutmeg	¹/₂ tsp.	2 mL
Pepper	¹/₈ tsp.	0.5 mL
Lean ground beef	1¹/₂ lbs.	680 g
Reserved tomato mixture	3 tbsp.	50 mL

In small bowl stir tomato sauce, corn syrup and mustard. Measure and reserve 3 tbsp. (50 mL) for topping.

Beat egg whites with spoon in large bowl. Add next 8 ingredients. Stir well.

Mix in ground beef. Turn into 9 x 5 inch (23 x 12 cm) loaf pan which has been sprayed with no-stick cooking spray. Cook, uncovered, in 350°F (175°C) oven for 1 hour.

Smooth reserved tomato mixture over top. Continue to cook for about 15 minutes more. Let stand 10 minutes before cutting into 10 slices.

NUTRITION GUIDE	1 slice contains:	
	Energy	185 Calories (775 kJ)
	Cholesterol	35 mg
	Sodium	553 mg
	Fat	6.3 g

SHIPWRECK WITH BEANS

A full meal with the addition of kidney beans for extra protein without added fat.

Chopped onions	3 cups	750 mL
Lean ground beef	1 lb.	454 g
Kidney beans with juice	14 oz.	398 mL
Chopped celery	1½ cups	375 mL
Long grain rice, uncooked	½ cup	125 mL
Medium potatoes, peeled and sliced	2	2
Condensed tomato soup	10 oz.	284 mL
Hot water	1¼ cups	275 mL

Layer first 6 ingredients in 3 quart (3 L) casserole in order given.

Stir soup and water together well. Pour over all. Cover. Bake in 350°F (175°C) oven for 2 to 2½ hours until vegetables are tender. Makes 9¼ cups (2 L).

NUTRITION GUIDE	1 cup (225 mL) contains:	
	Energy	222 Calories (931 kJ)
	Cholesterol	25 mg
	Sodium	425 mg
	Fat	4.9 g

1. Special Day Ribs, page 128
2. Shrimp Creole, page 92
3. Brandied Fruit, page 102
4. Baked Chop Suey, page 12

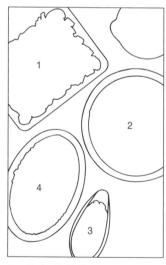

Props Courtesy Of: The Bay

CHOPPED BEEF CASSEROLE

A colorful full meal in a dish. Good way to use leftovers.

Chopped onion	1 cup	250 mL
Chopped celery	⅓ cup	75 mL
All-purpose flour	1 tbsp.	15 mL
Skim milk	1 cup	250 mL
Dry elbow macaroni	1 cup	250 mL
Boiling water	1½ qts.	1.5 L
Condensed tomato soup	10 oz.	284 mL
Cooked carrot coins	2 cups	500 mL
Cooked peas	1 cup	250 mL
Lean chopped cooked roast beef	2 cups	500 mL
Grated low-fat sharp Cheddar cheese (less than 21% MF)	3 tbsp.	50 mL

Spray frying pan with no-stick cooking spray. Add onion and celery. Sauté until soft.

Mix in flour. Stir in milk until it boils and thickens. Remove from heat.

Cook macaroni in boiling water in large uncovered saucepan for 5 to 7 minutes until tender but firm. Drain.

Stir next 4 ingredients together in large bowl. Add onion mixture and macaroni. Mix. Turn into 2 quart (2 L) casserole. Bake, uncovered, in 350° (175°C) oven for about 30 minutes until hot.

Sprinkle with cheese. Bake about 5 minutes more until cheese melts. Makes 6½ cups (1.5 L).

NUTRITION GUIDE	1 cup (225 mL) contains:	
	Energy	258 Calories (1081 kJ)
	Cholesterol	33 mg
	Sodium	434 mg
	Fat	4.4 g

A magic crust topped with hamburger and cheese.

PIZZA CRUST		
All-purpose flour	1½ cups	350 mL
Baking powder	2 tsp.	10 mL
Fast rising yeast	2 tsp.	10 mL
Cooking oil	2 tbsp.	30 mL
Warm water	⅔ cup	150 mL
TOPPING		
Lean ground beef	½ lb.	250 g
Tomato paste	½ cup	125 mL
Water	⅓ cup	75 mL
Onion powder	¼ tsp.	1 mL
Garlic powder	⅛ tsp.	0.5 mL
Oregano	¼ tsp.	1 mL
Granulated sugar	1 tsp.	5 mL
Basil	⅛ tsp.	0.5 mL
Salt	½ tsp.	2 mL
Pepper	⅛ tsp.	0.5 mL
Grated part-skim mozzarella cheese (35% less fat)	1 cup	250 mL
Sliced fresh mushrooms	1 cup	250 mL
Green pepper, in short slivers	1	1
Red pepper, in short slivers	1	1
Grated part-skim mozzarella cheese (35% less fat)	1 cup	250 mL

Pizza Crust: Stir flour, baking powder and yeast together in bowl.

Add cooking oil and water. Mix. Knead on lightly floured surface 25 to 30 times until smooth. Spray 12 inch (30 cm) pizza pan with no-stick cooking spray. Roll and stretch dough to fit pan.

Topping: Spray frying pan with no-stick cooking spray. Add ground beef. Scramble-fry until no pink remains.

Add next 9 ingredients. Stir. Spread over crust.

(continued on next page)

Sprinkle with first amount of cheese.

Arrange mushrooms, green and red peppers over top.

Sprinkle with remaining cheese. Bake on bottom rack in 425°F (220°C) oven for 12 to 15 minutes. Cut into 8 wedges.

NUTRITION GUIDE	1 wedge contains:	
	Energy	267 Calories (1118 kJ)
	Cholesterol	39 mg
	Sodium	335 mg
	Fat	11 g

BEEF HASH

An easy dish and a good way to use leftover roast beef.

Beef bouillon powder (35% less salt)	4 tsp.	20 mL
Finely chopped onion	1 cup	250 mL
Grated raw potato	2¹/₂ cups	575 mL
All-purpose flour	2 tbsp.	30 mL
Pepper	¹/₂ tsp.	2 mL
Finely chopped lean cooked roast beef	2 cups	500 mL
Water	2 cups	500 mL

Salt to taste

Combine bouillon powder, onion, potato and flour in bowl. Mix. Add pepper, beef and water. Stir. Turn into 2 quart (2 L) casserole. Bake, uncovered, in 350°F (175°C) oven for 1 hour or more until cooked.

Salt to taste. Makes 4¹/₂ cups (1 L).

NUTRITION GUIDE	1 cup (225 mL) contains:	
	Energy	210 Calories (877 kJ)
	Cholesterol	44 mg
	Sodium	305 mg
	Fat	3.9 g

LASAGNE

With a real tomato sauce.

MEAT SAUCE

Lean ground beef	1 lb.	454 g
Chopped onion	1 cup	250 mL
Tomato paste	2 × 5½ oz.	2 × 156 mL
Water	1¾ cups	400 mL
White vinegar	1½ tbsp.	25 mL
Chili powder	2 tsp.	10 mL
Oregano	1 tsp.	5 mL
Salt	1 tsp.	5 mL
Garlic powder	¼ tsp.	1 mL
Pepper	¼ tsp.	1 mL
Liquid sweetener	¾ tsp.	4 mL

CHEESE FILLING

Low-fat cottage cheese (less than 1% MF)	2 cups	500 mL
Grated Parmesan cheese	⅓ cup	75 mL
All-purpose flour	2 tbsp.	30 mL
Dried chives	2 tsp.	10 mL
Salt	½ tsp.	2 mL
Pepper	⅛ tsp.	0.5 mL
Skim milk	½ cup	125 mL
Lasagne noodles	9	9
Boiling water	3 qts.	3 L
Grated part-skim mozzarella cheese (35% less fat)	1½ cups	350 mL

Meat Sauce: Spray frying pan with no-stick cooking spray. Add ground beef and onion. Sauté until no pink remains in meat and onion is soft. Transfer to large pot.

Add next 9 ingredients. Heat, stirring occasionally until it boils. Boil slowly for 30 minutes. Add a bit more water if tomato flavor is too strong.

Cheese Filling: Stir first 7 ingredients together in bowl in order given. Set aside.

(continued on next page)

Cook noodles in boiling water in large uncovered pot 14 to 16 minutes until tender but firm. Drain.

To assemble, spray 9 x 13 (22 x 33 cm) pan with no-stick cooking spray and layer as follows:

1. Layer of 3 noodles
2. ½ meat sauce
3. Layer of 3 noodles
4. Cheese filling
5. Layer of 3 noodles
6. ½ of meat sauce
7. Mozzarella cheese

Bake, uncovered, in 350°F (175°C) oven for 45 to 55 minutes until browned. Lay foil over top if cheese browns too soon. Cut into 12 pieces.

NUTRITION GUIDE	1 piece contains:	
	Energy	230 Calories (962 kJ)
	Cholesterol	31 mg
	Sodium	656 mg
	Fat	7 g

A hypnotist used public tranceport to get around.

MEATBALL STEW

Different to have ground beef in a stew. Tasty.

MEATBALLS

Frozen egg product, thawed (low-fat and cholesterol-free)	**¼ cup**	**60 mL**
Regular or quick rolled oats (not instant)	**½ cup**	**125 mL**
Water	**⅓ cup**	**75 mL**
Pepper	**¼ tsp.**	**1 mL**
Lean ground beef	**¾ lb.**	**335 g**

VEGETABLES

Bite size carrot pieces	**2 cups**	**500 mL**
Bite size potato pieces	**2 cups**	**500 mL**
Sliced celery	**1 cup**	**250 mL**
Sliced onion	**1 cup**	**250 mL**
Frozen cut green beans	**1 cup**	**250 mL**
Canned tomatoes	**19 oz.**	**540 mL**
Beef bouillon powder (35 % less salt)	**4 tsp.**	**20 mL**

Meatballs: Place egg product in bowl. Stir in rolled oats, water and pepper.

Add ground beef. Mix. Shape into 24 balls. Arrange on baking sheet. Bake in 425°F (220°C) oven for about 10 minutes to brown.

Vegetables: Combine all 7 ingredients in small roaster. Stir. Cover. Bake in 350°F (175°C) oven for 30 minutes. Add meatballs. Bake about 30 minutes more until carrots are cooked. Makes 6 servings.

NUTRITION GUIDE	**1 serving contains:**	
	Energy	208 Calories (869 kJ)
	Cholesterol	22 mg
	Sodium	439 mg
	Fat	4.7 g

Simply put all in a roaster and bake. Deep brown tender chunks of meat.

Beef stew meat, trimmed of fat	2 lbs.	900 g
Tomato paste	5½ oz.	156 mL
Water	1 cup	250 mL
Chopped onion	1 cup	250 mL
White vinegar	2 tbsp.	30 mL
Brown sugar	2 tbsp.	30 mL
Light soy sauce (40% less salt)	2 tbsp.	30 mL
Ground ginger	½ tsp.	2 mL
Dry mustard	1 tsp.	5 mL
Beef bouillon powder (35% less salt)	1 tsp.	5 mL
Pepper	¼ tsp.	1 mL

Arrange stew meat in small roaster.

Stir remaining ingredients together in small bowl. Mix. Pour over meat. Cover. Bake in 325°F (160°C) oven for 2½ to 3 hours until very tender. Makes 8 servings.

NUTRITION GUIDE	1 serving contains:	
	Energy	148 Calories (621 kJ)
	Cholesterol	44 mg
	Sodium	244 mg
	Fat	3.7 g

Variation: Short ribs, about 4 lbs. (1.8 kg) may be used instead of stew meat. Fat content will be much higher.

Is a fjord a Norwegian car?

CHILI CON CARNE

This oven chili may also be simmered on top of the stove. Extra chili powder may be added if desired.

Lean ground beef	2 lbs.	900 g
All-purpose flour	2 tbsp.	30 mL
Water	2 cups	500 mL
Tomato paste	5½ oz.	156 mL
Chopped onion	3 cups	700 mL
Kidney beans with juice	2 × 14 oz.	2 × 398 mL
Chili powder	1 tbsp.	15 mL
Celery flakes	1 tsp.	5 mL
Cumin	1 tsp.	5 mL
Pepper	¼ tsp.	1 mL
Garlic powder	¼ tsp.	1 mL
Liquid sweetener	1 tsp.	5 mL

Spray frying pan with no-stick cooking spray. Add ground beef. Scramble-fry until browned.

Mix in flour. Add water and tomato paste. Stir until it boils and thickens.

Add remaining ingredients. Stir. Turn into 3 quart (3 L) casserole. Cover. Bake in 350°F (175°C) oven for about 1 hour until flavors are blended. Makes 9¼ cups (2.1 L).

NUTRITION GUIDE	1 cup (225 mL) contains:	
	Energy	271 Calories (1133 kJ)
	Cholesterol	50 mg
	Sodium	386 mg
	Fat	8.7 g

Slices of this are very attractive. Ask your meat cutter to slice meat thin enough to roll.

Boiling water	**¼ cup**	**60 mL**
Instant rice, uncooked	**¼ cup**	**60 mL**
Dry bread crumbs	**¾ cup**	**175 mL**
Finely chopped onion	**2 tbsp.**	**30 mL**
Poultry seasoning	**½ tsp.**	**2 mL**
Parsley flakes	**½ tsp.**	**2 mL**
Salt	**½ tsp.**	**2 mL**
Water	**2 tbsp.**	**30 mL**
Lean round steak, thin enough to roll	**2 lbs.**	**900 g**
Canned tomatoes, mashed	**19 oz.**	**540 mL**
Granulated sugar	**½ tsp.**	**2 mL**

Pour boiling water over rice in bowl. Cover. Let stand 5 minutes.

Add next 6 ingredients. Stir.

Lay meat on working surface. Divide rice mixture over meat. Roll up as for jelly roll. Tie with string. Arrange in 3 quart (3 L) casserole.

Stir tomatoes and sugar together and pour over top. Cover. Bake in 350°F (175°C) oven for 1½ to 2 hours until beef is tender. Makes 8 servings.

NUTRITION GUIDE	1 serving contains:	
	Energy	195 Calories (814 kJ)
	Cholesterol	52 mg
	Sodium	390 mg
	Fat	4.8 g

Pare Pointer

Why don't crabapples taste like seafood?

OVEN BEEF STEW

A good, convenient meaty stew.

Lean beef stewing meat or round steak, cut bite size	1 lb.	454 g
Large onion, cut up	1	1
Medium potatoes, peeled and cut bite size	2	2
Yellow turnip cubes	1 cup	250 mL
Thickly sliced celery	½ cup	125 mL
Medium carrots, cut bite size	3	3
Tomato paste	5½ oz.	156 mL
Beef bouillon powder (35% less salt)	4 tsp.	20 mL
Pepper	¼ tsp.	1 mL
Water	1½ cups	375 mL
White vinegar	2 tbsp.	30 mL
Liquid sweetener	¾ tsp.	4 mL

Combine first 6 ingredients in small roaster.

Mix remaining ingredients together in bowl. Pour over top. Cover. Bake in 300°F (150°C) oven for 3 to 4 hours until meat is tender. Makes 4 servings.

NUTRITION GUIDE	1 serving contains:	
	Energy	279 Calories (1166 kJ)
	Cholesterol	45 mg
	Sodium	433 mg
	Fat	4.4 g

An autobiography is really a life history of a car.

Mashed potatoes would add the finishing touch or bake some along side of roaster.

Lean beef pot roast, boneless	4 lbs.	1.8 kg
White wine (or alcohol-free wine)	½ cup	125 mL
Water	½ cup	125 mL
Peppercorns	½ tsp.	2 mL
Bay leaves	2	2
Whole cloves	2	2
Garlic clove, minced	1	1
Salt	1 tsp.	5 mL
Sliced onion	1½ cups	375 mL
Sliced carrots	2 cups	500 mL
Low-fat sour cream (7% MF)	½ cup	125 mL
All-purpose flour	3 tbsp.	50 mL
Boiling water as needed		

Place meat in small roaster. Add next 7 ingredients. Cover. Bake in 325°F (160°C) oven for 1½ hours.

Add onion and carrot. Continue to bake for 1 hour or until meat and vegetables are tender.

Remove vegetables with slotted spoon to bowl. Remove meat to plate. Mix sour cream and flour together. Stir into juice in pan. Heat and stir until it boils and thickens. Turn into measuring cup. Stir in boiling water to make 2 cups (450 mL). Makes 8 servings.

NUTRITION GUIDE	1 serving contains:	
	Energy	315 Calories (1320 kJ)
	Cholesterol	108 mg
	Sodium	443 mg
	Fat	9.7 g

BEEFY CHEESE STEAK

Tender meat in creamy gravy.

Lean round steak, cut in 4 pieces	1 lb.	454 g
Water	⅔ cup	150 mL
Chopped onion	¾ cup	175 mL
Chopped celery	½ cup	125 mL
Grated low-fat sharp Cheddar cheese (less than 21% MF)	½ cup	125 mL
Condensed cream of mushroom soup	10 oz.	284 mL
Medium potatoes, peeled and sliced	4	4
Salt and pepper to taste		

Spray frying pan with no-stick cooking spray. Add steak. Brown both sides. Turn into small roaster.

Add water to frying pan. Loosen any brown bits. Pour over meat.

Mix onion, celery, cheese and soup in bowl. Set aside.

Layer potato over meat. Top with soup mixture. Cover. Bake in 350°F (175°C) oven for 1½ to 2 hours until meat is very tender.

Add salt and pepper to taste. Makes 4 servings.

NUTRITION GUIDE	1 serving contains:	
	Energy	414 Calories (1730 kJ)
	Cholesterol	63 mg
	Sodium	764 mg
	Fat	13.2 g

By the time you learn to make the most of life, most of it's gone!

Creamy gravy with yogurt rather than sour cream.

Lean beef sirloin or round steak	**1 lb.**	**454 g**
All-purpose flour	**⅓ cup**	**75 mL**
Beef bouillon powder (35% less salt)	**4 tsp.**	**20 mL**
Garlic powder	**¼ tsp.**	**1 mL**
Water	**1½ cups**	**350 mL**
Low-fat plain yogurt (less than 1% MF)	**1 cup**	**250 mL**
Sliced onion	**1 cup**	**250 mL**
Sliced fresh mushrooms	**1 cup**	**250 mL**
Sherry (or alcohol-free sherry)	**2 tbsp.**	**30 mL**

Spray frying pan with no-stick cooking spray. Cut beef into 4 serving pieces. Brown both sides. Arrange in 2 quart (2 L) casserole.

Combine flour, bouillon powder and garlic powder in saucepan. Mix. Stir in part of the water until no lumps remain. Add rest of water and yogurt. Heat and stir until it boils and thickens.

Add onion, mushrooms and sherry. Stir. Pour over meat. Cover. Bake in 325°F (160°C) oven for 2 hours until meat is tender. Makes 4 servings.

NUTRITION GUIDE	1 serving contains:	
	Energy	231 Calories (965 kJ)
	Cholesterol	54 mg
	Sodium	372 mg
	Fat	5 g

History is a record of events that never should have happened.

CHUNKY CHILI

A different variety. Brown meat, combine with other ingredients and the oven does the rest.

Lean boneless beef, cut in bite size cubes	**1½ lbs**	**680 g**
Diced fresh tomatoes (see Note)	**2½ cups**	**575 mL**
Canned kidney beans, with juice	**14 oz.**	**398 mL**
Chopped onion	**1½ cups**	**375 mL**
Chili powder	**1 tbsp.**	**15 mL**
Garlic powder	**¼ tsp.**	**1 mL**
Pepper	**¼ tsp.**	**1 mL**
Oregano	**¼ tsp.**	**1 mL**
Granulated sugar	**1 tsp.**	**5 mL**

Brown meat under broiler. Drain any juice into small roaster. Turn and brown other side. Transfer meat to roaster.

Mix all remaining ingredients in bowl. Pour over meat. Stir. Cover. Bake in 325°F (160°C) oven for 2 to 2½ hours until meat is very tender. Makes 6 servings.

Pictured on page 53.

NUTRITION GUIDE	1 serving contains:	
	Energy	203 Calories (851 kJ)
	Cholesterol	44 mg
	Sodium	304 mg
	Fat	4 g

Note: One 14 oz. (398 mL) can of tomatoes can be substituted for fresh tomatoes, but sodium content will be higher.

Paré Pointer

The reason there are so many fat dentists is that almost everything they touch is filling.

Similar to a mild chili. Dark reddish color. Add a salad and a dinner roll for a complete meal.

Round steak, fat removed, cut bite size	**1 lb.**	**454 g**
Chopped onion	**1 cup**	**250 mL**
Canned tomatoes, mashed	**19 oz.**	**540 mL**
Instant rice, uncooked	**1 cup**	**250 mL**
Canned kidney beans, with juice	**14 oz.**	**398 mL**
Condensed beef consommé	**10 oz.**	**284 mL**
Chili powder	**1 tsp.**	**5 mL**
Granulated sugar	**½ tsp.**	**2 mL**
Salt	**½ tsp.**	**2 mL**
Pepper	**¼ tsp.**	**1 mL**
Oregano	**¼ tsp.**	**1 mL**

Spray frying pan with no-stick cooking spray. Brown steak and onion. Turn into large bowl.

Stir tomatoes into frying pan to loosen brown bits. Add to bowl.

Add remaining ingredients. Stir well. Turn into 2 quart (2 L) casserole. Cover. Bake in 350°F (175°C) oven for 1½ to 2 hours until meat is tender. Makes 6⅔ cups (1.5 L).

Pictured on page 89.

NUTRITION GUIDE	1 cup (225 mL) contains:	
	Energy	222 Calories (929 kJ)
	Cholesterol	32 mg
	Sodium	819 mg
	Fat	3 g

Paré Pointer

A man wears trousers, a dog pants.

STEAK MEAL IN A DISH

No pre-browning of meat. Similar to stew.

Boneless sirloin steak, fat removed, cut in slivers	1 lb.	454 g
Thinly sliced onion	1 cup	250 mL
Medium potatoes, peeled and cubed, about 1¼ lbs. (570 g)	4	4
Medium carrots, sliced, about ¾ lb. (340 g)	5	5
Condensed tomato soup	10 oz.	284 mL
Water	1 cup	250 mL
Worcestershire sauce	2 tsp.	10 mL
Salt	1 tsp.	5 mL

Layer steak, onion, potato and carrot in 3 quart (3 L) casserole.

Mix soup, water, Worcestershire sauce and salt in bowl. Pour over top. Cover. Bake in 350°F (175°C) oven for 2 hours or until vegetables are tender. Makes 7⅓ cups (1.65 L).

NUTRITION GUIDE	1 cup (225 mL) contains:	
	Energy	212 Calories (885 kJ)
	Cholesterol	29 mg
	Sodium	735 mg
	Fat	3.1 g

1. Whole Wheat Biscuits, page 101
2. Cauliflower-Broccoli Casserole, page 148
3. Quick Tamale Casserole, page 15
4. Pineapple Ham Pizza, page 114
5. Chunky Chili, page 50

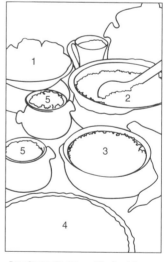

Props Courtesy Of: Cottswood Furniture & Home Interiors, Scona Clayworks

Prepare rice and chicken ahead to save time.

Chopped fresh mushrooms	2 cups	500 mL
Sesame seeds	2 tbsp.	30 mL
All-purpose flour	3 tbsp.	50 mL
Salt	½ tsp.	2 mL
Skim milk	2 cups	500 mL
Cooked rice	2 cups	500 mL
Chopped cooked chicken breast, skin and fat removed	2 cups	500 mL
Paprika	½ tsp.	2 mL
White wine (or alcohol-free white wine)	¼ cup	60 mL
Hard margarine	1 tbsp.	15 mL
Dry bread crumbs	⅓ cup	75 mL

Spray frying pan with no-stick cooking spray. Add mushrooms and sesame seeds. Sauté until mushrooms are soft.

Mix in flour and salt. Stir in milk until it boils and thickens.

Add rice, chicken, paprika and wine. Stir. Pour into 1½ quart (1.5 L) casserole.

Melt margarine in small saucepan. Stir in bread crumbs. Spread over all. Bake, uncovered, in 350°F (175°C) oven for about 30 to 35 minutes until heated through. Makes 4½ cups (1.1 L).

NUTRITION GUIDE	1 cup (225 mL) contains:	
	Energy	505 Calories (2111 kJ)
	Cholesterol	58 mg
	Sodium	504 mg
	Fat	8.6 g

Paré Pointer

A sleeping child could be a kidnapper.

CHICKEN ZUCCHINI DISH

Serve to your favorite people. Excellent choice.

Dry fettuccine, broken in quarters	4 oz.	125 g
Boiling water	2 qts.	2 L
Boneless chicken breasts, skin and fat removed	1 lb.	454 g
Boiling water to cover		
Chopped onion	$^2/_3$ cup	150 mL
Medium zucchini with peel, cut bite size	1	1
Condensed cream of mushroom soup	10 oz.	284 mL
Skim milk	$^1/_2$ cup	125 mL
Grated part-skim mozzarella cheese (35% less fat)	1 cup	250 mL
Garlic powder	$^1/_4$ tsp.	1 mL
Imitation bacon bits	1 tbsp.	15 mL
Paprika, sprinkle		

Cook fettuccine in first amount of boiling water in large uncovered saucepan about 5 to 7 minutes until tender but firm. Drain.

Cook chicken in second amount of boiling water until tender. Drain. Chop.

Spray frying pan with no-stick cooking spray. Add onion. Sauté until almost soft before adding zucchini. Cover and sauté, stirring often, until zucchini is cooked.

Stir next 5 ingredients together in large bowl until mixed. Add fettuccine, chicken and onion mixture. Stir. Turn into 2 quart (2 L) casserole.

Sprinkle with paprika. Bake, uncovered, in 350°F (175°C) oven for 35 minutes until hot. Makes 6 servings.

NUTRITION GUIDE	1 serving contains:	
	Energy	297 Calories (1244 kJ)
	Cholesterol	60 mg
	Sodium	593 mg
	Fat	9.4 g

Variation: Omit paprika. Sprinkle with 1 to 2 tbsp. (15 to 30 mL) grated Parmesan cheese.

One of the best choices you can make. Very good.

Sliced fresh mushrooms	2 cups	500 mL
Dry linguini, broken (or other pasta)	1/2 lb.	250 g
Boiling water	3 qts.	3 L
Coarsely chopped cooked chicken, skin and fat removed	2 cups	500 mL
Minced onion	2 tbsp.	30 mL
Sliced or chopped pimiento-stuffed green olives	1/3 cup	75 mL

SAUCE

All-purpose flour	1/4 cup	60 mL
Salt	3/4 tsp.	4 mL
Pepper	1/4 tsp.	1 mL
Paprika	1/4 tsp.	1 mL
Skim milk	3 cups	750 mL
Grated low-fat medium or sharp Cheddar cheese (less than 21% MF)	1 cup	250 mL
Sherry (or alcohol-free sherry), optional	1 1/2 tbsp.	20 mL

TOPPING

Hard margarine	1 tbsp.	15 mL
Dry bread crumbs	1/3 cup	75 mL

Cook mushrooms and linguini in boiling water in large uncovered pot for 11 to 13 minutes until linguini is tender but firm. Drain.

Add chicken, onion and olives. Stir.

Sauce: Stir flour, salt, pepper and paprika in saucepan. Mix in enough milk to make smooth. Stir in rest of milk and cheese. Add sherry, if desired. Heat and stir until it boils and thickens. Pour over pasta mixture. Stir. Transfer to 3 quart (3 L) casserole.

Topping: Stir margarine and bread crumbs together. Sprinkle over top. Bake, uncovered, in 350°F (175°C) oven for about 30 minutes. Makes 7 cups (1.58 L).

NUTRITION GUIDE	1 cup (225 mL) contains:	
	Energy	360 Calories (1504 kJ)
	Cholesterol	44 mg
	Sodium	708 mg
	Fat	10 g

SPEEDY CHICKEN

A snap to make.

Boneless chicken breasts, skin and fat removed	1½ lbs.	680 g
Ketchup, see page 99	⅓ cup	75 mL
Water	2½ tbsp.	40 mL
Beef bouillon powder (35% less salt)	2 tsp.	10 mL
Onion flakes	2 tsp.	10 mL
Liquid sweetener	½ tsp.	2 mL

Lay chicken in 3 quart (3 L) casserole in single layer.

Stir next 5 ingredients together in bowl. Spoon evenly over chicken pieces. Cover. Bake in 350°F (175°C) oven for 1 to 1½ hours until very tender. Makes 6 servings.

NUTRITION GUIDE	1 serving contains:	
	Energy	158 Calories (660 kJ)
	Cholesterol	70 mg
	Sodium	247 mg
	Fat	3 g

HOT CHICKEN SALAD

Enjoy a change. A mild salad tartness. Serve with hot biscuits and plump red tomatoes.

Dry vermicelli (or other thin noodle)	½ lb.	250 g
Boiling water	3 qts.	3 L
Chopped cooked chicken breasts, skin and fat removed	2 cups	500 mL
Thinly sliced celery	1½ cups	375 mL
Sesame seeds, browned in 350°F (175°C) oven, about 5 minutes	1 tbsp.	15 mL
Minced onion	2 tbsp.	30 mL
Chopped pimiento	2 tbsp.	30 mL
Salad dressing, page 98	½ cup	125 mL
Lemon juice, fresh or bottled	1 tbsp.	15 mL
Salt	½ tsp.	2 mL
Grated low-fat sharp Cheddar cheese (less than 21% MF)	2 tbsp.	30 mL
Paprika, sprinkle		

(continued on next page)

Cook vermicelli in boiling water in large uncovered pot for about 4 to 6 minutes until tender but firm. Drain.

In large bowl combine next 8 ingredients. Add vermicelli. Stir well. Turn into 2 quart (2 L) casserole. Bake, uncovered, in 350°F (175°C) oven for 25 minutes until hot.

Sprinkle with cheese then paprika. Continue to bake for about 5 minutes until cheese is melted. Makes 6 servings.

NUTRITION GUIDE	1 serving contains:	
	Energy	332 Calories (1391 kJ)
	Cholesterol	44 mg
	Sodium	432 mg
	Fat	7.6 g

SMOKEY CHICKEN

Try this for campfire flavor.

Boneless chicken breasts, skin and fat removed	2 lbs.	900 g
Condensed cream of mushroom soup	10 oz.	284 mL
Low-fat sour cream (7% MF)	1 cup	250 mL
Liquid smoke	1/4 tsp.	1 mL

Spray frying pan with no-stick cooking spray. Brown chicken. Arrange in 3 quart (3 L) casserole.

Mix soup, sour cream and liquid smoke. Pour over chicken. Cover. Bake in 350°F (175°C) oven for about 1 to 1½ hours until tender. Push chicken to the side. Stir sauce to smooth. Makes 8 servings.

NUTRITION GUIDE	1 serving contains:	
	Energy	201 Calories (843 kJ)
	Cholesterol	76 mg
	Sodium	379 mg
	Fat	7.9 g

CHICKEN TETRAZZINI

This is very good even though it doesn't contain the thick cream and rich cheese it usually calls for.

Chicken breasts, halved	1½ lbs.	680 g
Boiling water	2 cups	500 mL
Dry spaghetti, broken	½ lb.	250 g
Boiling water	3 qts.	3 L
Sliced fresh mushrooms	2 cups	500 mL
Red pepper strips	½ cup	125 mL
Sliced green onions	⅓ cup	75 mL
Water	¼ cup	60 mL
All-purpose flour	2 tbsp.	30 mL
Chicken bouillon powder (35% less salt)	2 tsp.	10 mL
Reserved broth	¾ cup	175 mL
Evaporated skim milk	½ cup	125 mL
Sherry (or alcohol-free sherry)	2 tbsp.	30 mL
Grated Parmesan cheese	⅓ cup	75 mL
Salt	½ tsp.	2 mL
Pepper	⅛ tsp.	0.5 mL
Grated low-fat sharp Cheddar cheese (less than 21% MF)	1 cup	250 mL

Cook chicken in first amount of boiling water for about 30 minutes until tender. Drain. Reserve broth. Discard skin and bone. Cut chicken into cubes.

Cook spaghetti in second amount of water in large uncovered saucepan for 11 to 13 minutes until tender but firm. Drain. Add chicken.

Spray frying pan with no-stick cooking spray. Add mushrooms, red pepper and green onion. Sauté until soft.

Mix third amount of water with flour and bouillon powder until no lumps remain. Stir in reserved broth. Pour over mushroom mixture, stirring until it boils and thickens.

(continued on next page)

Add next 5 ingredients. Stir. Add to spaghetti. Stir. Turn into 3 quart (3 L) casserole. Bake in 350°F (175°C) oven for 30 minutes.

Sprinkle with cheese. Bake, uncovered, for about 5 minutes to melt cheese. Makes 7 cups (1.58 L).

NUTRITION GUIDE	1 cup (225 mL) contains:	
	Energy	324 Calories (1354 kJ)
	Cholesterol	57 mg
	Sodium	531 mg
	Fat	7.3 g

CHICKEN RICE BAKE

Colorful with bits of pimiento and parsley showing.

Boneless chicken breasts, skin and fat removed	2 lbs.	900 g
Paprika	½ tsp.	2 mL
Celery salt	½ tsp.	2 mL
Garlic powder	½ tsp.	2 mL
Boiling water	2 cups	500 mL
Chicken bouillon powder (35% less salt)	1 tbsp.	15 mL
Long grain rice, uncooked	1 cup	250 mL
Chopped pimiento	2 tbsp.	30 mL
Parsley flakes	½ tsp.	2 mL

Spray frying pan with no-stick cooking spray. Brown chicken on each side, sprinkling with ½ mixture of paprika, celery salt and garlic powder. Turn and sprinkle with second ½ of mixture.

Pour water into 3 quart (3 L) casserole. Stir in bouillon powder. Add rice, pimiento and parsley. Stir. Lay chicken on top. Cover. Bake in 350°F (175°C) oven for about 1 hour until rice is cooked, water is absorbed and chicken is tender. Makes 8 servings.

Pictured on page 107.

NUTRITION GUIDE	1 serving contains:	
	Energy	212 Calories (888 kJ)
	Cholesterol	70 mg
	Sodium	214 mg
	Fat	3.1 g

CHICKEN ASPARAGUS BAKE

A great combination. The asparagus is hidden beneath the chicken.
A cheesy topping covers it all.

Boneless chicken breasts, skin and fat removed	2 lbs.	900 g
Water	2½ cups	525 mL
Frozen asparagus	2 × 10 oz.	2 × 284 g
Boiling water		
SAUCE		
All-purpose flour	½ cup	125 mL
Reserved chicken broth	2 cups	500 mL
Salad dressing, page 98	½ cup	125 mL
Lemon juice, fresh or bottled	2 tsp.	10 mL
Curry powder	½ tsp.	2 mL
Salt	¼ tsp.	1 mL
Grated low-fat sharp Cheddar cheese (less than 21% MF)	½ cup	125 mL
Dry bread crumbs	1 tbsp.	15 mL

Cook chicken breasts in first amount of water for about 30 minutes until tender. Drain. Reserve broth. Remove bones. Chop chicken.

Cook asparagus in some boiling water until tender crisp. Drain. Cut into 1 inch (2.5 cm) lengths. Place in 3 quart (3 L) casserole. Cover with chicken.

Sauce: Mix flour with a little reserved broth in saucepan until no lumps remain. Stir in rest of reserved broth, salad dressing, lemon juice, curry powder and salt. Heat and stir until it boils and thickens. Pour evenly over asparagus.

Stir cheese and bread crumbs together. Sprinkle over top. Cover. Bake in 350°C (175°C) oven for about 30 minutes. Makes 8 servings.

NUTRITION GUIDE	1 serving contains:	
	Energy	233 Calories (976 kJ)
	Cholesterol	74 mg
	Sodium	277 mg
	Fat	4.7 g

Serve over rice or noodles. Lots of vegetables in this.

Boneless chicken breasts, skin and fat removed	1½ lbs.	680 g
Water to cover		
Lemon juice, fresh or bottled	2 tbsp.	30 mL
Sliced celery	1 cup	250 mL
Sliced fresh mushrooms	1 cup	250 mL
Green pepper, seeded and chopped	1	1
Fresh bean sprouts, packed	4 cups	1 L
Chopped onion	¾ cup	175 mL
Water chestnuts, drained and chopped	10 oz.	284 mL
All-purpose flour	3 tbsp.	50 mL
Chicken bouillon powder (35% less salt)	1 tbsp.	15 mL
Pepper	⅛ tsp.	0.5 mL
Reserved broth	1½ cups	350 mL
Light soy sauce (40% less salt)	3 tbsp.	50 mL

Combine first 3 ingredients in large saucepan. Cover. Bring to a boil. Simmer 15 minutes.

Add next 6 ingredients. Return to a boil. Cook for about 10 minutes until tender. Drain. Reserve broth. Remove bones. Cut meat into cubes or slices. Turn chicken and vegetables into 2 quart (2 L) casserole.

Stir flour, bouillon powder and pepper in saucepan. Mix in a little of reserved broth until smooth. Stir in rest of reserved broth and soy sauce. Heat and stir until it boils and thickens. Pour over casserole. Stir lightly. Bake, uncovered, in 350°F (175°C) oven for 25 to 30 minutes. Makes 7 cups (1.58 L).

N U T R I T I O N G U I D E	1 cup (225 mL) contains:	
	Energy	181 Calories (757 kJ)
	Cholesterol	60 mg
	Sodium	471 mg
	Fat	2.9 g

CHICKEN SQUARES

Mild flavored and moist. Red and green specks are attractive showing through the top.

Chopped cooked white chicken meat, skin and fat removed	2 cups	500 mL
Cooked rice	1 cup	250 mL
Dry bread crumbs	¾ cup	175 mL
Chopped celery	¼ cup	60 mL
Frozen egg product, thawed (low-fat and cholesterol-free)	¾ cup	175 mL
Egg white (large)	1	1
Condensed cream of mushroom soup	10 oz.	284 mL
Skim milk	½ cup	125 mL
Chopped pimiento	2 tbsp.	30 mL
Salt	¾ tsp.	4 mL
Thyme	¼ tsp.	1 mL

Combine first 4 ingredients in bowl.

Mix remaining ingredients in bowl. Add to chicken mixture. Stir. Turn into 9 x 9 inch (22 x 22 cm) pan sprayed with no-stick cooking spray. Bake, uncovered, in 350°F (175°C) oven for 50 to 60 minutes until set. Cut into 16 squares to serve.

NUTRITION GUIDE	1 square contains:	
	Energy	99 Calories (415 kJ)
	Cholesterol	16 mg
	Sodium	362 mg
	Fat	2.6 g

If you could only combine old automobiles with nylons, you would have cars that run.

Garlic is very light. You may want to strengthen it. Colorful.

Boneless chicken breasts, skin and fat removed	2 lbs.	900 g
Chopped onion	1¼ cups	275 mL
Green pepper, seeded and coarsely chopped	1	1
Sliced fresh mushrooms	1 cup	250 mL
Canned tomatoes, broken up	14 oz.	398 mL
Salt	½ tsp.	2 mL
Pepper	⅛ tsp.	0.5 mL
Garlic powder	¼ tsp	1 mL
White wine (or alcohol-free white wine)	3 tbsp.	50 mL

Arrange chicken in 2 quart (2 L) casserole.

Spray frying pan with no-stick cooking spray. Add onion, green pepper and mushrooms. Sauté until soft. Add to chicken.

Place remaining 5 ingredients in frying pan. Stir to loosen any brown bits. Pour over casserole. Cover. Bake in 350°F (175°C) oven for 1½ hours or until chicken is tender. Makes 8 servings.

Pictured on page 71.

NUTRITION GUIDE	1 serving contains:	
	Energy	162 Calories (679 kJ)
	Cholesterol	70 mg
	Sodium	310 mg
	Fat	3.0 g

A one liner is a Mini Ha Ha.

TOMATO CHICKEN

A different variety of ingredients combine to make this unusual casserole. Currants add to the taste.

Boneless chicken breasts, skin and fat removed	**1½ lbs.**	**680 g**
Canned tomatoes	**14 oz.**	**398 mL**
Slivered green pepper	**¼ cup**	**60 mL**
Chopped onion	**½ cup**	**125 mL**
Curry powder	**1 tsp.**	**5 mL**
Garlic powder	**¼ tsp.**	**1 mL**
Thyme	**¼ tsp.**	**1 mL**
Currants	**¼ cup**	**60 mL**

Spray frying pan with no-stick cooking spray. Add chicken. Brown both sides. Transfer to 2 quart (2 L) casserole.

Stir remaining ingredients together in bowl. Pour over top. Cover. Bake in 350°F (175°C) oven for 1½ hours until tender. Makes 6 servings.

NUTRITION GUIDE	**1 serving contains:**	
	Energy	177 Calories (741 kJ)
	Cholesterol	70 mg
	Sodium	168 mg
	Fat	3.0 g

WORTHY CHICKEN

A mild mustard-carrot mixture covers this chicken before being topped with crushed cornflakes.

Boneless chicken breasts, halved, skin and fat removed	**1½ lbs.**	**680 g**
Salad dressing, page 98	**½ cup**	**125 mL**
Chopped onion	**½ cup**	**125 mL**
Grated carrot	**½ cup**	**125 mL**
Prepared mustard	**1 tbsp.**	**15 mL**
Liquid sweetener	**½ tsp.**	**2 mL**
Chives	**2 tsp.**	**10 mL**
Thyme	**¼ tsp.**	**1 mL**
Basil	**¼ tsp.**	**1 mL**
Coarsely crushed corn flakes	**½ cup**	**125 mL**

(continued on next page)

Lay chicken in pan large enough to hold single layer.

Mix next 8 ingredients in bowl. Spoon over chicken, getting some on each.

Sprinkle corn flake crumbs over top. Bake, uncovered, in 375°F (190°C) oven for 50 to 60 minutes until tender. Makes 6 servings.

NUTRITION GUIDE	1 serving contains:	
	Energy	209 Calories (872 kJ)
	Cholesterol	71 mg
	Sodium	289 mg
	Fat	3.2 g

CURRIED CHICKEN BAKE

Only a hint of curry. More can easily be added. Also a hint of sweetness and mustard.

Boneless chicken breasts, skin and fat removed	1½ lbs.	680 g
Water	⅓ cup	75 mL
Prepared mustard	1 tbsp.	15 mL
Curry powder	¼ tsp.	1 mL
Cornstarch	2 tsp.	10 mL
Liquid sweetener	½ tsp.	2 mL

Arrange chicken pieces on foil lined baking sheet.

Mix next 5 ingredients in saucepan. Heat and stir until it boils and thickens. Remove from heat. Brush over chicken. Bake, uncovered, in 350°F (175°C) oven for 30 minutes. Turn chicken over. Brush tops. Bake about 15 minutes more or until tender. Makes 6 servings.

NUTRITION GUIDE	1 serving contains:	
	Energy	142 Calories (595 kJ)
	Cholesterol	70 mg
	Sodium	95 mg
	Fat	3.1 g

CHICKEN IN SAUCE

Rich looking gravy with mushrooms and onion.

Boneless chicken breasts, skin and fat removed	1½ lbs.	680 g
Sliced fresh mushrooms	1 cup	250 mL
Sliced onion	1 cup	250 mL
Water	½ cup	125 mL
Tomato paste	1½ tbsp.	25 mL
Sherry (or alcohol-free sherry)	2 tbsp.	30 mL
Paprika	½ tsp.	2 mL
Salt	½ tsp.	2 mL
Pepper	¼ tsp.	1 mL

Spray hot frying pan with no-stick cooking spray. Add chicken. Brown both sides. Transfer to 2 quart (2 L) casserole.

Add mushrooms and onion.

Stir next 6 ingredients together in bowl. Pour over top. Cover. Bake in 350°F (175°C) oven for about 1 hour until tender. Makes 6 servings.

NUTRITION GUIDE	1 serving contains:	
	Energy	158 Calories (662 kJ)
	Cholesterol	70 mg
	Sodium	288 mg
	Fat	2.9 g

CLUB CHICKEN CASSEROLE

A little salad dressing perks up the flavor in this dish.

Chopped, cooked chicken, skin and fat removed	2 cups	500 mL
Cooked rice	1 cup	250 mL
Salad dressing, page 98	¼ cup	60 mL
Condensed cream of chicken soup	10 oz.	284 mL
Lemon juice, fresh or bottled	1 tbsp.	15 mL
Chopped celery	½ cup	125 mL
Chopped onion	3 tbsp.	50 mL
Sliced fresh mushrooms	1 cup	250 mL
Coarsely crushed corn flakes	½ cup	125 mL

(continued on next page)

Combine first 5 ingredients in bowl.

Spray frying pan with no-stick cooking spray. Add celery, onion and mushrooms. Sauté until soft. Add to chicken mixture. Stir. Turn into 1½ quart (1.5 L) casserole.

Sprinkle corn flake crumbs over top. Bake, uncovered, in 350°F (175°C) oven for 30 to 40 minutes. Makes 4 cups (900 mL).

NUTRITION GUIDE	1 cup (225 mL) contains:	
	Energy	358 Calories (1499 kJ)
	Cholesterol	72 mg
	Sodium	868 mg
	Fat	10.2 g

CHICKEN IN WINE

Just like a classic meal. So easy. A good company casserole.

Boneless chicken breasts, skin and fat removed	2 lbs.	900 g
Condensed cream of mushroom soup	10 oz.	284 mL
Fresh button mushrooms	2 cups	500 mL
White wine (or alcohol-free white wine)	½ cup	125 mL
Pepper	⅛ tsp.	0.5 mL
Paprika	¼ tsp.	1 mL

Arrange chicken in 3 quart (3 L) casserole.

Stir remaining ingredients in bowl. Spoon over top. Bake, covered, in 350°F (175°C) oven for about 1 hour or until tender. Makes 8 servings.

Pictured on cover.

NUTRITION GUIDE	1 serving contains:	
	Energy	181 Calories (757 kJ)
	Cholesterol	70 mg
	Sodium	363 mg
	Fat	5.7 g

CHICKEN COLA

Excellent choice. Lots of juice and carrot sticks to spoon over rice or potatoes.

Boneless chicken breasts, skin and fat removed	**1½ lbs.**	**680 g**
Thinly sliced onion	**½ cup**	**125 mL**
Ketchup, page 99	**½ cup**	**125 mL**
Diet cola beverage	**1 cup**	**250 mL**
Medium carrots, cut in matchsticks	**2**	**2**

Spray hot frying pan with no-stick cooking spray. Add chicken. Brown. Arrange in 2 quart (2 L) casserole.

Combine next 4 ingredients in bowl. Mix. Pour over chicken. Cover. Bake in 350°F (175°C) oven for 1¼ to 1½ hours until tender. Makes 6 servings.

Pictured on page 125.

NUTRITION GUIDE	1 serving contains:	
	Energy	184 Calories (770 kJ)
	Cholesterol	70 mg
	Sodium	231 mg
	Fat	3 g

1. Corny Biscuits, page 103
2. Crowd Pleasing Chili, page 14
3. Pork Chops Supreme, page 127
4. Chicken Cacciatore, page 65
5. Green Pepper Steak, page 10

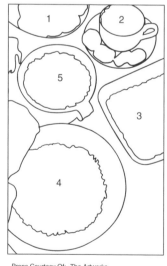

Props Courtesy Of: The Artworks

Meat and potatoes in one dish. Each person can add salt to taste.

Chicken breasts, halved, skin and fat removed	2 lbs.	900 g
Water	4 cups	900 mL
Medium potatoes, peeled and halved	3	3
Water		
Chopped onion	½ cup	125 mL
Chopped red or green pepper	½ cup	125 mL
Chicken bouillon powder (35% less salt)	2 tsp.	10 mL
All-purpose flour	2 tbsp.	30 mL
Pepper	⅛ tsp.	0.5 mL
Reserved broth	¾ cup	175 mL
Evaporated skim milk	¼ cup	60 mL
Prepared horseradish	2 tsp.	10 mL

Cook chicken in first amount of water about 30 minutes until tender. Drain, reserving broth. Remove bones. Chop meat. Place in bowl.

Cook potatoes in some water until barely tender. Drain. Cool until you can handle them. Grate coarsely. Add to meat.

Spray frying pan with no-stick cooking spray. Add onion and pepper. Sauté until soft. Add to meat.

In saucepan stir bouillon powder, flour and pepper with enough broth to mix smooth. Add rest of measured broth, milk and horseradish. Heat and stir until it boils and thickens. Add to meat. Stir lightly. Turn into 2 quart (2 L) casserole. Bake, uncovered, in 350°F (175°C) oven for 35 to 45 minutes until hot. Makes 5½ cups (1.24 L).

NUTRITION GUIDE	1 cup (225 mL) contains:	
	Energy	228 Calories (953 kJ)
	Cholesterol	67 mg
	Sodium	180 mg
	Fat	3 g

CHICKEN EGGS

These eggs are round meatballs served in sauce.

Chicken breasts, halved, skin and fat removed	2¼ lbs.	1 kg
Dry bread crumbs	¾ cup	175 mL
Finely chopped celery	⅓ cup	75 mL
Finely chopped onion	⅓ cup	75 mL
Ground walnuts	⅓ cup	75 mL
Salt	½ tsp.	2 mL
Pepper	⅛ tsp.	0.5 mL
Paprika	¼ tsp.	1 mL
Thyme	⅛ tsp.	0.5 mL
Water	¼ cup	60 mL
SAUCE		
All-purpose flour	2 tbsp.	30 mL
Chicken bouillon powder (35% less salt)	2 tsp.	10 mL
Pepper	⅛ tsp.	0.5 mL
Water	⅔ cup	150 mL
Evaporated skim milk	½ cup	125 mL

Cut meat from bone. Grind meat into bowl.

Add next 9 ingredients. Mix. Shape into 40 balls. Arrange on baking tray. Bake in 350°F (175°C) oven for 25 minutes or until cooked. Turn into 1½ quart (1.5 L) casserole.

Sauce: Stir flour, bouillon powder and pepper together in small saucepan. Add enough water to mix into smooth paste. Stir in rest of water and milk. Heat and stir until it boils and thickens. Pour over chicken eggs. May be held in 200°F (95°C) oven or reheated later. Makes 40 eggs.

Pictured on page 89.

NUTRITION GUIDE	4 eggs contain:	
	Energy	158 Calories (661 kJ)
	Cholesterol	41 mg
	Sodium	306 mg
	Fat	4.6 g

FAMILY CHICKEN CASSEROLE

A good tasting, good size dish. A whole meal.

Dry elbow macaroni	1½ cups	375 mL
Boiling water	3 qts.	3 L
Thinly sliced carrots	1½ cups	375 mL
Water		
Frozen peas	1 cup	250 mL
Canned chunk chicken (low fat)	2 × 5 oz.	2 × 142 g
SAUCE		
Condensed cream of mushroom soup	10 oz.	284 mL
Evaporated skim milk	1 cup	250 mL
Skim milk	½ cup	125 mL
White vinegar	2 tbsp.	30 mL
Garlic powder	¼ tsp.	1 mL
Liquid smoke (optional)	⅛ tsp.	0.5 mL

Cook macaroni in boiling water in large uncovered saucepan for 5 to 7 minutes until tender but firm. Drain.

Cook carrots in some water until tender-crisp.

Add peas. Cook 2 to 3 minutes more. Drain. Add to macaroni.

Add chicken. Turn into 2 quart (2 L) casserole.

Sauce: Mix all ingredients in bowl. Pour over macaroni mixture. Cover. Bake in 350°F (175°C) oven for 30 minutes until bubbly hot. Makes 8 cups (1.8 L).

NUTRITION GUIDE	1 cup (225 mL) contains:	
	Energy	240 Calories (1004 kJ)
	Cholesterol	24 mg
	Sodium	553 mg
	Fat	6.2 g

CHICKEN POT PIE

Little onions and chicken are in a gravy beneath a golden biscuit crust.

Boneless chicken breasts, skin and fat removed	1½ lbs.	680 g
Water	3 cups	700 mL
Thyme	½ tsp.	2 mL
Marjoram or rosemary	¼ tsp.	1 mL
Celery flakes	1 tsp.	5 mL
Salt	½ tsp.	2 mL
Pepper	½ tsp.	2 mL
Small whole onions	18	18
Water		
All-purpose flour	⅓ cup	75 mL
Skim milk	½ cup	125 mL
Reserved chicken broth	1 cup	250 mL
Chicken bouillon powder (35% less salt)	2 tsp.	10 mL
Gravy browner	⅛ tsp.	0.5 mL
CRUST		
All-purpose flour	½ cup	125 mL
Baking powder	1 tsp.	5 mL
Vegetable cooking oil	1 tbsp.	15 mL
Skim milk	3 tbsp.	50 mL

Combine first 7 ingredients in saucepan. Cook 30 to 45 minutes until chicken is tender. Remove chicken and chop. Reserve broth.

Cook onions in some water until tender. Cook gently to keep onions whole. Drain.

Mix flour and milk in saucepan until no lumps remain. Add chicken broth, bouillon powder and a bit of gravy browner for color. Heat and stir until it boils and thickens. Pour into 3 quart (3 L) casserole. Add chicken and onions. Stir lightly.

Crust: Mix all 4 ingredients into a ball. Roll out thinly on lightly floured surface. Place crust over chicken mixture inside casserole. Cut several slits in top. Bake in 425°F (220°C) oven for 15 to 20 minutes until hot and top is browned. Makes 4 servings.

NUTRITION GUIDE	1 serving contains:	
	Energy	485 Calories (2028 kJ)
	Cholesterol	106 mg
	Sodium	627 mg
	Fat	9 g

Good with or without bacon bits. Rice is added before cooking.

Condensed cream of chicken soup	10 oz.	284 mL
Water	1½ cups	375 mL
Juice drained from salmon		
Lemon juice, fresh or bottled	1 tsp.	5 mL
Large hard-boiled eggs, whites only, chopped	2	2
Cut green beans, fresh or frozen	2 cups	500 mL
Canned pink salmon (no added salt), drained, skin and round bones removed	7½ oz.	213 g
Finely chopped onion	⅓ cup	75 mL
Long grain rice, uncooked	1 cup	250 mL
Parsley flakes	1 tsp.	5 mL
Imitation bacon bits (optional)	1 tbsp.	15 mL
Salt to taste (optional)		
Pepper	⅛ tsp.	0.5 mL
Paprika	¼ tsp.	1 mL

Combine all ingredients in order given. Mix. Turn into 3 quart (3 L) casserole. Cover. Bake in 350°F (175°C) oven for 1 to 1¼ hours, stirring at half time to distribute beans, until rice is cooked. Makes 5½ cups (1.24 L).

NUTRITION GUIDE	1 cup (225 mL) contains:	
	Energy	234 Calories (980 kJ)
	Cholesterol	13 mg
	Sodium	530 mg
	Fat	6.5 g

Too bad the nuclear scientist swallowed some uranium. Now he has atomic ache.

SALMON RICE BAKE

Contains carrot, onion, broccoli and rice to make a full meal-type casserole.

Water	3 cups	675 mL
Grated carrot, packed	1½ cups	350 mL
Finely chopped onion	1 cup	250 mL
Chicken bouillon powder (35% less salt)	2 tsp.	10 mL
Small broccoli florets	1 cup	250 mL
Instant rice, uncooked	2¼ cups	500 mL
Condensed cream of mushroom soup	10 oz.	284 mL
Canned pink salmon (no added salt), drained, skin and round bones removed	7½ oz.	213 g

Paprika, sprinkle

Combine water, carrot, onion and bouillon powder in saucepan. Cover and cook until onion is almost tender.

Add broccoli. Cook for 4 minutes more. Do not drain.

Stir in rice. Cover. Let stand 5 minutes.

Add soup. Stir to mix. Break up salmon. Stir in. Turn into 2 quart (2 L) casserole.

Sprinkle with paprika. Cover. Bake in 350°F (175°C) oven for 30 minutes. Makes 6⅓ cups (1.43 L).

NUTRITION GUIDE	1 cup (225 mL) contains:	
	Energy	254 Calories (1065 kJ)
	Cholesterol	8 mg
	Sodium	538 mg
	Fat	6.6 g

Paré Pointer

A sign by a tree and fire hydrant said "Get a lawn, little doggie, get a lawn".

Although this should be served immediately, the topping will stay soft and tasty for a lengthy spell.

All-purpose flour	½ cup	125 mL
Paprika	¼ tsp.	1 mL
Celery salt	¼ tsp.	1 mL
Salt	¼ tsp.	1 mL
Skim milk	1½ cups	350 mL
Water packed tuna, drained and flaked	6½ oz.	184 g
Parsley flakes	½ tsp.	2 mL
Egg whites (large), room temperature	4	4
Baking powder	½ tsp.	2 mL

Stir flour, paprika, celery salt and salt together in saucepan. Mix in some of the milk until no lumps remain. Add rest of milk. Heat and stir until it boils and thickens. Remove from heat.

Add tuna and parsley.

Beat egg whites and baking powder in mixing bowl until stiff. Fold into tuna mixture. Pour into 2 quart (2 L) casserole that bottom has been sprayed with no-stick cooking spray. Bake in 350°F (175°C) oven for 30 to 35 minutes until it looks puffy and golden brown. Center will be soft. Makes 4 servings.

NUTRITION GUIDE	1 serving contains:	
	Energy	170 Calories (712 kJ)
	Cholesterol	10 mg
	Sodium	528 mg
	Fat	.6 g

At an auction sale you can very easily get something for nodding.

TUNA SHELL CASSEROLE

Stuffed shells over creamed spinach. A tasteful go-together.

Giant pasta shells	18	18
Boiling water	3 qts.	3 L
All-purpose flour	3 tbsp.	50 mL
Salt	1/4 tsp.	1 mL
Pepper	1/8 tsp.	0.5 mL
Nutmeg	1/8 tsp.	0.5 mL
Skim milk	1 cup	250 mL
Frozen chopped spinach, cooked and drained	10 oz.	284 g
Part-skim ricotta cheese, broken up	1/2 lb.	227 g
Water packed tuna, drained and flaked	6 1/2 oz.	184 g
Paprika, sprinkle		

Cook shells in boiling water in uncovered Dutch oven about 12 to 15 minutes until tender but firm. Drain. Rinse with cold water. Drain well.

Measure next 4 ingredients into saucepan. Whisk in some milk until no lumps remain, then whisk in rest of milk. Heat and stir until it boils and thickens.

Stir in spinach. Turn into 8 x 8 inch (20 x 20 cm) baking dish.

Mash cheese and tuna together. Carefully stuff shells. Arrange over spinach.

Sprinkle with paprika. Cover. Bake in 350°F (175°C) oven for 20 to 30 minutes until heated through. Makes 6 servings.

NUTRITION GUIDE	1 serving contains:	
	Energy	225 Calories (940 kJ)
	Cholesterol	18 mg
	Sodium	334 mg
	Fat	3.8 g

Sometimes it doesn't matter who you know but who you yes.

Serve this with noodles for a satisfying meal.

All-purpose flour	1/3 **cup**	**75 mL**
Skim milk	1/3 **cup**	**75 mL**
Skim milk	1 1/2 **cups**	**350 mL**
Chives	**2 tsp.**	**10 mL**
Onion flakes	**2 tsp.**	**10 mL**
Salt	1/2 **tsp.**	**2 mL**
Pepper	1/4 **tsp.**	**1 mL**
Sherry (or alcohol-free sherry)	1/4 **cup**	**60 mL**
Frozen peas	**1 cup**	**250 mL**
Cooked shrimp, chopped	**12 oz.**	**340 g**
Grated low-fat sharp Cheddar cheese (less than 21% MF)	1/2 **cup**	**125 mL**

Stir flour and first amount of skim milk together in saucepan until no lumps remain.

Add next 5 ingredients. Heat and stir until it comes to a boil and thickens.

Stir in remaining ingredients. Turn into 1 quart (1 L) casserole. Bake, uncovered, in 350°F (175°C) oven for about 45 minutes. Makes 4 servings.

NUTRITION GUIDE	**1 serving contains:**	
	Energy	271 Calories (1132 kJ)
	Cholesterol	174 mg
	Sodium	688 mg
	Fat	5.3 g

When liars die they lie still.

SEAFOOD CASSEROLE

Casual deluxe.

Long grain rice	¾ cup	175 mL
Boiling water	1½ cups	350 mL
Sliced fresh mushrooms	2 cups	500 mL
Diced celery	1 cup	250 mL
Diced green pepper (optional)	⅓ cup	75 mL
All-purpose flour	3 tbsp.	50 mL
Salt	½ tsp.	2 mL
Skim milk	2½ cups	600 mL
Salad dressing, page 98	½ cup	125 mL
Cooked peas	1 cup	250 mL
Onion flakes	1 tbsp.	15 mL
Worcestershire sauce	1 tbsp.	15 mL
Curry powder	½ tsp.	2 mL
Imitation crabmeat, sliced	¼ lb.	120 g
Cooked shrimp	¼ lb.	120 g
TOPPING		
Hard margarine	1 tbsp.	15 mL
Dry bread crumbs	⅓ cup	75 mL

Cook rice in boiling water until tender and water is absorbed.

Spray frying pan with no-stick cooking spray. Add mushrooms, celery and green pepper. Sauté until soft.

Mix in flour and salt. Stir in milk until it boils and thickens.

Add next 7 ingredients along with rice. Stir. Turn into 2 quart (2 L) casserole.

Topping: Melt margarine in small saucepan. Stir in bread crumbs. Spread over casserole. Bake, uncovered, in 350°F (175°C) oven for about 45 minutes until very hot. Makes 6½ cups (1.5 L).

NUTRITION GUIDE	1 cup (225 mL) contains:	
	Energy	246 Calories (1029 kJ)
	Cholesterol	39 mg
	Sodium	663 mg
	Fat	3.2 g

ORIENTAL TUNA CASSEROLE

Slightly crunchy, this really stretches a can of tuna.

Condensed cream of mushroom soup	10 oz.	284 mL
Water	⅔ cup	150 mL
Cooked noodles	1 cup	250 mL
Finely chopped celery	1 cup	250 mL
Finely chopped onion	½ cup	125 mL
Finely chopped green pepper	¼ cup	50 mL
Chopped water chestnuts, drained	5 oz.	142 mL
Cracker crumbs (unsalted)	¾ cup	175 mL
Water-packed tuna, drained and flaked	2 × 6½ oz.	2 × 184 g
Pepper	⅛ tsp.	0.5 mL
Chow mein noodles	¼ cup	60 mL

Mix soup and water in medium bowl.

Add next 8 ingredients. Stir. Turn into 1½ quart (1.5 L) casserole.

Sprinkle with noodles. Bake, uncovered, in 350°F (175°C) oven for about 45 minutes. Makes 5 cups (1.13 L).

Pictured on page 17.

NUTRITION GUIDE	1 cup (225 mL) contains:	
	Energy	287 Calories (1199 kJ)
	Cholesterol	14 mg
	Sodium	941 mg
	Fat	7.6 g

People who sculpt, bathe often so they won't be known as dirty chiselers.

FISH PIE

Complete the meal with a green vegetable.

Sole, cod or other white fish fillets **Water to cover**	**1 lb.**	**454 g**
Medium potatoes, peeled and halved **Water**	**3**	**3**
Skim milk	**¼ cup**	**60 mL**
All-purpose flour **Skim milk**	**3 tbsp.** **⅔ cup**	**50 mL** **150 mL**
Reserved fish stock **Parsley flakes** **Grated low-fat sharp Cheddar cheese** **(21% less MF)**	**½ cup** **½ tsp.** **½ cup**	**125 mL** **2 mL** **125 mL**
Onion flakes	**2 tbsp.**	**30 mL**
Paprika, sprinkle		

Cook fish in water for about 5 minutes until it flakes easily. Drain, reserving ½ cup fish stock. Flake fish. Set aside.

Cook potatoes in some water until tender. Drain. Mash.

Add first amount of milk. Mash again.

Mix flour with some of the second amount of milk until no lumps remain. Stir in remaining milk. Heat and stir until it boils and thickens.

Add next 4 ingredients. Add fish. Stir. Turn into 1½ quart (1.5 L) casserole. Cover with potatoes.

Sprinkle with paprika. Bake, uncovered, in 350°F (175°C) oven for about 40 minutes until hot and browned. Makes 4 servings.

NUTRITION GUIDE	**1 serving contains:**	
	Energy	279 Calories (1167 kJ)
	Cholesterol	59 mg
	Sodium	199 mg
	Fat	4 g

*This looks so fancy yet is so easy to make. Not actually a ⸻
but you serve it from the oven.*

Canned pink salmon (no added salt), drained, skin and round bones removed	2 × 7½ oz.	2 × 213 g
Finely chopped celery	⅔ cup	150 mL
Salad dressing, page 98	⅓ cup	75 mL
Onion powder	½ tsp.	2 mL
Chives	1½ tsp.	7 mL
BISCUIT DOUGH		
All-purpose flour	2 cups	450 mL
Baking powder	4 tsp.	20 mL
Salt	¼ tsp.	1 mL
Cayenne pepper	⅛ tsp.	0.5 mL
Vegetable cooking oil	2 tbsp.	30 mL
Skim milk	⅞ cup	200 mL

Combine first 5 ingredients in bowl. Stir well.

Biscuit Dough: Measure flour, baking powder, salt and cayenne pepper into a separate bowl. Stir.

Add cooking oil and milk. Mix until soft ball forms. Knead on lightly floured surface 6 to 8 times. Roll out to 12 inch (30 cm) square. Spread with salmon mixture. Roll up like jelly roll. Dampen and seal seam. Cut into 12 slices. Arrange cut side down on pan that has been sprayed with no-stick cooking spray. Bake in 400°F (205°C) oven for 20 to 25 minutes until browned. Makes 12 servings.

Pictured on cover.

NUTRITION GUIDE	1 serving contains:	
	Energy	159 Calories (664 kJ)
	Cholesterol	9 mg
	Sodium	136 mg
	Fat	5.2 g

SHRIMP NOODLE CASSEROLE

Also contains kernel corn. Creamy with a browned cheese topping.

Dry fettuccine	8 oz.	250 g
Boiling water	2 qts.	2 L
Frozen kernel corn, cooked	1½ cups	375 mL
Sliced fresh mushrooms	1 cup	250 mL
Frozen cooked shrimp	½ lb.	250 g
SAUCE		
All-purpose flour	3 tbsp.	50 mL
Salt	½ tsp.	2 mL
Pepper	⅛ tsp.	0.5 mL
Powdered skim milk	⅓ cup	75 mL
Skim milk	2 cups	500 mL
Reserved juice from shrimp		
Paprika	¼ tsp.	1 mL
Grated low-fat sharp Cheddar cheese (less than 21% MF)	1½ cups	375 mL

Cook fettuccine in boiling water in large uncovered pot for 5 to 7 minutes until tender but firm. Drain. Turn into 3 quart (3 L) casserole.

Spread corn over noodles followed by mushrooms then shrimp.

Sauce: Measure flour, salt, pepper and powdered milk (which adds extra richness) into saucepan. Add enough milk to mix until no lumps remain. Stir in rest of milk, juice from shrimp and paprika. Heat and stir over medium heat until it boils and thickens.

Stir in 1 cup (250 mL) of the grated cheese. Pour over shrimp. Bake, uncovered, in 350°F (175°C) oven for 30 minutes until heated through. Sprinkle with remaining cheese. Return to oven for about 5 minutes to melt cheese. Makes 7½ cups (1.7 L).

Pictured on page 143.

NUTRITION GUIDE	1 cup (225 mL) contains:	
	Energy	331 Calories (1386 kJ)
	Cholesterol	80 mg
	Sodium	463 mg
	Fat	6.6 g

A tuna-based sauce cooked over broccoli makes for a great meal.

Sliced fresh mushrooms	**2 cups**	**500 mL**
Skim milk	**1¼ cups**	**275 mL**
Salt	**½ tsp.**	**2 mL**
Pepper	**⅛ tsp.**	**0.5 mL**
Garlic powder	**⅛ tsp.**	**0.5 mL**
Sliced green onion	**¼ cup**	**60 mL**
Chopped pimiento	**2 tbsp.**	**30 mL**
Water-packed tuna, drained and flaked	**2 × 6½ oz.**	**2 × 184 g**
All-purpose flour	**¼ cup**	**60 mL**
Skim milk	**¼ cup**	**60 mL**
Broccoli, cut bite size	**1 lb.**	**454 g**
Boiling water		
Grated low-fat sharp Cheddar cheese (less than 21% MF)	**¼ cup**	**60 mL**
Dry bread crumbs	**¼ cup**	**60 mL**

Spray frying pan with no-stick cooking spray. Add mushrooms. Sauté until moisture has evaporated.

Add next 7 ingredients. Stir.

Mix flour and second amount of skim milk in small bowl until no lumps remain. Stir into tuna mixture until it boils and thickens. Remove from heat.

Cook broccoli in some boiling water until barely tender. Drain. Scatter over bottom of 3 quart (3 L) casserole. Pour tuna mixture over top.

Sprinkle with cheese, then bread crumbs. Bake, uncovered, in 350°F (175°C) oven for 30 minutes until bubbly hot. Makes 5½ cups (1.25 L).

NUTRITION GUIDE	1 cup (225 mL) contains:	
	Energy	200 Calories (835 kJ)
	Cholesterol	16 mg
	Sodium	611 mg
	Fat	2.2 g

BAKED FILLETS

The red pepper makes this tasty dish quite colorful.

Cod fish fillets	1 lb.	454 g
Light soy sauce (40% less salt)	2 tsp.	10 mL
Lemon juice, fresh or bottled	2 tsp.	10 mL
Garlic powder	1/8 tsp.	0.5 mL
Ginger, just a pinch		
Granulated sugar	3/4 tsp.	4 mL
Chopped green onion	1/3 cup	75 mL
Sliced fresh mushrooms	1 1/2 cups	375 mL
Small red pepper, seeded and cut in slivers	1	1

Arrange fish fillets in 2 quart (2 L) casserole.

Mix next 5 ingredients. Brush over fish. Reserve rest of marinade.

Sprinkle with onion, mushrooms and red pepper. Cover. Bake in 400°F (205°C) oven for 20 to 30 minutes. Dab with marinade mixture at half time. When fish flakes easily with a fork it is done. Makes 4 servings.

NUTRITION GUIDE	1 serving contains:	
	Energy	114 Calories (478 kJ)
	Cholesterol	49 mg
	Sodium	176 mg
	Fat	1 g

1. Green Pea Bake, page 145
2. Tuna Squares, page 96
3. Chicken Eggs, page 74
4. Meat And Rice Casserole, page 51

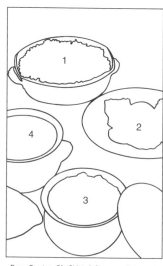

Props Courtesy Of: Chintz & Company, Cottswood
Furniture & Home Interiors,
Le Gnome

Add a salad to make this more complete.

Water	2¹/₂ cups	575 mL
Chopped onion	²/₃ cup	150 mL
Grated carrot	1 cup	250 mL
Chopped fresh mushrooms	¹/₂ cup	125 mL
Lemon juice, fresh or bottled	2 tsp.	10 mL
Instant rice, uncooked	1¹/₄ cups	300 mL
Skim milk	¹/₃ cup	75 mL
All-purpose flour	¹/₃ cup	75 mL
Chicken bouillon powder (35% less salt)	1 tsp.	5 mL
Cayenne pepper	¹/₈ tsp.	0.5 mL
Paprika	¹/₈ tsp.	0.5 mL
Skim milk	1 cup	250 mL
Peas, fresh or frozen, thawed	10 oz.	284 g
Canned pink salmon (no added salt), drained, skin and round bones removed	7¹/₂ oz.	213 g
TOPPING		
Grated low-fat sharp Cheddar cheese (less than 21% MF)	¹/₄ cup	60 mL
Dry bread crumbs	¹/₄ cup	60 mL

Measure first 5 ingredients into saucepan. Cover. Cook until vegetables are tender. Do not drain.

Add rice. Stir. Let stand 5 minutes.

Whisk first amount of milk with flour, bouillon powder, cayenne pepper and paprika until smooth. Add second amount of milk. Heat and stir until it boils and thickens.

Stir in peas and salmon. Add to rice mixture. Stir. Turn into 2 quart (2 L) casserole. Bake, uncovered, in 350°F (175°C) oven for 25 minutes.

Topping: Stir cheese and bread crumbs together. Sprinkle over casserole. Continue to bake for about 15 minutes more. Makes 7 cups (1.58 L).

NUTRITION GUIDE	1 cup (225 mL) contains:	
	Energy	222 Calories (931 kJ)
	Cholesterol	10 mg
	Sodium	537 mg
	Fat	6.8 g

SHRIMP CREOLE

This is a runny mixture that is served over rice. Excellent. Serve from stove top or from oven.

Chopped onion	**2 cups**	**500 mL**
Chopped celery	**2 cups**	**500 mL**
Boiling water		
Skim milk	**1 cup**	**250 mL**
All-purpose flour	**2 tbsp.**	**30 mL**
Skim milk	**2 tbsp.**	**30 mL**
Condensed tomato soup	**10 oz.**	**284 mL**
Salt	**¼ tsp.**	**1 mL**
Pepper	**⅛ tsp.**	**0.5 mL**
Fresh medium shrimp, cooked	**¾ lb.**	**375 g**

Cook onion and celery in some boiling water until tender. Drain through sieve.

Heat first amount of milk in saucepan until it boils.

Mix flour with second amount of milk until no lumps remain. Stir into boiling milk until it returns to a boil and thickens.

Stir in soup, salt and pepper.

Add shrimp to soup mixture reserving a few for garnish. Turn into 1½ quart (1.5 L) casserole. Cover. May be held in 200°F (95°C) oven for at least 2 hours or may be chilled in refrigerator for next-day use. Heat in 350°F (175°C) oven for 25 to 30 minutes until hot. Garnish with shrimp the last 5 to 10 minutes. Makes 4⅓ cups (1 L).

Pictured on page 35.

NUTRITION GUIDE	½ cup (125 mL) contains:	
	Energy	133 Calories (555 kJ)
	Cholesterol	91 mg
	Sodium	483 mg
	Fat	1.8 g

Variation: Omit fresh shrimp. Use 2 x 4 oz. (2 x 113 g) cans of medium cleaned shrimp. Sodium per serving will increase.

A meal in one. Good flavor.

Chopped onion	1 cup	250 mL
Chopped fresh mushrooms	1 cup	250 mL
Chopped green pepper	1/3 cup	75 mL
Worcestershire sauce	1 tsp.	5 mL
Chopped celery	1/2 cup	125 mL
Water	2 cups	500 mL
Condensed cream of mushroom soup	10 oz.	284 mL
Reserved juice, plus water if needed	1/2 cup	125 mL
Long grain rice	2/3 cup	150 mL
Boiling water	1 1/3 cups	300 mL
Cooked fresh shrimp	2 cups	500 mL
Corn flake crumbs	3 tbsp.	50 mL

Combine first 6 ingredients in saucepan. Cook until tender. Drain and reserve juice.

Stir in soup and reserved juice.

Cook rice in boiling water for about 15 minutes until tender and water is absorbed. Add to vegetable mixture.

Stir in shrimp. Turn into 2 quart (2 L) casserole.

Sprinkle corn flake crumbs over top. Cook, uncovered, in 350°F (175°C) oven for 20 to 30 minutes until bubbly hot. Makes 5 2/3 cups (1.28 L).

NUTRITION GUIDE	1 cup (225 mL) contains:	
	Energy	212 Calories (888 kJ)
	Cholesterol	92 mg
	Sodium	577 mg
	Fat	5.4 g

SHRIMP IMPERIAL

A special luncheon dish.

Low-fat cottage cheese (less than 1% MF)	½ cup	125 mL
White vinegar	1½ tsp.	7 mL
All-purpose flour	3 tbsp.	50 mL
Dry mustard	⅛ tsp.	0.5 mL
Chicken bouillon powder (35% less salt)	1 tsp.	5 mL
Skim milk	1 cup	250 mL
Canned chicken, broken up	6¼ oz.	184 g
Canned medium shrimp, drained	4 oz.	113 g
Sherry (or alcohol-free sherry)	2 tbsp.	30 mL
Paprika	¼ tsp.	1 mL
TOPPING		
Hard margarine	1 tbsp.	15 mL
Dry bread crumbs	⅓ cup	75 mL

Smooth cottage cheese, vinegar, flour, mustard and bouillon powder in blender.

Heat milk in saucepan until it boils. Stir cottage cheese mixture into boiling milk until it returns to a boil and thickens.

Add next 4 ingredients. Stir. Turn into 1 quart (1 L) casserole.

Topping: Melt margarine in small saucepan. Stir in bread crumbs. Sprinkle over top. Bake, uncovered, in 350°F (175°C) oven for 20 to 25 minutes until bubbly hot. Makes 4 servings.

NUTRITION GUIDE	1 serving contains:	
	Energy	238 Calories (996 kJ)
	Cholesterol	74 mg
	Sodium	602 mg
	Fat	8 g

Good tomato flavor with lots of shrimp.

Long grain rice	⅔ **cup**	**150 mL**
Boiling water	1⅓ **cups**	**300 mL**
Medium shrimp, shelled and deveined	**1 lb.**	**454 g**
Boiling water	1½ **cups**	**375 mL**
Chopped onion	½ **cup**	**125 mL**
Chopped green pepper	¼ **cup**	**60 mL**
Sliced fresh mushrooms	**1 cup**	**250 mL**
Tomato paste	5½ **oz.**	**156 mL**
Water	¾ **cup**	**175 mL**
Granulated sugar	**1 tsp.**	**5 mL**
Salt	½ **tsp.**	**2 mL**
Pepper	¼ **tsp.**	**1 mL**
TOPPING		
Hard margarine	**1 tbsp.**	**15 mL**
Dry bread crumbs	⅓ **cup**	**75 mL**

Cook rice in first amount of water about 15 minutes until tender and water is absorbed. Set aside.

Cook shrimp in second amount of water for about 5 minutes until pinkish and curled a bit. Drain. Cut up into bite size pieces. Set aside.

Spray frying pan with no-stick cooking spray. Add onion, green pepper and mushrooms. Sauté until soft.

In medium size bowl mix tomato paste, third amount of water, sugar, salt and pepper. Add prepared rice, shrimp and onion mixture. Stir. Turn into 1½ quart (1.5 L) casserole.

Topping: Melt margarine in small saucepan. Stir in bread crumbs. Spread over casserole. Bake, uncovered, in 350°F (175°C) oven for 30 minutes. Makes 5 cups (1.13 L).

NUTRITION GUIDE	**1 cup (225 mL) contains:**	
	Energy	257 Calories (1076 kJ)
	Cholesterol	138 mg
	Sodium	508 mg
	Fat	4.8 g

OVEN FRIED FISH

What a nice change to have this cooked in the oven.

Lemon juice, fresh or bottled	1½ tsp.	7 mL
Low-fat cottage cheese (less than 1% MF)	½ cup	125 mL
Dry onion soup mix	1 tbsp.	15 mL
Fine dry bread crumbs	½ cup	125 mL
Grated Parmesan cheese	1 tbsp.	15 mL
Parsley flakes	½ tsp.	2 mL
Paprika	¼ tsp.	1 mL
Fish fillets, 4 oz. (112 g) size	4	4

Run lemon juice and cottage cheese through blender to smooth. Turn into bowl.

Stir dry soup mixture well, then measure required amount. Stir into cottage cheese mixture.

In another small bowl mix bread crumbs, cheese, parsley and paprika.

Spray baking pan with no-stick cooking spray. Spread fish with cottage cheese mixture then roll in crumb mixture. Arrange on baking pan. Bake in 400°F (205°C) oven about 20 minutes until browned and fish flakes easily with fork. Makes 4 servings.

NUTRITION GUIDE	1 serving contains:	
	Energy	188 Calories (787 kJ)
	Cholesterol	51 mg
	Sodium	659 mg
	Fat	2.3 g

TUNA SQUARES

This could almost pass for chicken.

Large eggs	2	2
Skim milk	1 cup	250 mL
Dry bread crumbs	1 cup	250 mL
Finely chopped onion	⅓ cup	75 mL
Parsley flakes	1 tsp.	5 mL
Lemon juice, fresh or bottled	1 tbsp.	15 mL
Salt	¾ tsp.	4 mL
Pepper	¼ tsp.	1 mL
Thyme, generous measure	¼ tsp.	1 mL
Water-packed tuna, drained and flaked	3 × 6½ oz.	3 × 184 g

(continued on next page)

Beat eggs in medium bowl until frothy.

Add remaining ingredients, stirring after each addition. Turn into 8 x 8 inch (20 x 20 cm) pan that has been sprayed with no-stick cooking spray. Bake in 350°F (175°C) oven for 40 minutes until firm. Cut into 9 squares.

Pictured on page 89.

NUTRITION GUIDE	1 square contains:	
	Energy	160 Calories (671 kJ)
	Cholesterol	59 mg
	Sodium	585 mg
	Fat	2 g

GARLIC TOAST

Tastes like the real thing but with very little fat.

Diet soft margarine	**4 tbsp.**	**60 mL**
Garlic powder	**½ tsp.**	**2 mL**
French loaf slices, 1 inch (2.5 cm) thick	**12**	**12**

Mix margarine with garlic powder in small bowl.

Arrange bread slices on baking sheet. Toast under broiler. Turn slices over. Spread each slice with 1 tsp. (5 mL) margarine mixture. Toast again under broiler. Makes 12 slices.

NUTRITION GUIDE	1 slice contains:	
	Energy	134 Calories (561 kJ)
	Cholesterol	trace
	Sodium	273 mg
	Fat	2.1 g

SEEDY TOAST

Quick and easy.

Diet soft margarine	4 tbsp.	60 mL
Celery seed	1 tsp.	5 mL
Onion powder	1/4 tsp.	1 mL
Paprika	1/4 tsp.	1 mL
Hot pepper sauce	1/4 tsp.	1 mL
French loaf slices, 1 inch (2.5 cm) thick	12	12

Mix first 5 ingredients in bowl.

Arrange bread slices on broiler tray. Broil to toast 1 side. Turn slices over. Spread untoasted side with 1 tsp. (5 mL) margarine mixture. Broil to toast. Serve hot. Makes 12 slices.

NUTRITION GUIDE	1 slice contains:	
	Energy	135 Calories (563 kJ)
	Cholesterol	trace
	Sodium	274 mg
	Fat	2.2 g

SALAD DRESSING

For the lowest fat content, make your own.

Granulated sugar	1/4 cup	60 mL
All-purpose flour	3 tbsp.	50 mL
Dry mustard powder	1/2 tsp.	2 mL
Salt	1/2 tsp.	2 mL
Skim milk	1 cup	250 mL
White vinegar	1/4 cup	60 mL

Stir first 4 ingredients together well in small saucepan.

Mix in part of the milk until smooth. Whisk in remaining milk and vinegar. Heat and stir until it boils and thickens. Pour into container when cooled a bit. Store in refrigerator. Makes 1 1/4 cups (275 mL).

NUTRITION GUIDE	1 tbsp. (15 mL) contains:	
	Energy	19 Calories (80 kJ)
	Cholesterol	trace
	Sodium	75 mg
	Fat	trace

KETCHUP

Use as a condiment or in recipes requiring ketchup.

Tomato paste	5½ oz.	156 mL
Water	⅓ cup	75 mL
White vinegar	½ cup	125 mL
Granulated sugar	¼ cup	60 mL
Onion powder	¾ tsp.	4 mL
Salt	¾ tsp.	4 mL
Ground cloves	⅛ tsp.	0.5 mL
Cornstarch	1 tbsp.	15 mL
Water	3 tbsp.	50 mL
Liquid sweetener	1½ tsp.	7 mL

Place first 7 ingredients in saucepan. Heat and stir on medium-high until it boils.

Mix cornstarch, water and sweetener together in small cup. Stir into boiling liquid until it boils and thickens. Cool. Makes 1¼ cups (300 mL).

NUTRITION GUIDE

1 tbsp. (15 mL) contains:

Energy	20 Calories (82 kJ)
Cholesterol	0 mg
Sodium	108 mg
Fat	trace

CRANBERRY SAUCE

Serve with meat, especially chicken and turkey.

Cranberries, fresh or frozen	2 cups	450 mL
Water	¾ cup	175 mL
Liquid sweetener	2 tsp.	10 mL

Place cranberries and water in saucepan. Bring to a boil. Boil slowly for about 10 minutes until berries pop their skins.

Stir in sweetener. Cool. Store in refrigerator. Makes 1⅓ cups (300 mL).

NUTRITION GUIDE

1 tbsp. (15 mL) contains:

Energy	4 Calories (19 kJ)
Cholesterol	0 mg
Sodium	trace
Fat	trace

BANNOCK BISCUITS MODERN

A different biscuit to be sure. Cooked in a modern appliance rather than over a fire.

Whole wheat flour	1½ cups	350 mL
Cornmeal	½ cup	125 mL
Baking powder	1 tbsp.	15 mL
Salt	½ tsp.	2 mL
Skim milk	1½ cups	350 mL
Granulated sugar	2 tbsp.	30 mL

Stir first 4 ingredients together in bowl.

Add milk and sugar. Stir just until mixture is moistened. Mixture should be thick and barely spreadable. Spray frying pan with no-stick cooking spray. Spread about ¼ cup (60 mL) batter in flattish circle. An ice cream scoop is ideal for this. Try 1 first to be sure pan isn't too hot. An electric frying pan would be 325°F (160°C). Cover. Cook for about 9 minutes without turning. Tops will feel dry and firm and bottoms will be browned. Makes 10 large biscuits.

Pictured on page 17.

NUTRITION GUIDE	1 biscuit contains:	
	Energy	108 Calories (451 kJ)
	Cholesterol	1 mg
	Sodium	163 mg
	Fat	.6 g

DROP CHEESE BISCUITS

Speckled with cheese. These are so easy.

All-purpose flour	2 cups	500 mL
Granulated sugar	1 tbsp.	15 mL
Baking powder	4 tsp.	20 mL
Salt	¼ tsp.	1 mL
Grated low-fat sharp Cheddar cheese (less than 21% MF)	1½ cups	375 mL
Vegetable cooking oil	2 tbsp.	30 mL
Skim milk	1 cup	250 mL

(continued on next page)

Measure first 5 ingredients into bowl. Stir.

Add cooking oil and milk. Stir until moistened. Drop by spoonfuls onto baking sheet that has been sprayed with no-stick cooking spray. Bake in 425°F (220°C) oven for about 12 to 15 minutes. Makes 16 biscuits.

Pictured on page 125.

NUTRITION GUIDE	1 biscuit contains:	
	Energy	120 Calories (501 kJ)
	Cholesterol	7 mg
	Sodium	127 mg
	Fat	4.2 g

WHOLE WHEAT BISCUITS

Looks so different from the usual white. So good! They look like little loaves of bread.

Whole wheat flour	2 cups	450 mL
Baking powder	1 tbsp.	15 mL
Salt	1/4 tsp.	1 mL
Vegetable cooking oil	2 tbsp.	30 mL
Mild molasses	1 tbsp.	15 mL
Skim milk	3/4 cup	175 mL

Stir flour, baking powder and salt together in bowl.

Add cooking oil, molasses and milk. Stir to form a soft dough. Knead 8 times on lightly floured surface. Roll or pat 3/4 inch (2 cm) thick. Cut into 1 x 2 inch (2.5 x 5 cm) rectangles. Arrange on ungreased baking sheet. Bake in 425°F (220°C) oven for 12 to 15 minutes. Makes 19 biscuits.

Pictured on page 53.

NUTRITION GUIDE	1 biscuit contains:	
	Energy	65 Calories (272 kJ)
	Cholesterol	trace
	Sodium	44 mg
	Fat	1.7 g

POTATO BISCUITS

Very moist. Serve warm with your favorite casserole.

All-purpose flour	1½ cups	350 mL
Baking powder	1 tbsp.	15 mL
Salt	½ tsp.	2 mL
Granulated sugar	1 tbsp.	15 mL
Skim milk	⅔ cup	150 mL
Cooked mashed potato	1 cup	225 mL
Vegetable cooking oil	3 tbsp.	50 mL

Measure first 4 ingredients into bowl. Stir.

Add remaining ingredients. Stir until soft ball forms. Knead 6 or 8 times on lightly floured surface. Roll out ¾ inch (2 cm) thick. Cut into 2 inch (5 cm) rounds. Arrange on baking sheet sprayed with no-stick cooking spray. Bake in 425°F (220°C) oven for 15 minutes until lightly browned and risen. Makes 16 biscuits.

Pictured on page 17.

NUTRITION GUIDE	1 biscuit contains:	
	Energy	80 Calories (335 kJ)
	Cholesterol	trace
	Sodium	94 mg
	Fat	2.7 g

BRANDIED FRUIT

Be different. Serve this hot thickened fruit with any meat to make the occasion more festive.

Canned unsweetened fruit salad or fruit cocktail with juice	14 oz.	398 mL
Brandy flavoring	1 tsp.	5 mL
Liquid sweetener	1 tbsp.	15 mL
Maple flavoring	¼ tsp.	1 mL
Cornstarch	2 tbsp.	30 mL
Water	2 tbsp.	30 mL

(continued on next page)

Heat first 4 ingredients in saucepan until it boils.

Mix cornstarch in water in small cup. Stir into boiling fruit until it returns to a boil and thickens. Serve hot. Makes 1²/₃ cups (375 mL).

Pictured on page 35.

NUTRITION GUIDE	¹/₄ cup (60 mL) contains:	
	Energy	43 Calories (182 kJ)
	Cholesterol	0 mg
	Sodium	4 mg
	Fat	trace

CORNY BISCUITS

Cornmeal gives these good little biscuits a bit of a crunch.

Cornmeal	³/₄ cup	175 mL
Onion flakes	1 tbsp.	15 mL
Skim milk	³/₄ cup	175 mL
Biscuit mix	2 cups	450 mL

Combine cornmeal, onion flakes and milk in bowl. Let stand 10 minutes.

Add biscuit mix. Stir to form a soft ball of dough. Knead 6 to 8 times. Roll ³/₄ inch (2 cm) thick on lightly floured surface. Cut into 2 inch (5 cm) circles. Arrange on ungreased baking sheet. Bake in 400°F (205°C) oven for 15 minutes or until browned. Makes 15 biscuits.

Pictured on page 71.

NUTRITION GUIDE	1 biscuit contains:	
	Energy	96 Calories (403 kJ)
	Cholesterol	trace
	Sodium	219 mg
	Fat	2.3 g

BEET RELISH

Pretty color. Serve with cold or hot meat.

Canned beets, drained, diced or ground	14 oz.	398 mL
Grated cabbage	1 cup	250 mL
Chopped onion	1/4 cup	60 mL
Prepared horseradish	3/4 tsp.	4 mL
White vinegar	1/2 cup	125 mL
Salt	1/2 tsp.	2 mL
Pepper	1/8 tsp.	0.5 mL
Liquid sweetener (or 6 tbsp., 100 mL, granulated sugar)	4 tsp.	20 mL

Combine first 7 ingredients in large pot. Bring to a boil, stirring often. Simmer for 3 minutes. Cool.

Stir in sweetener. Store in refrigerator. Makes 2 cups (450 mL).

N U T R I T I O N G U I D E	1 tbsp. (15 mL) contains:	
	Energy	4 Calories (18 kJ)
	Cholesterol	0 mg
	Sodium	72 mg
	Fat	trace

PASTRY

Cholesterol-free crust.

All-purpose flour	1 cup	250 mL
Vegetable cooking oil	1/4 cup	60 mL
Salt	1/4 tsp.	1 mL
Water	3 tbsp.	50 mL

Combine all ingredients in bowl. Stir to mix and form a ball. Roll between 2 sheets of waxed paper. Fit into 9 inch (22 cm) pie plate.

N U T R I T I O N G U I D E	1/8 single crust contains:	
	Energy	121 Calories (507 kJ)
	Cholesterol	0 mg
	Sodium	85 mg
	Fat	7 g

Oranges and juice add a slightly different flavor. Rice is added raw which is a great time saver.

Boneless lamb shoulder steak, trimmed of fat	1½ lbs.	680 g
Long grain rice, uncooked	1 cup	250 mL
Canned mandarin oranges, drained, juice reserved	10 oz.	284 mL
Reserved orange juice plus boiling water to make	3 cups	750 mL
Beef bouillon powder (35% less salt)	4 tsp.	20 mL

Spray hot frying pan with no-stick cooking spray. Add lamb steak. Brown both sides. Place in 2 quart (2 L) casserole.

Pour rice evenly over top followed by orange segments.

Stir juice-water mixture with bouillon to dissolve. Pour over casserole. Cover. Bake in 325°F (160°C) oven for 1¼ to 1¾ hours until rice is cooked and meat is tender. Makes 6 servings.

NUTRITION GUIDE	1 serving contains:	
	Energy	268 Calories (1122 kJ)
	Cholesterol	74 mg
	Sodium	245 mg
	Fat	6.4 g

BEEF STEAK CASSEROLE: Use beef instead of lamb.

Old used batteries don't cost anything. They're free of charge.

LAMB CREOLE

Just the right blend of spices.

Boneless lamb, cubed, trimmed of fat	2 lbs.	900 g
Sliced fresh mushrooms	2 cups	500 mL
Canned tomatoes, broken up	14 oz.	398 mL
Red wine (or alcohol-free red wine)	1 cup	250 mL
Sliced onion	1 cup	250 mL
Green pepper, seeded and cut in slivers	1	1
Bay leaf	1	1
Salt	¾ tsp.	4 mL
Pepper	¼ tsp.	1 mL
Thyme	¼ tsp.	1 mL
Garlic powder	¼ tsp.	1 mL

Combine all ingredients in 3 quart (3 L) casserole. Stir well. Cover. Bake in 325°F (160°C) oven for 3 hours until meat is tender. Discard bay leaf. Makes 8 servings.

NUTRITION GUIDE	1 serving contains:	
	Energy	178 Calories (745 kJ)
	Cholesterol	73 mg
	Sodium	385 mg
	Fat	6 g

BEEF CREOLE: Use beef instead of lamb.

1. Chicken Rice Bake, page 61
2. Green Chili Quiche, page 150
3. Pork Casserole, page 123
4. Tomato Scallop, page 142

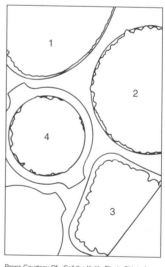

Props Courtesy Of: Call the Kettle Black, Chintz & Company, The Bay

Colorful with a mild taste similar to lasagne. Lean ground beef may be used instead of lamb.

Lean ground leg of lamb	1 lb.	454 g
Finely chopped onion	½ cup	125 mL
Canned tomatoes	14 oz.	398 mL
Garlic powder	¼ tsp.	1 mL
Salt	½ tsp.	2 mL
Pepper	¼ tsp.	1 mL
Granulated sugar	½ tsp.	2 mL
Sliced carrots	1½ cups	375 mL
Boiling water		
Dry colored fusilli (or other pasta)	2⅔ cups	600 mL
Boiling water	3 qts.	3 L
Low-fat plain yogurt (less than 1% MF)	1 cup	250 mL
Low-fat cottage cheese (less than 1% MF)	1 cup	250 mL
All-purpose flour	2 tbsp.	30 mL
Parsley flakes	2 tsp.	10 mL
Grated low-fat sharp Cheddar cheese (less than 21% MF)	1 cup	250 mL

Spray frying pan with no-stick vegetable spray. Add ground lamb and onion. Sauté until browned and onion is soft.

Add next 5 ingredients. Stir.

Cook carrots in some boiling water until tender. Drain.

Cook fusilli in second amount of boiling water in large uncovered pot about 10 minutes until tender but firm. Drain. Add carrots.

Stir yogurt, cottage cheese, flour and parsley together well. Add to fusilli. Stir. Place ½ meat mixture in 3 quart (3 L) casserole followed by ½ noodle mixture, second ½ meat and second ½ noodles. Cover. Bake in 350°F (175°C) oven for 25 to 30 minutes.

Sprinkle with cheese. Bake for 5 to 8 minutes more until cheese melts. Makes 8¼ cups (1.85L).

Pictured on cover.

NUTRITION GUIDE	1 cup (225 mL) contains:	
	Energy	296 Calories (1237 kJ)
	Cholesterol	44 mg
	Sodium	532 mg
	Fat	6.5 g

MOUSSAKA

Sweet spices are added to this Greek dish.

Medium eggplants, cut ½ inch (12 mm) thick	2	2
Chopped onion	2 cups	500 mL
Lean ground leg of lamb	1½ lbs.	680 g
Tomato paste	2 tbsp.	30 mL
Salt	1 tsp.	5 mL
Pepper	½ tsp.	2 mL
Garlic powder	¼ tsp.	1 mL
Cinnamon	¼ tsp.	1 mL
Parsley flakes	1 tsp.	5 mL
Water	½ cup	125 mL
CREAM SAUCE		
All-purpose flour	¼ cup	60 mL
Salt	½ tsp.	2 mL
Pepper	¼ tsp.	1 mL
Nutmeg	⅛ tsp.	0.5 mL
Skim milk	2 cups	450 mL
Low-fat cottage cheese (less than 1% MF), mashed with fork	1 cup	225 mL
Grated Parmesan cheese	½ cup	125 mL

Broil eggplant to cook and brown both sides.

Spray frying pan with no-stick cooking spray. Add onion. Sauté until soft and clear. Transfer to bowl.

Spray frying pan again. Add ground lamb. Scramble-fry until no pink remains in meat. Remove from heat.

Add next 7 ingredients to meat. Add onion. Stir.

(continued on next page)

Cream Sauce: Combine flour, salt, pepper and nutmeg in saucepan. Add a bit of milk and stir until no lumps remain. Add rest of milk. Heat and stir until it boils and thickens. Remove from heat.

Stir in cottage cheese. Layer in 9 x 13 inch (22 x 33 cm) pan:

1. ½ eggplant slices
2. ½ meat sauce
3. ⅓ Parmesan cheese
4. ½ eggplant slices
5. ½ meat sauce
6. ⅓ Parmesan cheese
7. All Cream Sauce
8. ⅓ Parmesan cheese

Bake, uncovered, in 350°F (175°C) oven for about 45 minutes until golden. Cut into 12 squares.

NUTRITION GUIDE	1 square contains:	
	Energy	156 Calories (652 kJ)
	Cholesterol	40 mg
	Sodium	564 mg
	Fat	4.8 g

Variation: Use beef instead of lamb.

Policemen who play tennis belong to the racket squad.

MEAL IN A DISH

Everything is mixed together raw. Lean ground beef may be used instead of lamb.

Chopped onion	1½ cups	375 mL
Frozen kernel corn	1 cup	250 mL
Grated carrot, packed	1 cup	250 mL
All-purpose flour	¼ cup	60 mL
Salt	1 tsp.	5 mL
Pepper	¼ tsp.	1 mL
Canned tomatoes	14 oz.	398 mL
Lean ground leg of lamb	1 lb.	454 g
Worcestershire sauce	1 tsp.	5 mL
Medium potatoes, peeled and cubed	4	4

Combine first 6 ingredients in large bowl. Stir well until flour is evenly mixed.

Add tomatoes, ground lamb and Worcestershire sauce. Mix.

Stir in potatoes. Turn into 3 quart (3 L) casserole. Cover. Bake in 350°F (175°C) oven for about 2 hours until potatoes are tender and meat is cooked. Makes about 7 cups (1.6 L).

NUTRITION GUIDE	1 cup (225 mL) contains:	
	Energy	213 Calories (893 kJ)
	Cholesterol	40 mg
	Sodium	541 mg
	Fat	4 g

Variation: Use beef instead of lamb.

Habits can be harmful. The carpenter broke his teeth by biting his nails.

Could be Irish Stew.

Lamb cubes, from neck or shoulder	1 lb.	454 g
Peeled cubed potatoes	2 cups	500 mL
Chopped onion	1 cup	250 mL
Sliced celery	1 cup	250 mL
Green pepper, seeded, cut in short slivers	1	1
Boiling water	1½ cups	375 mL
Beef bouillon powder (35% less salt)	4 tsp.	20 mL
Frozen peas	2 cups	500 mL

Spray frying pan with no-stick cooking spray. Add lamb. Brown. Turn into 2 quart (2 L) casserole.

Add next 4 ingredients.

Mix water with bouillon powder. Pour into frying pan, loosen brown bits and pour over lamb. Cover. Bake in 350°F (175°C) oven for 1½ hours.

Add peas. Stir lightly. Continue to bake for 15 minutes until peas are cooked and meat is tender. Makes 6 cups (1.35 L).

NUTRITION GUIDE	1 cup (225 mL) contains:	
	Energy	210 Calories (878 kJ)
	Cholesterol	49 mg
	Sodium	296 mg
	Fat	4.5 g

BEEF DINNER DISH: Use beef instead of lamb.

After he was made a ruler, he was the straightest man around.

PINEAPPLE HAM PIZZA

This has a rice crust covered with cheese, ham and pineapple.

RICE CRUST

Long grain rice	½ cup	125 mL
Boiling water	1 cup	250 mL
All-purpose flour	1½ cups	350 mL
Fast rising instant yeast	1½ tsp.	7 mL
Warm water	½ cup	125 mL

TOPPING

Tomato paste	½ x 5½ oz.	½ x 156 mL
Water	⅓ cup	75 mL
Onion powder	¼ tsp.	1 mL
Oregano	¼ tsp.	1 mL
Liquid sweetener	¼ tsp.	1 mL
Basil	¼ tsp.	1 mL
Garlic salt	½ tsp.	2 mL
Grated part-skim mozzarella cheese (35% less fat)	¾ cup	175 mL
Unsweetened pineapple tidbits, drained	14 oz.	398 mL
Ham cubes	⅔ cup	150 mL
Green pepper, seeded and cut in slivers	½	½
Grated part-skim mozzarella cheese (35% less fat)	¾ cup	175 mL
Grated low-fat medium or sharp Cheddar cheese (less than 21% MF)	½ cup	125 mL

Rice Crust: Cook rice in boiling water until tender and water is absorbed. Measure 1¼ cups (275 mL) into bowl. Cool a little.

Add flour and yeast. Stir well. Add water. Mix. Knead 25 times on lightly floured surface mixing in a bit more flour if sticky. Roll and stretch to fit 12 inch (30 cm) pizza pan that has been sprayed with no-stick cooking spray.

(continued on next page)

Topping: Stir first 7 ingredients together. Spread over cr

Sprinkle with first amount of mozzarella cheese, pineapp
green pepper. Bake on bottom shelf of 450°F (230°C)
minutes.

Sprinkle with second amount of mozzarella cheese. Add   ~ddar
cheese. Continue to bake for 5 to 10 minutes more until cheese is
melted and crust is browned. Cut into 8 wedges.

Pictured on page 53.

NUTRITION GUIDE	1 wedge contains:	
	Energy	241 Calories (1009 kJ)
	Cholesterol	22 mg
	Sodium	400 mg
	Fat	5.9 g

SWEET AND SOUR HAM BALLS

Amazing morsels. Great for company.

Lean ground cooked ham	1 lb.	454 g
Lean ground pork	1 lb.	454 g
Dry fine bread crumbs	2 cups	500 mL
Skim milk	1 cup	250 mL
All-purpose flour	1/4 cup	60 mL
Dry mustard powder	1 tsp.	5 mL
Brown sugar	1 1/2 cups	350 mL
White vinegar	3/4 cup	175 mL
Water	3/4 cup	175 mL
Pineapple or orange juice	3/4 cup	175 mL

In large bowl mix first 4 ingredients together well. Shape into 1 inch
(2.5 cm) balls. Place on shallow baking sheet. Bake, uncovered, in
375°F (190°C) oven for 20 minutes. Drain. Place in 3 quart (3 L)
casserole.

Mix flour, mustard and brown sugar in small saucepan. Stir in
remaining ingredients until it boils and thickens. Pour over meatballs.
Bake, uncovered, for another 20 minutes. Makes 84 meatballs.
Serves 12.

NUTRITION GUIDE	1 serving (7 meatballs) contains:	
	Energy	241 Calories (1008 kJ)
	Cholesterol	30 mg
	Sodium	650 mg
	Fat	3.5 g

...M PASTA CASSEROLE

Creamy yellow in color. The ham and tomato add even more color to this tasty dish.

Chopped onion	½ cup	125 mL
Dry elbow macaroni	2 cups	500 mL
Boiling water	3 qts.	3 L
Grated low-fat sharp Cheddar cheese (less than 21% MF)	¾ cup	175 mL
Lean cooked ham slice, cubed (¼ lb., 125 g)	¾ cup	175 mL
Medium tomatoes, diced	2	2
Condensed cream of chicken soup	10 oz.	284 mL
Skim milk	½ cup	125 mL
Prepared mustard	1 tsp.	5 mL

Cook onion and macaroni in boiling water in large uncovered saucepan until macaroni is tender but firm. Drain. Return to saucepan.

Add cheese, ham and tomato.

In bowl whisk soup, milk and mustard together. Stir into macaroni mixture. Turn into 2 quart (2 L) casserole. Bake, uncovered, in 350°F (175°C) oven for 20 minutes until quite hot. Makes 6⅓ cups (1.43 L).

NUTRITION GUIDE	1 cup (225 mL) contains:	
	Energy	259 Calories (1085 kJ)
	Cholesterol	21 mg
	Sodium	735 mg
	Fat	7.0 g

Incredibly good. The stuffing makes them taste like more.

STUFFING

Chopped onion	⅓ cup	75 mL
Chopped celery	2 tbsp.	30 mL
Water	½ cup	125 mL
Dry bread crumbs	2 cups	500 mL
Parsley flakes	1 tsp.	5 mL
Poultry seasoning	¾ tsp.	4 mL
Salt	¼ tsp.	1 mL
Pepper	⅛ tsp.	0.5 mL
Water	1 cup	250 mL
Lean cooked ham slices (see Note)	16	16
Paprika, sprinkle		
Grated low-fat sharp or medium Cheddar cheese (less than 21% MF)	3 tbsp.	50 mL

Stuffing: Cook onion and celery in first amount of water until soft. Do not drain.

Add bread crumbs, parsley, poultry seasoning, salt, pepper and second amount of water. Stir well. Add more water as needed so it will hold together.

Place 2 tbsp. (30 mL) filling down center of each ham slice. Roll. Place seam side down in 9 x 13 inch (22 x 33 cm) pan, making 2 long rows side by side.

Sprinkle with paprika. Cover. Bake in 350°F (175°C) oven for 20 minutes.

Sprinkle cheese down center of each row. Cover. Bake 5 minutes more. Makes 16 rolls.

Note: Square cooked ham slices, 6 per 6 oz. (175 g) package, were used for this recipe.

NUTRITION GUIDE	1 roll contains:	
	Energy	100 Calories (416 kJ)
	Cholesterol	14 mg
	Sodium	564 mg
	Fat	2.4 g

ZUCCHINI PORK BAKE

So colorful with green and orange showing through the top.

Lean ground pork	1 lb.	454 g
Salt	½ tsp.	2 mL
Onion powder	¼ tsp.	1 mL
Sage	⅛ tsp.	0.5 mL
Thyme	⅛ tsp.	0.5 mL
Pepper	⅛ tsp.	0.5 mL
Zucchini with peel, cubed, about 1¼ lbs. (570 g)	4 cups	900 mL
Water		
Sweet potato, peeled and cubed	2 cups	450 mL
Water		
Frozen egg product, thawed, (low-fat and cholesterol-free)	½ cup	125 mL
Egg white (large)	1	1
Cracker crumbs (unsalted)	¼ cup	60 mL
Grated low-fat sharp Cheddar cheese (less than 21% MF)	½ cup	125 mL

Spray frying pan with no-stick cooking spray. Add ground pork. Scramble-fry. Mix in next 5 ingredients.

Cook zucchini in some water until tender crisp. Drain.

Cook sweet potato in some water until tender crisp. Drain.

Combine egg product, egg white, cracker crumbs and cheese in large bowl. Add ground pork, zucchini and sweet potato. Toss lightly to distribute evenly. Turn into 2 quart (2 L) casserole. Cover. Bake, in 350°F (175°C) oven for about 30 minutes. Makes 6½ cups (1.5 L).

NUTRITION GUIDE	1 cup (225 mL) contains:	
	Energy	182 Calories (760 kJ)
	Cholesterol	28 mg
	Sodium	379 mg
	Fat	4.2 g

Breakfast in a pan.

SAUCE

All-purpose flour	2 tbsp.	30 mL
Salt	1/4 tsp.	1 mL
Pepper	1/8 tsp.	0.5 mL
Skim milk	1 cup	250 mL
Sliced green onion	2 tbsp.	30 mL
Sliced fresh small mushrooms	1 cup	250 mL
Frozen egg product, thawed (low-fat and cholesterol-free	1 1/2 cups	375 mL
Egg whites (large)	2	2
Medium potatoes, cooked, peeled and grated	2	2
Lean ham cubes	1/2 cup	125 mL

TOPPING

Hard margarine, melted	1 tbsp.	15 mL
Dry bread crumbs	1/2 cup	125 mL
Water	1 tbsp.	15 mL

Sauce: Combine flour, salt and pepper in saucepan. Whisk in milk gradually until smooth. Heat and stir until it boils and thickens.

Spray frying pan with no-stick cooking spray. Add onion and mushrooms. Sauté until soft. Add to sauce.

Spray frying pan again. Add egg product and egg whites. Scramble-fry until cooked. Stir into sauce.

Add potato and ham. Stir. Turn into 9 x 9 inch (22 x 22 cm) pan which has been sprayed with no-stick cooking spray.

Topping: Stir all 3 ingredients together well. Sprinkle over top. Bake in 350°F (175°C) oven for about 40 minutes. Cut into 9 squares.

NUTRITION GUIDE	1 square contains:	
	Energy	119 Calories (498 kJ)
	Cholesterol	4 mg
	Sodium	354 mg
	Fat	2.4 g

HAM SCALLOP

Good flavor. A green salad complements this dish.

Lean ham slice, about ½ inch (12 mm) thick, cubed or slivered	1 lb.	454 g
Potatoes, peeled and thinly sliced	2 lbs.	900 g
Cauliflower florets	1 cup	250 mL
Chopped or sliced onion	1 cup	250 mL
Peas, fresh or frozen	1 cup	250 mL
SAUCE		
All-purpose flour	⅓ cup	75 mL
Pepper	¼ tsp.	1 mL
Cayenne pepper	⅛ tsp.	0.5 mL
Parsley flakes	½ tsp.	2 mL
Skim milk	2½ cups	575 mL

Put first 5 ingredients into large bowl.

Sauce: Stir flour, pepper, cayenne pepper and parsley together in saucepan. Whisk in part of the milk until no lumps remain. Whisk in rest of milk. Heat and stir on medium-high until it boils and thickens. Pour over contents in bowl. Stir. Pour into 3 quart (3 L) casserole. Cover. Bake in 350°F (175°C) oven for about 60 minutes until potato is tender. Makes 9 cups (2 L).

NUTRITION GUIDE	1 cup (225 mL) contains:	
	Energy	221 Calories (924 kJ)
	Cholesterol	24 mg
	Sodium	706 mg
	Fat	2.6 g

PORK CHOP BAKE

Fantastic flavor in both meat and gravy.

Boneless pork chops, fat removed	2 lbs.	900 g
Condensed cream of mushroom soup	10 oz.	284 mL
White wine (or alcohol-free wine)	¼ cup	60 mL
Beef bouillon powder (35% less salt)	2 tsp.	10 mL
Onion flakes	1 tbsp.	15 mL

(continued on next page)

Arrange pork chops in 3 quart (3 L) casserole.

Mix remaining ingredients in small bowl. Spoon over and between pork chops. Cover. Bake in 350°F (175°C) oven for 1½ hours or until very tender. Makes 8 servings.

NUTRITION GUIDE	1 serving contains:	
	Energy	131 Calories (550 kJ)
	Cholesterol	37 mg
	Sodium	413 mg
	Fat	5.4 g

PORK POT

Pork and vegetables with a stroganoff gravy.

Lean pork, cut bite size	1 lb.	454 g
Sliced carrots	1½ cups	375 mL
Peeled sliced potatoes	2 cups	500 mL
Chopped onion	⅓ cup	75 mL
Low-fat sour cream (7% MF)	1 cup	250 mL
Water	1 cup	250 mL
Beef bouillon powder (35% less salt)	4 tsp.	20 mL

Spray frying pan with no-stick cooking spray. Add pork. Sauté to brown well. Turn into 2 quart (2 L) casserole.

Add carrots, potatoes and onion.

Stir sour cream, water and bouillon powder together in frying pan to loosen brown bits. Pour into casserole. Stir lightly. Cover. Bake in 350°F (175°C) oven for about 1½ hours until meat and vegetables are tender. Makes 5 cups (1.13 L).

NUTRITION GUIDE	1 cup (225 mL) contains:	
	Energy	206 Calories (860 kJ)
	Cholesterol	39 mg
	Sodium	332 mg
	Fat	5.8 g

RY FIRST RIBS

ntastic. Served with a dark reddish sauce. Pre-boiling ribs
reduces fat content.

Lean meaty pork back ribs Water to cover	4 lbs.	1.82 kg
Water	1 cup	250 mL
Chopped onion	½ cup	125 mL
White vinegar	¾ cup	175 mL
Worcestershire sauce	2 tbsp.	30 mL
Granulated sugar	½ cup	125 mL
Dry mustard	1 tsp.	5 mL
Salt	1½ tsp.	7 mL
Pepper	¼ tsp.	1 mL
Ground cloves	⅛ tsp.	0.5 mL
Tomato paste	5½ oz.	156 mL

Cut ribs into 2 rib servings. Place in large pot. Add water. Cover. Bring to a boil. Boil for 30 minutes. Drain.

Measure remaining ingredients into saucepan. Heat, stirring frequently until it simmers. Simmer gently until onion is soft. Using tongs, transfer ribs to roaster. Pour sauce over top. Cover. Bake in 350°F (175°C) oven for 1 hour. Makes 8 servings.

Pictured on page 125.

NUTRITION GUIDE	1 serving contains:	
	Energy	289 Calories (1209 kJ)
	Cholesterol	52 mg
	Sodium	610 mg
	Fat	10.5 g

If you are hired to make a bandstand, just take away all the chairs.

Apples lend a different flavor while carrots add color.

Lean pork steaks, fat removed, cut bite size	1½ lbs.	680 g
Chopped onion	2 cups	500 mL
Bite size carrot chunks	2 cups	500 mL
Peeled, chopped and cored apple	2 cups	500 mL
All-purpose flour	3 tbsp.	50 mL
Chicken bouillon powder (35% less salt)	1 tbsp.	15 mL
Pepper	¼ tsp.	1 mL
Water	2 cups	500 mL
Gravy browner as needed	¼ tsp.	1 mL

Spray frying pan with no-stick cooking spray. Brown steaks.

Combine pork, onion, carrot and apple in 3 quart (3 L) casserole.

Stir flour, bouillon powder and pepper in saucepan. Mix in a small amount of water until no lumps remain. Add rest of water. Add a bit of gravy browner to make a richer color. Heat and stir until it boils and thickens. Pour over casserole. Cover. Bake in 350°F (175°C) oven for about 2 hours until vegetables and meat are tender. Makes 6 servings.

Pictured on page 107.

NUTRITION GUIDE	1 serving contains:	
	Energy	200 Calories (839 kJ)
	Cholesterol	37 mg
	Sodium	236 mg
	Fat	3.3 g

Chicken noodle is actually a cowardly pasta soup.

ᴇNER PASTA BAKE ▬▬▬

ta is added raw. Convenient and very good.

Condensed tomato soup	2 × 10 oz.	2 × 284 mL
Boiling water	2½ cups	625 mL
Chili powder	2 tsp.	10 mL
Small fresh mushrooms (slice bigger ones)	1½ cups	375 mL
Dry elbow macaroni	2 cups	500 mL
Wieners, cut in 6 pieces each	1 lb.	454 g

Mix soup, water and chili powder in 3 quart (3 L) casserole until smooth.

Add remaining ingredients. Stir. Cover. Bake in 350°F (175°C) oven for about 45 to 60 minutes until macaroni is tender. Makes 8 servings.

Pictured on page 17.

NUTRITION GUIDE	**1 serving contains:**	
	Energy	343 Calories (1435 kJ)
	Cholesterol	28 mg
	Sodium	1167 mg
	Fat	18.3 g

1. Very First Ribs, page 122
2. Drop Cheese Biscuits, page 100
3. Teener's Dish, page 19
4. Chicken Cola, page 70

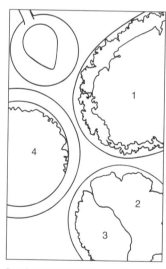

PORK CHOPS SUPREME

Delicious casserole. Chops with mushrooms, onion and gravy.

Boneless pork chops, fat removed, 2 lbs. (900 g)	8	8
Skim milk	1 cup	250 mL
Water	²/₃ cup	150 mL
All-purpose flour	¼ cup	60 mL
Parsley flakes	½ tsp.	2 mL
Garlic powder	¼ tsp.	1 mL
Beef bouillon powder (35% less salt)	1 tsp.	5 mL
Water	6 tbsp.	100 mL
Chopped fresh mushrooms	2 cups	500 mL
Chopped onion	1 cup	250 mL

Spray hot frying pan with no-stick cooking spray. Brown chops on both sides. Remove to plate.

Add milk and first amount of water to frying pan. Stir to loosen brown bits.

Stir next 4 ingredients together in bowl. Mix in remaining water until no lumps remain. Stir into liquid until it boils and thickens.

Add mushrooms and onion. Arrange pork chops in 3 quart (3 L) casserole spooning sauce between and over top. Cover. Bake in 350°F (175°C) oven for 1½ hours or until tender. Makes 8 servings.

Pictured on page 71.

NUTRITION GUIDE	1 serving contains:	
	Energy	129 Calories (541 kJ)
	Cholesterol	37 mg
	Sodium	90 mg
	Fat	2.8 g

SPECIAL DAY RIBS

These are dressed up with fruit. Excellent sweet and sour flavor. Pre-boiling reduces fat.

Lean meaty pork back ribs	**4 lbs.**	**1.82 kg**
Water to cover		
White vinegar	¼ **cup**	**60 mL**
Light soy sauce (40% less salt)	¼ **cup**	**60 mL**
Reserved juice from pineapple		
Reserved juice from apricots		
Chopped onion	⅔ **cup**	**150 mL**
Garlic powder (or 1 clove minced)	¼ **tsp.**	**1 mL**
Brown sugar, packed	½ **cup**	**125 mL**
Liquid sweetener	**1 tbsp.**	**15 mL**
Cornstarch	**2 tbsp.**	**30 mL**
Water	**2 tbsp.**	**30 mL**
Canned unsweetened pineapple tidbits, drained, juice reserved	**14 oz.**	**398 mL**
Canned unsweetened apricots, drained, juice reserved	**14 oz.**	**398 mL**

Cut ribs into 2-rib portions. Boil in water for 30 minutes. Drain. Place in roaster.

Combine next 8 ingredients in saucepan. Stir. Bring to a boil.

Mix cornstarch and water together in small cup. Stir into boiling liquid until it boils and thickens.

Pour sauce over ribs. Cover. Cook in 350°F (175°C) oven for 1 hour. Spoon drained fruit over ribs. Cover and cook 15 minutes more. Makes 8 servings.

Pictured on page 35.

N U T R I T I O N G U I D E	**1 serving contains:**	
	Energy	339 Calories (1420 kJ)
	Cholesterol	52 mg
	Sodium	361 mg
	Fat	10.3 g

Variation: If you aren't watching sugar intake, omit sweetener and add 1 cup (250 mL) brown sugar. Of course it's delicious.

Scrumptious rolls stuffed with a mild curried rice covered with a curried raisin sauce.

Long grain rice	½ cup	125 mL
Boiling water	1 cup	250 mL
Finely chopped onion	1 tbsp.	15 mL
Parsley flakes	½ tsp.	2 mL
CURRY SAUCE		
All-purpose flour	4 tbsp.	60 mL
Curry powder	¾ tsp.	4 mL
Salt	½ tsp.	2 mL
Skim milk	2 cups	450 mL
Raisins	¾ cup	175 mL
Prepared rice		
Prepared sauce	½ cup	125 mL
Lean ham slices (see Note)	16	16

Cook rice in water about 15 minutes until tender and water is absorbed.

Stir in onion and parsley.

Curry Sauce: Measure flour, curry powder and salt into saucepan. Whisk in enough milk to mix until no lumps remain. Add rest of milk and raisins. Heat and stir until it boils and thickens.

Stir rice and ½ cup (125 mL) sauce together.

Place 2 tbsp. (30 mL) rice mixture down center of ham. Roll. Place seam side down in 9 x 13 inch (22 x 33 cm) pan, making 2 long rows side by side. Spoon remaining sauce over top. Cover. Bake in 350°F (175°C) oven for about 20 minutes until hot. Makes 16 rolls.

Note: Square cooked ham slices, 6 per 6 oz. (175 g) package, were used for this recipe.

Pictured on page 17.

NUTRITION GUIDE

1 roll contains:

Energy	94 Calories (393 kJ)
Cholesterol	14 mg
Sodium	508 mg
Fat	1.6 g

HAM ASPARAGUS BAKE

Serve with mashed potatoes and a salad and you will have a real hit.

All-purpose flour	3 tbsp.	50 mL
Salt	¼ tsp.	1 mL
Pepper	⅛ tsp.	0.5 mL
Skim milk	1⅓ cups	300 mL
Cubed cooked lean ham	1cup	250 mL
Onion powder	¼ tsp.	1 mL
Frozen asparagus spears, cut in 1 inch (2.5 cm) lengths	10 oz.	284 g
Boiling water		
Sesame seeds, toasted in 350°F (175°) oven, about 5 minutes	1½ tsp.	7 mL

Measure flour, salt and pepper in saucepan. Whisk in part of milk until no lumps remain. Add rest of milk. Heat and stir until it boils and thickens.

Stir in ham and onion powder. Remove from heat.

Cook asparagus in some boiling water until tender. Drain. Add to ham mixture. Stir lightly. Turn into 1½ quart (1.5 L) casserole.

Sprinkle with sesame seeds. Bake, uncovered, in 350°F (175°C) oven for 20 to 25 minutes. Makes 6 servings.

NUTRITION GUIDE	1 serving contains:	
	Energy	81 Calories (340 kJ)
	Cholesterol	12 mg
	Sodium	461 mg
	Fat	1.8 g

HAM CAULIFLOWER BAKE: Add about 1 lb. (454 g) cooked cauliflower instead of asparagus. Excellent combination.

Paré Pointer

Ships carry most vegetables in their dining room, except leeks that is.

You will hesitate to take out the first spoonful from this picturesque dish.

Grated peeled potato (1 medium)	1 cup	250 mL
Chopped onion	1/4 cup	60 mL
Chopped green pepper	1/4 cup	60 mL
Chopped mushrooms	1 cup	250 mL
Skim milk	2/3 cup	150 mL
All-purpose flour	2/3 cup	150 mL
Chicken bouillon powder (less than 35% salt)	1 tsp.	5 mL
Paprika	1/8 tsp.	0.5 mL
Cayenne pepper	1/8 tsp.	0.5 mL
Skim milk	2 cups	500 mL
Lean diced ham (about 9 oz., 255 g)	1 1/2 cups	350 mL
CHEESE BISCUITS		
All-purpose flour	1 1/2 cups	350 mL
Baking powder	2 1/2 tsp.	12 mL
Grated low-fat sharp Cheddar cheese (less than (21% MF)	1/3 cup	75 mL
Vegetable cooking oil	2 tbsp.	30 mL
Skim milk	2/3 cup	150 mL

Spray saucepan with no-stick cooking spray. Add potato, onion, green pepper and mushrooms. Sauté until soft. Set aside.

Whisk first amount of milk with flour, bouillon powder, paprika and cayenne pepper in saucepan until smooth. Add second amount of milk. Heat and stir until it boils and thickens. Stir into onion mixture.

Add ham. Stir. Turn into 2 quart (2 L) casserole. Place in 425°F (220°C) oven to heat while making biscuit topping.

Cheese Biscuits: Stir first 3 ingredients together in bowl.

Add cooking oil and milk. Mix until it forms a soft ball. Roll out 1/2 inch (12 mm) thick on lightly floured surface. Cut with doughnut cutter. Arrange on top of casserole with small center rounds still in place. Bake, uncovered, for about 15 minutes until browned. Makes 6 servings.

NUTRITION GUIDE	1 serving contains:	
	Energy	357 Calories (1492 kJ)
	Cholesterol	25 mg
	Sodium	707 mg
	Fat	8.5 g

BARBECUED PORK CHOPS

Tomato ketchup flavor with onion and mushrooms.

Boneless loin pork chops, all fat removed, about 4 oz. (114 g) each	8	8
SAUCE		
Tomato paste	**½ cup**	**125 mL**
White vinegar	**⅔ cup**	**150 mL**
Salt	**½ tsp.**	**2 mL**
Ground cloves	**⅛ tsp.**	**0.5 mL**
Liquid sweetener	**3 tbsp.**	**45 mL**
Prepared mustard	**1 tbsp.**	**15 mL**
Sliced fresh mushrooms	**2 cups**	**500 mL**
Chopped onion	**2 cups**	**500 mL**

Spray frying pan with no-stick cooking spray. Brown pork chops on both sides.

Sauce: Stir next 6 ingredients in medium saucepan. Heat until it boils.

Add mushrooms and onion. Arrange pork chops in small roaster or large casserole, spooning sauce between and over chops. Cover. Bake in 350°F (175°C) oven for about 1½ hours. Makes 8 servings.

NUTRITION GUIDE	**1 serving contains:**	
	Energy	230 Calories (963 kJ)
	Cholesterol	51 mg
	Sodium	264 mg
	Fat	10 g

Give a banana a suntan and it peels.

A lean bean dish.

Dried white beans	**2 cups**	**450 mL**
Water	**6 cups**	**1.5 L**
Chopped onion	**1 cup**	**250 mL**
Molasses	**2 tbsp.**	**30 mL**
Prepared mustard	**1 tsp.**	**5 mL**
Salt	**¹/₂ tsp.**	**2 mL**
Water	**3¹/₂ cups**	**800 mL**
Liquid sweetener	**1 tsp.**	**5 mL**
Liquid smoke	**¹/₂ tsp.**	**2 mL**
Maple flavoring	**¹/₁₆ tsp.**	**0.5 mL**

Combine beans and first amount of water in large pot. Bring to a boil. Boil for 3 minutes. Remove from heat. Cover. Let stand 1 hour. Drain.

Add next 8 ingredients. Stir. Bring to a boil. Cover. Simmer for about 1 hour. Turn into 2 quart (2 L) casserole or bean pot. Cover. Bake in 300°F (150°C) oven for about 2 hours until tender. Makes 4¹/₂ cups (1 L).

NUTRITION GUIDE	1 cup (225 mL) contains:	
	Energy	156 Calories (653 kJ)
	Cholesterol	0 mg
	Sodium	328 mg
	Fat	trace

A rolling stone may not gather moss but it squashes bugs.

BAKED SHELF BEANS

These doctored-up beans make a quick change.

Baked beans in tomato sauce	2 × 14 oz.	2 × 398 mL
Onion flakes	3 tbsp.	50 mL
Ketchup, page 99	1 tbsp.	15 mL
Prepared mustard	1 tsp.	5 mL
Mild molasses	1 tbsp.	15 mL
Liquid sweetener	½ tsp.	2 mL
Maple flavoring	⅛ tsp.	0.5 mL
Worcestershire sauce	½ tsp.	2 mL

Combine all ingredients in large bowl. Stir well to distribute everything evenly. Turn into 1 quart (1 L) casserole. Bake, uncovered, in 350°F (175°C) oven for about 1 hour, stirring twice during baking. Makes 3 cups (675 mL).

NUTRITION GUIDE	½ **cup (125 mL) contains:**	
	Energy	155 Calories (650 kJ)
	Cholesterol	0 mg
	Sodium	602 mg
	Fat	.7 g

ASPARAGUS PUFF

Light and good flavor.

Medium potatoes, peeled and quartered	2	2
Water		
Frozen asparagus, chopped	10 oz.	284 g
Water		
All-purpose flour	1 tbsp.	15 mL
Green onions, sliced	2	2
Grated Parmesan cheese	¼ cup	60 mL
Prepared mustard	1 tsp.	5 mL
Salt	½ tsp.	2 mL
Pepper	⅛ tsp.	0.5 mL
Egg whites (large), room temperature	2	2

(continued on next page)

Cook potatoes in some water until tender. Drain. Mash.

Cook asparagus in some water until tender. Drain. Add to

Add next 6 ingredients. Mix.

Beat egg whites in small mixing bowl until stiff. Fold into asparagus mixture. Turn into 1 quart (1 L) casserole. Bake in 350°F (175°C) oven for about 25 minutes until an inserted knife comes out clean. Makes 2½ cups (575 mL).

N U T R I T I O N G U I D E	½ cup (125 mL) contains:	
	Energy	100 Calories (417 kJ)
	Cholesterol	4 mg
	Sodium	408 mg
	Fat	1.8 g

OVEN FRIES

If you have never tried using sweet potatoes, you will enjoy this method. Regular potatoes may be used.

Sweet potatoes, peeled	**1½ lbs.**	**680 g**
Vegetable cooking oil	**1 tbsp.**	**15 mL**

Cut potatoes into sticks. Place in bowl.

Add cooking oil, tossing to coat. Arrange in single layer on baking sheet that has been sprayed with no-stick cooking spray. Bake in 450°F (230°C) oven for 15 minutes. Turn and bake 10 to 15 minutes more. Makes 4 servings.

N U T R I T I O N G U I D E	1 serving contains:	
	Energy	209 Calories (875 kJ)
	Cholesterol	0 mg
	Sodium	22 mg
	Fat	4 g

Variation: Omit vegetable cooking oil. Toss potatoes as you spray them with no-stick cooking spray. No cholesterol, low in calories and sodium and only a trace of fat.

CHEESY RICE CASSEROLE

Green chilies add zip to the rice.

Long grain rice	1 cup	250 mL
Boiling water	2 cups	500 mL
Low-fat cottage cheese (less than 1% MF)	2 cups	500 mL
Skim milk	½ cup	125 mL
Lemon juice, fresh or bottled	2 tbsp.	30 mL
Canned chopped green chilies	4 oz.	114 mL
Salt	½ tsp.	2 mL
Pepper	⅛ tsp.	0.5 mL
Grated part-skim mozzarella cheese (35% less fat)	½ cup	125 mL
Grated low-fat sharp Cheddar cheese (less than 21 % MF)	½ cup	125 mL

Cook rice in water until tender and water is absorbed, about 15 minutes.

Smooth cottage cheese, milk and lemon juice in blender. Turn into bowl. Add rice.

Stir chilies, salt and pepper into rice.

Layer ½ rice mixture then ½ mozzarella cheese. Repeat. Bake, uncovered, in 350°F (175°C) oven for about 25 minutes.

Sprinkle with cheddar cheese. Bake 5 to 8 minutes more to melt. Makes 5½ cups (1.24 L).

NUTRITION GUIDE	½ cup (125 mL) contains:	
	Energy	240 Calories (1006 kJ)
	Cholesterol	17 mg
	Sodium	885 mg
	Fat	5.1 g

MUSHROOM CASSEROLE

Unusual and ever so tasty.

Fresh button mushrooms	2 lbs.	900 g
Lemon juice, fresh or bottled	2 tbsp.	30 mL
Salt	½ tsp.	2 mL
Pepper	⅛ tsp.	0.5 mL
Water	¾ cup	175 mL
All-purpose flour	3 tbsp.	50 mL
Chicken bouillon powder (35% less salt)	2 tsp.	10 mL
Thyme	⅛ tsp.	0.5 mL
Pepper	⅛ tsp.	0.5 mL
Water	¼ cup	60 mL
Evaporated skim milk	½ cup	125 mL
Sherry (or alcohol-free sherry)	2 tbsp.	30 mL

Place first 5 ingredients in large saucepan. Heat until it simmers. Cover. Simmer for about 10 minutes, stirring occasionally.

Mix flour, bouillon powder, thyme and pepper with second amount of water until no lumps remain. Stir into boiling mushroom mixture until it boils and thickens.

Add milk and sherry. Stir. Turn into 2 quart (2 L) casserole. Bake, uncovered, in 350°F (175°C) oven for 20 to 25 minutes. Makes 4 cups (900 mL).

NUTRITION GUIDE	½ cup (125 mL) contains:	
	Energy	47 Calories (198 kJ)
	Cholesterol	1 mg
	Sodium	263 mg
	Fat	.5 g

Paré Pointer

Yes, postage is more expensive. But at least it sticks to one thing until it gets there.

BROCCOLI CASSEROLE

Colorful with its cheesy topping.

Chopped onion	1 cup	250 mL
Sliced fresh mushrooms	2 cups	500 mL
Water		
Frozen egg product, thawed (low-fat and cholesterol-free)	¼ cup	60 mL
Egg white (large)	1	1
Salad dressing, page 98	¼ cup	60 mL
Condensed cream of mushroom soup	10 oz.	284 mL
Salt	½ tsp.	2 mL
Pepper	⅛ tsp.	0.5 mL
Dry bread crumbs	⅓ cup	75 mL
Frozen chopped broccoli, thawed	2 × 10 oz.	2 × 284 g
Grated low-fat sharp Cheddar cheese (less than 21% MF)	1 cup	250 mL
Dry bread crumbs	⅓ cup	75 mL

Cook onion and mushrooms in some water for 20 to 30 minutes until tender. Drain.

In large bowl, spoon beat egg and egg white until mixed. Stir in next 6 ingredients. Add onion-mushroom mixture. Turn into 3 quart (3 L) casserole.

Mix cheese with remaining bread crumbs. Sprinkle over top. Cover. Bake in 350°F (175°C) oven for 35 minutes. Remove cover. Continue to bake about 10 minutes more until cheese melts. Makes 5⅔ cups (1.28 L).

NUTRITION GUIDE	½ cup (125 mL) contains:	
	Energy	137 Calories (580 kJ)
	Cholesterol	10 mg
	Sodium	551 mg
	Fat	5.8 g

GREEN BEAN CASSEROLE

The secret of the good flavor is the addition of soy sauce. Serve with hot rolls.

Chopped fresh mushrooms	**2 cups**	**500 mL**
Chopped onion	**½ cup**	**125 mL**
All-purpose flour	**3 tbsp.**	**50 mL**
Pepper	**⅛ tsp.**	**0.5 mL**
Skim milk	**1½ cups**	**375 mL**
Light soy sauce (40% less salt)	**2 tbsp.**	**30 mL**
Grated low-fat sharp Cheddar cheese (less than 21% MF)	**1 cup**	**250 mL**
Sliced water chestnuts, drained	**5 oz.**	**142 mL**
Frozen beans, cooked, whole, cut or French style	**2 × 10 oz.**	**2 × 284 g**
Sliced almonds, browned in 350°F (175°C) oven about 5 minutes	**2 tbsp.**	**30 mL**

Spray frying pan with no-stick cooking spray. Add mushrooms and onion. Sauté until soft.

Measure flour and pepper in bowl. Mix in a little milk until no lumps remain. Add rest of milk and soy sauce. Stir into mushroom mixture until it boils and thickens.

Stir in cheese, water chestnuts and beans. Turn into 2 quart (2 L) casserole.

Sprinkle with almonds. Bake, uncovered, in 350°F (175°C) oven for 30 minutes until bubbly hot. Makes 5¼ cups (1.18 L).

NUTRITION GUIDE	½ cup (125 mL) contains:	
	Energy	90 Calories (377 kJ)
	Cholesterol	7 mg
	Sodium	220 mg
	Fat	3.1 g

THREE CHEESE MANICOTTI

Shells are stuffed with a tasty filling covered with a meatless tomato sauce.

Manicotti shells	8	8
Boiling water	3 qts.	3 L
FILLING		
Low-fat cottage cheese (less than 1% MF)	1½ cups	350 mL
Grated part-skim mozzarella cheese (35% less fat)	1 cup	250 mL
Grated Parmesan cheese	¼ cup	60 mL
Large egg	1	1
All-purpose flour	1 tbsp.	15 mL
Oregano	½ tsp.	2 mL
Chives	1 tbsp.	15 mL
Salt	¼ tsp.	1 mL
Pepper	⅛ tsp.	0.5 mL
Garlic powder	¼ tsp.	1 mL
Skim milk	3 tbsp.	50 mL
TOMATO SAUCE		
Canned tomatoes, mashed	14 oz.	398 mL
Chopped onion	½ cup	125 mL
Chopped celery	¼ cup	50 mL
Granulated sugar	½ tsp.	2 mL
Parsley flakes	½ tsp.	2 mL
Salt	½ tsp.	2 mL
Pepper	⅛ tsp.	0.5 mL
Oregano	¼ tsp.	1 mL
Basil	¼ tsp.	1 mL
Garlic powder	¼ tsp.	1 mL

Cook manicotti in boiling water in large uncovered Dutch oven about 5 to 6 minutes until barely tender. Drain. Rinse with cold water. Drain.

Filling: Stir all ingredients in bowl in order given. Carefully stuff shells.

(continued on next page)

Tomato Sauce: Combine all ingredients in saucepan. Stir. Bring to a boil. Simmer, stirring occasionally about 20 minutes until liquid reduces. Pour about ⅓ sauce in 9 x 9 inch (22 x 22 cm) pan. Arrange manicotti over top in single layer. Cover with remaining sauce. Cover. Bake in 350°F (175°C) oven for about 40 minutes until hot and bubbly. Makes 8 manicotti.

NUTRITION GUIDE	1 manicotti contains:	
	Energy	191 Calories (800 kJ)
	Cholesterol	40 mg
	Sodium	667 mg
	Fat	5 g

QUICK BAKED BEANS

Good flavor. Rich dark brown color. So easy.

Baked beans in tomato sauce	2 x 14 oz.	2 x 398 mL
Unsweetened crushed pineapple	1 cup	250 mL
Instant coffee granules	1 tsp.	5 mL
Prepared mustard	1 tsp.	5 mL
Liquid smoke	¼ tsp.	1 mL
Liquid sweetener	1 tsp.	5 mL
Chopped onion	½ cup	125 mL
Sliced fresh mushrooms	1 cup	250 mL
Diced green pepper (optional)	¼ cup	60 mL

Combine first 6 ingredients in bean pot or 1½ quart (1.5 L) casserole.

Spray frying pan with no-stick cooking spray. Add onion, mushrooms and green pepper. Sauté until soft. Add to bean mixture. Stir. Bake, uncovered, in 350°F (175°C) oven for about 1 hour until browned and bubbly. Makes 4¼ cups (950 mL).

NUTRITION GUIDE	½ cup (125 mL) contains:	
	Energy	121 Calories (506 kJ)
	Cholesterol	0 mg
	Sodium	409 mg
	Fat	.6 g

...ATO SCALLOP

...d, old recipe that is still good today. Quick and easy.

Canned tomatoes, broken up	28 oz.	796 mL
Dry bread crumbs	2⅓ cups	525 mL
Finely minced onion	1½ tbsp.	25 mL
Dry mustard	1 tsp.	5 mL
Granulated sugar	1 tsp.	5 mL
Salt	¼ tsp	1 mL
Pepper	¼ tsp.	1 mL
White bread slices (or brown)	2	2
Hard margarine, softened	2 tsp.	10 mL

Combine first 7 ingredients in 2 quart (2 L) casserole.

Spread bread thinly with margarine. Cut into cubes. Spread over tomatoes. Bake, uncovered, in 350°F (175°C) oven for about 30 minutes until bubbly. Makes 8 servings.

Pictured on page 107.

NUTRITION GUIDE	**1 serving contains:**	
	Energy	170 Calories (713 kJ)
	Cholesterol	1 mg
	Sodium	518 mg
	Fat	2.8 g

1. Shrimp Noodle Casserole, page 86
2. Porcupines, page 20
3. Cabbage Scallop, page 151
4. Barley Bake, page 148

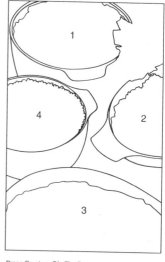

Props Courtesy Of: The Bay

Changes peas from ordinary to extraordinary.

Chopped onion	½ cup	125 mL
Boiling water		
Sliced fresh mushrooms	1 cup	250 mL
Frozen peas	2 cups	500 mL
CREAM SAUCE		
All-purpose flour	4 tsp.	20 mL
Skim milk	1 cup	225 mL
Salt	½ tsp.	2 mL
Pepper	⅛ tsp.	0.5 mL
Paprika	¼ tsp.	1 mL
Hard margarine	1 tbsp.	15 mL
Dry bread crumbs	¼ cup	60 mL

Cook onion in some boiling water until almost done.

Add mushrooms and peas. Cook for 3 to 4 minutes. Drain. Pour into 1 quart (1 L) casserole.

Cream Sauce: Place flour in small saucepan. Mix in a small amount of milk until no lumps remain. Add remaining milk, salt, pepper and paprika. Heat and stir until it boils and thickens slightly. Pour over vegetables. Stir lightly.

Melt margarine in small saucepan. Stir in bread crumbs. Sprinkle over top. Bake in 350°F (175°C) oven for 20 to 30 minutes until hot and browned lightly. Makes 2½ cups (575 mL).

Pictured on page 89.

NUTRITION GUIDE	½ cup (125 mL) contains:	
	Energy	132 Calories (553 kJ)
	Cholesterol	1 mg
	Sodium	425 mg
	Fat	2.9 g

SCALLOPED POTATOES

Just good potatoes. Just a trace of fat.

All-purpose flour	**¼ cup**	**60 mL**
Dill weed	**½ tsp.**	**2 mL**
Salt	**¾ tsp.**	**4 mL**
Pepper	**⅛ tsp.**	**0.5 mL**
Skim milk	**2 cups**	**500 mL**
Medium potatoes, sliced ¼ inch (6 mm) thick	**6**	**6**
Large onion, thinly sliced	**1**	**1**

Stir flour, dill weed, salt and pepper together in saucepan. Mix in milk gradually until no lumps remain. Heat and stir until it boils and thickens. Remove from heat.

Place ½ potatoes and ½ onion in 2 quart (2 L) casserole. Pour ½ sauce over top. Repeat. Cover. Bake in 350°F (175°C) oven for about 1½ hours or until potatoes are tender. Remove cover for a few minutes to brown if desired. Makes 6 servings.

NUTRITION GUIDE	**1 serving contains:**	
	Energy	206 Calories (861 kJ)
	Cholesterol	2 mg
	Sodium	392 mg
	Fat	trace

Astronauts have their launch at noon.

MACARONI AND CHEESE

An old-timer pared down to suit today's lifestyle.

Dry elbow macaroni	2 cups	500 mL
Boiling water	3 qts.	3 L
All-purpose flour	3½ tbsp.	50 mL
Salt	¾ tsp.	4 mL
Pepper	⅛ tsp.	0.5 mL
Paprika	¼ tsp.	1 mL
Skim milk	2⅓ cups	575 mL
Grated low-fat sharp Cheddar cheese (less than 21% MF)	1 cup	250 mL
Onion flakes	2 tbsp.	30 mL
Dry mustard	½ tsp.	2 mL
TOPPING		
Hard margarine	1 tbsp.	15 mL
Dry bread crumbs	⅓ cup	75 mL

Cook macaroni in boiling water in large uncovered pot about 5 to 7 minutes until tender but firm. Drain. Return macaroni to pot.

Stir flour, salt, pepper and paprika together in saucepan. Mix in part of the milk until no lumps remain. Add rest of milk. Heat and stir until it boils and thickens.

Add cheese, onion flakes and mustard. Stir well. Add to macaroni. Stir. Pour into 2 quart (2 L) casserole.

Topping: Melt margarine in small saucepan. Stir in bread crumbs. Sprinkle over top. Bake, uncovered, in 350°F (175°C) oven for about 30 minutes until hot and bubbly. Makes 6 cups (1.35 L).

NUTRITION GUIDE	1 cup (250 mL) contains:	
	Energy	298 Calories (1247 kJ)
	Cholesterol	14 mg
	Sodium	584 mg
	Fat	7.1 g

RLEY BAKE

makes a nice change from potatoes and rice.

Beef bouillon powder (35% less salt)	2 tbsp.	30 mL
Boiling water	3½ cups	875 mL
Barley, pot or pearl	1 cup	250 mL
Chopped onion	1½ cups	375 mL
Parsley flakes	2 tsp.	10 mL
Chopped green onions	¼ cup	60 mL
Pepper	¼ tsp.	1 mL
Pine nuts or slivered almonds, browned in 350°F (175°C) oven for about 5 minutes, for garnish	2 tsp.	10 mL

Stir bouillon powder into water in 2 quart (2 L) casserole.

Add next 5 ingredients.

Garnish with pine nuts. Cover. Bake in 350°F (175°C) oven for about 2 hours until barley is tender. Makes about 4¼ cups (950 mL).

Pictured on page 143.

NUTRITION GUIDE	½ cup (125 mL) contains:	
	Energy	79 Calories (329 kJ)
	Cholesterol	trace
	Sodium	207 mg
	Fat	3.4 g

CAULIFLOWER-BROCCOLI CASSEROLE

Fast and easy. Vegetables are used in the frozen state. Good.

Frozen cauliflower	10 oz.	284 g
Frozen broccoli	10 oz.	284 g
Finely chopped onion	⅓ cup	75 mL
Condensed cream of mushroom soup	10 oz.	284 mL
Grated low-fat sharp Cheddar cheese (less than 21% MF)	⅓ cup	75 mL
Corn flake crumbs	¼ cup	60 mL

(continued on next page)

Layer cauliflower, broccoli and onion in 2 quart (2 L) casserole. Cut large chunks with sharp knife.

Place soup in bowl. Add cheese. Stir. Spoon over casserole.

Sprinkle with corn flake crumbs. Bake, uncovered, in 350°F (175°C) oven for about 60 minutes. Makes 3½ cups (800 mL).

Pictured on page 53.

NUTRITION GUIDE	½ cup (125 mL) contains:	
	Energy	95 Calories (397 kJ)
	Cholesterol	3 mg
	Sodium	432 mg
	Fat	4.4 g

LUNCH SPECIAL

Begin with a convenience food, add vegetables and you have a quick, easy luncheon dish.

Packaged macaroni and cheese dinner	**7¼ oz.**	**200 g**
Sliced fresh mushrooms	**1½ cups**	**375 mL**
Skim milk	**⅓ cup**	**75 mL**
All-purpose flour	**⅓ cup**	**75 mL**
Chicken bouillon powder (35% less salt)	**1 tsp.**	**5 mL**
Paprika	**⅛ tsp.**	**0.5 mL**
Cayenne pepper	**⅛ tsp.**	**0.5 mL**
Skim milk	**1 cup**	**250 mL**
Peas, fresh or frozen, cooked	**1 cup**	**250 mL**
Salt and pepper to taste		

Prepare macaroni according to directions on package, omitting salt and margarine or butter and adding mushrooms to macaroni to cook at the same time. Drain. Stir in cheese packet and milk.

Whisk first amount of milk with flour in saucepan until smooth. Add bouillon powder, paprika and cayenne pepper. Add second amount of milk. Heat and stir until it boils and thickens. Add to macaroni mixture.

Add peas. Stir. Turn into 2 quart (2 L) casserole. Bake, uncovered, in 350°F (175°C) oven for 20 to 30 minutes. Makes 5⅓ cups (1.2 L).

NUTRITION GUIDE	1 cup (225 mL) contains:	
	Energy	271 Calories (1132 kJ)
	Cholesterol	7.4 mg
	Sodium	298 mg
	Fat	3.6 g

GREEN CHILI QUICHE

Wedges are topped with green and yellow. Easy.

Unbaked 9 inch (22 cm) pastry shell, page 104	1	1
Grated part-skim mozzarella cheese (35% less fat)	1½ cups	350 mL
Grated low-fat sharp Cheddar cheese (less than 21% MF)	½ cup	125 mL
Canned chopped green chilies	4 oz.	114 mL
Egg white (large)	1	1
Frozen egg product, thawed (low-fat and cholesterol-free)	½ cup	125 mL
All-purpose flour	2 tbsp.	30 mL
Salt	¼ tsp.	1 mL
Cumin	¼ tsp.	1 mL
Evaporated skim milk	1 cup	250 mL

Prepare pastry shell. Do not prick.

Sprinkle next 3 ingredients in layers in pastry shell.

Mix egg white, egg product, flour, salt and cumin in bowl. Add milk. Stir. Pour over top. Bake in 350°F (175°C) oven for about 40 minutes until set. Freezes well. Makes 8 servings.

Pictured on page 107.

NUTRITION GUIDE	1 serving contains:	
	Energy	245 Calories (1024 kJ)
	Cholesterol	18 mg
	Sodium	490 mg
	Fat	12 g

Variation: May be baked in a pie plate without pastry shell. Spray pie plate with no-stick cooking spray. One serving will contain only 5 g of fat.

Paré Pointer

A foot is a great device for finding furniture in the dark.

This economical vegetable is transformed.

Head of cabbage, cut in 6 wedges, core intact	**1½ lbs.**	**800 g**
Boiling water		
All-purpose flour	**¼ cup**	**60 mL**
Salt	**¾ tsp.**	**4 mL**
Pepper	**¼ tsp.**	**1 mL**
Garlic powder	**⅛ tsp.**	**0.5 mL**
Onion powder	**⅛ tsp.**	**0.5 mL**
Skim milk	**2 cups**	**500 mL**
Grated low-fat sharp Cheddar cheese (less than 21 % MF)	**½ cup**	**125 mL**
Grated low-fat sharp Cheddar cheese (less than 21 % MF)	**½ cup**	**125 mL**

Cook cabbage in some boiling water for about 10 minutes until tender. Using slotted spoon, lift out wedges as best you can and place in 3 quart (3 L) casserole. Pile loose leaves on top.

Measure next 5 ingredients into saucepan. Mix in part of milk until no lumps remain. Add rest of milk. Heat and stir until it boils and thickens.

Stir in first amount of cheese. Pour over cabbage.

Sprinkle with remaining cheese. Cover. Bake in 350°F (175°C) oven for 20 to 30 minutes until hot. Makes 6 servings.

Pictured on page 143.

NUTRITION GUIDE	1 serving contains:	
	Energy	155 Calories (647 kJ)
	Cholesterol	14 mg
	Sodium	551 mg
	Fat	4.7 g

◢ MEASUREMENT TABLES ▬▬▬

Throughout this book measurements are given in Conventional and Metric measure. To compensate for differences between the two measurements due to rounding, a full metric measure is not always used. The cup used is the standard 8 fluid ounce. Temperature is given in degrees Fahrenheit and Celsius. Baking pan measurements are in inches and centimetres as well as quarts and litres. An exact metric conversion is given below as well as the working equivalent (Standard Measure).

OVEN TEMPERATURES

Fahrenheit (°F)	Celsius (°C)
175°	80°
200°	95°
225°	110°
250°	120°
275°	140°
300°	150°
325°	160°
350°	175°
375°	190°
400°	205°
425°	220°
450°	230°
475°	240°
500°	260°

SPOONS

Conventional Measure	Metric Exact Conversion Millilitre (mL)	Metric Standard Measure Millilitre (mL)
1/8 teaspoon (tsp.)	0.6 mL	0.5 mL
1/4 teaspoon (tsp.)	1.2 mL	1 mL
1/2 teaspoon (tsp.)	2.4 mL	2 mL
1 teaspoon (tsp.)	4.7 mL	5 mL
2 teaspoons (tsp.)	9.4 mL	10 mL
1 tablespoon (tbsp.)	14.2 mL	15 mL

CUPS

	Metric Exact Conversion Millilitre (mL)	Metric Standard Measure Millilitre (mL)
1/4 cup (4 tbsp.)	56.8 mL	60 mL
1/3 cup (5 1/3 tbsp.)	75.6 mL	75 mL
1/2 cup (8 tbsp.)	113.7 mL	125 mL
2/3 cup (10 2/3 tbsp.)	151.2 mL	150 mL
3/4 cup (12 tbsp.)	170.5 mL	175 mL
1 cup (16 tbsp.)	227.3 mL	250 mL
4 1/2 cups	1022.9 mL	1000 mL (1 L)

PANS

Conventional Inches	Metric Centimetres
8x8 inch	20x20 cm
9x9 inch	22x22 cm
9x13 inch	22x33 cm
10x15 inch	25x38 cm
11x17 inch	28x43 cm
8x2 inch round	20x5 cm
9x2 inch round	22x5 cm
10x4 1/2 inch tube	25x11 cm
8x4x3 inch loaf	20x10x7.5 cm
9x5x3 inch loaf	22x12.5x7.5 cm

DRY MEASUREMENTS

Conventional Measure Ounces (oz.)	Metric Exact Conversion Grams (g)	Metric Standard Measure Grams (g)
1 oz.	28.3 g	28 g
2 oz.	56.7 g	57 g
3 oz.	85.0 g	85 g
4 oz.	113.4 g	125 g
5 oz.	141.7 g	140 g
6 oz.	170.1 g	170 g
7 oz.	198.4 g	200 g
8 oz.	226.8 g	250 g
16 oz.	453.6 g	500 g
32 oz.	907.2 g	1000 g (1 kg)

CASSEROLES (Canada & Britain)

Standard Size Casserole	Exact Metric Measure
1 qt. (5 cups)	1.13 L
1 1/2 qts. (7 1/2 cups)	1.69 L
2 qts. (10 cups)	2.25 L
2 1/2 qts. (12 1/2 cups)	2.81 L
3 qts. (15 cups)	3.38 L
4 qts. (20 cups)	4.5 L
5 qts. (25 cups)	5.63 L

CASSEROLES (United States)

Standard Size Casserole	Exact Metric Measure
1 qt. (4 cups)	900 mL
1 1/2 qts. (6 cups)	1.35 L
2 qts. (8 cups)	1.8 L
2 1/2 qts. (10 cups)	2.25 L
3 qts. (12 cups)	2.7 L
4 qts. (16 cups)	3.6 L
5 qts. (20 cups)	4.5 L

INDEX

RECIPE NOTES

THE COMPANY'S COMING STORY

Jean Paré grew up understanding that the combination of family, friends and home cooking is the essence of a good life. From her mother she learned to appreciate good cooking, while her father praised even her earliest attempts. When she left home she took with her many acquired family recipes, a love of cooking and an intriguing desire to read recipe books like novels!

"never share a recipe you wouldn't use yourself"

In 1963, when her four children had all reached school age, Jean volunteered to cater the 50th anniversary of the Vermilion School of Agriculture, now Lakeland College. Working out of her home, Jean prepared a dinner for over 1000 people which launched a flourishing catering operation that continued for over eighteen years. During that time she was provided with countless opportunities to test new ideas with immediate feedback—resulting in empty plates and contented customers! Whether preparing cocktail sandwiches for a house party or serving a hot meal for 1500 people, Jean Paré earned a reputation for good food, courteous service and reasonable prices.

"Why don't you write a cookbook?" Time and again, as requests for her recipes mounted, Jean was asked that question. Jean's response was to team up with her son, Grant Lovig, in the fall of 1980 to form Company's Coming Publishing Limited. April 14, 1981, marked the debut of "150 DELICIOUS SQUARES", the first Company's Coming cookbook in what soon would become Canada's most popular cookbook series.

Jean Paré's operation has grown steadily from the early days of working out of a spare bedroom in her home. Full-time staff include marketing personnel located in major cities across Canada. Home Office is based in Edmonton, Alberta in a modern building constructed specially for the company.

Today the company distributes throughout Canada and the United States in addition to numerous overseas markets, all under the guidance of Jean's daughter, Gail Lovig. Best-sellers many times over in English, Company's Coming cookbooks have also be published in French and Spanish. Familiar and trusted in home kitchens around the world, Company's Coming cookbooks are offered in a variety of formats, including the original softcover series.

Jean Paré's approach to cooking has always called for quick and easy recipes using every ingredients. Even when travelling, she is constantly on the lookout for new ideas to share with her readers. At home, she can usually be found researching and writing recipes, or working in the company's test kitchen. Jean continues to gain new supporte by adhering to what she calls "the golden rule of cooking": never share a recipe you wouldn't use yourself. It's an approach that works— *millions of times over!*